More Praise for
Small Business Taxes M

Winner—2017 Gold Award from Axiom in Bu

"I started my business 10 years ago, and by luck and the kindness of friends, strangers, and professionals, I was able to hobble together less than half the wealth of information and great advice in this book. Eva's book is insightful, timely, and a must-read for anyone starting or already in a small business. Thank you!"

—Deborah M. Pratt, Director/Producer/Writer—
known for the popular TV series *Quantum Leap*

"Eva has the uncanny gift of making the arcane world of taxes easy to understand, fun, and engaging. This book does just that. This is a great resource and guidebook for any small business owner and independent contractor who wants to get a better handle on how their business is really doing. This book helps empower people to understand their business's financial health."

—Michael Rozbruch, CPA, CTRS, Founder, Michael
Rozbruch's Tax & Business Solutions Academy

"I personally work closely with dozens of serious entrepreneurs one-on-one, and tens of thousands in group coaching sessions and via my newsletters.

Whenever I get a question about choosing a business structure, business planning, keeping proper records without too much *pain*, and minimizing taxes legally, my answer is always the same. I point them to Eva Rosenberg.

The best advice that I offer is to point them to Eva Rosenberg's *Small Business Taxes Made Easy*, and the best gift that I can and do give any of my entrepreneurial clients is a copy of Eva's book, *Small Business Taxes Made Easy*."

—Willie Crawford, 20+ Year Online Marketing Mentor

"Failing to plan is planning to fail. Ignoring The TaxMama = Epic Fail."

—Brent Clanton, CPO, Clanton Communications, LLC,
and former host of CBS Radio's *Talk650 Morning Show*, Houston, Texas

"TaxMama provides a comprehensive overview of small business accounting and taxation issues in a fun and easy-to-read format."

—Michael T. Hanley, CPA–Managing Partner of Michels & Hanley, LLP,
and author of *Effective Tax Planning for the MicroBusiness*

"TaxMama's book provides not only a bit of laughter but also a lot of straightforward information about operating a small business within the guidelines set by the IRS."

—Jan Zobel, EA, author of *Minding Her Own Business*

"As a business owner you must have this book. If you're a work-at-home mother or an Internet marketer or a bricks-and-mortar business owner, this book has answers and instructions presented in TaxMama's irreverent, entertaining, and fun (yes, I said fun) style."

—Stephanie L. Watson, Virtual Assistant Moms

"Every US business owner will benefit from Rosenberg's clear, well-written explanations of complex, arcane tax concepts. You'll run your business more effectively and you'll stay out of trouble with the IRS. Buy this book."

—Shel Horowitz, author of *Principled Profit:
Marketing That Puts People First* and owner of frugalmarketing.com

"Here is a book that is short on theory and long on practical, plainspoken advice. From how to buy office supplies to how to deal with the IRS, Rosenberg taps decades of business savvy to walk readers through the minefields of new business ownership."

—Al Tompkins, author, teacher, consultant

"When I started my career as a CPA, one of the most valuable lessons I learned was to simplify and explain the basics. Eva has managed to take a complex subject and simplify it for all."

—Ken Leebow, The Incredible Internet Guy, author, speaker, TV personality

"From the very beginning, this excellent book clearly sets itself apart from other tax books. As the title implies, Eva's book gives the small business person a good handle on tax issues, and the checklists make it easy to follow through on what you learn. This is a must-have book for every small business person and anyone wanting to start his or her own small business."

—Dennis Gaskill, BoogieJack.com

"Eva Rosenberg counsels new entrepreneurs that they'll need a business plan if they want to succeed. *Small Business Taxes Made Easy* should be the first step in that plan."

—Kay Bell, tax editor at Bankrate.com

Small Business Taxes

Taxes

Fourth Edition

Made Easy

HOW TO INCREASE
YOUR DEDUCTIONS,
REDUCE WHAT
YOU OWE,
AND BOOST
YOUR PROFITS

EVA ROSENBERG, MBA, EA

New York   Chicago   San Francisco   Athens   London   Madrid   Mexico City
Milan   New Delhi   Singapore   Sydney   Toronto

1 2 3 4 5 6 7 8 9   LCR   25 24 23 22 21 20

ISBN: 978-1-260-46818-2
MHID: 1-260-46818-6

e-ISBN: 978-1-260-46819-9
e-MHID: 1-260-46819-4

TaxMama® is a registered service mark of Eva Rosenberg and may not be used without written permission.

This publication is designed to provide accurate and authoritative information in regard to the subject matter covered. It is sold with the understanding that neither the author nor the publisher is engaged in rendering legal, accounting, securities trading, or other professional services. If legal advice or other expert assistance is required, the services of a competent professional person should be sought.

> —From a Declaration of Principles Jointly Adopted by a Committee of the American Bar Association and a Committee of Publishers and Associations

McGraw-Hill Education books are available at special quantity discounts to use as premiums and sales promotions, or for use in corporate training programs. To contact a representative, please visit the Contact Us pages at www.mhprofessional.com.

This edition of *Small Business Taxes Made Easy* is dedicated to all the people I love who have been neglected in the last couple of years. You know who you are—and know how much I really appreciate you.

And special thanks and love to Mel Kreger, attorney and Enrolled Agent, who has taught us all so much and who has been so generous in his support of our breakfast meeting members for decades beyond memory.

CONTENTS

ACKNOWLEDGMENTS

This book was first conceived by the original editor Donya Dickerson, who called me out of the blue. Michele R. Wells initiated the second update, then went off to the world of pictures at Penguin. Mary Therese Church brought that edition to fruition. The third edition was nurtured by Cheryl Segura, as a newly minted full-fledged editor. She has been a spot of sunshine. Now, in 2019, Amy Li stepped up to take on this project on very, very short notice. I really want to thank Amy for doing such a great job putting this book together in weeks, instead of months.

When it comes to taxes, nothing happens in a vacuum. It's impossible for any one person to know it all. TaxMama relies on many people to keep me in the loop. Key among them are the hardworking public relations firms for all the top tax software, tax preparation, and publishing companies. They are generous with information, resources, and experts, often on a moment's notice. You make my job look easy.

I want to thank the entire family at TaxMama.com and Team TaxMama and the students at my enrolled agent school IRSExams.School. Everyone who asks a question, or answers it, contributes to experiences that helped shape this book. All my friends on the Internet, around the world, in a variety of fields tell me their stories, help me build and improve my websites, and become the source of stories and cases you're about to enjoy.

During the past few years, I have had to slow down as I recovered from cancer. The great news is, it's been more than five years now. But my doctors (whom I will not name, in respect of their privacy) have continued to keep me under their care. It's such a relief to have them and that continuity.

In the meantime, several people have stepped up to help visitors to TaxMama .com and to answer questions. Chief among them is Jean Mammen, EA, author of the definitive book and blog for taxpayers with international tax issues—http://iTax Mama.com/1040NR _Book. You can find Jean dispensing wisdom and generous advice at TaxMama.com to visa holders, taxpayers with foreign spouses, resident aliens living in the United States, and Americans working overseas.

Thanks to the wealth of talented, passionate tax professionals who have been part of my advisory team for the past decades—Michael Rozbruch, CPA; Larry Lawler, CPA; L. G. Brooks, EA; Jamie Buchwald, CPA; Irinia Bobrova, EA; David Stone, EA; Bruce Drooks, JD; Mel Kreger, EA/LLM; Doug Thorburn, EA; Sharoj Sharma, EA; Galina Metelitsa, EA; Rita Lewis, EA; Fred Daily, tax attorney; David L. Mellem, EA; Tom Blair, EA; Linda Dorfmont, EA; "Uncle" Bill Porter, EA; Mike Reed, EA; and Jim Faucett—a future EA. And the mysterious ClemRick and TeeEarls who provide valuable insights. Special thanks to Susan Holtgrefe, EA, who mentors my EA students, and teaches several of my classes. And thanks to the countless others who inspire me or bring me laughter each day.

Thanks to Robert Kerr and the special teams of folks at the National Association of Enrolled Agents (NAEA) and the National Association of Tax Professionals (NATP) who advocate tirelessly for enrolled agents' rights and to make the income tax system more helpful to taxpayers—and who provide the enrolled agents who create the questions for the Special Enrollment Examination (also known as the EA Exam). And to Lynn Freer and Spidell Publishing and the California Society of Tax Consultants (CSTC) who keep us up-to-date on California laws.

In recent years, a new organization has appeared on the scene, LatinoTaxPro .com. They have attracted many young people to the tax community and are doing a great job with their many educational programs and events. They are a breath of fresh air to the tax community—and I hope to see many new Enrolled Agents, CPAs, and tax attorneys inspired by this group.

I especially want to thank all the folks at the IRS and the Taxpayers Advocate Service who are always so generous to me with their time and humor—both personally and on the job. My gratitude also goes to the team at the Los Angeles Stakeholder Liaison teams who work long hours to keep people informed, fix errors when we find them, and do it all with grace and good spirit. Thanks also to those special, dedicated folks at the IRS who actually go out of their way to help complete strangers solve their problems. They prove that a tax system can be administered fairly.

INTRODUCTION

A Letter from Eva Rosenberg to You, the Business Owner

Dear Entrepreneur,

(Yes, *you*. If you're starting or operating a business, please start thinking of yourself right now as an *entrepreneur*.)

Since the first edition of this book was first published in 2004, TaxMama has received many letters or emails from business owners with two themes:

1. I wish I had read this book before starting my business. It would have saved me a fortune in time, money, taxes—and errors.
2. Even though I've been in business for many years, this book has helped me cut my taxes and increase my profits. It's my new business bible.

Why are people saying things like that? Because *Small Business Taxes Made Easy* is a book you can use on a day-to-day basis to keep your business on a path to profits and success. So, please do exactly that.

Many books on the market tell you how to organize your business records, prepare your tax returns, even how to make decisions or choices. Some are excellent.

So why does the world need yet another book on small business taxes? Because even the best books focus primarily on the record-keeping or legal aspects of small business taxes. For your business to succeed, you must *also* understand how the reporting requirements can be used to improve your business management, provide better decision-making tools, and increase your profits. Providing that information is what makes this book different.

With all the resentment and resistance toward paying taxes and toward the flood of reporting requirements, you've got to see what's in it for you. What do *you* get from your investment of time and money? It doesn't only benefit the IRS and your state and local governments.

While each chapter of this book explains tax concepts and responsibilities, it also helps you understand how you benefit from following those guidelines.

You're not in business to supply a flood of paperwork to the government. Nor are you sweating blood trying to meet your business, financial, and family obligations in order to buy your tax pro a new BMW.

You're in business to have more control of your life and time; to earn more money than you could on a job; and to build a future—and a legacy—for your family and future generations.

Otherwise, why work so hard? Just go back to your traditional nine-to-five job. Seriously, there's more to running a business than appears on the surface. Some people make it appear effortless—and they often go out of business quickly as a result. Others make it seem a gargantuan burden—and they end up hating every minute of it. They destroy their family and relationships in the process, blaming everyone else for their failures.

Then there are those people who start up, and everything goes right. Life is good. Family and social relationships remain solid, and they maintain balance in their lives. That's what I want for you.

Listening to the news, you often hear when large businesses fail. You're probably still shaking your head over the whole dot-com bust several years ago, wondering how all those businesses failed after raising millions of dollars in venture capital or through their initial public offering. Well, the venture capitalists learned a hard lesson from that, too. And they are far more discerning about how they invest their funds these days. So, if you want their investment in your business, you will need to show well-thought-out structures and planning.

The businesses that failed went wrong in one, or all, of three ways:

1. They didn't have a realistic business plan.
2. They didn't plan for success.
3. They were run by immature and inexperienced people who simply blew all the money without looking for reasonable returns on their spending.

You're buying this book to avoid all those mistakes. Use this book to learn from others' failures and successes. Please, make a commitment to devote all the time and resources needed to make *your* business work.

Otherwise, put this book back on the shelf. It's not for you.

Using This Book

I didn't write this book to bore you, bully you, or enable your failure.

If you can't make a serious commitment to create your business plan, set up and use a proper accounting system, and be ethical in tax reporting—please don't start the business. You'll earn much more, with less effort, less stress, and less risk, with a job working for someone else. Really, you will.

Let Me Tell You a Story About a Very Successful and Brilliant Film Editor

Marie was at the top of her industry, earning a healthy six-figure income. She was popular with the filmmakers and knew she could attract clients if she went out on her own. In fact, her own employer was willing to subcontract to her. Sounds good, right? And it was, at first. Marie always had enough work to support the costs of hiring several editors and other staff members. Unfortunately, she hired a good friend as her office manager and bookkeeper. Sally did a great job. Until she didn't. Sally was an alcoholic and, well, let's say she got distracted. Bills weren't being paid. Worst of all, payroll taxes weren't being paid. By the time Marie called me, in a panic, she needed to cover close to $50,000 worth of delinquent payroll taxes! Fine—I had a good friend managing a bank, and we got her a quick line of credit to get her out of trouble with the IRS and state of California. But from then on, she was never able to get the right administrator—and stressed out for years, with one business problem after another. Marie learned that she just wasn't good at running a business, with all the myriad of administrative nonsense. But she was great as a film editor and team manager. Finally, she decided to leave the bureaucracy to someone else and got reemployed. Since then, she's had the opportunity to be the head of the production team designing visual effects for an Academy Award–winning film, edit many TV shows with which you are familiar, and create compelling trailers for many films.

So be honest with yourself. If you're not a capable administrator, maybe you should just renegotiate your compensation or position at work—or look for a better job, if you're unhappy at work.

But if you still want to start a business (or stay in a business you've already started), here's your next important consideration. Take into account how much you could earn on a job or on the money you're investing to get this business going. Even if you borrow the money, think of how many hours of work it will take to pay it back.

Those are called "opportunity costs." It's important to understand what you're giving up to start your business. When I started my business, I knew what I was getting into. I relish the independence and the lack of office politics. I love my clients, the people I work with, and the people whom I consult. And I am free to turn down clients when my instincts suggest they will be trouble (whether professionally or personally). Despite being constantly behind in my workload, I rejoice in the flood of new work and fresh ideas that comes pouring in each day from friends and readers.

Here are the two most important things I want you to know going in:

- Love what you do.
- Don't delude yourself into thinking your goal is to pay the least amount of tax possible. Your real goal is to end up with the *highest disposable income possible*—and to be in great physical and mental health when you get there.

That's what I'd like to help you achieve.

You're about to learn how following the IRS's rules for small business owners will make you richer, happier, and less stressed.

TaxMama's warning: Although I can make changes at the IRS, I can't change grammatical rules. So wherever you see web addresses (URLs) in this book that seem to have colons, commas, or periods as the last character, ignore that final character when typing them into your browser. If you are using an electronic edition, links that span more than one line often break when you click on them. You might have to retype the link into your device.

Comparing a Job and a Business

Be sure to understand these distinctions between a job and a business. People starting out on their own rarely realize just how many things they've taken for granted on a job. These are the things that just happened invisibly, in the background, taken care of by your employer's infrastructure. Even if you felt as though you were doing most of it for him or her, when you're on your own, the sidebar will show you just how many more things you'll need to oversee—things that will drain your time, patience, and resources.

One of the biggest complaints from people working for others is that they do not have control over their income. Their bosses can cut their commissions, territories, or bonuses at will—and often do. When you're in business for yourself, if you earn it, *you* reap the rewards.

When You Have a Traditional Job

THE *GOOD* THINGS IN A JOB

- Your boss ensures there's money coming in, that it gets into the bank, and that your payroll is covered.
- Your boss pays your payroll taxes, your workers' compensation insurance, your vacations, and sick pay, possibly even health insurance.
- Your boss, or staff paid by your boss, gets the customers; orders and pays for the supplies you use; buys and sets up your computer, telephone, and the other tools you take for granted every day—and arranges to keep them all in good working order.
- Your job has a structure and a schedule. You know what's expected of you each day, week, or month.
- Your boss arranges to take care of all the billing, the administrative paperwork, all the day-to-day trivia needed to run a business. All you have to do is show up and do your job—you get your paycheck, leave, and don't have to think about things once you're off the clock.

THE *BAD* THINGS IN A JOB

- What if you have to leave for a little while or need the day off? You have to ask permission—which you sometimes don't get. Or you have to lie about situations such as . . .

    You've got a doctor's appointment.
    Your kids have a recital.
    You're not feeling well.
    You just don't feel like working.

- You hate a customer or client—you're stuck dealing with people if they're important to your boss.
- You don't like a business practice or policy? If you want to keep your job, you've got to do it your boss's way.
- Your boss assigns the workload. How many times has someone dumped stuff on you at the last minute that's been sitting there for weeks? You have to work overtime you hadn't anticipated.
- You don't get raises when you feel you've earned them—or you have to go hat-in-hand to request them.
- You have to work with managers who don't know what they're doing—and you have to cover for their mistakes.
- You face periodic employee reviews—or none at all, when you really should be meeting with the boss to discuss key issues that should be reviewed.
- Your company leaders might not offer logical employee benefits—like flexible spending accounts or retirement plans—and they won't listen to your explanations about how beneficial they can be to the employer.
- With the new Tax Cuts and Jobs Act, if your employer doesn't reimburse your out-of-pocket job-related expenses, you can no longer deduct those costs on your tax return. For some employees, those non-deductible expenses add up to thousands of dollars.
- You don't have power.

When You Have a Business

THE *BAD* THINGS IN A BUSINESS

- You have to take the time to do all those things listed in "The Good Things" column under "When You Have a Traditional Job."
- Or, you have to pay people to do all those things. So you must generate enough extra income to cover their compensation.
- Trying to do it all yourself won't give you time to sell, and to build your customer or client base.
- Or, if you do have the time, you won't have time to do the work.
- So you'll need to learn the most cost-effective use of your time. You'll want to learn what to outsource, or hire staff to do, and what is worth doing yourself.
- Or, you'll need to create a solid budget and business plan to determine how much money you'll need to raise to cover your operating costs and staff until your business starts to turn a profit.
- Remember, while being in business for yourself does mean you work your own hours; *it could mean you work all of them*. Expect to put in 50 to 75 percent more hours than you worked having a traditional job.

THE *GOOD* THINGS IN A BUSINESS

- You can take time off anytime that suits you— no excuses or lies needed.
- You don't have to keep clients or customers who treat you without respect. (Or you can charge them lots more to make it worth your while.)
- You set the policies. You never have to do anything against your morals or ethics.
- You get to try out new ideas and take chances to enhance your customers' or clients' experience with your company.
- You get to deduct all your business-related expenses—and can plan your life to make many of your travels and activities deductible.
- You get to build retirement savings—and reduce your tax hit.
- You get to hire your family or friends (if qualified) without having to be concerned about nepotism.
- You can help clients or customers for free, when you feel they need special attention or help.
- You can take advantage of various opportunities to get your business involved in helping to improve your community.
- You manage your own time, so you can and should get involved with solid networking opportunities in your community—especially your Chamber of Commerce.

YOU GET TO ENJOY YOUR LIFE!

Before we continue, if you're presently an employee, please read one of TaxMama's TaxQuips about what employees give up when they want to switch to owning their own business—even if they are assured about getting a stream of income by contracting with their former employer (http://iTaxMama.com/What_U_Lose_Self _Employed). With the current provisions of the Tax Cuts and Jobs Act (TCJA) that prevent employees from deducting all their job-related expenses (though 2025), this switch to self-employment is tempting. But, please remember Marie's story. Not everyone is cut out to run a business and to live a less-structured life.

Be sure to read the previous lists to understand the additional demands that owning a business places on you—and your family. Think deeply how all the extra time you spend working will affect your relationships with your parents, spouse, children, and friends. Will you miss the important moments in your children's lives? Or will your business give you the freedom to be present? Before you tackle a new business, visualize how your life will look and feel once you've embarked on this challenge.[1]

Did you want a little more hand-holding? Join me at *Wolters Kluwer's CCH CPELink—https://www.cchcpelink.com/teamtaxmama*. We are starting a series of classes based on the chapters in this book. You can ask questions about your own business during these classes.

Meanwhile, remember to use the downloadable To-Do Lists at http://www .YourBusinessBible.com to help you stay focused and organized.

If you're still prepared to go forward, if I can't talk you out of it, if you're getting really excited about your business—then let's get to work.

You're going to do great!

Join me for your adventure in building a business—and a legacy.

Best wishes,
Eva Rosenberg, MBA, EA
Your TaxMama

---

1 Robert MacPhee, *Manifesting for Non-Gurus*, 2010.

LIGHTEN UP

Youʼre about to venture into dangerous and terrifying territory—the World of Taxes.

It's not as bad as you think. Get comfortable with the humor and ironies in this ever-shifting world. It will make all the onerous rules easier to bear.

Believe it or not, these quotes come to you courtesy of the Internal Revenue Service and other fine folks. Come back to this page any time your spirits need a boost of humor.

Did you ever notice that when you put the words "The" and "IRS" together, it spells "THEIRS"?
—Unknown

He who gets his tax advice out of a Cracker Jack box doesnʼt always get crackerjack advice.[1]
—LINDA DORFMONT, Enrolled Agent

I like to pay taxes. With them I buy civilization.
—OLIVER WENDELL HOLMES JR.,
US Supreme Court Justice

The government that robs Peter to pay Paul can always depend on the support of Paul.
—GEORGE BERNARD SHAW, Irish playwright

Taxes are indeed very heavy, and if those laid on by the government were the only ones we had to pay, we might more easily discharge them; but we have many others, and much more grievous to some of us. We are taxed twice as much by our idleness, three times as much by our pride, and four times as much by our folly.
—BENJAMIN FRANKLIN, *Poor Richard's Almanac*

---

1 Cracker Jack™ is a registered trademark of Frito-Lay.

Alexander Hamilton started the US Treasury with nothing, and that was the closest our country has ever been to being even.

       —WILL ROGERS, writer and humorist

The only difference between a tax man and a taxidermist is that the taxidermist leaves the skin.

       —MARK TWAIN, writer and humorist

Excellence is a good habit. But do not strive for perfection—it will prevent you from ever finishing anything.

       —EVA ROSENBERG, Your TaxMama

The seven deadly sins . . . food, clothing, firing, rent, taxes, respectability, and children. Nothing can lift those seven millstones from man's neck but money; and the spirit cannot soar until the millstones are lifted.

       —GEORGE BERNARD SHAW, Irish playwright

The hardest thing in the world to understand is the income tax.

       —ALBERT EINSTEIN, physicist

The only thing that hurts more than paying an income tax is not having to pay an income tax.

       —THOMAS DEWAR, First Baron Dewar

A good tax return is like a good mystery novel. You follow the clues, make deductions, and arrive at a profitable conclusion.

       —EVA ROSENBERG, Your TaxMama

"Post Tax Season Blues,"
an original poem by TaxMama, for April 15 of each year.

> *I finally filed my tax return.*
>
> *Through sleepless nights, how my eyes burn.*
>
> *I dug and searched before I filed.*
>
> *But let me tell you, I am riled.*
>
> *I work too hard and pay a ton.*
>
> *But, hey, . . . for now, my tax return's done.*
>
> *. . . is yours?*

Visit TaxMama.com for more humor in the Money Funnies column http://taxmama.com/category/asktaxmama/money-funnies. Please feel free to submit your clean jokes, too.

HOW TO USE THIS BOOK

At the beginning of each chapter, you will find a To-Do List and Questionnaire. Read the list and keep it in mind while you read the chapter. As you go along, perform the tasks on the list. If you put everything you do into this book, it will become your business bible. In fact, you can pick up a complete set of these To-Do Lists at www.YourBusinessBible.com.

- Enter the dates you complete the tasks.
- Enter the dates you schedule the meetings.
- Set the deadlines.
- Enter the answers to the questions.
- Fill out the forms.
- Enter the relevant ID numbers as you apply for the licenses or government IDs and programs.
- Make copies of all relevant documents and place them behind the To-Do List page.
- Use the resources at the end of each chapter to help you save taxes, operate your business, and increase your profits.

Incidentally, as you may have realized, tax laws change constantly, and most deductions, exemptions, and limits change annually. In fact, by the time this book reaches your hands, there may already be changes and updates. To get a quick summary of the updates, please visit www.YourBusinessBible.com.

Note About Links in This Book

As you go through the book, you will find that it is full of resources. The links and contact information for all the resources in each chapter will be found at the end of each chapter, to avoid cluttering up the text as we go along.

Many of the URLs in this book start out with iTaxMama.com. These are tiny.cc URLs that allow me to edit the underlying link. Too often, links on the Internet change, especially on the IRS website. So if one of these links doesn't work, please let me know and I can fix the underlying link without needing to change the link in the book. Ain't technology grand!

Disclosure: Some of the links in the book go to sites that pay me a commission. I don't recommend the sites because of the commission. They are recommended because they are good resources. But getting a referral fee never hurts. In fact, it's a good idea for you to learn how to use affiliate marketing yourself—both to earn commissions and to build a referral base to help you sell your products or services. A good place to learn about this is at Affiliate Summit, http://iTaxMama.com/Affiliate Summit.

PROLOGUE

Update on the Latest Tax Laws

When it comes to taxes, we live in ever-changing landscape. Even when we think we are up-to-date, some legislation or court comes along and changes the entire picture. In fact, just before this book went to print, we got a whole new set of changes. We were able to hold the presses long enough to include all the relevant changes in this Prologue and throughout the book.

Incidentally, about the most recent set of laws that were passed—the House and Senate versions of these laws have been, more or less, ready since May and July. Consider asking your legislators why they couldn't get their acts together to pass the SECURE Act early enough in the year so everyone doesn't have to rewrite all their software (including the IRS) and so it is possible to get some explanations and procedures from the IRS before tax season. Remember, when your refunds are being held up, the blame falls squarely on the shoulders of your Senators and Representatives—not the IRS.

As I write this introduction, I will give you a list of the most current laws our businesses need to take into consideration. The chapters in this book have been updated to take these laws into account. Since laws will continue to change, please subscribe to TaxMama.com to get news and updates throughout the year.

Although these laws also affect your personal tax returns, for now, we will primarily focus on the business effects:

- In December 2015 Congress passed a comprehensive set of laws—**the PATH Act of 2015—Protecting Americans from Tax Hikes Act of 2015** https://www.finance.senate.gov/download/summary-of-the-protecting -americans-from-tax-hikes-path-act-of-2015. You will see references throughout the book using only the acronym PATH Act.

- In 2017, Congress gave us the **Tax Cuts and Jobs Act (TCJA)**, which became law on December 22, 2017. http://docs.house.gov/billsthisweek /20171218/CRPT-115HRPT-%20466.pdf. You will see references throughout the book using only the acronym TCJA.
- On February 2, 2018, Congress passed the **Bipartisan Budget Act of 2018**. https://www.congress.gov/115/bills/hr1892/BILLS-115hr1892enr.pdf. This was mostly an Extender Bill, extending some tax provisions through the end of the year. Most of these provisions have expired.
- On July 1, 2019, Congress passed the **Taxpayer First Act (TFA)** https:// www.congress.gov/bill/116th-congress/house-bill/3151. This law primarily affects representation, not preparation of returns.
- On December 20, 2019, Congress passed the 715-page law called the Further Consolidated Appropriations Act. It includes two tax-related provisions that affect individual and small business taxpayers: the **Setting Every Community Up for Retirement Enhancement Act (SECURE Act)** and the **Taxpayer Certainty and Disaster Tax Relief Act (TCDTRA)**. (To save time, we'll be calling it the SECURE Act.) https://www.congress.gov/bill /116th-congress/house-bill/1865/text.

Some changes are permanent. Some are temporary and may get renewed or extended every few years. And some phase out gradually, over time. Let's start with the permanent changes.

C Corporations

Tax Rate—The tax rate is now a flat 21 percent—all those other nasty brackets are gone. This includes personal service corporations.

Alternative Minimum Taxes (AMT)—This tax is permanently repealed for corporations. (But not for individuals.)

Dividends Received Deductions—A corporation that receives dividends because they own stock in another corporation has always gotten a break. They could avoid paying taxes on most of those dividends—to avoid triple taxation. (Tax paid by the corporation issuing the dividends; tax paid by the corporation receiving the dividends; and tax paid by the shareholders of the corporation that received the dividends.)

- If the corporation receiving the dividends owns 20 percent or more of the paying corporation, the exclusion from income is 65 percent of the dividends (down from 80 percent).

- If the receiving corporation owns less than 20 of the paying corporation (think about buying stock through a brokerage), the exclusion from income is 50 percent of the dividends (down from 70 percent).

Qualified Small Business Stock (QSBS) Exclusion from Income—This makes owning or forming a C corporation very attractive. For qualified stock purchased after September 27, 2010, and held for more than five years, you can exclude 100 percent of the capital gains—up to $10 million. The PATH Act made this provision permanent. And it also eliminated the alternative minimum taxes that were previously assessed on the untaxed gains. You can learn more about this in Chapter 3.

S Corporations

Built-in Gains Tax (BIG)—When a C corporation elected to become an S corporation, it may have had some untaxed increases in the values of some assets. That's called a built-in gain. In the past, if the S corporation sold that property within 10 years after electing S status, the corporation would have to pay an extra BIG tax. The PATH Act reduced that time frame to five years. We don't really get into this in this book, but you can find information on the IRS website at http://iTaxMama.com /Built_In_Gains_Tax.

Partnerships

Technical Terminations Eliminated—In the past, if 50 percent or more of a partnership interest changed hands—for any reason—the partnership was considered terminated. This could apply equally if a partner died and heirs took over his or her interest, or if shares in the partnership were sold. This was such an inconvenient law—and most small businesses didn't even realize that was the case. So they didn't terminate the partnership and start a new one. The TCJA eliminated this annoying technical termination.

Businesses in General

Section 199A—The 20 Percent Qualified Business Income Deduction—This is a tax deduction, not a tax credit. This gets deducted after all the income has been computed and reduced by either the standard deduction or the itemized deductions. The next line after those deductions is the Section 199A deduction. This is available to sole proprietorships, partnerships, S corporations, certain trusts, and limited liability corporations (LLCs) filing their tax returns as any of these entities. There are income limitations for Specified Service Trades or Businesses. For more details, read Chapter 5.

The Definition of a Small Business—A business that has average annual gross receipts of $25 million or less for the past three years (increased by inflation). This affects several accounting rules and deductions for small businesses—like the next two provisions.

Accounting Rule Change—Businesses meeting the definition of a "Small Business" may elect to use the cash accounting method, instead of accrual. This applies even if your business has an inventory. Please read Chapter 4 for guidance.

Business Interest Deduction—The deduction for interest expenses is limited to 30 percent of business income for businesses with gross receipts in excess of the "Small Business" definition. Surprisingly enough, this may affect you if your business has losses (considered a tax shelter), or if you have pass-through investments, like partnerships or S corporations with losses. Read more on the IRS website's FAQs, available at http://iTaxMama.com/Bus_Interest_163j.

Entertainment Expenses—These are no longer deductible at all. However, if you can get a separate invoice for the food and beverages at your entertainment event—those are still deductible as meals.

Lobbying Expenses—All deductions for this are eliminated. And if you pay dues to any organization that's involved in lobbying, the part of the dues allocated to lobbying or political activities is not deductible. (OK, I admit that I am baffled by this one. I thought this was always the law. Perhaps it needed to be more specific?)

Section 1031 Exchanges—These tax-deferred exchanges are now limited to trades of business or investment real estate. We used to use this provision to exchange equipment and vehicles and to avoid paying taxes on the gains from the sale of the asset—something you commonly do is to trade in your business vehicle. It's no longer an option to defer the gain from that transaction.

Transportation Fringe Benefits—These are no longer a tax-free benefit or deductible to the employer. There's an exception when the transportation expenses are necessary for employee safety. So find a way to prove that the transportation fringe is related to employee safety. That shouldn't be hard in the big city.

Bicycle Commuting Benefits—These are no longer a tax-free benefit. These payments must now be included in employees' wages in order for an employer to continue to claim this deduction.

Qualified Moving Expenses—These are no longer a tax-free benefit. These payments must now be included in employees' wages in order for an employer to continue to claim this deduction unless the costs are for active-duty military.

Employee Awards—You can no longer give employee achievement awards of cash, gift cards, and other non-tangible personal property. Special rules allow an employee to exclude certain achievement awards from their wages if the awards are tangible personal property.

Self-Created Property—These assets do not get capital gains treatment if sold by any creator (the artist, writer, composer, inventor, etc.), or anyone to whom the creator gifted the property.

Long-Term Rental Agreements—"Long-term" was defined as 75 percent of the life of the building. The TCJA redefines "long-term" as 25 years.

Costs Related to Sexual Harassment Lawsuits—If there is a nondisclosure agreement as part of the settlement, none of the settlement payments are deductible to the payor.

Fines, Penalties, and Settlements—Congress has disallowed deductions for payments that the taxpayer establishes are either restitution (including remediation of property) or amounts required to come into compliance with any law that was violated or involved in the investigation or inquiry, that are identified in the court order or settlement agreement as restitution, remediation, or required to come into compliance. In other words, if you're paying a fine of any kind for violating any laws—none of those payments are tax deductible.

Net Operating Losses (NOLs)—Can no longer be carried back. They are carried forward only. They are no longer limited to a 20-year carryforward. They may be carried forward indefinitely.

Depreciation—There are many changes to the depreciation deductions and capitalization rules. All kinds of depreciation have increased. See Chapter 6 for most of the relevant changes that apply to the average business. Take an in-depth course on capital assets and depreciation if you want to learn all the details. There are many.

Opportunity Zones—This is a new term "Opportunity Zones." We have had similar concepts in the past, with different types of tax breaks. The current version is designed to allow businesses to defer paying taxes on certain kinds of income if they invest in depressed areas. They need to invest in or open a business in the area, or construct buildings, ideally to provide jobs and improve the economic conditions of specific areas. They can defer the gains until 2026. Or if they hold on to the investment for at least 10 years, they might be able to defer the gains permanently. Incidentally, you can roll over opportunity zone investments from one project to another. It's rather complicated and we are not covering this topic in this book. Beware. I expect there to be a lot of sharks creating projects to steal investors' money. So, please, please be careful. If you don't understand the project and cannot actually see the business in operation, stay away. For more information about this tax break visit this area of the IRS website at http://iTaxMama.com/Opportunity_Zones.

Rehabilitation Credits—For rebuilding and improving existing historic structures. The 10 percent credit for other buildings has been repealed. But the 20 percent credit for the historic structures remains in effect. The main difference is that the credit is taken over five years instead of in the year the building is placed into service. We will not be discussing this. You can find more information on the IRS website at http://iTaxMama.com/Rehab_Credit.

Wrongful IRS Levy—What a surprise. Sometimes the IRS levies funds or seizes assets from a taxpayer when they should not be doing so. Sometimes, it's quite a battle to get the money back—or time runs out before the taxpayer understands how to get the money back. The TCJA give us additional time to file our claims. We now have up to two years. In fact, if the IRS has sold the assets they seized, we might still be able to get those back! We are not covering this. But I thought it was important for you to know. Read more on the IRS website at http://iTaxMama.com/Wrong_IRS_Levy.

Provisions That Expire

Meals—The biggest change here is the elimination of the 100 percent deduction for food provided by employers at the company's facilities. That deduction has dropped to 50 percent. This provision will sunset after December 31, 2025. *Note:* The taxpayer must be present for the meals to be deductible. You cannot simply send a client off to a great restaurant and pick up the tab.

Employee Retention Credit Form 5884—https://www.irs.gov/instructions/i5884a. This is available to employers in certain disaster areas in 2017, 2018, and 2019. The employers can get up to $2,400 per employee that they retained after the relevant disaster (fire, flood, hurricane, etc.). This has been extended to December 31, 2020.

Employer Credit for Paid Family and Medical Leave—Employers who provide leave time (not sick pay) to their employees and continue to pay them for at least half of their wages for at least two weeks, up to 12 weeks, can qualify for this credit. This credit ranges between 12.5 and 25 percent of the wages of employees. This credit was extended by the SECURE Act through December 31, 2020. Please see Chapter 10.

Health Insurance Coverage Credit Form 8885—https://www.irs.gov/pub/irs-pdf/f8885.pdf. This has been extended for one more year, through December 31, 2020. We do not discuss this in Chapter 10 because the topic is somewhat complicated and is not often used by employers with fewer than 25 employees. But if you're planning to add health care coverage for all your employees, this is definitely worth exploring.

Since some states are mandating health insurance coverage, make sure to file for both the IRS and state credits.

Work Opportunity Tax Credit—This is a tax incentive for hiring disadvantaged workers—like veterans, disabled people, ex-felons, and so on. This credit was extended by the SECURE Act through December 31, 2020. See Chapter 10.

Business-Related SECURE Act Provisions

These all take effect for years after December 31, 2020, unless otherwise indicated.

Small Employer Pension Plan Credit Form 8881—https://www.irs.gov/forms-pubs /about-form-8881. The amount of the credit was raised from $500 to $5,000. This is for employers who start new pension plans after December 31, 2020. The credit is good for each year, for up to three years.

Small Employer Automatic Enrollment Credit (no form yet)—This credit is in addition to the Small Employer Pension Plan Credit. This is for employers that either set up a new pension plan or that add the automatic enrollment provision to an existing plan.

What is an automatic enrollment provision? That's where all your new employees must automatically start contributing part of their paycheck to their own pension plan. Employees are allowed to opt out. But if they don't read the hiring packet, they will see part of their paychecks disappearing into a retirement account. This is both good and bad for the individual employee. It forces savings. But not everyone can afford it. So read your employment packets when starting a new job.

Part-Timers May Contribute to 401(k)—Employers must now include part-time employees in their 401(k) plans, if they have worked for the company for at least 500 hours a year, for three years in a row. They must be age 21 by the end of the three-year period.

Multiple-Employer Plans (MEP)—Unrelated employers may now pool their resources to participate in shared health plans. Hopefully, this will help bring the costs down for all the employees.

Certain Personal Provisions in the SECURE Act Relevant to This Book

Adoption Benefits—The SECURE Act added a new twist to adoption benefits. Taxpayers may withdraw up to $5,000 from their IRAs or retirement accounts without penalty after December 31, 2019. How does that work? Parents who adopt a child, or give birth to a child, may withdraw that $5,000, penalty-free, as long as the withdrawal is within 12 months of the date of birth or adoption. They don't have to prove the money was used for the birth or adoption costs. The taxes on those distributions will still be due—but not the 10 percent early withdrawal penalty.

Section 529 Plans—The SECURE Act added two new provisions for these plans:

- Costs related to registered apprenticeships qualify as educational costs.
- Up to $10,000 may be withdrawn from a Section 529 plan to pay student loans. That total may be applied to principal or interest. And it's only a once-in-a-lifetime limit. In other words, if you use $5,000 to pay toward a student loan in 2020, you still have up to $5,000 to use in the future. Incidentally, if any Section 529 funds are used to pay the student loan interest, the taxpayer cannot deduct that interest on their tax return.

A Few Words About the Taxpayer First Act (TFA)

The IRS is very excited about the passage of this set of laws. The IRS and the Taxpayer Advocate Service have been working hard to get some of these provisions passed. They are designed to improve things for taxpayers, believe it or not.

For instance, IRS Appeals will become a separate, independent division of the IRS. This will help you get more objective results when you file an appeal. Though I must tell you this. In all the years I have brought cases before IRS Appeals, in every instance, they were professional, ethical, and helpful. So, I think this takes some of the pressure off the Appeals team from having to deal with interactions or interference from other IRS divisions, like collections, . . . perhaps?

There are provisions requiring improved customer service to taxpayers. Don't we all wish that would happen!

There are provisions to limit the IRS's right to seize your property or to issue arbitrary summonses. Innocent spouses will get more of a fair break when they file for relief. Taxpayers who are living on disability or are low-income will not be bothered by the independent collection agencies that the IRS is allowed to use.

There is another provision making the IRS responsible to help taxpayers track down refunds that have been deposited to the wrong account. Presently, the IRS encourages taxpayers to get their refunds deposited directly into our bank accounts. Sometimes it goes to the wrong account. Why? Not generally because of any IRS error. The error comes from the taxpayer or tax preparer entering the wrong bank account (sometimes it's off by one or two digits or a transposition). Perhaps the taxpayer provides the account number of an account they used to have. (One woman did that and more than $80,000 went to someone else's account.) Due to this, the IRS doesn't really have the power to recover the money from the person who received it.

This is really something the bank should do because they allowed a deposit to go to an account with someone else's name. (The account numbers and the names are required to match.) *But* . . . Congress put a provision into the Taxpayer First Act holding the IRS responsible for getting the money back to the taxpayer. It remains to be seen just how this will be implemented. In the meantime, to get *your* refunds, make sure you use the correct bank account number.

Whistleblowers may now get more information about the status of cases they submit the IRS. Until now, you submit a report and might never learn if the IRS followed up or not.

However, minimum late filing penalties are increased from $210 to $330 if there is an unpaid tax. The overall penalty is still 5 percent of the tax per month, up to 25 percent, when taxes are paid late.

Taxpayers who owe the IRS more than $50,000 (increased for inflation) and ignore IRS notices will get their passports revoked—or won't be able to renew them. In the past, if they opened a case with the Taxpayer Advocate Service, the IRS would release the passports. However, due to manipulation, the IRS will only release passports if a payment plan is set up—and payments are kept up.

As you know, the IRS keeps closing Taxpayer Assistance Centers (TACs). They will have to provide substantial notice (90 days) to the community before closing any more TACs.

The IRS is also required to modernize and increase their cybersecurity measures. From my standpoint, one of the more useful provisions is expanding the electronic, do-it-yourself taxpayer tools. Since it really is so hard to reach someone at the IRS during filing season (practically all year), being able to log in and get information saves a ton of time. Better yet, I am waiting for the ability to respond to IRS notices and audits by uploading replies directly to the taxpayer's own IRS account. It's coming. Really it is!

All of this is terrific . . . but I didn't see any provision to pay for any of these improvements.

In the meantime, let's get to work on setting up or improving your business!

Overall, There Will Always Be More . . .

There are a great many provisions in these laws that only affected individuals, including certain energy credits that haven't quite expired. Since this is a book about business taxes, those provisions are not covered here. I will be covering them in the TaxMama's TaxQuips podcast, and in my classes at CCH CPELink. However, you know that if you have questions about anything related to taxes, all you need to do is ask—http://iTaxMama.com/AskQuestion.

CHAPTER 1: **SMALL BUSINESS CHECKLIST**

To-Do List and Questionnaire

Fill in this worksheet as you work your way through the book. Each chapter will contribute information to help you complete this. This will be your master summary of the key information related to your business. Consider using an expandable file with A–Z pockets for this purpose. The files come in paper or plastic for under $15.

☐ 1. Set up your Advisory Team and meeting schedule. List the names and contacts of all the members on an attached sheet.

☐ 2. Contact small business advocacy groups, chambers of commerce, and research your industry. Lay the groundwork for your business. List the new resources you've just learned about.

☐ 3. What is your business focus? List the top two things your business will do or sell.
_____   _____

☐ 4. Start the outline for your business plan. What is your first business target?
_____

☐ 5. Start thinking about your business structure—to incorporate or . . . ?
Which business entity do you think is the best for you? _____
Why? _____

☐ 6. Select a business name. _____

☐ 7. Set up a corporation, partnership, or LLC—if you plan to be one.

☐ 8. Open a business bank account.
Bank name: _____
Account #: _____

☐ 9. Select your accounting system(s). _____

☐ 10. Research your business licenses. Make a list of all the licenses you need and have on an attached sheet of paper. Include the agency, license number, expiration date (if any), cost, and contact information.

☐ 11. Research state taxes and licenses, if applicable. List the secretary of state information, state income, sales tax, and payroll ID numbers. List other related agencies.

☐ 12. What insurance coverages do you need? Make a list of all the policies you need and have on an attached sheet of paper. Include the name of the insurance company, broker, policy number, expiration date, cost, and contact information. For auto insurance, keep a copy of the policy data in your car and here.

☐ 13. Where will you be working? From home or an outside office? Do a cost-benefit analysis to see which one works better for you.

☐ 14. What business equipment do you need? Make a list of the equipment you need, including vehicles. Split the list up between equipment you will buy and equipment you will lease. On each list include the name of the equipment, license or serial number, purchase date, cost, warranty contact and expiration, loan or lease amount, and monthly payment. Include a copy of the purchase document in this file.

☐ 15. Arrange for inventory. Where will you get the best prices and terms from those who sell you the merchandise that is the primary source of income for your business?

☐ 16. Research your vendors. Make a list of the main vendors or suppliers your business will use. List each vendor's name, the vendor's phone number and website (if applicable), the key contact (the top executive you can reach), the types of products or services the vendor will provide, the discount it will give you, and the payment terms.

☐ 17. Make a list of all the service providers you need and have. Include on the list each vendor's name, the vendor's phone number and website (if applicable), the key contact (the top executive you can reach), the types of products or services the vendor will provide, the discount it will give you, and the payment terms.

☐ 18. What legal issues affect you? Make a list of the contracts and forms you need in your business for customers or clients, vendors, subcontractors or freelancers, etc. Keep a master copy in this file.

☐ 19. Find ways to consolidate your communications vendors and the related bills.

☐ 20. When it comes to image and marketing, lay out your marketing plan. What are the first two things you will do to promote your business, besides the website? _____   _____

☐ 21. Address the money issues. Will you accept credit cards? PayPal? Square? Will you factor your receivables? What key strategies do you plan to use to get paid soonest? _____ _____

Remember to put a copy of each document into your expanding file—and scan it for your permanent electronic file.

You can download and print a copy of this checklist—and all the others in this book at www.yourbusinessbible.com.

SMALL BUSINESS CHECKLIST

Checklists are a helpful tool. Don't turn them into a crutch or limitation. When something is missing from your life or business checklist—add it!

—TaxMama

Before we start our small business checklist, let me just remind you that this book is full of resources. The links and contact information for all the resources will be found at the end of each chapter, to avoid cluttering up the text as we go along.

Ready? Let's talk about your business!

Starting a business is really easy. Many small business owners are in business before they even realize it. Someone likes something you make or do and offers to pay for it. Then another person asks. Pretty soon, something that started out as a hobby or family meal is bringing in a stream of income, even though you never intended to be in business. This is particularly true for the millions of people starting their own personal websites. Sure, the sites might start out as personal interest pages. But as they are filled with so much good information, they are suddenly discovered by hordes of people, and income starts rolling in. Oops, you're in business and didn't even know it. It is a wonderful feeling, though, isn't it?

Other times businesses are started with a clear purpose. Some people, for example, get frustrated because a type of product isn't available or because a service that should be there isn't obtainable. These smart people see the void and fill it. Sometimes, they simply start doing it for friends, like a carpool service, and a business grows from there.

Other people come up with a great idea to hit it rich and start building the business around the idea. Usually, they get so excited, their friends and family get caught up in the excitement and give them money. Or if they're really aggressive, they'll raise the money from strangers or through banks, loans, or venture capital—or, these days, through various forms of crowdfunding

And then there are those people who really want to start a business but don't know what business to start. If you don't have a clue but want one, read Paul and Sarah Edwards's book *The Best Home Businesses for the 21st Century: The Inside Information You Need to Know to Select a Home-Based Business That's Right for You*, published by Jeremy P. Tarcher. It will not only give you ideas, but it will tell you what skills and tools you need to make that business work for you.

Folks who prefer to run a business from home, here's another great resource filled with ideas—Raven Blair Davis's *Careers from the Kitchen Table*. The book has morphed into a radio show. (TaxMama Family members can get a free copy of the 2010 edition, filled with great business ideas, with TaxMama included on page 235.)

Which of these businesses will succeed? Which will fail? Can you tell just by reading about the personalities involved and the nature of the start-up? Not really.

Three Indicators Will Predict the Success of the Business

There are three key factors that will predict the success of any business. Look at the descriptions below and see how they fit your business.

1. **How big should your business be?** If a business stays small—such as a mom-and-pop operation—it may never make a fortune, but it can generate a nice, modest cash flow without a fuss. If handled properly, some of these businesses will support a household forever—without much stress—in modest, happy style, allowing for family time, vacations, and community involvement.

2. **Has the business developed a plan—something to map out how it is organized and, when it grows, how to deal with success?** The people who have the foresight to treat their businesses as real enterprises generally grow them properly, make excellent profits, often more than a million dollars, and have something solid to pass on to their children. Or they sell out to larger companies, for millions, when they are ready to retire or exit.

3. **Did the business owners take all the right compliance steps to learn of their tax and licensing obligations and stay on top of them?** Too many small business owners, even those who aren't home-based, just never take the time to look into the laws and rules that regulate their businesses. They just trip along blithely, doing what they do, and not dealing with licenses, payroll issues, or, sometimes, even filing issues, until these issues come and bite them in the derriere. I'm not kidding. I've seen too many nice people come to me because they were in such trouble with the IRS (or city licensing people or sales tax departments) that they were about to lose their businesses—even though they were successful. Or maybe these people were in trouble precisely because their businesses were successful and had finally come to the attention of the authorities.

Remember, *ignorance of the law is no excuse*. It's your responsibility to learn what your business must do—it's not the government's responsibility to tell you. On the other hand, most cities and states offer excellent free information on their websites and through local training sessions at colleges or other outreach programs. Or there are nonprofit organizations, like SCORE, ready to provide advice. This wealth of information and help is often free or costs very little. Using those resources, you'll also build a good contact network of the officials and bureaucrats who administer many of the programs. The small effort is well worth the trouble.

Let's ensure that your business is one of those that succeed. This book will help make sure you're one of the winners. Even if you're already in business, and have been for decades, the information you'll find here will help you.

Dennis Gaskill of BoogieJack.com said, "If you're already in business for yourself don't be fooled into thinking you can't learn plenty from this book. I've been in business for myself since 1997, and my eyes were opened wide in several places. In addition to gaining a greater understanding of tax issues, I found oodles of great business advice and a vast array of valuable resources that multiply the end value of the book. If I'd had this book when I started my business I'd have been able to spend more time growing it because I'd have spent less time working it. When you're working your business you're keeping it going, but when you grow your business you're increasing your income. With this book at hand, I'm giving myself a raise!"

It's not too late to get it right—to protect the time and dollar investment you've already made.

So What Do You Need to Do?

Before you get started, use the checklist in this chapter to get on track and make sure you are doing everything right. Try to follow the steps in the order they are presented. As you go along, you may think of some other things that need to be done at that particular point for your specific business or industry. Keep a stack of self-stick notes handy so you can record your thoughts when you think of them. (Did you know that Post-it Notes came about as an error? 3M found a brilliant use for a glue that didn't stick.)

Many of the resources mentioned in this book will take you to the Internet. When I was starting my business, I had to drive 50 miles to the nearest US Department of Commerce office in Los Angeles, or spend days in the little glassed-in room in the back of the Santa Ana law library to do my tax research. Today, you can get the same answers in a few minutes using the Internet. Most of the resources are free—at least, the ones I've found for you and included in this book. If you don't have Internet access, go to your public library. Most public libraries offer free Internet access, and the librarians can be very helpful. Perhaps it's time you were reacquainted with those libraries you loved as a kid.

You don't need a computer to start a business (e.g., house-sitting or dog-walking). You don't even need Internet access. But it helps. As Chapter 6 points out, the costs of a computer and Internet access are deductible as business expenses.

You'll be coming back to the Small Business Checklist at the beginning of this chapter often. You would be wise to photocopy the pages and put them on a clipboard so you can work with them as you go along. In fact, make a few extra copies so you can use them in the first exercise. Each chapter will have a to-do list for you to use. Be sure to do everything that applies to you.

Step 1. The first time you read the checklist, keep your mind open. Free-associate with the ideas and treat the time as a brainstorming session. Don't do anything yet—just add your notes. You can use self-stick notes to track and move your ideas around.

Step 2. Read the list through again. Treat the second read-through the same way. Only this time, make your notes more specific. Write the names of vendors or suppliers you already know, the ones you'll be contacting to implement the steps on the checklist. Add new vendors you find during your research efforts.

Step 3. Finally, start taking the actions and check them off when they are completed. Cross off anything that doesn't apply to you so that you're not distracted.

Ready? Let's go.

The Checklist in To-Do Order

Set Up an Advisory Team

Even if you're not incorporating your business, you need something similar to a board of directors. No one can run a business in a vacuum. Call upon professionals and people in your social or family circle or people in your community who've achieved success in the industries or fields you'll be servicing. You can't be expected to know everything, so don't try. Find an expert in each field to help your business succeed.

Plan to meet at least every month until the business is established. Then meet at least every quarter during the first year or two as the business develops. Meet at least once each year after that. Be sure these are people who are available for you to call upon throughout the year. Expect to pay them for their time. You might even want to keep them on retainer. Questions will come up that they can answer quickly and easily, saving you hours of research time, and perhaps quite a bit of money, in the process.

Who should be on your team? Your insurance broker, business attorney, tax professional, bookkeeper (if you have one), office manager, banker, largest vendor or supplier, largest customer, website manager, at least two people who have successful businesses in your community, perhaps your favorite marketing guru, and your spouse. Include at least one person who has been successful in your industry, too. Once you start hiring employees outside the family, add a human resources expert to your team.

While some people may find setting up an advisory board impractical, I disagree. True, you can certainly start a business without this step, but let's look at the people who are highly successful in their businesses, who don't seem to be stressed or struggling, and who seem to always have things go their way. What do we see in most of them? It's that they have advisors or mentors who have helped them build their business. The folks who are doing just "OK," or making just enough to live on—they were independent and did it all themselves. Like me. I achieved my successes by working too many hours and not finding the right marketing and business development people to help my business grow to its full potential. Building the right advisory team, I would have ended up with two lucrative deals—that I didn't know how to negotiate or present on my own. I would have worked fewer hours, built a larger teaching team, and made larger profits.

Let me tell you about two of my friends who did use advisors and informal advisory boards. Meet Lynn Freer and Michael Rozbruch.

Currently, Lynn Freer, an enrolled agent (EA), is president of Spidell Publishing, Inc. in Anaheim, California (https://www.caltax.com/). How she achieved this position is an interesting story—perhaps for another time. For now, let's talk about how she took a solid, existing, tax seminar business dealing only with California state tax issues and grew it to the remarkable, multimillion-dollar California and IRS *and* accounting resource it is today. Spidell now offers seminars and webinars on several hot topics. Their courses include the best written materials in the industry. The annual Spidell year-end tax update book is my primary resource for the year.

How did Lynn manage this? She did her research and networked to find an advisory group. The group she found at the time was Vistage. Members of the Vistage team paid a monthly fee (then, $1,000 per month), and a small, select group of business owners met each month to discuss their business goals, issues, problems, and ask for vendor or contact recommendations. Essentially, they shared their contacts, ideas, expertise, and resources with one another. Vistage provided a business coach to the group, who also met privately with each member during the month for additional consultations. Looking up Vistage, here's what I found—https://www.vistage .com/membership/programs/, in case you're interested in getting their guidance. Although Lynn is no longer part of Vistage, she is still a member of a small advisory group. Even after all these years, they meet each month and help each other reevaluate their respective progress, and to open doors for one another. Lynn says she has always worked with a business coach and an advisory team.

It's Time to Meet Michael

Meet Michael Rozbruch, CPA. He had built up a multimillion-dollar business helping people who owed too much money to the IRS. But, around 2013, the partnership went sour and he felt compelled to start over. But doing what? Right around that time, I invited Michael to teach some online classes with me. He was a natural! He loved the medium. He was intrigued. At that same time, three different people told him to read *The Millionaire Messenger* by Brendon Burchard. Reading that book gave him his "Aha!" moment. But he needed more than that—Michael needed a plan. He invested a couple of thousand dollars in a three-and-half-day expert academy to learn how to reach a million dollar level of gross revenue. Michael also followed up with the long-term team of advisors he had built up during his years in his previous business. People like Dan Kennedy and a mastermind group, like the Titanium Mastermind group. (When he started his original business, he invested more than $30,000 to make his business start-up effective quickly.) We'll talk more about Michael in Chapter 2, when we discuss business plans. I just wanted to introduce him here, to tell you that by having an advisory team, Michael was able to build two multimillion-dollar businesses—and to help other tax professionals increase their incomes dramatically (https://www.rozstrategies.com/success-stories/). I asked him, "Would you have started this business without your advisors' guidance?" Michael replied, "Without my advisors, I would not have attempted to start the new business at all. If I had started on my own, I would have wasted a lot of money—and time. And probably walked away from the project."

Where can you find these professionals? Ask people you know for recommendations. You'd be surprised at the important, successful people who are willing to help you grow your business. Look for mastermind groups that accept people at your level of expertise and investment. After all, many mastermind groups have minimum requirements, so members don't waste the team's time and resources. Or visit the websites of your professional organization(s). These are the best places to find key tax and financial professionals:

- **Enrolled agents (EAs).** For tax specialists licensed to represent taxpayers before the IRS, people whose license allows them to work anywhere in the nation, contact the National Association of Enrolled Agents (NAEA), http://taxexperts.naea.org, (855) 880-NAEA (6232).
- **Certified public accountants (CPAs).** CPAs are authorized to perform certified audits and issue financial statements. For a referral, contact the American Institute of Certified Public Accountants (AICPA), https://cpapowered .org/find-a-cpa, (888) 777-7077.
- **Attorneys with the American Bar Association (ABA).** For tax attorneys, business attorneys, and intangibles experts (patents and copyrights), contact the ABA, http://iTaxMama.com/ABA_Attorney_Search, (800) 285-2221 or (312) 988-5000.
- **National Association of Tax Professionals (NATP).** You'll find a cross section of all kinds of tax professionals here—EAs, CPAs, attorneys, and licensed tax professionals. You can use NATP's online search function to find a local tax professional at http://www.natptax.com, or call the association's toll-free number, (800) 558-3402.
- **Certified Tax Coach (CTC).** To get higher level, more complex tax planning done, you need the help of a trained CTC. The CTC is able to help you

set up everything we discuss in this book—and so much more—especially if your business is generating profits of a million dollars or more. https://www .certifiedtaxcoach.com/.

- **Insurance agents and brokers.** To locate insurance professionals, try the Independent Insurance Agents and Brokers of America (IIAA), http://www .independentagent.com, (800) 221-7917.
- **Certified financial planners.** To locate trained financial managers, contact the Certified Financial Planner Board of Standards, http://www.cfp.net, (800) 487-1497.

Incidentally, if a really big part of your business involves shipping, see if you can get your shipping company's representative on your team. People rarely think about including representatives from the shipping companies, but they often have worldwide contacts. They may be able to help you find the best vendors, as well as customers, for your business. And they can even design custom packaging for you at little or no cost if you're doing volume. For example, UPS created really beautiful packaging for Randazzo's King Cakes in New Orleans.

Get started now assembling your team; you'll need all these people to help you with the rest of this checklist.

Contact Small Business Advocacy Groups

Two of the most helpful advocacy groups for small businesses have websites with invaluable information. They are the Small Business Administration (SBA) at https:// www.sba.gov/ and SCORE, also known as the "Service Corps of Retired Executives," at https://www.score.org/.

On their websites, you'll receive lots of useful information about the business climate, your industry, and general business start-up help. SCORE even provides free advisors, or coaches, to help your business follow the right paths. Bear in mind that most of the people volunteering at SCORE come from the corporate world and have little experience with small businesses. But they have good contacts, and if you let them guide you, they can help groom your business to grow in ways you couldn't do alone. What's the key thing to do with SCORE volunteers? Listen.

Decide Your Business Focus

Focus on one or two things you do well or products or product lines you want to sell or produce. If you think of many, list them so you don't forget about them. Then select only the top one or two things you can implement most easily. Once the business is running smoothly, you can always add products or services. Starting with too many services or product lines dilutes your focus and your market.

Think about McDonald's. It started with a core product line—hamburgers, fries, shakes, and Filet-O-Fish. That was it for decades until the company had built a solid reputation and market saturation. McDonald's does field-test new products in certain of its company restaurants. But these products are often dropped before they can be distributed nationally. The company only adds new products after successful consumer testing.

Prepare a Business Plan

We'll explain why you need a business plan and show you how to create one in Chapter 2.

Decide on Your Business Structure

Will you be a sole proprietor, corporation, or what? We'll help you decide in Chapter 3.

Decide on the Name or Names You Will Use

How do you decide on a name? Perform some searches first. Try looking online to make sure there isn't another company with the same name already in operation. Here are some other steps to take when selecting a name:

- **Trademark your name.** If you are planning for the long term or ever want to take your business public, this is an excellent precaution. You can do it yourself with the US Patent and Trademark Office. Before you file, even before you settle on your name, however, it may be worthwhile to run a trademark search to see if anyone is using it. A great web resource for this is the Patent Office's trademark database, which you can search. Once you've decided on a name, you may submit your application online. If you don't do it right up front, you may have to spend a fortune fighting to protect it. Because I didn't file right up front, it took me about three years to get TaxMama registered (see Figure 1.1). You can see the history of the battle at the US Trademark and Patent office website. Search for "TaxMama."

FIGURE 1.1 TaxMama Trademark

United States Patent and Trademark Office	**Reg. No. 3,426,814** Registered May 13, 2008

TRADEMARK
SERVICE MARK
PRINCIPAL REGISTER

TaxMama

ROSENBERG, EVA (UNITED STATES INDIVI-DUAL)
P.O. BOX 280549
NORTHRIDGE, CA 91328

FOR: DOWNLOADABLE ELECTRONIC PUBLI-CATIONS IN THE NATURE OF A SYNDICATED COLUMN DEALING WITH TAXATION, PERSO-NAL FINANCE AND SMALL BUSINESS, IN CLASS 9 (U.S. CLS. 21, 23, 26, 36 AND 38).

FIRST USE 7-10-1998; IN COMMERCE 12-11-1999.

FOR: PRINTED SYNDICATED COLUMNS DEAL-ING WITH TAXATION, PERSONAL FINANCE AND SMALL BUSINESS, IN CLASS 16 (U.S. CLS. 2, 5, 22, 23, 29, 37, 38 AND 50).

FIRST USE 7-10-1998; IN COMMERCE 12-11-1999.

FOR: PROVIDING A NON-DOWNLOADABLE ONLINE COLUMN DEALING WITH TAXATION, PERSONAL FINANCE AND SMALL BUSINESS; EDUCATION SERVICES, NAMELY, PROVIDING INTERNET-BASED AND E-MAIL COURSES IN THE FIELD OF TAXATION, PERSONAL FINANCE AND SMALL BUSINESS, IN CLASS 41 (U.S. CLS. 100, 101 AND 107).

FIRST USE 7-10-1998; IN COMMERCE 12-11-1999.

THE MARK CONSISTS OF STANDARD CHAR-ACTERS WITHOUT CLAIM TO ANY PARTICULAR FONT, STYLE, SIZE, OR COLOR.

SER. NO. 78-727,175, FILED 10-5-2005.

SUZANNE BLANE, EXAMINING ATTORNEY

- **Get an Internet domain name to match your business name.** Even if you're not planning to have a website right away, buy the name now and hold it until you need it. Otherwise, it will be gone when you're ready. Do-mains are cheap. GoDaddy.com sells domain names for about $10 per year. When operating online is important to your business, your business name might depend on what's available as a domain name. The very memorable TaxMama.com was chosen after just such a search. The boring tax-related domains I wanted were no longer available. So, to our everlasting delight, we came up with something clever and original.

TaxMama Tip

The most important type of domain is the ".com" because it's the one most people automatically type. So if you use a domain with any other ending (or "extension")—without also owning the .com—people will be taken to someone else's website.

- **File fictitious name announcements in your local newspaper, if necessary.** This step will protect your name at the local level. This is what people call "doing business as" or "DBA." It lets the community know who is using the business name that you are announcing. If you are purely using your own name, you don't need to file. For instance, if your business name is "Georgia Brown," no DBA is needed. But if it is "Georgia Brown Consultant Extraordinaire!," you need to file the DBA information. Generally, if you incorporate, you can skip the fictitious name filings because the corporate name is protected at the state level.

Set up a Corporation, Partnership, or LLC—If You Plan to Be One

There are several documents that you have to fill out to become a corporation, partnership, or limited liability corporation (LLC). You'll need certain of those documents in order to take several of the next steps. So save yourself some time by filling out these documents now. You could use an attorney to handle the setup for you. I've found that attorneys tend to charge about $1,500 to $3,000 to set up your entity. They provide about an hour of advice and order the kit from an outside service that creates all the documents. The law firm turns it all over to you; then you have to get your own federal identification number or your tax professional has to get it for you. Attorneys rarely remember to file the S-corporation election. That problem keeps cropping up consistently when clients come to me with their new corporations. What can you do instead? Pay your attorney for the hour of consultation about your business structure. Better yet, include your tax professional in that meeting, too. Then use one of these services to set up your entity. They are the same ones your attorney would use (see the Resources at the end of this chapter for the links):

- **Incorp Services Inc. in Nevada.** (800) 2 INCORP: You'll get 20 percent off on formation services and registered agent services when you use the coupon code TAXMAMA (and TaxMama gets a commission).

- **The Company Corporation.** (800) 315-9420: Register your corporation, LLC, or other formal structure at this site, which is one of the oldest incorporators in the country. Mention that TaxMama sent you to get a $25 discount.
- **Hubco.** (800) 443-8177: Hubco has the *cheapest prices for entity setup.* Attorneys who prepare some of their own bylaws and articles use these folks. Hubco services the public, too, but you'll need to take care of several aspects of the setup yourself. (It is also a good source for supplies, such as corporate seals, stock certificates, etc.)

It's essential to get the guidance of your team's attorney and tax pro on this issue before you take action. Read Chapter 3 to better understand why you need guidance.

Before you start working with a partner or an investor who plans to participate actively in your business, consider reading Doug Thorburn's *Drunks, Drugs & Debits: How to Recognize Addicts and Avoid Financial Abuse.* Deciding to work with a recovering addict or obvious addict is easy. Once you know the person's condition, you can make your decision with your eyes open. It's the hidden addict who will destroy your business and your own emotional stability. Read the book and you'll know the signs going in; then you'll be able to decide if you want to go forward.

Open a Separate Bank Account for Your Business

Open a unique bank account for your business even if you plan to operate as a sole proprietor. Remarkably, many people overlook this fundamental business step. But it is crucial so that your personal money doesn't get confused with funds from your business. If you are ever audited, having a separate account can help you gather your paperwork quickly.

When you are picking a bank, shop around. Find a local bank with nationwide ATMs, willing to waive first-year fees on business accounts. Arrange to get copies of your canceled checks. Many banks are discouraging this service or charging for it. Pay the fee. Having those canceled checks available will save you a lot of time and money in audits and tough situations. Arrange for online access and downloads. Often with online banking, you'll get free accounting software. If you are given a choice, opt for Sage 50c or QuickBooks, not Quicken (we'll cover this topic in detail in Chapter 4). You're welcome to establish a business savings account or an investment account to store your profits or start-up loans until you need the money.

Select an Accounting System or Software

Chapter 4 will guide you through the record-keeping process.

Research the Licenses You Need and Agencies to Which You'll Be Reporting

Gather all the forms and determine what your costs will be—both initially and annually. You'll need all this for your business plan and budget (we'll discuss this more in Chapter 2). In brief, though, here are several forms you'll probably need to fill out:

- **City or county license.** Even a home-based business may need one. Call your city, county, or parish clerk's office for more information. The SBA has a resource linking to small business information in each state; see the State Resources list at the end of this chapter. Read your local government's business website carefully. Most localities have inexpensive licenses, around $25 to $75 per year. Be aware, however, that the Los Angeles license, for example, is based on a percentage of sales and could cost hundreds of dollars each year. And Los Angeles aggressively collects those funds. Do you have the same multiplicity of jurisdictions where you live?
- **IRS registration for an employer identification number (EIN).** File Form SS-4 online yourself. You'll find a link at TaxMama.com's Resource Center. *Note:* If you are a sole proprietor who doesn't plan to have employees, say you will have them, just to get the identification number issued. Having that EIN will make the difference between looking like a real business and looking like a hobby. (More about this in Chapter 2.)
- **IRS online payment system.** Sign up with the IRS's online payment system at https://www.eftps.gov/eftps/. You can deposit your estimated tax payments, pay payroll taxes, and conduct other business tax transactions online.

Research State Taxes and Licenses

A variety of agencies may be regulating your industry, and you should learn the details about taxes, licensing, zoning, unions, and so on before you start. The fastest way to get the information you need is on the Internet. Start with your state's official website. When you get to the state's home page, look for a business link. If you need information about other states, you will find a link to all state tax agencies in this chapter's resources section including the website for the Federation of Tax

Administrators. The link goes to the federation's tax forms pages, but if you do a little backtracking, you'll find the tax home page of the state you are interested in.

If you don't have access to the Internet, pull out your residential telephone book. In the front, you'll find pages listing all your local and state agencies. Spend some time reading that whole section. You'd be surprised at the agencies you'll find. Some of them may even become a source of funding or contracts. Who knows? At least you'll find the key agencies that affect your industry. Be sure to call your city clerk (or local equivalent) about local licensing. For state issues, call your secretary of state's office. If that office is not the one you need to speak with, someone there will tell you whom you should call.

- **State income tax registration.** This is generally necessary only if you have formed an entity other than a sole proprietorship.
- **Sales tax.** You'll need to know about sales taxes even if all your sales are online sales. (Chapter 12 explains why.) You must collect sales taxes if you are selling products to the end user. Some states might charge sales taxes on services. Check with your state's department of revenue or its equivalent.
- **Payroll taxes.** Register with your state's payroll tax department if you plan to have employees. Your children might be employees—if they actually do the work they're supposed to do. (Chapter 9 will explain who is and isn't an employee.)
- **State licenses.** State licenses are usually required for childcare providers, cosmeticians, most professionals, contractors, those selling alcohol, anyone dealing with hazardous substances, truckers, and who knows what other industries. It's best to check before you find you're operating without a license. The SBA has an excellent resource to help you look up your state's requirements at https://www.sba.gov/starting-business/business-licenses-permits /state-licenses-permits.
- **Other.** Check to see what else your industry needs or requires. If you can't find answers online, interview people who are successful in your industry. Or just call your state and ask the folks there to point you to a list of your obligations. Better yet, have them mail the list to you. Save the list and use it as a checklist. Of course, hiring a good tax professional with expertise in your industry will save you hours or even weeks of research. A good tax professional already knows what you must do. Another way to save time researching all the licenses you need is to use http://iTaxMama.com/BusLicense. It will do the research for you. For an extra fee, it will even fill in the forms for you.

Research Your Costs—Especially Insurance

One of the first things you'll need to get quotes on is insurance costs. Consider working with good business insurance brokers. They'll know where the deals are and your coverage requirements:

- **Business liability, fire, theft.** Get a combined policy. For malpractice insurance, check with your professional association for the best prices.
- **Auto.** A good local broker can find you the best rates. You may be able to cut your rates by having one company carry several of your policies. Check several sources for better rates, but be sure that the coverage you're pricing is equivalent across all carriers. Visit the American Automobile Association to find your local automobile club or call information to get the number of a local office. AAA offers some of the most complete insurance coverage and great service in case of accidents. GEICO offers different discounts for members of organizations such as government workers, AARP, and so on. I started with a "Good Sam" discount. When I obtained a letter from my alma mater, the "university discount" cut my policy by another $116 for six months. Seniors taking driving classes can get another discount from most insurers. Mercury Insurance runs great commercials. It has good prices, but its policies do not cover other people driving your car or accessories on your car, even if the accessories were from the dealer. Read the proposed coverage before buying!
- **Health.** You'll probably need health coverage for yourself and your employees. Start out small. If you can't afford to pay for your employees' insurance, consider setting up a Health Savings Arrangement (HSA) plan. Find an insurance carrier in your state at https://www.ehealthinsurance.com/. HSAs were signed into law in 2003 and have become very popular. Read Chapter 10 for information on insurance benefits and tax credits. *Note:* HSAs consist of two parts, both of which are abbreviated as HSA. There is the Health Savings Arrangement (the plan) and the Health Savings Account (the bank account that comes with the plan).
- **Workers' compensation (WC).** Find a local carrier. Some WC carriers, especially the quasi-state agencies, will pay you dividends if the fund makes money. Those dividends can reduce your net premiums by 10 percent or more per year. If you belong to an association or a professional or trade organization, contact it. Some organizations have negotiated deals for their members. I got a substantial rate reduction through one of my accounting

associations. For a comprehensive list of state agencies and carriers across the country, visit http://www.workerscompensationinsurance.com/links/index .htm or call your state insurance commissioner for carriers in your area.

- **Disability.** If you can qualify, get covered. You'll need a source of income if you get sick or hurt and can't work for several weeks. Check with your state if you can't get covered commercially. Many states offer state disability insurance coverage for small business owners that are similar to employees' coverage. The cost may be higher if you're on Schedule C rather than on payroll. The benefits tend to be good for only around one year. So, if you can, try to get private disability coverage that will pay you benefits for several years—or even for life. Another way to get coverage if you don't meet the minimum health requirements is to buy a group policy for yourself and your employees. It usually requires a minimum of three people, but there are no medical exams. If you can find a really good policy, you'll be able to live on it if—heaven forbid—you become permanently disabled. If you don't have employees, look to your union or professional or trade association for group coverage. If that organization has not arranged for coverage, bug it until it does.
- **Life.** Work with your advisory team on life insurance. Don't go overboard, but get the coverage you need. For instance, seriously consider getting key person insurance, which allows you to buy out partners or their heirs in case of catastrophic injury or death.
- **Other.** There may be other insurance you will need, depending on your area, your business, and your industry. Your advisory team can alert you to the right coverage.

Select Facilities

Will you work from home, or will you buy or rent space? Whenever possible, look at the long-term picture. If you can afford to buy a place, do it. If you outgrow it, you can always rent it or sell it. Be unconventional, if you can. Will your business work if you put it into a house or an apartment? If it will, buy one. Many law firms and professionals take over old houses and fix them up as stately offices. If buying isn't an option, be creative. Can you share space with a vendor in exchange for some service? If the service doesn't interfere too much with your time, that may be a way to fund your first office space. (Read Chapter 5 about barter income.) If you must rent, negotiate. Offer to accept a higher monthly rent than you'd like in exchange for free months each year. That helps the landlord show a high monthly rental rate in case he or she wants to sell the building. Meanwhile, you end up paying a lower overall average rate.

The other option is to set up an office in your home, which has some excellent tax benefits—but could be too distracting to allow you to work. We'll discuss this in depth in Chapter 7.

One of my EA Exam students graduated and passed all three of the IRS's Special Enrollment Examinations. He met a man in church who ran a chain of check cashing outlets. They worked out a deal. Joe set up a tax office in one of the check cashing stores and did tax returns for the patrons. In exchange, Joe agreed to double his tithe to their church—paying the church 20 percent of his income instead of 10 percent. The arrangement worked out so well that the following year Joe had to hire staff and expand the arrangement to all the check cashing stores in the chain. Perhaps you can work out a mutually beneficial rental arrangement, too.

Make Lease-or-Buy Decision on Equipment and Vehicles

When it comes to the equipment and vehicles you'll use, your first step is deciding whether you want to lease or buy. For equipment that either becomes obsolete quickly or is older and more subject to breaking down, a lease may be preferable. You can deduct the lease costs. Leases will often include service contracts, which will save you some money on that score. There are also benefits to buying automobiles you need for your job. We'll cover this in more depth in Chapter 8.

Arrange for Inventory

When manufacturing a product, inventory is the heart of your operation. Though you'll find suppliers around the world on the Internet, don't rely on people you've never seen at facilities you've never visited to make your main products. Legwork is critical. Inspect the facilities and talk to their customers. Once you have prices, plug them into your business plan. Let your advisory team help you find the right sources. Always be on site when the factory manufactures your products—or have a representative there to inspect the finished products—before shipping.

Several years ago, when computer ports were precious and not to be wasted, Chris invented the EasyStick, a mechanical joystick that could be strapped over the number pad on the keyboard instead of having to be plugged into the computer. He knew this device would only have a brief life before it became outmoded—perhaps two to three years at the most. It garnered rave reviews from the *Computer Shopper* and other major computer and gaming magazines. Chris found a major wholesaler who contracted with him to buy all the units he could produce. He raised money from a handful of investors, knowing he'd be able to give them a generous profit. Chris found a company in China to manufacture it, using Lexan™, a hard plastic that would withstand the heavy-duty use. Well . . . Chris wasn't there to oversee the process on the day the Chinese factory did its production run. It didn't use Lexan but instead used a cheaper material. When people used them, the EasySticks broke almost immediately. The wholesaler canceled the contract. The company went bankrupt, and the investors got nothing back.

Establish Supplies Accounts

Establish accounts with office supply houses, both locally and online. My company has worked with Quill and Office Depot for decades. Unfortunately, Quill has been bought up by Staples and they no longer offer the same level of service, pricing, or value. Whenever a product is wrong or damaged, both companies will generally take the materials back. Consider also Costco, Sam's Club, or other volume discount stores.

Develop a reasonable budget for the things you need, and be careful not to spend money on things you don't need. Don't get things because they're cute.

Consider Your Services Needs

Even if you decide not to hire employees initially, you'll still need help. There are many people who can assist you with their services. Get an answering service so that you're not constantly interrupted by calls. You may even need a virtual assistant. Certainly, you'll need an attorney and a tax professional, and you might need a consultant or two. For instance, you may not want to ship all your own products. Will you need a fulfillment house? Price out all the services you're going to need. However, be careful about treating your "assistant" as a contractor rather than as an employee. If the individuals are not actually in business for themselves, you may need to put them on payroll. Some states are passing stricter legislation about staffing issues—especially as a result of the Uber driver lawsuits. Chapter 9 will give you a hiring setup checklist for freelancers and employees, and will provide you with more information on paying taxes for the people who work for you.

Research Legal Issues

A variety of legal issues will affect your business. For instance, you'll need to know about your area's labor laws—so call your state's employment department:

- **Contract law.** Everything you sell is under contract, even if it is implied. Understand how to limit your responsibilities to your customers—to only the specifics of your contracts. Include references to additional fees for any changes to the goods or services once the contract has been signed. The attorney on your advisory team can help.
- **Bad debts.** Customers don't always pay on time . . . or ever. Set up protections in your invoices and contracts before the problems arise. Search online for contracts similar to those you expect to use. Modify them for your business. Also speak to your attorney about additional protections. Some contracts can be protected with UCC lien filings (http://iTaxMama.com/UCC_Filings). The rules are different in each state. The fees tend to be low. The disclosure must be included in the contract. If your client doesn't pay you—that UCC lien will make you a secured creditor. You might be able to collect your fees, even if they file for bankruptcy.
- **Liability laws.** When you have an online presence, your business is exposed to liability in a number of ways—sometimes through actions of others. As you're beginning your business planning, read Jonathan I. Ezor's *Clicking Through: A Survival Guide for Bringing Your Company Online*. It will give you a handle on the legal areas you'll need to address so that you can develop your legal budget. There's lots of practical information in his book—if only he'd written it before I went online. Yes, I know, this book has a 2000 copyright and is out of print. So you can probably only find used copies. But, honestly, I haven't seen anyone else write a book like this for the small business owner. Also, read Chapter 12 of this book to learn more about the nexus issues you face due to your Internet presence.

Select Communications

If there's a way to integrate your telephone, cell phone, Internet, and fax into one billing plan, do it. It's easier to get one bill from one service provider. On the other hand, it doesn't hurt to duplicate some of these services in case of trouble. For instance, my company has AT&T U-verse for the Internet. In case it goes down, we have Verizon's wireless thumb drive for our laptops, which we can use to run the entire business. Since services like U-verse use your office's electrical supply, keep at least one old-fashioned phone line that is powered by the phone company's electrical supply at the socket. It doesn't hurt to also have a smartphone. That way, you have triple power redundancy.

Find the best vendors, providing good service at fair prices. Be willing to sacrifice a bit of price to get personal service. For instance, our toll-free line is through National Comtel, a small local company at (800) 987-0100. We can call the office and speak to the same two or three people every time, even the company president. No long waits on hold. No random customer service people who keep getting it wrong. I pay five cents per minute for incoming calls on my toll-free line. Small companies are willing to negotiate, which is great. But don't make them cut their prices low enough to put them out of business. With a little bit of work, you'll be able to find good suppliers in your own neck of the woods.

Start to Work on Image and Visibility

Establishing brand awareness among your clientele and in the marketplace will help you keep your customer base in tough times. When they're devoted to your brand, you become their only choice:

- **Build your brand.** Rob Frankel's *The Revenge of Brand X* provides invaluable guidelines that you can use to cement your identity from day one.
- **Develop a presence in the marketplace.** Public relations is less costly than advertising—and more effective. Good PR will get you established as an expert in your industry. If you can't afford a public relations firm but you're able to speak clearly and eloquently about your business, sign up for Dan Janal's PR Leads service and Cision's free HelpAReporter.com. Having both services will give you access to the broadest base of journalists and publicists. Be prepared to invest a lot of time, at least initially. But if you write good responses to journalists' requests for experts, you'll be flooded

with calls. Press releases also generate attention when written well. For that, you will need an expert. Your advisory team can help you find the best person locally—or consult Dan Janal or Shel Horowitz.

- **Consider advertising.** It's the lifeblood of a growing business. But don't shotgun your ads all over the place. Target your audience carefully and find the most effective, least expensive publications. If you're on a tight budget, *Guerrilla Marketing to Heal the World: Combining Principles and Profit to Create the World We Want by* Jay Conrad Levinson and Shel Horowitz offers twenty-first-century tips for getting the most attention for your product or service, while also helping your business make a big impact solving problems like hunger, poverty, war, violence, and catastrophic climate change while making a healthy profit—also found at http://www.FrugalMarketing.com.

Take Care of Money Issues

Some businesses or industries have a really long accounts receivable lag. Some businesses require you to advance money on merchandise or services. Then you must wait 30, 60, 90, or even 120 days to get paid—that's industry standard. Unless you have a charming and clever way to speed up the payments, you will need financing. Look into all the options available to you. In some industries, like the schmatte industry (the textile trade), "factoring" is common. Factoring is the practice of selling your accounts receivable to another company at a slight discount. Essentially, you're paying interest on your accounts receivable so you can get the cash in advance. The factor becomes responsible for collecting the money from your customers. Consider factoring or accounts receivable financing if you're planning to sell to any government agencies. They are notoriously slow pays—often 90 days or more.

This checklist (shown in shorter form in Table 1.1) is probably more comprehensive than you expected from a tax book, but you'll soon find that good tax planning goes hand in hand with good business planning. Without a solid business, who needs to worry about taxes? You'll have nothing but losses, and that requires a whole different set of plans—for failure. Well, this book isn't about failing. It's designed to make you a stunning success, without expending too much money or stress on your part.

TABLE 1.1 The Carry-with-You Checklist in To-Do Order

☐ 1. Set up an advisory team.
   Tax advisors
   Attorneys
   Insurance agents and brokers

☐ 2. Contact small business advocacy groups and research your industry.
   Small Business Administration: www.sba.gov
   Service Corps of Retired Executives (SCORE): www.score.org

☐ 3. Decide your business focus.

☐ 4. Prepare a business plan.

☐ 5. Decide on your business structure.

☐ 6. Decide on the name or names you will use.
   Trademark the name with the US Patent Office: www.uspto.gov/index.html.
   Get an Internet domain name to match your business name.
   File fictitious name announcements in your local newspaper, if necessary.

☐ 7. Set up a corporation, partnership, or LLC—if you plan to be one.

☐ 8. Open a separate bank account for your business.

☐ 9. Select an accounting system or software.

☐ 10. Research the licenses you need and the agencies to which you'll be reporting.
   City or county license
   IRS registration for an employer identification number (EIN)
   Sign up with the IRS's online payment system: www.eftps.gov.

☐ 11. Research state taxes and licenses.
   State income tax registration if you are not a sole proprietorship
   Sales tax
   Register with your state's payroll tax department
   State licenses
   Other: Check to see what else your industry needs

☐ 12. Research your costs, especially insurance.
   Business liability, fire, theft
   Auto: www.aaa.com to find your local automobile club; GEICO, (800) 861-8380, www.geico.com
   Health—for yourself and your employees: www.ehealthinsurance.com
   Workers' compensation (WC): http://iTaxMama.com/WorkComp_by_State
   Other—depending on your area, your business, and your industry

☐ 13. Select facilities: Will you work from home, rent space, or buy it?

☐ 14. Make a lease-versus-buy decision on equipment and vehicles.

☐ 15. Arrange for inventory.

☐ 16. Establish supplies accounts.

☐ 17. Consider your services needs.

☐ 18. Research legal issues.

☐ 19. Select communications: telephone, cell phone, Internet, fax.

☐ 20. Start to work on image and visibility.

    Brand recognition

    Public relations

    Advertising

☐ 21. Take care of money issues.

    Loans

    Other financing

Resources

In this chapter, you saw a variety of resources. Here's a summary of them, so you can find them quickly and easily. The resources are not necessarily in alphabetical order in each category. They are in order of their importance or usefulness, in TaxMama's opinion.

US Government Resources

- **IRS.** https://www.irs.gov/. For IRS forms and publications. Use the links on the navigation bar at the top of the page to find things quickly, or use the two search boxes to search the site or the forms and publications database.
- **IRS Employer ID Number.** http://iTaxMama.com/IRS_EIN. This site explains how to fill out your SS-4 application and file for your EIN online.
- **IRS Online Payment System.** https://www.eftps.gov/eftps/. Sign up with the IRS's online payment system here.
- **US Patent and Trademark Office.** https://www.uspto.gov/. This is the place to go for patents and trademarks. You can search the database for similar patents or trademarks, and you can apply for yours online.

State Resources

- **State Tax Forms.** http://www.taxadmin.org/state-tax-forms. This site links to the tax agencies of all 50 states.
- **State-by-State Business Start-Up Information.** http://www.taxadmin.org /state-tax-agencies

- **SBA.** https://www.sba.gov/starting-business/business-licenses-permits
/state-licenses-permits. An excellent resource to help you look up your
state's requirements.
- **Business Licenses.** http://iTaxMama.com/BusLicense. Save time researching all the licenses you need. BusinessLicenses.com will do the research for
you. For an extra fee, it will even fill in the forms for you.

Business and Legal Resources

- **Incorp Services Inc. in Nevada.** http://iTaxMama.com/InCorpTM,
(800) 2 INCORP. You will get 20 percent off the price of formation services
and registered agent services if you use coupon code TAXMAMA.
- **The Company Corporation.** https://www.incorporate.com/, (800) 315-9420.
Register your corporation, LLC, or other formal structure at this site, which
is one of the oldest incorporators in the country. Mention that TaxMama
sent you to get a $25 discount.
- **Hubco.** http://www.inc-it-now.com, (800) 443-8177. Register your corporation, LLC, or other formal structure, and handle most of it yourself, a cheap
option. It is also a great source of corporate supplies, such as corporate seals,
binders, and so on.
- **Certified Tax Coach (CTC).** https://www.certifiedtaxcoach.com/. Tax planning for successful businesses. Once you reach the point where your business is profitable and you feel that you're paying way too much in taxes, you
need a CTC to sit down and help you reduce your tax burden and build up
your savings—ethically and legally.
- *Clicking Through: A Survival Guide for Bringing Your Company Online*
by Jonathan I. Ezor (Bloomberg Press). http://iTaxMama.com/Ezor_Book.
The best book about how Internet issues affect your business. If you read
nothing else I recommend, you must read this book. Ezor provides practical
information in plain English about the issues you face the minute your business opens its website.
- *The Best Home Businesses for the 21st Century: The Inside Information
You Need to Know to Select a Home-Based Business That's Right for You* by
Paul and Sarah Edwards (published by Jeremy P. Tarcher). http://iTaxMama
.com/Paul_Sarah_Edwards.

- *Guerrilla Marketing to Heal the World: Combining Principles and Profit to Create the World We Want* by Jay Conrad Levinson and Shel Horowitz (Morgan James Publishing). http://www.frugalmarketing.com. This book will help you focus your marketing efforts to get the most attention for the least amount of money, while still being socially responsible. http://iTax Mama.com/Guerrila_Marketing.
- *Careers from the Kitchen Table* by Raven Blair Davis (self-published). http://iTaxMama.com/Raven_Blair_Edwards.
- *The Revenge of Brand X* by Rob Frankel (Frankel & Anderson Publishers). http://iTaxMama.com/Frankel_Revenge_Brand_X. Find out how to make your company the only choice.
- **Dan Janal's PR Leads.** http://www.prleads.com. Janal explains how to get interviewed by the top publications in the country.
- **Help a Reporter.com.** https://www.helpareporter.com/. A great way to be interviewed or even for you to find expert sources to interview or write about.
- *Drunks, Drugs & Debits: How to Recognize Addicts and Avoid Financial Abuse* by Doug Thorburn (Galt Publishing). http://www.preventragedy .com. This book will help you avoid going into business with hidden addicts—or do it with your eyes open and precautions in place.
- **The Small Business Advocate.** http://iTaxMama.com/TaxMama-on -JBSBA. Jim Blasingame has a wealth of interviews and resources on his website, and in his daily radio show.
- **UCC Filings.** http://iTaxMama.com/UCC_Filings. Use this to secure your accounts receivable when you have clients who will be paying you over time, or on a monthly basis for your ongoing work.
- *The Millionaire Messenger* by Brendon Burchard. http://iTaxMama.com /Millionaire_Messenger. This resource helps you transform your knowledge and expertise into a very profitable business.
- **Vistage.** https://www.vistage.com/membership/programs/. A well-organized mastermind group with a coach and contacts and resources to help you build and grow your business most effectively.

Internet Resources

- **GoDaddy.** http://iTaxMama.com/GoDaddy. Domain names are often less than $10 per year. Even though there are other designations you could choose to buy (e.g., *.biz* or *.org*), if you can't get the *.com* version of the name, choose another name. Otherwise, whoever owns the .com site will get all your traffic.
- **Yahoo!** https://smallbusiness.yahoo.com/domains. Yahoo.com has entered the domain name business. So if you're more comfortable with a brand name you recognize, Yahoo! is selling domains for about $12 per year. Naturally, it has added a host of website tools.
- **LogoNerds.** http://iTaxMama.com/Logo_Nerds. A great place to get a new or updated logo at a reasonable price. You can get a complete package for your website, business stationery, advertisements, and more, in just three to five days.
- **National Comtel.** (800) 987-0100, http://www.telecommunicationsdenver.com/. Long-distance toll-free numbers.
- **SoloBuildIt (SBI).** buildit.sitesell.com/taxmama.html. Ken Evoy has built an all-inclusive online business package. It includes the website, hosting, domain name, mailing lists, merchant accounts, shopping cart, all the tools you need to build a website and make it pay—even if you don't have a clue about programming or Internet mysteries. It even has a built-in affiliate program that lets you track and pay for referrals. For little more than the price of hosting a website, you're going to get tools I've paid thousands of dollars to use. You really can put up your own site—even without the help of your 10-year-old.

Office Supplies for Accounting and Taxes

- **Avery Labels.** http://avery.com, (800) GO-AVERY, (800) 462-8379.
- **Costco.** http://costco.com, (800)-774-2678. Shop online or visit a warehouse nearby.
- **Greatland.** http://www.greatland.com, (800) 968-1099. For accounting forms and supplies.
- **Office Depot.** http://iTaxMama.com/Office_Depot, (800) GO DEPOT. Shop online or visit a store nearby.
- **Staples.** http://www.staples.com, (800) 3STAPLE. Shop online or visit a store nearby.
- **UPS—Custom Packaging.** http://iTaxMama.com/UPS_Custom_Package

TaxMama Resources

- **TaxMama's Quick Look-Ups.** http://iTaxMama.com/TM_QuickLookUp. You will find all kinds of useful reference materials, webinars you can replay, e-books, and more.
- **Your Business Bible.** http://www.yourbusinessbible.com. Look for worksheets, printable checklists, and other goodies and resources.

CHAPTER 2: **BUSINESS PLANS YOU KNOW AND TRUST**

To-Do List and Questionnaire

☐   Have you prepared your preliminary Business Plan? _____

- Will it be for your own use only? If yes, *use a short version.*

- Will you use it with your Advisory Team or investors? *Use a longer version with more details and explanations.*

- Will you be using it to raise money? *Use a software tool (see the "Business Plan Books and Resources" section at the end of this chapter) to develop a formal Business Plan.*

☐ 1.   Review it with your Advisory Team.   Date: _____

- Separate out the short- and long-term recommendations.

- Revise your Business Plan with the new information.

☐ 2.   List the first *five* things you must do *this week* (repeat this list each week):

(1) _____

(2) _____

(3) _____

(4) _____

(5) _____

☐ 3.   What must you do *today*? _____

☐ 4.   Enter your target tasks on your calendar for the next 12 months.

☐ 5.   Schedule the first two dates to reevaluate and rebalance your Business Plan.

Date #1: _____   Date #2: _____

Remember to put a copy of each document behind this page, folded in half.

2

BUSINESS PLANS
YOU KNOW AND TRUST

I've been rich and I've been poor. Believe me, rich is better.

—MAE WEST

Create a Business Plan

We're just starting out, and already you're ready to turn the page. You're thinking, I don't need a business plan. I know what I'm doing. It's just me, basically working from notes in my back pocket.

You might just do all right playing it by ear. But why not do great?

Frankly, you're going to need a business plan if you want to succeed. You will especially need a business plan if you fail (to protect your tax deductions—I'll explain in a moment). Without a plan, you're courting failure. There are so many details to remember in a business, it's hard to keep track of them without a scorecard, especially when you're working alone. Why sabotage your chances for success? Are you one of those people who are secretly afraid to succeed? Get over it! Take the time to sit down, make a few notes, and shoot for success.

Why You Need a Business Plan

The main reason you need a business plan (for tax purposes) is that the IRS will want to see it when your tax return shows losses for the first several years.

I know. You don't plan to have losses. But even the best-laid plans sometimes go wrong. When you run losses for more than two or three years, that business plan is going to make the difference between getting to keep those deductions and having the IRS disallow them all under the "hobby loss rules." We'll talk about those next.

You're almost asking for an audit if your business shows a loss for more than two years out of five (or five years out of seven if you're dealing with the breeding, training, showing, or racing of horses). With the country in financial crisis and with a tax gap of $441 billion and growing, the IRS is putting more energy into audits that it knows it can win. The IRS's audit software can be aimed to select returns that really do have something wrong with them. Businesses with constant losses are a prime target.

Why? What's the point of being in business if you cannot make a profit? You might as well go out and get a job! This makes perfect sense, doesn't it? After all, if this is your business, how are you going to live on losses? You certainly won't make it up in volume!

Of course, if this is a hobby, that's another story. In that case, you are not entitled to be deducting those losses. In fact, the Tax Cuts and Jobs Act (TCJA) had totally eliminated the right for hobbyists to claim any deductions at all. That's where the IRS gets you—eliminating or limiting your deductions for what you thought were your business expenses.

A business plan can help overcome the "hobby loss" argument during an audit.

What Is a Hobby Loss, and Why Do We Care?

Let's look at the information straight out of the tax code:

> IRC §183(d) Presumption: If the gross income derived from an activity for 3 or more of the taxable years in the period of 5 consecutive taxable years which ends with the taxable year exceeds the deductions attributable to such activity (determined without regard to whether or not such activity is engaged in for profit), then, unless the Secretary establishes to the contrary, such activity shall be presumed for purposes of this chapter for such taxable year to be an activity engaged in for profit. In the case of an activity which consists in major part of the breeding, training, showing, or racing of horses, the preceding sentence shall be applied by substituting "2" for "3" and "7" for "5."

When the IRS considers your business to be a hobby, you have several strikes against you:

1. Your expenses were only deductible to the extent of your gross income until your 2017 tax return. So if you have $10,000 worth of expenses, but your income is only $2,000, you waste all $10,000 of expenses. Now none of those costs are deductible anywhere. Those costs don't get carried forward, suspended, or anything. They're just gone. Poof!

2. You can't use Schedule C. You can no longer report your expenses on Schedule A as miscellaneous itemized deductions, aside from the expenses you lost because they were limited to your gross income.

3. You have to report the income on Schedule 1 of Form 1040 on the "Other income" line, which increases your adjusted gross income (AGI). That could cause you to lose a variety of credits and deductions—and could throw your taxes into the alternative minimum tax (AMT) bracket.

Now that you understand a little about why you don't want hobby losses, here's how to avoid them. Look at these nine factors that the IRS considers important and make sure you address these issues in your business's tax return files for every year in which you have losses. Better yet—don't have losses!

1. The manner in which the taxpayer carried on the activity
2. The expertise of the taxpayer or his or her advisors
3. The time and effort expended by the taxpayer in carrying on the activity
4. The expectation that the assets used in the activity may appreciate in value
5. The success of the taxpayer in carrying on other similar or dissimilar activities
6. The taxpayer's history of income or loss with respect to the activity
7. The amount of occasional profits, if any, which are earned
8. The financial status of the taxpayer
9. The elements of personal pleasure or recreation in this business

Real Business—Planned Losses

What if you know, at the outset, that it will take you 5 or 10 years of losses, as you build up your product or your market, before you make a profit? What if you know that if you can hang on for those 10 years, you're going to make millions?

The IRS doesn't know that. It has no way of knowing. But when the IRS comes along with its audit, the strongest defense you can have is your solid business plan in hand. Oh, you'll need a few more tools, as you'll see in Chapter 13, but the foundation of your audit defense will be your plan.

General Benefits

You're clear on the tax reason for the business plan, right? What other benefits can it give you? The five Cs:

- **Clarity and focus.** A plan can save you lots of time. You won't be floundering, wondering what to do next. You will understand your own business better.
- **Cost control.** A plan can help you keep your costs under control because you're not just shotgunning your spending. You only spend money on those things that are part of your plan.
- **Capital.** Except for small amounts of money, you won't get a bank loan or attract investors unless you have a business plan. Of course, you could use your credit cards . . . and with the no-interest or low-interest rate cards, that might even be a good option. But, at best, you're not going to get more than $5,000 to $50,000 that way. If you want real money—enough to fund your operation and let you fill large orders (for products or services)—you need a plan. No one will give you money if you don't understand your own business.
- **Confidence.** It's amazing the way your self-respect and confidence soar when you know what you're doing. You can look people in the eye and give them straight answers when they ask you how your business is doing.
- **Copiousness and growth.** Decide up front just how large you'd like your business to be. You may as well put the correct systems in place for the future—leaving room for expansion of software, phone systems, and so on. Decide if you plan to go public, build the business just so far and sell it, leave it to your children, or turn it into a franchise or a multilevel marketing operation. You can always decide to keep it small later. But to grow, when you haven't planned for it, will cost much more down the road.

The Fine Line Between Success and Failure

Running a business was easy as long as I just had my tax practice and no employees. It was a cinch to plan out what needed to be done by what date, how many clients I had to see, by when, and so on. One of the things I've discovered since operating on the Internet is that the world is full of distractions, temptations, and opportunities. You're going to find yourself being pulled in many directions. They all look like exciting opportunities. If you give in to those offers and invitations of quick money, you will slowly learn that if you had just stuck with your own business and your own plan, you'd be much further ahead.

Even if you do focus purely on your own business, it needs an online presence. That means you need to schedule time to deal with all the social media sources. Either you have to do it, or you must hire someone else to do it for you. Regardless, without some kind of online presence, your clients won't find you easily. They won't know what hours you're open (or available for interaction). They won't be able to pay your for your products or services easily—so you end with accounts receivable, waiting to get paid. How big an online presence do *you* have? And who keeps it up to date?

Here's my online presence (not always up to date):

- http://yourbusinessbible.com/—the website for this book
- http://www.TaxMama.com—my website where I answer your questions
- http://www.irsexams.school—my main source of income
- https://www.cchcpelink.com/teamTaxMama—where I teach a series of classes about the chapters in this book
- http://www.taxquips.com/—my podcast
- Twitter—https://twitter.com/TaxMama—where I post quick notes and updates, and help out with certain twitter-chats each year
- https://www.facebook.com/TaxMama—where I post copies of my podcast
- YouTube—https://www.youtube.com/TaxMama—where my audio podcast becomes video
- LinkedIn—https://www.linkedin.com/in/TaxMama/—where I oversee a special discussion group for tax professionals

Sheesh! Can you see how much time is involved—and that's without Instagram or other visual media.

The price of distraction is more than mere dollars. Time is also a finite, nonrenewable commodity. My husband is too kind to point out that by simply focusing on my tax practice, I'd have more evenings and most weekends free. Instead, because I am guilty of succumbing to those alluring temptations, I work 12 to 15 hours each day, including most evenings and practically every weekend and holiday.

Sure, I love what I do—*all* the things I do. But sometimes it would be really nice to do a bit less—quite a bit less. That's my price of success, spreading myself too thin. However, I have a plan in place that will let me gradually reduce my workload and raise my income to the point where, in another year or two, my time and life will be in balance again. (That's what I wrote in 2016. But . . .) Again, more interesting projects cropped up. More time has been invested. Once again, I must redefine my time budget! (I really am working on a way to delegate more and get some free time. Really.)

Is trying to do everything worth it? That's a personal decision. You'll have to decide. Let's see what happened to a few people and how they did or didn't focus.

Success

In the 2004 edition of this book, we introduced you to Brad Waller and his partners, who started EPage (http://epage.com/) in 1996. Brad and EPage just boringly focused on their business plan and deflected distractions. All their energies went into building an online classified system for websites to use as their own. They were pioneers in income-sharing programs like affiliate commissions (Amazon.com's came later).

In 2004, they had 27,000 merchant sites, had run nearly half a million ads, and had attracted more than 5 million page views a month, with more than three-quarters of a million visitors. EPage never needed to get venture capital. The business has been supporting all the original founders, plus several employees, full-time for years. Better yet, Brad's marketing efforts require that he take an annual cruise to the Bahamas and trips to Hawaii and other exotic locations—as part of marketing conferences. Yes, life is tough.

What has happened since then? Growth is slow, but business is steady. EPage.com still serves more than a million ads (double the number in 2016). It has more than 37,000 affiliates still telling the world about EPage.com (up from 28,000 in 2016)—still growing.

And there's been a vision change—Brad recognized a powerful opportunity with telephone applications. He created a series of iPhone applications relating to online auctions and shopping. As a result of this success, Brad's team has moved the company into a new market with a do-it-yourself iPhone application site—http:// iTaxMama.com/uBuildApp. Now, their main classified site and all their activities have gone mobile—leaving Brad time to get politically active in his school district and community.

Giving It Away Means More Profits

Philip Tirone's business ventures have done really well over the years, after a few bumps here and there. These days, he's feeling very fortunate. But Philip has seen others struggling through the credit disasters that befell them when they lost jobs and homes and destroyed their credit. He set up a free credit resource (http://www.720 creditscore.com) to provide information to help people fix their own credit. There's a glossary with an explanation of the FICO system and credit scores, information about recovering from bankruptcy, the various laws that apply to credit ratings, and more. The service is still going strong, helping thousands of people pull up their credit scores without being concerned about games and identity theft schemes.

That's a bit like how TaxMama started *waaay* back when—teaching people to do their own tax returns. Most people, once they saw how much work was involved, hired TaxMama to do it for them. The same thing happened to Philip Tirone's well-done site with free resources. The free resources led to sales of his paid service. Giving away high-quality information builds confidence in the marketplace. People get to know who you are and the quality of your work. Incorporating the right set of free products or services, managed properly, can lead to financial independence. Today,

Philip works when he wants, where he wants (with an Internet connection, you can work from practically anywhere on the planet), and he relishes the time he spends with his wife and young children.

Too Much Success Equals Failure

Carolin Benjamin had the most charming idea for a site. You can see what it was like by looking back into the past using the Wayback Machine: http://iTaxMama.com /DujourDotCom_Wayback. (The site at that domain today is a totally different operation and concept—not hers.) When she started the site, it told visitors the holiday of the day. It was a place where you could play games for free, test your knowledge, compete against other people, and win prizes. Participants registered for free. Starting in November 1996, Carolin got the idea to invite merchants who wanted exposure to donate prizes, daily, weekly, or monthly, depending on the kind of visibility they wanted. The site was an instant hit, attracting more than 80,000 visitors a day, myself included. I loved to play there and won an elegant wooden pen and pencil set as well as other handcrafted items. I still use the handmade soup mugs I won. Well, Carolin had the traffic and the prizes. But where was the revenue? She and her partner were too busy with their day jobs to plan how to make money.

Frankly, even with all the traffic, it was hard to find paying advertisers. Carolin maintained the site for several years, staying up most of the night to post daily and weekly winners, send out prize announcements, and respond to volumes of email. She nearly collapsed from exhaustion. Carolin had to sell the site. Why was the workload too much? She made the same mistake many companies make—even large ones: she didn't plan for success. She had traffic but not the means or resources to respond to her members' needs—or the income to cover the costs of additional help.

Carolin finally gave up the URL. These days, she runs a real estate business with her husband in Arizona.

Failure, Well, Almost

In Australia, Ian Purdie started putting up articles about electronics, ham radios, audio devices, and all kinds of related technical and hobby information. His site, http://electronics-tutorials.com, became so popular that universities were using his free technical articles in their courses. Ian believed that if he put high-quality information out there, people would be sensible enough to contribute funds, or tip him, to support keeping the site alive. Even small sums would be welcome. Amazon offered a payment system, so Ian didn't need to incur the cost of merchant credit card accounts. His costs weren't high. Living on a pension, he could, essentially, get by.

Though users sent him many letters of high praise, few—if any—made donations. Few people used his links to buy their books or supplies, which would have let him generate commissions from their purchases. They'd buy those things—but not so he got the credit. Ian never diminished the quality of the articles he provided, despite years of frustration at the lack of financial support. Finally, he just about gave up.

Why did he fail? He didn't have a business plan. Ian never arranged for a way to charge students and readers for his how-to articles. He never thought through the issue of where his income was going to come from. He just believed that people would be honorable and make contributions to support his useful site. To his credit, unlike Carolin, he didn't have to spend hours each night dealing with time-sensitive prizes and things. He could choose to add articles or not, as he saw fit. But he didn't have any money, either.

He was just about to do something violent to his computer when he got really lucky. The Google folks came along with AdSense, which provides a stream of advertising revenues. But that's another story for another time. Today, Ian is in clover, and his business is a labor of love again. And if you can handle his sense of humor, drop by and laugh—https://www.electronics-tutorials.com/humour/humour.htm.

Utter Failure

Mike was a very popular Realtor in Southern California, earning a six-figure income as a sales manager for a real estate brokerage, when a friend invited him to open a business leasing private homes and condominiums. When Mike broached the idea to me, I did my best to persuade him to do two things: (1) work out a business plan and (2) keep his day job. He could build up his new business slowly, from home, with a low overhead until it generated enough money to support him. In fact, if he'd told his boss about it, chances were, he'd have supported him, even to the point of helping him capitalize the business. No one else was making a concerted effort to tap into the San Fernando Valley market (in Los Angeles, California—where the Brady Bunch lived) with a comprehensive service providing leasing and management for owners of single units. There was a demand for this service, not just among the homeowners needing tenants, but by people looking for places to rent. Renters would keep running into those bait-and-switch ads, offering attractive houses, condos, or guesthouses—then telling the renters they'd have to pay a fee to get the address. When they finally did get the addresses, those units were already taken (probably always were) or didn't exist.

So with this great potential market, off he went, returning to me several months later. Mike had skipped doing a business plan. He also had quit his job and opened an expensive office. His overhead, before he got to take home a single dime, was more than $17,000 a month, but his income was nowhere near that. He was lucky to generate $2,000 per month. To support his business, Mike was drawing money from savings.

Mike begged me to help, so I stepped in and cut his costs by $10,000 a month, even after my fees. It turns out that although he was an expert in real estate sales, he didn't understand how the leasing business worked. Mike was still paying out of his own pocket for expenses that the homeowners should be paying. The owners paid them willingly once we rewrote the contracts.

We doubled his sales overnight by getting some high-end brokerages to refer their low-commission home leasing business to him. In fact, one luxury home brokerage owner told his staff that they must forward all leases to Mike. If he ever saw them wasting their time with a lease, they'd be fired. (You have to understand the economics. It takes about the same amount of time to find tenants as it does to find buyers, showing them lots and lots of houses. But where leasing a luxury home might garner a commission of $3,000, selling that same home will generate more than $30,000.)

Those referrals doubled Mike's revenues, but it was too late. His business was still hemorrhaging money. Even though he'd been in business less than a year, Mike had dipped so deeply into his financial reserves that within a few more months, he had to file for bankruptcy. It's a real shame. He was one of the most popular members of the local Board of Realtors. The other members would have been very happy to refer their leasing business to someone reliable. Had Mike started out with a business plan, a budget, low overhead, and better information, he'd literally be a millionaire today.

Speaking of a Business Plan, Let's Visit with Michael Again

Remember Michael Rozbruch from Chapter 1? Let's talk about his business plan for his new business. I told you that once he got the idea to use his knowledge to build an entirely new business, he and his wife went to an expert academy for three and a half days. During that time, they built a very specific business plan to launch the new business. The program provided them with the contacts and resources they needed, including a video production studio in Colorado, where he scheduled a live launch—an interactive broadcast. Michael admits it was a bit daunting to have that definite date looming over his head. There were a million details to take care of—forming the new company, getting banking and credit card arrangements, launching the website and order system, and building the marketing team and the sales funnel. The easiest part was to write the manuals—the ultimate product that he would be selling. Michael said, that actually flowed from his brain onto paper (or pixels) in an solid stream of ideas and information. It was up to his wife, Roslyn, to organize it and make sense of it. (Isn't that always the way?) Seriously, though. While the deadline was a bit frightening, having that broadcast deadline established meant that he had to meet that target and complete all the myriad tasks in time.

I was in the studio that day, along with three of his CPA educators. All the details came together. Because of all the groundwork, I saw him sell more than $100,000 in memberships and manuals that day. Since then, he has launched other products to the audience he built up. Michael is always using and refining his business plan. In November 2019, I saw him sell more than $200,000 worth of his latest product—in two hours.

In 2019, five years after he launched this new business, Roz Marketing Group earned their place in the Inc 5000—*that* is what the right business plan can do for you.

Exit Strategy—Taking It Public

A few years ago, Kevin Reeth and Ben Curren, both former Intuit employees, were immersed in their own web development company. Seeing that the increasingly complex and function-packed software left the really small business owner totally confused, they took a gamble. They developed a versatile application to provide the individual business owner with simplified online bookkeeping services at Outright .com. A free application, it was funded by additional services they provided the business owner to make life simple. Nearly from the outset, they structured the business for venture capital. The first round of investors came easily. By May 2010, they had processed more than $2 billion in transactions. Their exit strategy was to take the company public, make millions of dollars, and stay involved because it was fun! In 2012, however, they sold the company to GoDaddy for a cash and stock package of nearly $20 million.

Exit Plans for Fun and Profit

Not everyone wants to die in the saddle. Many of us want to taper down our business activities, sell the business, or turn it over to the next generation. You can see how good the results can be if you actually plan your exit, instead of just letting it happen. After all, without a plan (like without a will), situations happen and you could lose control.

How many people have you seen who became incapacitated or died and there was no plan in place to have someone take over the business or the customers or clients? The heirs didn't even know where to begin to save the business—and it became worthless or was sold for pennies on the dollar. That's a shameful waste.

So, how do you start an exit plan? I suggest you sit down with a business professional who specializes in exit plans or venture capital (if that's the direction you want to go). Or, the SBA has a resource for you—http://iTaxMama.com/SBA_Exit.

One friend of mine has successfully created a series of tech-related businesses that he builds up and sells for millions—every five years. He is what I would call, a "serial exiter." Knowing someone like that can be great for your financial health, don't you think? This is another reason to build a team of advisors. They can help you make the contacts you need to develop a viable exit plan.

Letting Your Ego Rule

Can you name one living person who personified great success, but turned it into a smashing failure for a time?

Yes, the answer is Martha Stewart. Her company, Martha Stewart Living, Omnimedia, Inc. (NYSE MSO), almost folded after her conviction. Large blocks of television stations dropped her show. Since the show was all Martha—and she was going to jail—even if they hadn't dropped her, who was in the wings to take her place? No one.

As a result, when she was indicted, then tried, and then convicted, the MSO stock went from more than $20 a share to below $10 in April 2004. In April 2010, the price was $7.30.

What's the criticism here? Surely, Martha had a business plan. No one could be more focused than she was. The problem is the excessive focus—on her, on Martha. Unlike most media businesses that plan to survive for the long run, everything was about Martha. She made no provisions, even after the indictment, to introduce someone else into her television show or on her radio features. There should have been someone groomed to become her replacement if she was convicted—or if she died. The MSO business plan didn't have any continuity built in.

However, when Martha stepped out of jail her personal reputation rebounded, and her popularity has soared. In June 2015, Martha Stewart Living Omnimedia sold for $353 million to Sequential Brands. Not bad for something that seemed doomed to fail!

In fact, Stewart was smart enough to cash out—but continue her media and other activities. Today, she is nearly 80 years old, worth in excess of half a billion dollars,[1] is an advisor to several companies, constantly establishes new television programs and contracts—and is still teaching the world how to cook, to garden, and to look good—with style.

But not everyone has Martha Stewart's charisma and drive. So, please be sure to treat your business as an entity of its own. Why build something up that no one can step into and take over if you get sick or die? If you tie it too closely to your irreplaceable personal services and your own name, your business won't have any value to anyone else. You won't be able to sell it.

---

1 The Street—https://www.thestreet.com/lifestyle/martha-stewart-net-worth-15064812.

Let's Not Fail Due to Success

Are you getting the idea? Even if you're on a success track, if you don't have a business plan in place to deal with that success, you're apt to fail. (Talk about a monotonous refrain!) These are the kinds of things to think about to prepare for success:

- Your ads are successful. Your phones are ringing off the hook. What do you do when the phone lines are jammed with customers wanting to give you money—but you haven't made any provisions for enough people to answer the phones?
- You get the largest order of your career. Where are you going to manufacture it? Or where will you get the trained staff to perform all those services on short notice?
- You get the largest order of the year. You can find the staff and facilities to fulfill it. But where are you going to get the money to pay for it all until you collect your accounts receivable from this sale—probably three to six months after you deliver the product or service?
- You introduce a new electronic product that can be downloaded from the web. It's all automated. No sweat, right? You get a great review in *PC Magazine*, and Seth Myers and Jimmy Fallon are all over it with their jokes in their nightly routines. You get so much traffic that your website crashes. Can you bring new bandwidth online in time to save the sales? Or count on mirror sites?

Make sure you have backup provisions to get the resources and/or funds you need, quickly, in the event of a sudden success. Without them, the business goes under. You can only get those things with foresight and planning.

Knowing What to Do—When

One of the major advantages of a business plan is—having a plan. You know exactly what to do at the start of the week. You don't have to start each week, or each day, wondering what do first—or just spend your time putting out fires. I used to be an executive recruiter, matching up financial and programming professionals with the perfect employer. The firm I worked for had printed a set of enormous writing pads, with 50 lines per page. On each line, we had to put the name of a prospective employee, with all the contact information about that person, and some relevant notes about his or her skills. Or we had to put the name of a potential employer, with all the contact information for the key hiring manager—and relevant information about the job or the company. We were required to fill that pad up by the end of each day.

As annoying and onerous as that task was at first, I came to really love it. That meant, the next morning, I walked in and started making my calls without hesitation. It's a great habit to build. Consider building that kind of a list yourself each day. You won't waste the first hour of every day just getting situated.

Outline of a Plan

Many different books, software, and websites are available to help you create a good business plan. Or you can invest in top experts, so you can achieve top results in a short time frame, like Michael Rozbruch. Whatever you use, even if it's only a simple list, there are 10 basic elements you'll need to consider (see Table 2.1). Answer these 10 questions. Use them to build your business plan using the books or tools that follow. With good planning, you are bound to succeed.

TABLE 2.1 Ten Fundamental Questions for a Business Plan

1. What kind of business will you be? (sole proprietorship, partnership, corporation)
2. What will the business do? (products, services)
3. Where will you get the money to start and fund the business until it generates income? (you, investors, loans, credit cards)
4. *How much money will you need to tide you over until income is generated? (to cover operations, wages, rents, supplies)*
5. How will the business generate income? (sales, rents, grants, dues)
6. When will the stream of income start? (research time, construction time, sales cycle)
7. When will you break even?
8. What contingency plans do you have to back you up if suppliers or investors fail you?
9. What contingency plans do you have to be able to fulfill orders or sales when you succeed beyond your wildest dreams?
10. What is your exit plan? (sell, go public, invite partners, shut down, give to children)

Important Things to Consider

When you sit down to develop your business plan, be sure to understand how you (and your partners) are going to be spending your time in this business. Face up to the tasks you hate to do. The simple fact is—if you hate to do something, you'll slough it off, do it poorly, or not do it at all. Don't economize by promising to do something you hate. The onerous tasks will be different for each person. Some people just dread having to sell. If you can't overcome that, delegate it. Or hire someone to do it. Others hate to do bookkeeping. If you have a mental block against it, don't torture yourself. Find someone on your team, or outside, who loves that task. Build the costs of delegation into your plan.

Sometimes, with the right team of people, it will work out perfectly. Be sure to have all the team members define their expectations—of themselves, of you, and of the company—so you're all going in the same direction. Have them put it in writing so everyone can see what each person expects to be doing—and what they think others' duties are. Sometimes, seeing what your partners' descriptions and expectations are, you will be surprised. You took for granted, for instance, that one of your partners is prepared to use his or her contacts to help you get contracts. But, it turns out that partner isn't comfortable imposing on his contacts—and has no intention of doing so. Oops! That was the main reason you wanted to partner with him. It's good to clear this up before investing a lot of time, money, and resources into a business that was based on his contacts. If you still want this person as a partner (perhaps he brings something else to the table, like money), then you're going to have to budget for a consultant or staff person to open doors for you. *And* you're going to have to find such a person. Wow. Without the right contacts, how will you do that? Time for that advisory team, isn't it?

This is not a vague, obscure example. Frankly, this kind of thing happens all the time.

Team Building in College

Working on my master's degree at California State University at Fullerton at night, I soon discovered that most of the courses required team projects. At first, I was incensed. My grade would depend on three other people, strangers, who were also working full-time during the day. Although most of them were men, somehow I always ended up being the group leader. That was fine with me. But assigning tasks would be touchy. Who was going to get the bad tasks or the grunt work? Well, drawing each person out, I learned that they each had a different idea of the chump job. There was usually someone who reveled in research. (Before the Internet, I hated that. Now, it's easy.) There was often someone who was a great typist (yes, before word processors and instant corrections) or had a secretary who was willing to type our papers, or someone who loved to create charts and analyze statistics. Most of them hated to write. For me, that was the easiest part of the job. *They* were relieved to be off the hook—*I* felt I was getting away with murder, sending them all out to dig up the information and present it to me. All I had to do was to organize it and write it up. Someone else was going to make it look pretty. We each did our share of the work gladly because we were each using our strengths. Those teams generally earned As.

Play to your strengths.

Of course, working to your strengths isn't just for college. Smart adults deeply engrossed in routine work will suddenly wake up to realize how much time they're expending on tasks that others should be doing. Robert MacPhee is the author of *Manifesting for Non-Gurus* (https://excellentdecisions.com/process/). He teaches a simple approach to attracting more of the results that people want in their lives. With his help, people learn to be clear about who they are, clear about their intended results, and connected to the feelings and emotions they want to experience. They learn to let go of attachments and consistently take inspired action. By doing this, they attract their desired results more quickly and easily. Robert says that the best part of teaching this work is getting the chance to practice what he preaches. That's how he ended up with his amazing assistant, Beth. I love this! Let's let Robert tell you his own story.

Manifesting My Assistant

I was sitting in my office one day, very busy as usual, feeling frustrated that I was unable to keep up with the demands of my workload. The thought occurred to me that I was spending way too much time working on things I did not need to be doing myself. I realized in that moment that I needed to get some help. But the thought of writing an ad, getting it printed, interviewing candidates, selecting someone, training that person, hoping he or she worked out. . . . It all seemed like even more work, and I was not even feeling optimistic about the result!

But then I realized what I was doing. I was imagining the exact outcome I didn't want—doing exactly what I coach others not to do. So I decided to practice what I preach. I asked myself what result I *did* want. I realized I wanted someone I could trust, who wanted to work from home, who wanted to work part-time, who could work independently, and who would be fun to work with. I paused and tapped into the feeling and emotion of what finding that person would mean, and then I let go of any attachment to needing it to happen in any certain way or by any certain time (mostly because I was so busy I had to get back to work!).

The very next day, I received an email from Beth, with whom I had worked before. She told me that she had recently had a baby and was looking for part-time work. Would I be interested in having her come back to work with me? She was able to work from home, only wanted part-time, and was fully capable of working independently. I knew I could absolutely trust her, and she was fun. Sound familiar?

There's a big advantage to having a reliable assistant, even part-time. The right person can make your company look bigger and more professional. That person can take over tasks that don't require your personal spark of creativity. And he or she can free you up to take on projects you wouldn't otherwise have time to tackle. In Robert's case, when the opportunity arose to become director of training for Jack Canfield's Training Group, he had Beth to help keep his own business running.

Rebalancing Your Business Plan for Tax Consequences

You're always hearing stockbrokers and investment advisors talking about rebalancing your investment portfolio. That means once you've agreed on an investment approach, with a specific percentage of your money in various risk levels of investment, you need to review it each year. As the values of the investments change due to price fluctuations, dividends, and capital gains, one group may become worth more or less in proportion to the other groups. To keep the proportions in balance, you may have to sell some units of one group or buy units of another.

Use the same concept with your business plan. Review it annually to make sure you're on track with your overall goals.

Then review it again to see how any tax law changes, phaseouts, or phase-ins affect your business. Particularly, look at depreciation rules—politicians like to change this area often, increasing or complicating the deductions or credits. Look at business credits. Are there new incentives in place for hiring, locations, or special industries? Expect changes in the areas of travel, meals, and gifts. Those need updating for this millennium.

What are the top three best things about having a good business plan in place?

1. You'll spend much less time and money running your business. By not floundering and wasting time and money going in too many directions, all your investment will go toward producing profits.

2. You'll be able to take the best advantage of tax benefits available to your business, income level, or industry.
3. You'll be in good shape if you're ever audited. The IRS so rarely sees business plans for small businesses. When it does see that level of organization and discipline in that area, it will believe you've carried that thoroughness through into your accounting and tax areas, too.

Business Plan Books and Resources

If you're going to get tools and resources, don't go cheap. Saving yourself $50 to buy a cheaper resource may cost you much more in the time you'll spend to find the information that's probably already in the more expensive tool. Whenever possible, get the material as an app or downloadable software so you can copy and paste or fill in forms. Go to workshops that make you think through your plan—and walk out with a tangible action list. It will save you more time than you can imagine. Besides, electronic media lets you click on links to resources to go directly to additional information as you need it.

Although this chapter is not directly about taxes, I believe this is the most important information in this book. Please, follow the wisdom of the people you've met here. Your time is precious. Why waste it working too hard, when you can be better organized and earn much more money? And have free time to do the things you love with the people you love.

Remember TaxMama's philosophy: You can always earn more money. But you can never recover wasted time.

Resources

In this chapter, you saw a variety of resources. Here's a summary of them, so you can find them quickly and easily. The resources are not necessarily in alphabetical order in each category. They are in order of their importance or usefulness, in TaxMama's opinion.

IRS Resources

- **IRS Resource—Starting a Business.** https://www.irs.gov/businesses /small-businesses-self-employed/starting-a-business. An overview of links to IRS resources to help structure and operate your business.

- **IRS Checklist for Starting a Business.** https://www.irs.gov/businesses /small-businesses-self-employed/checklist-for-starting-a-business. This includes links to get your Employer Identification Number (EIN), and other initial steps you need to take—most of which are also outlined in Chapter 1 of this book.
- **IRS Audit Technique Guide for Hobbies.** https://www.irs.gov/pub/irs-utl /irc183activitiesnotengagedinforprofit.pdf. A secret glimpse into how the IRS audits your business when they don't think you really have a profit motive. Don't wait to get audited to read this. Use this guide to help structure your business to avoid getting caught in the hobby-loss audit trap.

Books and CDs

- *Business Plan Pro* (CD). https://www.businessplanpro.com/. This includes sample business plans, financial statements for thousands of industries, SBA loan documents, and links to loan sources and venture capital.
- *Fix Your Business* by Melinda Emerson. https://succeedasyourownboss .com/. You've been in business for a while now, and you're doing OK. Just OK. But you want to do better. Melinda's guidance can help you take your business to the next level.
- *The Millionaire Messenger* by Brendon Burchard. http://iTaxMama.com /Millionaire_Messenger. This book provides tangible information on how to turn your expertise into a marketable product. How to communicate, develop, and sell your knowledge.
- Nolo's *Tax Savvy for Small Business* by Frederick W. Daily. www.nolo.com or www.Amazon.com. Looks at setting up a business and selecting a business entity from an attorney's point of view. It's an excellent companion piece to this book.
- Nolo's *How to Write a Business Plan* by Mike McKeever. www.nolo.com or www.Amazon.com. This book helps you evaluate your idea's profitability, estimate your expenses, and prepare your cash flow forecasts. It offers tips about sources of funds—and where *not* to get them.

Online Resources

- **IRS Audios and Videos on Disaster Planning and Continuity Planning.** http://www.tax.gov/Professional/DisasterInformation
- **CFS TaxTools.** http://iTaxMama.com/TaxTools. Lots of worksheets and templates to help you with tax planning.

- **Links to Business Plans.** http://iTaxMama.com/SBA_BusPlan
- *Inc.* **Magazine.** http://www.inc.com or http://iTaxMama.com/Inc_Bus
  _Plan. *Inc.*'s business plan resources give you information on creating and
  using a business plan.
- *Entrepreneur* **Magazine.** https://www.entrepreneur.com/. A series of arti-
  cles and guides, including tips from Wharton's Business Plan competition, is
  available at https://www.entrepreneur.com/article/247574.
- **The Small Business Administration.** https://www.sba.gov/
- **The Small Business Advocate.** http://www.smallbusinessadvocate.com/.
  Jim Blasingame's radio show offers a flood of helpful information, and
  there's a wealth of articles, links, and interviews archived on his site. The
  "Gentleman of the Airwaves" (my title for him) is accessible for guidance
  if you need help. TaxMama has been a member of Jim's Brain Trust since the
  very beginning. Listen to 18 years of interviews at http://www.smallbusiness
  advocate.com/small-business-experts/eva-rosenberg-222.
- **"The Myth of Being Successfully Solo in Business"** by Mark Silver, founder
  of Heart of Business.com. http://iTaxMama.com/Heart_of_Business.
  Articles and information you will find interesting, along with a spiritual perspective on business. Although this particular article is about a decade old—
  the information is totally relevant today. The rest of the site is, of course,
  more current.
- **GQueues.** https://www.gqueues.com/features. A new resource recommended by a tax pro as we were getting this book ready for publication. Use
  this for more than collaboration. Use it to track client information and to get
  organized.

TaxMama Resources

- **TaxMama's Quick Look-Ups.** http://iTaxMama.com/TM_QuickLookUp.
  You will find all kinds of useful reference materials, webinars you can replay,
  e-books, and more.
- **Your Business Bible.** http://www.yourbusinessbible.com. Look for worksheets, printable checklists, and other goodies and resources.

To-Do List and Questionnaire

☐ 1. What entity is your business now?

☐ 2. What entity have you decided to be? _____

☐ 3. In which state(s) must you register? _____

List the contact information for each secretary of state:
URL(s): _____
Phone (s): _____
Renewal due date(s): _____
Renewal Fee(s): _____

☐ 4. What service are you using? Name/URL: _____,
Contact person: _____, Phone(s): _____,
Cost: _____, CK#/CC: _____, Filing date: _____

☐ 5. File IRS Form SS-4 online. TIN: _____, Date: _____
Remember to print the page before *saving it.*

Must IRS Form 2553 be filed for an S Corporation?
If yes, date filed: _____
Must IRS Form 8832 be filed for an LLC?
If yes, date filed: _____

☐ 6. Now you can open your bank account(s) and sign the signature card for the correct business entity.

List each bank and bank account: _____
Account number(s): _____
Who is signing on each account: _____
Make a copy of each signature card and put the copy with this checklist.

Remember to put a copy of each document behind this page, folded in half.

3

ENTITIES: SELECTING YOUR BUSINESS STRUCTURE

A house divided against itself cannot stand.

—ABRAHAM LINCOLN
(FROM *MATTHEW* 12:25)

To complete your business start-up and operations checklist as well as your business plan, you need to know what kind of body your business will wear. Why body? That's what *corporation* means:

> *Incorporate—1398, "to put [something] into the body or substance of [something else]," from L.L. incorporatus, pp. of incorporare "unite into one body," from L. in- "into" 1 corpus (gen. corporis) "body." The legal sense first recorded in Rolls of Parliament, 1461.*
>
> —FROM THE *ONLINE ETYMOLOGY DICTIONARY,*
> HTTP://WWW.ETYMONLINE.COM

Decisions, Decisions, Decisions

Once you get past all the setup and planning, your business will be a joy to run. You'll love what you're doing. Everything will fall right into place, and you soon won't have to stop and make decisions each time you must make a move. So far, you've been doing drudge work, getting set up, but that will change. You have one more big decision to make. Then you'll be ready to go forth and conquer the world. (Of course, that one big decision comes only after lots more little decisions.)

What Do You Want to Be When You Grow Up?

The official term for the form—or body—of your business is *business entity*. There are two ways to decide what kind of business entity you are: decide for today or decide for the long run. Those not making plans, by default, decide only for today. But you—you have great plans. You want a dynasty! Better yet, you want a piece of that initial public offering (IPO) pie so you can build a business worth millions of dollars.

There's no reason not to get it. According to Crunchbase.com, venture capital (VC) firms, worldwide, are being more selective in their choice of investments. There is a 1.2 percent drop in investment volume. Who is still getting the angel funding and seed money? It is going to well-organized businesses with clear business plans showing how they plan to grow and generate revenue. In the United States, venture capital firms get great tax breaks, potentially, 0 percent taxes on their capital gains since they can roll the gains over into another specialized small business investment company (SSBIC) http://iTaxMama.com/SSBIC. The money has to go somewhere. Why not tap into that?

You can't tap into VC money by being sloppy. To get it, you've got to start out with a corporation or limited liability company (LLC), and you must have the right accounting team. Your advisory team can help you find the right firm to lay the foundation.

Not everyone wants the stress of venture capital oversight. You might want the freedom to succeed or fail on your own strengths. That doesn't mean you can't have investors. You may—but you can keep them at a distance with smaller LLCs or limited partnerships composed of people you know. Before you decide, let's see what your choices are.

First, understand that what is presented here is just an overview of your options. To fully list all your options would take volumes. Use this information as a starting point for a discussion with your advisory team. There's just enough information here to help you frame intelligent questions.

Misplaced Generosity

Jerry, a new client, came to me one day to help him set up his brand-new business. After telling me a little bit about his new guitar lesson business, he proudly showed me the California LLC documents that Andrew, a friend of his, had paid for on his behalf. I cringed in horror.

His dear friend Andrew, though meaning well, had just obligated Jerry to a life of needless separate tax returns, an extra $800 annual fee to the California Franchise Tax Board, and a potential gross receipts tax. Plus Andrew had only loaned Jerry the money for the new LLC. Jerry also had to pay that back. All this, before Jerry even opened his doors. What a great friend!

Jerry and I sat down and outlined his business plan, determining his anticipated client base and potential income for the first three years, and then we outlined the expenses it would take to generate that income. In the end it was clear that with Jerry having a full-time job, this business would grow slowly but steadily. It would not earn enough income to make it worthwhile to incorporate, or set up any other entities, for at least the first three years. Perhaps, with some diligent marketing and referrals, Jerry would be in a position to quit his job and run the guitar business full-time in about five years. Not sooner.

Since a guitar business is not likely to cause expensive lawsuits, there was no reason not to operate as an uncomplicated sole proprietor.

We thanked Andrew for the LLC—and told him to either keep it or have his incorporator instantly revoke it before it started generating a mountain of paperwork for Jerry. Fortunately, the incorporator was able to revoke it quickly. But it did not return Andrew's money. After all, the incorporator had done its job!

An Overview of Certain Tax Considerations Related to Entities

Presently, in the United States, there are only two basic types of entities—those that pay taxes and those that pass the taxes over to the owner's personal tax return. Some entities swing either way. Once a small business decides what type of entity it is, it must stay with that decision. For some entities, like S corporations, there are exceptions, but they may only change once every five years. Here are three of the key issues you'll need to understand before going deeper into the body of your business.

Taxation. Table 3.1 displays your tax-paying options. As you can see, corporations are the only businesses that must pay their own taxes. The current corporate tax rate is a flat 21 percent for all C corporations, including personal service corporations (PSC). Income or losses from all other business forms are, or may be, passed on to you via a Schedule K-1 from most entities. You report the income or losses on your tax return and pay taxes at your highest tax bracket. These businesses are called "pass-through" entities.

TABLE 3.1 How Income Taxes Are Handled by the Entity

You Pay	It Pays	Either Way
Sole proprietorship	Corporation	Limited liability companies
General partnership		Other limited liability–type entities
Limited partnership		Trusts
Limited liability partnership		
S corporation		

Personal Holding Company

Personal holding companies are subject to an additional tax on any undistributed personal holding company income. (IRS Code Section 541.) The additional tax is reported on Form 1120, Schedule PH.

Year	Rate
2013–present	20.0 percent
2003–2012	15.0 percent
2002	38.6 percent

Accumulated Earnings Tax

In addition to the regular tax, a corporation may be liable for an additional tax on accumulated taxable income in excess of $250,000 ($150,000 for personal service corporations) (IRS Code Section 531).

Year	Rate
2013–present	20.0 percent
2003–2012	15.0 percent
2002	38.6 percent
2001	39.1 percent
2000 and prior years	39.6 percent

None of the other entities pay tax at the federal level.

Note: Filing partnership returns late will result in penalties of $205 per partner per month, for up to 12 months. There is also a penalty for providing K-1s late. The penalty is $270 per partner per month—with a limit in excess of $3,000,000 per calendar year. If you have a good enough reason for being late, do take the time to write to the IRS requesting abatement of penalties. The IRS is less likely to abate these days. Try using Rev. Proc. 84-35 if all partners reported their share of partnership income on their tax returns. Penalties are increased on a regular basis.

Unless you're currently in a high personal tax bracket, you're better off not forming a corporation. Corporations are not eligible for the new 20 percent qualified business income deduction (IRC Section 199A). Corporations are notorious for double taxation—corporations pay tax and then you pay tax on the dividends or wages they pay you. However, if you are in a high tax bracket, a corporation might be a great idea. Especially with the current 21 percent flat tax rate. You can run lots of employee benefits through the corporation to bring down profits. And the tax on the "qualified dividends" will be 0–20 percent, depending on your tax bracket. That might actually be a substantial savings when you are personally in a 22 percent or higher tax bracket.

Self-employment taxes. Chapter 11 goes into self-employment taxes in depth. For now, all you need to know is that they cost you 15.3 percent of your business profits, even if your overall taxable income is zero. Income from all the "You Pay" entities is subject to self-employment tax, except one—the S corporation.

Payroll. Working officers of corporations, S corporations, and LLCs filing as corporations are required to take a reasonable salary. With a $441 billion "tax gap" looming over the country, the IRS has hired an army of auditors. The newly trained auditors are reviewing corporate books, looking for unreasonably low wages. (We will explain "adequate compensation" in a moment.) They are looking for hobbies reported as businesses, incorrectly reported retirement deductions, unreported tips, and unreported eBay-type transactions, among other things. For all the other types of entities, wages are not permitted for the owners. Owners' families may be paid, if appropriate, as Chapter 9 explains. Owners may be required to receive "guaranteed payments." (See the Glossary in Chapter 4 for an explanation.) Those are not subject to payroll taxes at the business level. But they are subject to self-employment taxes. (Remember that 15.3 percent we mentioned a moment ago?)

It's a real shame. Most working partners, even sole proprietors, would prefer to have a clear, definite payroll to deal with, rather than having to remember to make quarterly estimated payments.

Incidentally, the IRS is using "big data analytics" to identify individual and business taxpayers that are likely to be tax evaders. At the 2019 UCLA Tax Controversy Institute, the IRS revealed that the analytics work. More key personnel have been assigned to this project. So, if you're underreporting your income, beware. "Big Brother"—or Uncle Sam will find you.

Major Issues Related to Entities

Before outlining the pros and cons of the various entity options, let's look at five major issues that are common to all of them. Rather than boring you by repeating them for each entity, let's summarize them in advance. The issues are: what is an investment;

partnership profits and compensation; adequate compensation; the liability protection myth; and raising money.

What Is an Investment?

An investment is money you receive from someone who will own shares of your business. In a partnership, this is called a partnership interest. In a corporation, this is called stock. In an LLC, this is called a membership unit or stock. When people make an investment, they expect to get a return on that investment. There are two types of returns. The first is the long-term expectation, which means that investors will make a healthy profit when they sell (or cash out) their partnership interests or stocks. The second is the periodic return during operations. Those periodic returns could be in the form of dividends (often quarterly or annually) when you have a corporation. For partnerships (or entities reporting as partnerships), the partners would get distributions (monthly, quarterly, or annually). It's important to note that if the business should fail, the investors generally get little or nothing back—beyond a proportionate split of whatever assets might be left over after creditors are paid. The good news for the people who started the business is that once the business is defunct, they won't owe the investors anything more. (If the "investment" had been a loan, on the other hand, the business owner or founder might still be on the hook to repay the loan after the business is closed or dissolved.)

Partnership Profits and Compensation

When it comes to any partnerships and LLCs (or other LL entities) the following considerations are important to understand.

Profits and losses may be split by formula, time devoted to the company, or other criteria, instead of only by ownership percentage. In fact, the Schedule K-1 (which transfers the partnership's income, expenses, and credits to the partners) has three separate lines to show the way things are split:

1. Profit sharing
2. Loss sharing
3. Capital ownership

Partners (or members) working in the business must receive a "guaranteed payment" to cover the value of their services. This payment comes to the working partner(s) before any profits are split:

- This guaranteed payment is subject to self-employment taxes.
- This prevents the working partner from reducing his or her share of profits and self-employment taxes by spreading the income—especially to family member owners, or others.

When it comes to the profit-sharing percentage, all partners will pay taxes on their share of the income whether the partnership or entity distributes any cash to them or not. Watch out! The partnership often doesn't file its Form 1065 until late in the year (by September 15th). So you may need to hold off filing your own tax return until you get your K-1. That may be the first time you learn how much income you must report. And, if the partnership didn't give you a distribution of your share of the profits, you might be caught short. So definitely stay in touch with the managing partners early in the year to get the numbers—and perhaps some cash to cover the taxes. *Note:* This same issue also applies to S corporations (and all pass-through entities).

When there are multiple owners, it's always wise to get "key person" insurance policies. These are insurance policies you take out on the life of each owner with the partnership as the beneficiary:

- When one of the owners dies, the policy pays the family of the deceased in order to buy out their interest in the business.
- This allows the survivor(s) to own and operate the business without suddenly becoming partners with the deceased's spouse or children.

Adequate Compensation

Adequate compensation is a universal theme in all entities—especially those that provide tax advantages. So just how much *is* adequate? You would think that this is purely subjective since the IRS never actually defines an amount in so many words. The IRS touches upon some of its considerations when it talks about S corporation compensation and health insurance benefits. Do you want something a little more definitive? Here is a resource you can use to pull reports about compensation in your own industry. The IRS has been known to accept these reports during business audits. There is a fee for each report. But if it will help you win an audit, the modest fees are certainly worth it. You can get the report from RCReports at http://www.rcreports.com.

We have a new consideration when it comes to compensation, as a result of the Tax Cuts and Jobs Act (TCJA). The Section 199A, qualified business income deduction is based on the net profit of the qualified business. So, businesses have a new incentive to keep the owners' compensation as low as legally possible. A great example of Congress passing tax laws that conflict with other tax laws. We'll talk more about Section 199A in Chapter 6, Common Deductions.

One thing you do need to know at this stage in your decision-making. The TCJA defined a new category of occupations—the Specified (or Specific) Service Trade or Business (SSTB). The affected occupations are similar to the previous definition for Personal Service Corporations (PSC), with some changes. SSTB includes services in the fields of health, law, accounting, actuarial science, performing arts, consulting, athletics, financial services, investing and investment management, trading, dealing in certain assets, or any trade or business where the principal asset is the reputation or skill of one or more of its employees or owners. Excluded are architects and engineers. They seem to have a good political lobby because they were subject to the PSC rules.

Why is this definition important? Because the Section 199A deduction for these occupations phases out when their Qualified Business Income exceeds certain limits. The TCJA defined the limits as $350,000 for married couples filing jointly, and $157,500 for all others. These amounts are increased by inflation. So for 2019, it's already at $321,400 (MFJ) and $160,700 (all others). You can find the most current information on Form 8995A. The deductions phase out as income rises above these limits by $100,000 for married filing jointly and $50,000 for all others. These numbers can help you with your decision.

Liability Protection Myth

Many people form corporations (C and S) and other entities specifically to limit their liability—but please understand that you don't really get personal liability protection at all. That's a major misunderstanding. Although you might be protected from the debts of the entity, you are not protected from lawsuits. Think about this. You are working in your business entity (especially if you are the one doing the primary work). You do something wrong. The customer or client sues. Who will they sue? Naturally, they will sue your business. But if you are the one who caused the problem, damage, loss, or harm, they will also name you in the lawsuit. Your corporation or limited liability entity gives you no protection at all. On the other hand, suppose one of your employees is responsible for the harm or damage. Are you protected? Nope. You've heard the old saying "The buck stops here." Ultimately, you are responsible for everything your employees do. Of course, you could always defend yourself in court and win. But at what cost? The monetary cost, time, and stress invested in litigation are enormous. Even when you win, it could deplete your savings—and destroy your health.

So if it's primarily liability protection you want, skip the entity altogether. Instead, get a solid liability insurance policy—and *read it!* Consider adding an umbrella policy to protect more of your assets if the liability policy can't go high enough to protect your life's savings (home, retirement accounts, investments, children's college funds, and so on).

Raising Money

These days, there are some creative ways you can raise money to start your business or to fund specific projects. By now, you've certainly heard about "crowdfunding." There are several major websites that can help you raise money, like Kickstarter.com, IndieGoGo.com, GoFundMe.com, and others. The money you raise can be handled one of three ways—as loans, as income to your business, or as investments in your business.

Generally, when someone gets a loan for their new business, even if they are a corporation, the lender will require the owners' personal guarantee on the loan. Well-established businesses can often qualify for loans directly to the business without the owners' personal guarantees. With a loan, the lender does not own any part of the business. But they must receive the loan payments as contracted. As we mentioned earlier, if the business fails, the lender might not get paid back unless the loan is secured by business assets or by the owner's personal assets. As a result, most lenders do look for security for their loans. There is no tax effect when receiving a loan. It's just a liability on the books. And there is no tax benefit for paying the loan's principal. Though, there is a deduction for the interest paid. *Note:* There are new restrictions on interest deductions. However, they do not apply to small businesses, which are defined as having an annual average income of less than $25 million for the three prior years. But there are always exceptions.

When you raise money by offering shares in your business, you are raising capital. Those people who buy in are investors. In order to sell shares or micro-shares in your company, you will most likely need to be a corporation. CrowdExpert.com has a directory of the top investment crowdfunding sites. Fundraising costs are low because these small capital offerings are generally not required to be filed with the Securities and Exchange Commission (SEC). However, it's well worth reading the SEC's interesting and detailed bulletin for investors using crowdfunding—http://iTaxMama.com /SEC_Crowdfund. Investors still need to meet certain qualifications, but they are not as stringent as those for publicly traded investments or venture capital investments. This can be a good avenue to get investors—especially if you only want to sell a small part of your business to raise operating, development, or research funds. Before doing this, do your research thoroughly.

You can also raise money from potential customers, fans, and friends who will not own a piece of your business at all. Woo them by promises of e-books, special benefits, samples of your products, or other enticements. When you raise money this way, the funds you generate will be income. One outstanding example of using Kickstarter to raise money for a project is the Veronica Mars movie. This project raised more than $5 million!

Entities, in All Their Glory

So how do you decide? This section discusses all the major business formats with a brief explanation of how they work. Read the pros and cons carefully. There is no one perfect entity.

Although one of the most common questions to TaxMama is "Should I incorporate?" there is no quick or simple answer. Your ideal business entity will depend on what you want out of your business.

Each entity type may have some advantages that are important to you. But there may be some other feature that makes it impossible for you to use. The following sections will help you narrow down your decision.

Sole Proprietorships

This entity type is just you, in business alone. You file your business tax return as a part of your personal tax return. (Some people call this a "DBA business.") Use the long version of Form 1040 and either Schedule C or Schedule C-EZ. If you're in business with your spouse, you're really a partnership, aren't you? The IRS thinks so and prefers that you report your income that way on Form 1065, U.S. Return of Partnership Income.

Pros
- It costs nothing to set up—unless you register a fictitious name, and then it's about $50 to $100 every few years.
- You have complete autonomy in business operations and decisions.
- You aren't required to keep a balanced set of books—but you should do it anyway.
- You aren't required to have a separate bank account—but you should.

Cons

- Your profits are subject to self-employment taxes.
- Your business gets no tax benefit for medical expenses and insurance, without the complication and expense of a special plan—and hiring your spouse, as described in Chapters 9 and 10.
- Without any structure, owners often get mentally lazy and don't think of their operation as a real business—so they rarely make long-term plans or grow the way they should.
- You are personally liable for everything that happens—and all the business debts. All of your assets, including your home and your savings, are at risk if you're sued—unless you buy adequate liability insurance to protect you (see Chapter 1).
- There is no continuity of life for the business. When you die, the business does, too.

General Partnerships

Two or more people in business together are considered a general partnership (GP), if they don't set up any other formal structure. Income is reported on Form 1065, with Schedule K-1s issued to partners.

Pros

- General partnerships are inexpensive to set up. You may even write your own agreement. That's not a great idea, but it is a good starting point from which your attorney may prepare your partnership agreement. Even if there is no agreement, if two or more people are working together, you're automatically a partnership in the eyes of the IRS.
- General partnerships pay no taxes.
- Partnership profits and losses may be split any way that is defined in the partnership agreement—and may change each year. They don't have to be split based on ownership (capital) percentage.
- Losses are fully deductible on personal returns, unless they are real estate losses; those face passive loss limits, as described in Chapter 6.
- Certain partnerships can get out of filing a tax return altogether. The partnership may file an election, which is a formal announcement to the IRS, that the partners chose to report the transactions on their personal tax returns. You may do this with investment clubs, certain real estate rentals, or groups of people simply sharing expenses but not in business together.
- Partnership profits may qualify for the new Section 199A 20 percent qualified business income deduction.

Cons

- All the partners must be consulted for decision making.
- If loans are required, all partners must provide their tax returns and financial statements. Many refuse because they don't really want their partners to know how rich—or poor—they are.
- Profits are generally subject to self-employment taxes.
- All partners are personally liable for everything that happens. All their assets, including homes and savings, are at risk if sued.
- All partners are liable for the acts of other partners and employees, too.
- There can be continuity-of-life issues. This means if your partner dies you're saddled with an heir (spouse or child) who's in a position to make business decisions. This usually results in conflict. Avoid this by using the key person insurance policies described earlier.

Limited Partnerships

Limited partnerships (LPs) are coming back into vogue. In a limited partnership, the limited partners put their money in and get complete protection from any liability or lawsuit of the business. However, limited partners don't get to participate in the decision making. There must always be at least one general partner who takes on the liability for the whole company.

Pros

- LPs are less complicated than corporations, LLCs, or LLPs.
- LPs don't pay federal taxes.
- They provide complete liability protection for all limited partners.
- Raising money from partners is easy. You don't have lots of general partners to answer to, or get approval from.
- Getting loans is easier with LPs than with GPs. Only the entity's and the general partner's financial reports need to be produced for the lenders. Usually, there is only one general partner, which makes financial applications easier.
- Profits and losses may be split by formula, instead of only by ownership percentage—just like general partnerships. Some partners may want losses—others may not be able to use them at all.
- A benefit for the general partner in the LP is that partnership agreements may have buyout clauses or prohibitions against selling the partnership interest without the general partner's approval. This makes it possible for the general partner to raise the money for business, then buy out the partners

after a reasonable return on investment is achieved for the limited partner investors.

- Limited partners' earnings are not subject to self-employment taxes.
- Although there must be a general partner, the general partner could be an LLC or other limited liability entity. That way the general partner can avoid personal liability for the LP's debts and lawsuits.
- Partnership profits may qualify for the new Section 199A 20 percent qualified business income deduction.

Cons

- LPs are more expensive to set up than GPs. You must get an attorney involved—whether it's yours or one recommended by the people investing with you. Make sure all understandings and expectations are defined. If you don't understand something—*ask*!
- Limited partners have no control over decisions. They could lose their investment if the general partner is inept or crooked. They won't know in enough time to do anything about it, since the general partner often doesn't keep them informed.
- Some states charge minimum annual taxes. (California's fee is $800 annually.)
- For the limited partners, partnership agreements may have buyout clauses or prohibitions against selling the partnership interest without the general partner's approval. This can make it impossible for the limited partners to get their money out of the investment if they need it or no longer trust the general partner. So evaluate these investments carefully.
- Limited partners' income or losses are considered passive. Loss deductions are limited to passive income from other sources.
- General partners are fully liable if the company is sued.

Limited Liability Partnerships

Limited liability partnerships (LLPs) are usually reserved for professional groups, such as attorneys, accountants, architects, and others with special licenses—or really good political lobbyists.

Pros

- LLPs don't pay federal taxes.
- They provide complete liability protection for all limited partners.
- They provide liability protection from the acts of other partners.

- No general partner is needed.
- Profits may be split by formula, time devoted to the company, or other criteria, instead of only by ownership percentage—and the same way that general partnerships may split profits on the K-1.
- There is continuity protection, so that even if a partner dies, the company continues. Do set up buy-sell agreements and key person insurance policies in case of death or disagreement.
- LLP profits may qualify for the new Section 199A 20 percent qualified business income deduction.

Cons

- They are expensive to set up properly. All partners have a say in the issues. And being professionals, they are all experts—so they do tend to put in their two cents' worth. All this "cooperation" pushes up attorney fees. It can also hamper change and growth—or enhance it!
- Some states, such as California ($800), charge minimum annual taxes.
- Rules are different in each state.
- Profits are subject to self-employment taxes.
- Profits are taxable whether all the income is distributed or not.
- Since the partners are all professionals, generally working for the LLP, guaranteed payments are mandatory.

Limited Liability Companies

Limited liability companies (LLCs) are an interesting creation. You'll see why when you read all the features in the "Pros" section that follows. LLCs are one of the most popular business forms with attorneys, since the attorneys can set them up easily using boilerplate forms. LLCs solve the problem of general partner liability. All partners, including managing partners, have liability protection from the debts of the business.

Pros

- Multiple-owner LLCs get to choose whether to report their business as a partnership, a corporation, or an S corporation.
- One-person LLCs may report either as an S or C corporation or on a personal Schedule C.
- LLCs may have multiple classes of ownership—this allows companies to give nonvoting shares to consultants and employees. Those members can share in profits but not decisions. Sharing profits with employees is a good way to attract workers without losing voting control.

- LLCs are permitted to issue shares that may not be sold. Again, this is perfect for consultants and employees. If they leave, you may buy them out at a prearranged price or formula, whether they like it or not.
- LLCs filing as a partnership don't pay federal taxes.
- They provide complete liability protection for all members from the LLC's debts.
- No general partner, with liability exposure, is needed.
- There is no requirement for keeping minutes, thus reducing paperwork. But only a fool doesn't maintain detailed records of all key business decisions, compensation changes, reimbursement policies, and employee or member benefits.
- Profits may be split by formula, time devoted to the company, or other criteria, instead of only by ownership percentage—just like general partnerships.
- Even if a member dies, the company continues. Remember to set up buy-sell agreements and key person insurance policies in case of death or disagreement, as described earlier.
- If the LLC is established as a pass-through entity for tax purposes, profits may qualify for the new Section 199A 20 percent qualified business income deduction.

Cons
- They are expensive to set up properly.
- They are rarely set up correctly—with elections not being made about the business structure in a timely fashion. This ends up causing complications with the IRS and state taxing agencies.
- Some states charge minimum annual taxes. For instance, in addition to California's minimum annual $800 fee, California also charges a gross revenue tax—which is due even if the LLC ends up with a net loss. (See this chapter's Resources for notes about how California taxes her entities.)
- Rules are different in each state.
- Profits are subject to self-employment taxes if the LLC files a Schedule C or a partnership return.

Corporations

Corporations (corps) are still the most common large business format used in the United States. Most publicly traded companies are corporations. Some, on the smaller stock exchanges, may be LLCs.

Pros

- All shareholders, including officers, have liability protection from corporate debt.
- Corps may have multiple classes of stockholders. Generally, preferred shareholders get a guaranteed rate of return, but they have no voting power. This allows companies to give preferred shares to consultants and employees. Those members get an assured stream of income but stay out of management decisions.
- Corporate dividends to shareholders have a preferred tax rate of 0 to 20 percent if the stock is held long enough.
- Corporations receiving dividends from other corporations they own may be able to exclude 50 to 65 percent of those dividends. (Or 100 percent for certain small business investment companies.)
- No general partner, with liability exposure, is needed.
- Shares are theoretically easy to sell, though in small corporations the stock may have restrictions—or no market.
- Even if a member dies, the company continues. Remember to set up buy-sell agreements and key person insurance policies in case of death or disagreement.
- Shareholders owning qualified small business stock (QSBS), purchased after September 27, 2010, for more than five years may exclude up to 100 percent of the capital gains on the sale (IRC Section 1202).[1] Setting up your new corporation to issue QSBS is a terrific strategy—especially since the PATH Act of 2015 also permanently removed the alternative minimum taxes that were formerly charged on the untaxed income.
- Shareholders of QSBS may deduct up to $50,000 ($100,000 for couples) on losses in the year of the loss, instead of having the losses limited to $3,000 in excess of capital gains. You can learn more about these rules on the IRS website. But we have some more information for you in this chapter's Resources.
- You may have unlimited shareholders.
- Anyone anywhere on the planet may own your corporate stock, subject to Homeland Security restrictions.

Cons

- Corporations are expensive to set up properly.
- Some states, such as California ($800), charge minimum annual taxes, even when you have a loss.

[1] In December 2015, Congress passed the PATH Act of 2015 excluding 100 percent of the profits from the sale of certain QSBS permanently. This article by Latham and Watkins LLP explains it well: http://iTaxMama.com/qsbs_100.

- Profits are subject to double taxation. The corporation pays tax, and the shareholders pay tax on dividends issued from those already-taxed profits.
- The IRS may impose taxes for constructive dividends if you draw too much money.
- The corporation may be subject to an accumulated earnings tax if you draw too little money.
- The IRS may decide your wages are too high or too low and penalize you accordingly.
- If the corporation's income comes primarily from the services of shareholders, you may be subject to more frequent audits.
- Undistributed income of personal holding companies may get hit with personal holding taxes.
- If the company fails, in order to claim the special $50,000 ($100,000) ordinary loss treatment on the stock, you first must have a $50,000 ($100,000) basis in the stock. Most small corporation owners' stock basis is $10,000 or less.
- C corporation profits do not get the benefit of the Section 199A 20 percent qualified small business income deduction.

S Corporations

S corporations (S corps) have all the protections of corporations, but most of the tax filing advantages of partnerships.

Pros
- All shareholders, including officers, have liability protection from corporate debts.
- S corporations don't need to keep detailed minute books, like a C corporation—though it would be wise to do so.
- No general partner, with liability exposure, is needed.
- Even if a member dies, the company continues. Remember to set up buy-sell agreements and key person insurance policies in case of death or disagreement.
- You may choose to switch to a C corporation format or back, once every five years, as long as you file Form 2553 by the fifteenth day of the third month of your fiscal year. But don't make a habit of switching. You pick up extra taxes and lose certain benefits in the process each time. Beware, doing so can generate Built-in Gains (BIG) taxes. Read more about this in the Glossary in Chapter 4.

- S corporation profits may qualify for the new Section 199A 20 percent qualified business income deduction.

Cons

- Corporations are expensive to set up properly.
- Attorneys and corporate setup paralegals rarely file the S corporation election. You must remember to file it yourself or have your tax pro do it for you. If you don't do it on time, you might lose the privilege of the S corporation status.
- When shareholders are added, all shareholders should sign the S corporation election, Form 2553, all over again. Companies often overlook this.
- Shares are not easy to sell because there is no public market. Generally, it's wise to place restrictions on the stock to keep outsiders from owning your business.
- There are restrictions on the employee benefits of shareholders who own more than 2 percent of the business.
- When it comes to health insurance for the 2 percent or more shareholders, there are special rules—a total pain. See Internal Revenue Bulletin 2008-2.
- Some states, such as California ($800), charge minimum annual taxes, even when you have losses.
- The IRS may decide your wages are too low and penalize you accordingly.
- S corps may only have one class of stockholders. Profits and losses are allocated solely by ownership percentage.
- S corporation stock is not eligible for the qualified small business stock benefits (QSBS).
- Nonresident aliens may not own S corporation stock.
- You may have no more than 100 shareholders.

Whew! That's a lot of data. How can you decide what your company will be? Photocopy these last pages. Draw a line through all the things that are unacceptable to you. Highlight the items you like. This will give you a visual feel for which entities will and won't work for you. To help you out, look at Tables 3.2 and 3.3, which give you a visual view of all the entities. Table 3.2 provides a side-by-side comparison of the primary tax considerations of all the entities. Table 3.3 provides a side-by-side comparison of the primary nontax considerations of all the entities.

A Brief Word About Nevada, Delaware, and Wyoming Corporations

You've probably heard many radio ads tempting you with the virtues of Nevada, Delaware, or Wyoming corporations. The ads encourage you to set up your corporation in one of these three states. These ads promise to fix your credit, get you loans without your personal guarantee, and help you do other things you could never do as a small business. Sure, there are good things about them—privacy, for one. The corporate registrars of Nevada, Delaware, and Wyoming won't reveal your identity, only the identity of your agent for service. If you're hiding out from creditors or a former spouse, this may be a way to tuck away your assets.

None of these states have corporate, LLC, or partnership income taxes. They don't even require state tax returns. All you have to do is fill in an annual report about the current officers and agent for service—and pay the state a franchise fee.

What's bad about using them? If you're not living in one of those states, you'll have to register your corporation to do business in your own state, too. Often, that will require you to reveal who you are. It will mean filing and paying your state's taxes. It will mean extra forms and registrations. Basically, you are duplicating all the work and fees, giving up the privacy you hoped to get by filing out of state, and on top of that, you won't save a dime in taxes.

What if you follow the advice of those aggressively pushing the Nevada and Delaware corporations and you don't register in your home state? If someone doesn't want to honor any of your contracts, he or she doesn't have to and you have no standing in your state. Someone who figures out your company is not registered to do business in your state can walk away from your bills, and you can't sue. Your own state, when it catches you, will charge you taxes, penalties, and interest for all the years you didn't file tax returns locally. Try getting the courts to hear your case. You won't have any luck. Why? Because in order to file a lawsuit to collect bad debts, or anything, you must have legal standing in the state where you are filing the lawsuit.

Perhaps you feel you must set one up, because you think "Someday I'm going to leave my state. Besides, nothing really happens in my state. It all happens on the Internet," it will cost you. To legitimately have all your transactions take place in Nevada, Delaware, or Wyoming, you'll need a local address in that state. All your mail must be delivered to that state and then forwarded to you. Not only does this cost you money, but it adds about a week of time to each of your orders or banking notices. You must have either a phone number in that state or a toll-free number. After all, you don't want your state to see you using a phone number in your own state if you are trying to avoid paying state and local taxes, right? Even local customers in

TABLE 3.2 Summary of Tax Considerations for C and S Corporations, Partnerships, and Family Trusts

Characteristics	C Corporation	S Corporation	General Partnership	Limited Partnership	LLC	LLP	Family Trust
TAX CONSIDERATIONS							
Taxation	Corporation is taxed on profits. Shareholders are taxed on dividends.	Corporation is generally not taxed. Shareholders are taxed on profits passed on as dividends.	Partners pay taxes on their pro-rata share of income or losses. All income is subject to self-employment (SE) tax.	Partnership is not taxed. Partners pay taxes on their pro-rata share of profits. Ltd partners have passive loss restrictions. No SE tax.	Taxation method depends on election either as a corporation or partnership. Default: one member is Schedule C; two or more is Form 1065.	Partnership is not taxed. Partners pay taxes on their share of profits. Subject to SE tax.	Generally, income allocated to beneficiaries at year-end. If taxed to trust, taxes are excessively high.
Pass-Through of Income/Loss	No	Yes	Yes	Yes	It depends	Yes	It depends
Property Exchanged for Ownership Interest	Nonrecognition treatment if control requirements satisfied under IRC § 351. Liabilities transferred in excess of basis may result in gain.		More flexibility than corporations. Generally no gain or loss recognized at either entity or partner level. Guidance under IRC § 721.	More flexibility than corporations. Generally no gain or loss recognized at either entity or partner level. Guidance under IRC § 721.	More flexibility than corporations. Generally no gain or loss recognized at either entity or partner level. Guidance under IRC § 721.		Property or money transferred into or sold to trust.
Initial Basis	Basis in stock = stock purchase price + cash + adjusted basis of property transferred to the corporation. Liabilities do not increase basis.		Like corporations, but accepting a partner's share of liabilities increases basis. Giving up liabilities reduces basis.	Determined in same manner as general partnerships.	Determined in same manner as general partnerships.	Determined in same manner as general partnerships.	Fair market value of assets at time of transfer to the trust.
Income Allocation to Family Members	Not applicable.	Family members providing services must be compensated prior to allocating income and loss to other family members.	Same as S corporations. Capital must be an income-producing asset in order for income to be allocated to a partner who is a family member and has received interest by direct or indirect gift. Subject to SE tax.		Same as partnerships.		Specified in terms of trust agreement.
Alternative Minimum Tax	Not applicable.	Not subject to AMT at entity level.	Not subject to AMT at entity level.	Not subject to AMT at entity level.	Not subject to AMT at entity level.	Not subject to AMT at entity level.	Yes, either to the trust or beneficiary(ies).

Passive Loss Rules	Can generally offset passive losses against nonpassive income. C corporations not subject to PAL rules except personal service corporations and closely held C corporations.	Shareholders may be subject to passive loss rules.	General partners are considered to participate materially if they meet any of seven tests in Reg. 1.469-5T, but LPs are more restrictive. Ltd partners have only three tests by which they can be considered to "materially participate."		LLC members are treated as a general partner who has to satisfy one of the seven tests.	LLP members are treated as a general partner who has to satisfy one of the seven tests.	Subject to passive activity loss rules.
Fringe Benefits	Few restrictions.	Restrictions on 2 percent or more S corporation shareholders (may pay tax on fringe benefits).	Insurance, health, and welfare programs paid by partnership on behalf of partners are taxable to individual partners, deductible by entity, and reported as guaranteed payments to partners subject to SE tax.		Same rules as a partnership.	Same rules as a partnership.	Generally same as corporations.
Double Taxation	Yes	No	No	No	No	No	No
Highest Marginal Tax Rate	Top rate: 21 percent	Flow through—depends on individual's tax rate bracket. Top rate: 37 percent.	Same rules as S corporation.	Same rules as S corporation.	Same rules as S corporation.	Same rules as S corporation.	Depends on the type of trust—Top rate: 37 percent.
Subject to Section 199A	No	Yes, subject to SSTB limits.	Yes, subject to SSTB limits.	Yes, subject to SSTB limits.	Yes, subject to SSTB limits—if not C corporation.	Yes, subject to SSTB limits.	It depends.
Filing Costs	Filing fee with the state.	Filing fee with the state.	None.	Filing fee with the state.	Filing fee with the state.	Filing fee with the state.	None.
Tax Forms & Applicable Publications	Form 1120 / IRS Pub. 542	Form 1120S / IRS Pub. 542	Form 1065 / IRS Pub. 541	Form 1065 / IRS Pub. 541	Form 1065 / IRS Pub. 541	Form 1065 / IRS Pub. 541	Form 1041 / IRS Pub. 559
Tax Return Due Date Effective after 2015 for Returns Through 2024	15th day of 4th month following entity's tax year end. Extension: five months (six months for fiscal year). *Note:* starting in 2025, extension is six months for calendar year.	15th day of 3rd month following entity's tax year end. Extension: six months.	15th day of 3rd month following entity's tax year end. Extension: six months.	15th day of 3rd month following entity's tax year end. Extension: six months.	15th day of 3rd month following entity's tax year end. Extension: six months.	15th day of 3rd month following entity's tax year end. Extension: six months.	April 15 + six-month extension. Trusts must use a calendar year—except for tax-exempt or charitable trusts, and grantor trusts treated as wholly owned by the grantor or another person.

TABLE 3.3 Summary of Nontax Considerations for C and S Corporations, Partnerships, and Family Trusts

Characteristics	C Corporation	S Corporation	General Partnership	Limited Partnership	LLC	LLP	Family Trust
NONTAX CONSIDERATIONS							
Ease of Formation	File and incorporate in any state for permission to conduct business.	File and incorporate in any state for permission to conduct business.	General partners must agree to form partnership. No state permission is required.	Certificate of Limited Partnership to be filed with the state.	File with state for permission to conduct business. Must follow specific procedures for formation and operations.	Register election of LLP with Secretary of the State.	Set up trust, appoint trustee, and identify beneficiaries.
Legal Status	Corporate legal identity independent of shareholders.	Corporate legal identity independent of shareholders.	Legal business identity independent from partners.	Legal business entity independent of partners.	Legal identity independent of members.	Legal business identity independent of partners.	Independent taxable entity.
Eligible Entity	No restrictions.	Citizens, resident aliens, estates, certain trusts only. Limit 100 shareholders.	No restrictions. Any person or entity qualifies as an eligible partner.	No restrictions. Any person or entity qualifies as an eligible partner.	No restrictions. Any person or entity qualifies as an eligible partner.	No restrictions. Any person or entity qualifies as an eligible partner.	No restrictions.
Management	Board of Directors and Officers elected or selected by shareholders.	Board of Directors and Officers are selected by shareholders.	Partners generally have equal voice in decision making.	General partners manage according to partnership agreement.	Operating agreement outlines management.	Partners generally have equal voice in decision making.	Trustee decides on most issues.

Choice of Tax Year	No restrictions.	Have certain restrictions in choosing a fiscal tax year. (Section 444 election)	Must adopt same year-end as partners or members with 50 percent interest or if none same year-end of principal partners or members with 5 percent interest in profits and capital. Otherwise, calendar year or show a business purpose.				IRC § 645 provides tax year as the calendar year. Exempted are tax-exempt trusts under 501(a) and charitable trusts under 4947(a)(1).
Dissolution or Liquidation	Perpetual life. Shareholder approval normally required. State law dictates approval procedure and necessary percentage of shareholders that can affect a liquidation.		When entity winds up business affairs.	Generally limited to a defined amount of time.	Generally limited to a defined amount of time.	Generally limited to a defined amount of time.	Generally limited to a defined amount of time.
Owners' Liability	Shareholders are typically not personally liable for the debts of the corporation.	Shareholders are typically not personally liable for the debts of the corporation.	Partners may have unlimited liability.	General partners have unlimited liability and limited partners have limited liability.	Members not typically liable for the debts of the LLC.	Partners not typically liable for the debts of the LLP.	Grantor responsible for debts of the trust.
Ability to Raise Capital	Sell shares of stock or bonds to raise capital.	Sell shares of stock or bonds to raise capital.	Additional partners or investments from existing partners; bank loans.	Additional partners or investments from existing partners; bank loans.	Possible to sell interests; subject to operating agreement restrictions.	Additional partners or investments from existing partners; bank loans.	Grantor can sell assets in trust; income from assets held in trust.
Transferability of Interest	Shares of stock in a corporation are easily transferable.	Yes, subject to shareholder consent.	Depends on partnership agreement.	Depends on partnership agreement.	Possibly but usually restrictive.	Limited partners may transfer their interests subject to partnership agreement.	Grantor may redefine beneficiary in a revocable trust.

your hometown must use that out-of-state phone number. Your bank account must be in that state. You must pay an agent for service. How much extra can you expect to pay so that you can avoid taxes in your own state? Here are some annual numbers:

Post office box (at least $25 per month)	$300
Postage—mail and package forwarding	$360
Agent for service	$150
Extra bank costs due to late notices	$240
Toll-free phone number or call forwarding	$300
Annual franchise fee (approximate)	$125
Total cost of tax-free corporation	$1,475

If you set up an out-of-state corporation or LLC to save the annual $800 minimum fee in California (one of the more expensive states), you've just outsmarted yourself. You've spent $675 more than the taxes would have been or much more than $1,000 in excess of the costs to operate openly in your own state. Plus, who knows how many extra banking fees and insufficient fund fees you incurred because you learned about a bounced check too late to cover it in time! The extra fees result from the delays in learning when some of your Internet sales have been questioned or deemed fraudulent. Due to the mail delay, you might not get the notice in time to respond and defend your sale—or your standing with the bank. If you're in a less expensive state, as far as corporations go, seeing how high the costs can run may make you think twice—the inconveniences generally outweigh the benefits.

The Real Benefit of Incorporating in Places Like Nevada or Other Tax-Free States

Sometimes you team up with partners, friends, or business associates who will work with you actively in a business. Your associates are all in different states. Set up the main entity in Wyoming, Nevada, or Delaware—or even Florida, another tax-free state. Then register as a foreign corporation in each state where your business associates live and operate. Remember to register in the state where your fulfillment takes place (storage and shipping of inventory), if that takes place in yet another state. (See Chapter 12, talking about "nexus" and the Wayfair decision.)

Another good reason? You are at a point where you want to establish a solid business. You know that you will be moving to a different state within the next two to five years. You're not sure where you will be moving. You can protect your company's name, trademark, identity, and presence by establishing the master incorporation

(LLC, etc.) in a neutral state. By setting up your business in neutral territory, you can move anywhere in the country without having to close your business and reincorporate elsewhere.

What About Nonprofits?

If you want to get attention and raise money quickly, a nonprofit organization is a great structure. The right cause will open lots of corporate doors and treasuries. Radio and television stations are required to run public service spots, so advertising can be free. The big drawback to being a nonprofit is that you can get voted out if you don't structure your organization properly. You don't actually "own" the "company." So don't set up your business as a nonprofit entity unless you're prepared to do it right. Otherwise, the IRS will come down on you like a ton of bricks.

You can start out with a nonprofit entity to establish yourself, your image, and your credibility. Use that as a jumping-off point to create a parallel business, funneling part of your profits to your nonprofit. Just be careful not to use your nonprofit to give your own business advantages and benefits. Self-dealing can void your exempt status.

Set up things properly, and you will be helping yourself and doing good at the same time. Simply take a decent compensation as director of your nonprofit and make a remarkable improvement in the world around you. That's what Fred Jordan did. His Fred Jordan Mission started by feeding and sheltering Los Angeles's skid row homeless. Today it helps people as far away as Africa and Hong Kong. Or take actress Carmen Zapata of the Bilingual Foundation of the Arts, which promotes cross-cultural understanding by bringing the Latino experience and culture, through the medium of bilingual theater, to English-speaking and Spanish-speaking audiences. And there's Rose Martin, whose Peace Neighborhood Center in Ann Arbor, Michigan, raises millions each year to help local people in need—and shares the wealth with other organizations in need.

The organization doesn't have to be a charity. It doesn't have to be depressing. You can start something that's fun or that's for people in specific professions or that gathers people with similar interests—like bowling, surfing, scrapbooking, video games, movies, eating—anything your imagination can dream up. Imagine devising a way to get paid for doing something you love!

Don't you admire people who can bring their passion to their work and create a win-win situation for all concerned? That could be you—and your family.

Entities We're Not Discussing

This book doesn't cover the use of trusts or cooperatives as a business format. There are advantages to all those forms, too, along with pitfalls. If you're feeling really aggressive, consider chatting with your advisory team about those alternatives.

All the Highlights in One Place

Let's summarize what you need to know about entities. First of all, avoid Nevada, Delaware, and Wyoming corporations, unless you're located in Nevada, Delaware, or Wyoming—or you run a business across several states. Don't start a business thinking you can hide income offshore. What does "offshore" mean to the IRS? To the IRS, "offshore" means "outside the United States." That includes Canada, Mexico, and all those tempting tax-free islands and havens like the Caymans and the Bahamas. See Chapter 5 for a discussion of offshore income and abusive schemes.

Cut taxes, but don't make that your only consideration. Factor in long-term issues, such as health, retirement, and your family's and staff's needs.

The following overview lays out reporting requirements for each type of entity discussed in this chapter.

Sole Proprietorships

Report income and expenses on the following forms:

- Use Schedule C for most businesses.
- Use Schedule F for farms, horticulturists, and ranches.
- Use Form 4835 if your farmland was leased to a tenant farmer—or you received crops or livestock instead of cash. Income from this form is not subject to self-employment tax.
- Use Schedule E, page 1, for rentals of real estate or personal equipment.
- Use Schedule C if your business is equipment rental—like cars, films, construction equipment, etc.
- Use Schedule E, page 1, to report your royalties from books, films, and other intangibles. *Note:* Report that income on Schedule C while you are creating those works or actively marketing them.
- Use Form 8829 to deduct your home office.
- Use Form 4562 to report depreciation.
- Use Form 8995 to claim the Qualified Business Income Deduction.

All Partnerships and LLCs Reported as Partnerships

Report income and expenses on the following forms:

- Form 1065 is the overall tax return. Use page 1 to report your general business income and expenses.
- Use Form 1040, Schedule F, to report farm and ranching income. Include it with Form 1065.
- Use Form 8825 to report your real estate rental activities. Include the form with your Form 1065 package.
- Schedule K-1 is issued to each partner or member, reporting the person's share of income, expenses, and credits.
- Use Form 4562 to report depreciation. *Note:* Section 179 depreciation will appear on a separate line on the K-1. It won't be included in the deductions on page 1 of the Form 1065.
- Use Form 8995 to claim the Qualified Business Income Deduction.

S Corporations

Report income and expenses on the following forms:

- Form 1120S is the overall return form.
- Use Form 8825 to report your real estate rental activities. Include the form with your Form 1120S package.
- Schedule K-1 is issued to each shareholder or member, reporting the person's share of income, expenses, and credits.
- Use Form 4562 to report depreciation. *Note:* As with partnerships, Section 179 depreciation will appear on a separate line on the K-1. It won't be included in the deductions on page 1 of the Form 1120S.
- Use Form 8995 to claim the Qualified Business Income Deduction.

Corporations

Report income and expenses on the following forms:

- Form 1120 is the overall return form.
- Use Form 8825 to report your real estate rental activities. Include the form with your Form 1120 package.
- You will generally need Form 4562 to report your depreciation, amortization, and business miles driven.

Your Big Decision

You have the tools to decide which entity you need right now—and if you plan to change that entity in the future. After all, you do have the right to start small and grow, right? The decision has become more complicated as a result of the TCJA. Now, you need to determine if your business can benefit from that 20 percent Section 199A deduction. You need to determine if you're better off with a C corporation, with a flat tax rate of only 21 percent—and dividends issued by the C corporation are taxed at capital gains rates. Or are you better off with an untaxed entity, like a partnership or S corporation? It may be necessary to do some profit projections and sample tax return projections to see which gives you the best tax benefit in coming years.

Before you go to the next chapter, reflect. How will you set up your business, your legacy? What will the body of your vision be? Will it be you alone or one of those alluring corporate or partnership entities? You'll need to know how your business will operate before you can set up the structure of your accounting system. Don't agonize over the decision. Please, don't let it paralyze you. Pick an entity. If you're wrong, it's OK. You can always change it later. Sure, it will cost a bit of money to convert to another entity. Don't worry about it. By then, you'll have the money. So before turning to Chapter 4, decide!

Resources

In this chapter, you saw a variety of resources. Here's a summary of them, so you can find them quickly and easily. The resources are not necessarily in alphabetical order in each category. They are in order of their importance or usefulness, in TaxMama's opinion.

IRS Resources

- **IRS Publication 334, *Tax Guide for Small Businesses*.** https://www.irs.gov/publications/p334/index.html
- **The IRS's Perspective on Compensation—Especially for S Corporations and Their 2 Percent Owners.** http://iTaxMama.com/IRS_Compensation1
- **Form 1040, U.S. Individual Income Tax Return.** https://www.irs.gov/pub/irs-access/f1040_accessible.pdf
- **Form 1040, Schedule C, Profit or Loss from Business.** https://www.irs.gov/pub/irs-pdf/f1040sc.pdf

- **IRS Publication 541,** *Partnerships.* https://www.irs.gov/publications/p541/index.html
- **Form 1065, U.S. Return of Partnership Income.** https://www.irs.gov/pub/irs-pdf/f1065.pdf
- **IRS Publication 542,** *Corporations.* https://www.irs.gov/publications/p542/index.html
- **Form 1120, U.S. Corporation Income Tax Return.** https://www.irs.gov/pub/irs-pdf/f1120.pdf
- **Form 1120, Schedule PH.** https://www.irs.gov/pub/irs-pdf/f1120sph.pdf
- **Form 1120S, U.S. Income Tax Return for an S Corporation.** https://www.irs.gov/pub/irs-pdf/f1120s.pdf
- **Form 4835, Farm Income and Expenses.** https://www.irs.gov/pub/irs-pdf/f4835.pdf
- **Form 8825, Rental Real Estate Income of a Partnership or S Corporation.** https://www.irs.gov/pub/irs-pdf/f8825.pdf
- **Form 8995 and Form 8995A—Qualified Business Income Deduction.** http://iTaxMama.com/Form8995A-Sec199A. Form 8995 is the short version of the form.
- **IRS—Starting, Operating, or Closing a Business.** http://iTaxMama.com/IRS_Biz_Start. The IRS has built a small business resource that features articles, tips, and information to help you start a business, operate your business, and close your business. You may even find some brief videos.
- **IRS—Life Cycle of an Exempt Organization (Nonprofit Entity).** http://iTaxMama.com/IRS_Exempt. Step-by-step information on setting up, operating, and dissolving your charitable institution, trade association, social welfare organization, labor organization, or agricultural or horticultural organization.
- **IRS—Gig Economy Tax Center.** http://iTaxMama.com/IRS_Share

State Resources and Entity Formation Resources

- **States' Business Start-Up Information.** http://iTaxMama.com/BkRt_BizSuccess. Bankrate.com provides fundamental information on licensing and start-up tips and links to various state agencies.
- **State Tax Forms.** http://www.taxadmin.org/state-tax-forms
- **Wyoming—50 States Resource.** http://soswy.state.wy.us/Business/Business50.aspx. One-stop access to the business registration sites for all 50 states.

- **State Guide: Forms and Fees for Business Formation.** http://iTaxMama
  .com/State_LLC. Has links to fees and filing requirements.
- **Incorp Services Inc. in Nevada.** http://iTaxMama.com/InCorpTM,
  (800) 2 INCORP: To get 20 percent off on formation services and registered
  agent services, use the coupon code TAXMAMA.
- **The Company Corporation.** https://www.incorporate.com/, (800) 315-9420.
  Register your corporation, LLC, or other formal structure at this site, which
  is one of the oldest incorporators in the country. Mention that TaxMama
  sent you to get a $25 discount.
- **Hubco.** http://www.inc-it-now.com, (800) 443-8177. Register your corporation, LLC, or other formal structure, and handle most of it yourself—the
  cheapest option. Also, a great source of new or replacement corporate supplies, such as the corporate seal, binders, and so on.
- **California Business Entity Rules to Watch.** https://www.ftb.ca.gov/forms
  /misc/3556.html. See LLC Fees. If you're operating a small business in California, stay away from LLCs. They are usually your most expensive choice
  due to all the state taxes and gross revenue fees.

Exempt Organization Resources

- **TechSoup.org.** http://www.techsoup.org/. Get free software, technology,
  and other resources if you are a nonprofit organization. Often, you can get
  several copies of software products for all the key members of your organization for free or at significant discounts.
- **GuideStar.org.** http://www2.guidestar.org. Look up most legitimate
  charities and nonprofits. You can find their financial reports and all public
  information in this master database. Some of it is available for free simply by
  registering. Other data may require a fee.
- **Candid** (The Foundation Center and GuideStar are now part of Candid).
  https://candid.org/research-and-verify-nonprofits/990-finder. A faster and
  easier Form 990 search tool than GuideStar's. You can look up the financial
  reports, including officer compensation on all United States charitable organizations.

Other Resources—Including Research Tools

- **Legalbitstream.** http://www.legalbitstream.com. This site is a free tax law
  research website offering comprehensive and timely updated searchable
  databases of federal tax law, consisting of tax cases from the federal courts

and IRS materials that were issued from the present back to 1990 in most cases (contains 50,000 documents).

- **What Is Adequate Compensation?** http://www.rcreports.com/. This site can provide definitive reports to use to back up your decisions for wages or guaranteed payments.
- **SEC Information About Crowdfunding.** http://iTaxMama.com/SEC _Crowdfund. This investor bulletin does an excellent job of showing how investor capitalization works.
- **CrowdExpert.** http://crowdexpert.com/. A useful resource to learn more about crowdfunding to raise investment capital or funds for projects. Explore their crowdfunding directory at http://crowdexpert.com /investment-crowdfunding-platform-directory/.
- **Kickstarter and How to Use It Effectively.** http://iTaxMama.com/Kick _V_Mars. One outstanding example of using Kickstarter to raise millions of dollars for a project is the Veronica Mars movie.
- ***Bottom Line/Personal.*** http://bottomlineinc.com/. This site has a searchable database with at least the last three to five years of issues online. This is an excellent place to start a search. Subscribe to *Bottom Line/Personal* for $39 per year for short, to-the-point financial articles, information about tax issues, and money-saving tips. They're written in plain English, so you'll have no trouble understanding them.
- **Qualified Small Business Stock (QSBS).** http://iTaxMama.com/qsbs_100. In December 2015, Congress passed the PATH Act of 2015 excluding 100 percent of the profits from the sale of certain QSBS permanently. This article by Latham and Watkins LLP explains it well.

TaxMama Resources

- **"Doing Tax Research Online for Free."** http://iTaxMama.com/TM _TaxResearch_Order. Learn to do tax research online, using free research tools available to you through this link.
- **TaxMama's Quick Look-Ups.** http://iTaxMama.com/TM_QuickLookUp. You will find all kinds of useful reference materials, webinars you can replay, e-books, and more.
- **Your Business Bible.** http://www.yourbusinessbible.com. Look for worksheets, printable checklists, and other goodies and resources.

To-Do List and Questionnaire

☐ 1. Will you be doing your own record keeping? _____ Yes _____ No
If no, enter contact information and dates you collected documents, as needed:

Will you hire an outside or virtual bookkeeper?
Hire an in-office assistant?
Hire an accounting or tax firm?
Name: _____ Phone(s): _____
Address: _____
Email: _____
W-2: _____ I-9: _____ W-9: _____

☐ 2. What accounting system will you use? List the name of the tool(s):
Paper-based: _____
Software: _____
Both: _____

☐ 3. What online accounts will be integrated?
Bank accounts: _____
Credit cards: _____
PayPal or shopping cart: _____
Other: _____

☐ 4. Are you using a _____ fiscal year or _____ calendar year?
End date: _____

☐ 5. _____ Accrual or _____ Cash basis?

Remember to put a copy of each document behind this page, folded in half.

4

RECORD KEEPING

Delegate your record keeping. But more importantly, make sure the person you are delegating to has impeccable ethics and independent oversight by a quarterly accounting audit.

—ADRYENN ASHLEY OF WOWISME.NET

You've probably never thought about it this way, but record keeping is a language. In fact, it's a series of different languages, depending on who will be using or reading your records. In Chapter 3, you made the big decision. You picked out the body your business will be wearing—even if it's just for the short term. Now, it's time for you to learn to communicate properly for the body you've chosen.

While the languages are different, they have the same roots. Just as French, Spanish, Portuguese, and Italian all come from Latin (Romance languages—because of the Roman roots), English also has a strong Latin influence. If you listen closely to those other languages, you'll find you can understand them a little because you speak English.

It's the same thing with your records. The basics are the same across the board. The words used to describe concepts and transactions are the same, but the nuances and details are different the higher up the food chain your business gets. Refer to the glossary later in this chapter to demystify the terminology that tax professionals and accountants use.

Keeping Records Is a Pain

Many small business owners are so busy trying to run their businesses, hold it all together, and keep the bills paid that there just isn't time for bookkeeping, too.

Besides, who knows how to do it correctly? If you can't do it correctly, it can be daunting, can't it?

But you have to do it—really, really, you do. If you don't keep decent records, how can you possibly know how your business is doing?

Some people operate on the principle that if there is money in the bank account, everything is fine. One set of business owners I knew used to call up the bank in the morning to find out their balance. (Today, of course, you can look it up online.) If there was money in the account, they wrote checks. They didn't take into account the fact that the checks they wrote yesterday had not cleared yet. As you can imagine, they were bouncing checks all over town without understanding why. Their employees understood. The minute they got paid, they ran to the bank to cash their paychecks before any of the owners' wild checks hit the bank.

Making It Painless

Adryenn Ashley has some tips for you. Adryenn is an award-winning author, filmmaker, and speaker, and the founder of Wow! Is Me (http://wowisme.net).

When you're just starting out, you do your own "expense reports" to give to the bookkeeper. OK, when you're really starting out, you hand over a shoebox full of receipts with a slightly apologetic look on your face and say, "Can you make sense of this?" Once you have a system in place, then it's up to you to mark your receipts. Well let me tell you, when you get to a certain earning level, it is actually more practical to have a savvy bookkeeper do it all, import the data from the bank (so that means limiting cash spending and using debit cards for easy tracking), match up the data to appointments in the calendar, and only spend 10 minutes asking you to identify the dozen or so transactions from the month that he or she can't figure out. Your time spent on bookkeeping per month? Ten minutes. It all boils down to having a bookkeeper who is a self-starter and understands your habits.

But don't forget quarterly audits, not done by the bookkeeper, but by a third party. I once discovered my bookkeeper had been writing herself checks (using my signature stamp) for her pay. Rather than putting herself on payroll, she had been deducting herself as office supplies so she wouldn't get a 1099 at the end of the year! Tsk-tsk! I would never have found that without the audit. So, yes, delegate, but more important, make sure the person you are delegating to has impeccable ethics and independent oversight by a quarterly accounting audit.

I use QuickBooks Accountants edition because I have multiple entities in different segments. I have the bookkeeper come in, and the auditor comes in quarterly on the sly. I don't want people to behave because they know they're being watched; I want them to do an honest job because they're honest people. I love my bookkeeper now! She's amazing. She used to work for a bank doing very complex stuff, and so I'm a walk in the park for her.

I hired a more expensive bookkeeper who is a QuickBooks guru to make sure that it was properly done. You can also have your CPA's office do it. It's just more expensive. For me, having things in the right category was the most important. I did a full 10-year audit of a company (I was a forensic accountant for the movies for a while), and it was amazing what I found . . . designer sunglasses written off as utilities . . . once you get a feel for how the company runs and what's normal, the abnormal stands out.

Types of Accounting Systems

It's very important to track your incoming funds and your expenditures if you want to have success as a small business. The simplest of accounting systems is just a summary of your various sources of income and a list of your expenses. Since that's essentially a list of numbers, there's no real way to tell if anything's missing. That's called a single-entry system. Whether you maintain these records manually or on a computer—using something like Quicken—you have no cross-reference to ensure your books are in balance.

Here's an example of a single-entry system's transactions. In August, John fixed his car for $250 and paid with his American Express card. He paid his printer $150 by check. John picked up office supplies for $75 using petty cash. His rent was $550, paid, as usual, by check. He bought a copy machine for $775 using his Visa credit card. John's expense records might look like this:

Description	Amount
Auto Expenses	$ 250
Printing	$ 150
Office Supplies	$ 75
Rent	$ 550
Copy Machine	$ 775
Total for August	$1,800

As you can see, there's nothing to show you how much money came from his bank account, from cash in his pocket, or from increasing the balance due on his credit card. There's nothing to tell you that the copy machine is an asset rather than an expense.

There's no balancing factor in single-entry systems. Being in balance is an obsession for accountants and bookkeepers. It tells us that all the pieces of the puzzle are there. That's why businesses generally use a double-entry accounting system. Both sides of each transaction are recorded, and when the numbers don't balance—we know something's missing or something's entered incorrectly. In a double-entry system, John's transactions for August would look like this (with some more detailed descriptions, of course):

Description	Amount
Asset—Bank Account	($700)
Asset—Petty Cash	($ 75)
Asset—Copy Machine	$775
Liability—Visa Card	($775)
Liability—Amex Card	($250)
Auto Expenses	$250
Printing	$150
Office Supplies	$ 75
Rent	$550
Total for August	-0-

Using a double-entry system, you always come out to zero, because assets = liabilities + capital.

Not everyone will need a double-entry bookkeeping system. Corporations will. Very small businesses can get by with the most casual of records. Although if you start out with a balanced bookkeeping system, even for a tiny business, you'll already have your system in place when growth is better than you expect. You can save the cost of converting or entering a year's worth of data—or data for several years.

While paper-based bookkeeping systems are perfectly adequate, I recommend that you don't use them. If you're starting a business in this millennium, do your accounting on a computer. It's much easier and faster to correct posting errors. Reports are at your fingertips whenever a banker, your tax professional, or anyone else asks. The software will give you enough information to prepare budgets or to catch fluctuations in costs or income.

One of the things I love about today's computerized accounting systems is that you no longer have to sort checks into numerical order or invoices into date order before you enter them. You just enter everything in any order you find it—and the computer puts each transaction into the right order. When working with people who haven't done bookkeeping for years, this is especially helpful. As I come across checks or invoices from other years, I can enter them into QuickBooks as I go along. I just need to remember to set the paper aside and file it in the box or drawer for the right year. You'll find that feature very helpful if you have receipts in your car or kitchen or with your children, boss, or staff. You know how you often get receipts and documents from your team in a piecemeal fashion? With a system that operates like QuickBooks, you don't need to stress about reorganizing the entries to get them to appear in the right month when you get yet one more document someone on your team forgot to tell you about.

Another advantage to the computerized system is that it will give you reports for any time period. If you need to get a profit and loss statement for January through May in order to compute your estimated tax payment, it takes seconds with a good software program.

One feature that some of the accounting software companies are offering these days is online accounting. You pay a monthly fee, and they keep the software updated. You can access your accounts from practically anywhere on this planet—or even from the International Space Station. All you need is Internet access. You and your tax professionals don't need to exchange files. You can go online together and discuss the accounting and make revisions or corrections any time you like. The only drawback is that when you use an online accounting system, you can only use it for one company. You must pay separately for each company you operate. When you buy bookkeeping software, on the other hand, you can generally use it for as many companies as you like.

Do yourself a favor and get the computer and the accounting software or use an online system—whatever works for you. Just be sure to automate your accounting.

Doing It by Hand

If, on the other hand, you really prefer to do your bookkeeping by hand, take a look at Tables 4.1 and 4.2, which show how to set up a multicolumn spreadsheet. (If you want to do this on paper, buy 13-column spreadsheets.) As you can see in both tables, all the numbers to the right of the totals must be added together to equal the total in Column D, the "Total Check" column.

If you're going to do your bookkeeping by hand, be sure to total each page separately. Then have a total page for the month for both cash receipts and cash disbursements reports. Once the month is balanced, total all 12 months to get the whole year.

Use the "Other" column (see Table 4.2, Column L) for expenses that are not necessarily recurring. At the end of the month, subtotal each item in the "Other" column. Add those sums together for the year.

TABLE 4.1 Company Do-Re-Mi Cash Receipts Journal, November 2020

A	B	C	D	E	F	G	H	I	J
Date	Item #	Received From	Total Check	Net Sales	Sales Tax	Shipping Income	Reimb. Exp.	Late Fee	Rental Income
11/1/2020	2245	Newman Sound Systems	650.00	577.37	47.63	25.00			
11/5/2020	813	Ansty Tenant	825.00						825.00
11/17/2020	11612	Speakers City	923.18				923.18		
11/25/2020	945	Later Tenant	803.85				−62.40	41.25	825.00
		Total November	3,202.03	577.37	47.63	25.00	860.78	41.25	1,650.00

Totals in Columns E through J must equal the total in Column D.

TABLE 4.2 Company Do-Re-Mi Cash Disbursements Journal, November 2020

A	B	C	D	E	F	G	H	I	J	K	L	M
Date	Check #	Paid To	Total Check	Product Purchases	Office Supplies	Travel	Meals and Ent.	Rent and Utilities	Phone, Fax, Internet	Auto	Other (Describe)	Amount
11/1/2020	811	Janice Janeway	321.83			200.00	75.83			46.00		
11/5/2020	812	Landlord	1,165.00					1,165.00				
11/17/2020	813	Electric Company	224.16					224.16				
11/21/2020	814	Sally Staff	115.94		32.00		61.99		21.95			
11/26/2020	815	City of LA	109.00								Bus. license	109.00
		Total November	1,935.93	0.00	32.00	200.00	137.82	1,389.16	21.95	46.00		109.00

Totals in Columns E through M must equal the total in Column D.

Hand over all these pages to your tax professionals, who can review them and use the information to complete your business taxes.

The IRS Says It All

If you prefer not to take a full-blown bookkeeping course, start out by reading (or skimming) two IRS publications. The first one is IRS Publication 583, *Starting a Business and Keeping Records*, and the second is IRS Publication 334, *Tax Guide for Small Business*. Keep a highlighter pen and a pad of small Post-it Notes handy to mark the passages that apply to you.

Fiscal Year

In general, you will set up your bookkeeping system using a calendar year for most entities. Sole proprietors may only use calendar-year bookkeeping systems. Partnerships and pass-through entities may use the year of the majority owner. If that owner is a person, it will be a calendar year. When corporations or other partnerships own the majority interest, the partnership may use the fiscal year of the owners.

Corporations may select any year that suits them. Once the year is established, however, you may only change it with written approval from the IRS.

Accounting Styles

You have a choice of using either cash or accrual accounting—right? Nope, there's also the hybrid method and percentage of completion.

The cash method of accounting is the simplest and the most confusing. As with all things tax, there's always a dichotomy. It's the easiest method for people to use because you only report income from money you've actually received. You only report expenses for bills you've paid.

If it's that simple, why is it confusing? Perhaps it has something to do with the definitions of what is considered "received" and what is considered "paid," and the exceptions to the rule. Chapter 5 will explain "constructive receipt"—or define when money is considered received. Chapter 6 will explain when the money is considered spent—and the few exceptions that crop up.

A key area of confusion for people who have not studied accounting (in other words, most of the business population) is why they can't write off bad debts—bills clients or customers never pay.

That's because you must be on an accrual basis to use bad debt write-offs. Even then, it's not as useful as you might think. You see, when using an accrual basis, you're reporting income when you send out the invoice to the client. So you're paying tax on income you haven't received—or may never receive. That's why you may write off bad debts when you can't collect the money. You've already included that debt in income.

Why would anyone want to use accrual accounting (aside from the times it's required by law)? Because you also get to deduct your bills before you pay them. Some companies have customers who compensate them quickly, so their accounts receivable (money from clients) is low. But they have 60- or 90-day terms on their accounts payable (bills they pay), so they have large unpaid balances due—that they get to deduct at the end of the year. In other words, when you can deduct a lot of money that you haven't spent yet but only need to pick up a small amount of income, the accrual system is ideal for you. Unfortunately, most small businesses are not in that position. Worse, if we do get enough credit so we don't have to pay bills for 90 days or so, it can get us into deep debt. So please be careful.

When is this kind of accounts payable time frame important to your business—and when does it make sense? In two primary instances. When your income comes from government contracts—or you sell large volumes of products to major national retailers like Sears, Walmart, and Macy's. When you contract with them, you generally have to spend a fortune to produce, package, and deliver your product—but won't get paid for 90 to 120 days *and* they feel free to return discards and damaged goods (that they were careless with). In fact, one client who finally got his products into Sears told me that he had to buy up his competitor's entire inventory (about $1.2 million) before Sears would make room for his merchandise. So even when your contract appears to show a big profit, you need a lot of credit or a lot of cash to carry those accounts receivable—and the other onerous terms of the contract. (Of course, if you know what you're doing, you could avoid this long delay in getting your money by learning how to get your sales factored . . . now that's a whole other interesting story! Perhaps for another book.) Remember, we told you to explore factoring in Chapter 1 when we talked about the schmatte industry?

Typically, businesses such as medical practices, which have large unpaid accounts receivable balances, should always be on a cash basis, for tax purposes. There are always more and more invoices that patients are refusing to pay or paying slowly. And, with Medicare and insurance companies setting limits on fees for various procedures, the medical practices don't actually ever receive all the fees they bill. By using the cash basis of accounting on its tax returns, a medical practice never has to report all the income it never received.

Let's pause for a second here. Please understand that my goal is to explain how to handle accounting for tax issues. But, for day-to-day business issues, smart businesses should use an accrual accounting system for their operations. Yes, you may use accrual for operations and the cash basis for tax reporting. That's not cheating, and it's not dishonest. It's perfectly permissible. Just make sure when you pull reports for taxes that they are cash basis—and that the balance sheet and profit and loss statement were printed the same day. (The reports will show the printed date.)

The accrual system means that you enter all the fees, sales, and charges constituting the business's income—even if you haven't been paid. You enter all the bills that need to be paid—even if they just arrived and you don't have to pay them for 20 or 30 days. By putting all these numbers into the system, you can get a variety of important reports:

1. **Budgets.** Knowing how much your overhead is each month helps you understand how much income you need to generate to cover expenses and to give you money to live on and play with.
2. **Accounts receivable aging reports.** These reports let you know when to send invoices and to whom—and when to send stronger notices or . . . sue.
3. **Accounts payable aging reports.** These tell you how much money you need to have, to pay all your bills. They also let you see which bills are still eligible for the special discounts you can get if you pay quickly.
4. **Profit and loss comparison reports.** Use these to compare income and expenses by month, quarter, year, and so on. You can see if income has gone down or expenses have gone up; seeing significant changes and patterns can alert you to trouble before it's too late to fix the problems. You can also see if you're not charging enough for your products and services to cover your costs.

Larger corporations tend to use the accrual method. This lets them enter all their purchase orders, purchases, and shipping manifests or bills of lading into accounts payable in their accounting system. Doing this makes it easier to match up purchase orders with what was actually delivered. The company then has the invoice in its cash management system and can do a better job of tracking when to pay the bill. Companies on the accrual system also enter all the invoices for their sales into the system. That way, if a customer pays off only part of an invoice, the computer can keep track of the amount of money the customer still owes.

If you use the accrual method and know how much cash you have, how much you expect to come in, and how much you have to spend, it becomes much easier to take advantage of vendors' discounts. (Do they still give you a 2 percent discount if you pay within 10 days?)

The hybrid method allows a business to use the accrual method for its stock and inventory, but the cash method for everything else.

Percentage of completion is generally used for large projects, like construction and engineering. You report your income and expenses based on the percentage of the project that has been completed. So if 15 percent of the bridge has been built, you'll report only 15 percent of the contractual income—even if you've received 30 percent of the payment. And since you often must buy half the materials in advance, you'll still only deduct 15 percent. The rest will be inventory.

Records You Must Keep

In our office, we keep everything. Our office and our storage area are overflowing with paper. Why? I don't trust magnetic media to be readable when I need it. It's happened in the past, when something we meticulously backed up was corrupted by time or heat or . . . never got backed up properly to begin with. Besides, how many times have you changed your backup devices? You've used discs, then Zip drives, tapes, CDs, DVDs, and now—flash drives. Do you still have a 5¼-inch floppy drive to read those old discs? Heck, my tiny flash drive has more storage on it than they used for the entire space program in the 1960s.[1]

These days, the technology is better, easier, and faster when it comes to scanning. If you're smart, you'll get a scanner with a feeder so that you don't have to scan each page by hand—or use your smartphone. When you store the images electronically, make sure you get the front and the back, as appropriate. The best format to use for long-term access is Adobe's PDF file format. Adobe seems to be smart enough to keep its technology backward-compatible. In other words, you can still read a PDF file from 2005 even though the PDF technology has advanced dramatically since then.

What Kind of Documents Should You Keep?

- **Most important, make copies of all checks.** When customers pay you, copy their checks. Then copy their checks again, this time with your deposit slip. Put the copies of the checks in your customer files, with their invoices. Put the deposit slip into your banking file. Later, when you reconcile your

---

1 http://www.computerweekly.com/feature/Apollo-11-The-computers-that-put-man-on-the-moon

bank account, if you've overlooked an entry, you can find the details quickly. (Shhh . . . don't tell anyone, but this practice also makes it easy to find your clients' bank accounts if they stiff you and you have to get a court judgment.)

Consider making two copies of the invoices you send to clients, one to go in the client's file and the other to go into a master invoice file. All the invoices in the master file should be in numerical or date order. If you use numbers on your invoices, make sure you have each one, even if it's voided. The IRS looks for gaps in numbering sequence. To them, that means you invoiced someone and pocketed the cash off the books. To you, it probably meant your printer ate it or you messed up and prepared a new one. Just reprint it, mark it "void," and add it to the stack.

Making copies will also help you during an audit if the check you're depositing happens to be a loan from you or a cash advance. It will be easy to prove to an auditor that this was not income.

- **Next, save the canceled checks as a record of your spending.** You don't need to copy them; just be sure to keep them safe and dry. You need them to prove you paid a bill when a vendor says it never received your check. You'll also need canceled checks for tax agencies. And you'll need the information for audits. Naturally, these days, we are not getting them from the bank at all. Instead, banks provide the copies of the canceled checks in their online databases. Get into the habit of downloading those statements and canceled check copies every three to six months. The bank will keep the database open to you for about a year or two. But, if you really need the copies for an audit or lawsuit, you will need something from the closed year, and would have to pay for it. Protect yourself from that problem by establishing smart habits.
- **It's very important to save paid bills.** Some people chill my soul: when they pay a bill, they throw it out. *Nooooooo!* The IRS wants to see what you're paying, not just how much. Do you like doing this with credit card bills? Please stop. Save all your paid invoices and your credit card statements. You're buying a lot of things online or electronically these days. Set up a filing system for all those electronic records. The nice thing about being able to save these records is that you can put them into multiple places, in seconds, such as folders for master purchases, all your transactions with that company, and the category of expenditure (software, gasoline, training, etc.).
- **Save bank statements.** Keep them all—from all accounts.
- **Save receipts.** Save receipts when you've been out of the office shopping. Bring back all the receipts for the money you took from petty cash and for

the things you charged on your credit cards. You'll be able to match up the invoices with the statements. If there are errors, you'll catch them and get your refunds. Sometimes, the computer system produces posting errors, or it gets hacked. With the receipt in hand, you have proof of the correct charge.

- **Keep copies of purchase contracts on all assets.** When you buy a car, a copy machine, a computer, or whatever, keep copies of all purchase contracts in a master file. You'll need copies of those invoices to support your depreciation expenses. Even though the IRS can, technically, only go back and audit you for three years, if there is something on a tax return that was bought six years ago, the IRS has a right to request the original documentation. For instance, you bought an editing machine for $30,000 in 2014. You didn't need the deduction the first year, so you depreciated it over seven years. Your last year will be in 2021. An auditor comes along to audit in 2020. He or she may audit 2017, but the year 2015 is not permitted. However, you bought this editing machine in 2014, and it's still generating a deduction. The auditor may ask to see the purchase document, even though you bought it five years before the date of the audit. The auditor is not being unreasonable. After all, you're still taking a deduction for it. Save time—just have it handy.

- **Keep information about loans.** Keep a copy of the full loan contract, with all the details on the payoff terms. To verify the interest deduction, the IRS will want to see the contract so it can do its own calculations. Having a copy will also be a big help to you in case the interest charges are in error. I have seen banks and finance companies make errors all too often. You can prove the correct interest using your paperwork and your own loan amortization schedule. Use Bankrate.com's loan calculators and print out the report.

- **Retailers, keep cash register receipts.** Always make sure that you match the information on your cash register receipts with the entries in your accounting system. If your cash register software is properly programmed, it should give you separate totals for cash and for credit card payments by customers. Match that up with your accounting entries. If the cash is short because you kept some of it to use for purchases and errands, record the total income received. Then deduct the amount you kept as a charge to petty cash on hand. Be sure to bring back the receipts. For some reason, I find that with retail establishments, somehow the income on the books rarely seems to match the tape. We spend a great deal of time tracking down inconsistencies. Please make sure your tax professional helps you reconcile any differences.

- **1099-Ks.** These come from your merchant credit card companies, PayPal, and other services that you use to collect money from customers or clients.

I am hearing from tax professionals that there are often significant discrepancies between the total sales reported on those 1099-Ks and the total sales on businesses' books. One of the problems is that the 1099-Ks report the income (only) from every transaction. They don't take into account the refunds or chargebacks, or other reductions of those sales. It's important for you to reconcile your income to those reports, and not just for tax purposes. But if there are large discrepancies, there might be some serious problems—like employee theft, identity theft (someone using your account to run charges through), or . . . who knows?

- **Save tax returns of all kinds.** You file paperwork with your city, county, state, and federal governments. Keep copies of each item in its own file in date order with the most recent on top. Add up all your sales tax returns to make sure you've reported the same income on your income tax return as you did on your sales tax return. The IRS is on a payroll audit kick. Be sure to keep all your payroll records, time cards, and paychecks or proof of electronic payments. Also, keep copies of all the expense reports and reimbursements—to prove those payments were not payroll.
- **Documentation of electronic transactions.** As I've pointed out, many of your transactions are happening electronically now. I keep hearing lame excuses from people saying they don't have receipts or records because they paid (or sold) electronically. Don't try to fool me or your tax professional. We live in this world, too. And we see the flood of emails that come in after each purchase—and the email confirmations that come in after each sale. Get organized and set filters to file these records. If you don't know how, invest in a technology wizard to set up systems for you. It's not rocket science . . . well, not yet.

How Long Should You Keep Records?

Keep all tax returns forever. Ignore what anyone else tells you. There have been too many times that the IRS or the state has made demands on tax returns filed 8 or 10 years ago, saying they were never filed. If you have a copy, you can insist it was filed.

If you send money in with those tax returns, keep a copy of the canceled check in the file with the returns. If you got a refund, make a copy of that, too. If the IRS grabbed your refund, you won't have any check copies, but you'll have a letter saying it grabbed the refund from a given year. One of these three items will prove that your return was filed. These days a lot of these transactions are happening electronically. Keep a copy of the electronic receipt when you pay online. If the transaction goes directly in or out of your bank account via the IRS's direct deposit or Direct Pay system, keep a copy of the relevant bank statement with your tax file.

Keep copies of all asset purchases for the life of the asset plus 10 years or for the life of the loan on the asset plus 10 years. If it's real estate, keep the paperwork until you sell it, plus 10 years.

Basically, keep everything for at least 10 years after its useful life or tax return filing date is past.

You realize, of course, there is this universal rule: as long as you keep something, you won't need it. The minute you throw it out, everyone will need it.

Until a few years ago, I kept all my client records from way back in the 1970s. Finally, I got bold and decided to give the records to the clients whose addresses I still had—and to shred the files of people I couldn't reach. I only shredded files that were at least five years old, plus my own personal records.

One hour after I finished shredding, a client who'd filed bankruptcy a couple of years earlier, owing me money, called. He wanted the paperwork on the money he owed me so he could pay it off. (He had never listed my debt in the bankruptcy.) Well, I didn't have the papers, so I couldn't prove what he owed me. If it had been anyone else, I could have waved goodbye to that money. Luckily with Adam, he just shrugged and sent me what he thought he owed me.

Glossary of Bookkeeping Terms

Above the line. Accounting industry jargon for expenses that are deducted on the first page of Form 1040. These expenses are generally deductible as adjustments to income. They reduce your adjusted gross income, which allows you to increase medical expenses and miscellaneous itemized deductions. (*Also see* Below the line.)

Accounts payable (or A/P). Invoices you've received, or are expecting, for things you have purchased or things you have had delivered to your place of business or to your clients. For record-keeping purposes, only accrual basis companies report A/P on their financial statements.

Accounts receivable (or A/R). Money owed to you by your customers or clients after you have sent them an invoice. A/R does not include loans that are being repaid to your business or anything else. It is just income due to you, in whatever form, as a result of a business transaction.

Accrual. An accounting method that includes all your company's sales and purchases, even if you haven't collected the money from clients or paid your vendors. Most people in business alone are wise to avoid this method. It involves an assortment of complexities and rules. (*See* Cash basis.) Accrual accounting is good when your outstanding business debt is high, but your accounts receivable are low.

Adjusted basis. The tax cost of your asset, with improvements added in and things such as depreciation and casualty losses deducted. This is the tax cost after all adjustments mandated by the tax code have been applied to the cost. (*See* Basis.)

Adjusted gross income (AGI). The last number on the first page of your Form 1040. The lower this number is, the more apt you are to be able to deduct IRAs, take advantage of various credits and losses, and use medical expenses and miscellaneous itemized deductions. Several other numbers use this as a starting point. Please get familiar with AGI. Also called "The Line."

Advances. Loans, often to employees or owners, that will be repaid from their next payroll check or from their draws. They could also be funds given to workers before they go on a trip or to a business event. In that case, the workers must submit an expense report with receipts or mileage data adding up to the amount of money advanced. If they have money left over, they must either return it or have it deducted from their compensation. They may opt to have it added to their compensation and taxed, instead.

AGI. *See* Adjusted gross income.

Amortization. Derived from the Latin word for "death," the value of certain designated assets prorated over a period of time. You deduct a portion of it each year, much like depreciation.

Assets. Things the business owns that aren't part of the product being sold. Assets include bank accounts, investment accounts, inventory, vehicles, loans to people, equipment. They also include intangibles such as patents, copyrights, client lists, and goodwill. Businesses on accrual will also report their accounts receivable under assets. Assets are the first section of the balance sheet.

Audit trail. The details of all the transactions behind a number on the financial statements, including all adjustments. Most consumer accounting or bookkeeping software has good audit-trail features. It lets you run reports and then click on the number to get the details within that account. However, it also lets you correct the entry directly. Once you do that, there is no evidence of the error. Professional accounting software requires you to make a journal entry to correct each error, leaving a history of entries.

Balance Sheet (BS). A report that shows the following relationship of your finances: assets = liabilities + capital (or equity). The balance sheet does not include your expenses or income—just the profit resulting from them. The "income" line on the balance sheet must equal the net income line on the profit and loss statement. All prior year's profits are rolled over into retained earnings.

Basis. Tax cost of an asset. It generally consists of the purchase price. For some assets, the basis is the fair market value (FMV). To keep things interesting, when it comes to depreciating business assets, the basis is the *lower* of cost or FMV. But for estates, it's often the *higher* of cost or FMV. (*See* Adjusted basis, Fair market value.)

Below the line. Accounting industry jargon for *itemized deductions*. These are expenses deducted on Schedule A. They don't reduce your adjusted gross income.

Burden (*also called* burdened costs). These are costs added to the inventory, including the labor costs and overhead associated with the production or warehousing of the inventory. Labor costs include the wages, payroll taxes, and costs of all employee benefits. Overhead would include the interest on loans to buy the inventory, rent, utilities, and any other costs associated with the production or warehousing of the inventory. AccountingCoach.com provides an excellent explanation (http://iTaxMama.com/COGS_Burden).

Built-in Gains tax (BIG tax). This is a tax assessed on C corporations that convert to S corporation status. If the C corporation had appreciated assets and sells those assets within a specific time frame (that time frame changes as tax laws change), there is an extra tax assessed. You can read more about the current rules on the IRS website (see http://iTaxMama.com/Built_In_Gains_Tax).

Capital (*also called* owner's equity). Capital represents investments in the company. Depending on the type of company, it might include stocks (corporations), shares (LLCs, LLPs, partnerships), or simply owner's equity. The capital section of the balance sheet includes the money invested in the business, the draws taken from the business, and the profits or losses of the business. It also includes any money spent to buy back company shares or stock from owners or partners.

Cash basis. The most common method of accounting. As income, you only include the money for which you have constructive receipt. (*See* Constructive receipt.) Under expenses, you include only the bills you've paid. Certain things that look like accruals also get picked up—payroll and sales taxes to be paid in January (or at the end of your quarter). Credit card purchases are included in cash basis reporting, even though you have not paid for the purchases. They are treated like loans you've taken out at the time you made the purchase.

Check register. That little booklet the bank sent you with your checks. You're supposed to list all the checks you write and the deposits you make. Add your deposits and deduct your checks and bank fees. *Et voilà!* You know how much money is in your bank account, at a glance.

Closing the books. When a company finishes the accounting for a month, quarter, or year, and reconciles all the accounts, it closes the books for that period of time. No more entries are made into those ledger or journal pages. If errors are found later, they must be corrected using a journal entry. You can't just go back and erase the wrong entry. You must either debit or credit the error to get it right. That's in formal accounting systems. Today's software doesn't require that you close the books. It lets you make corrections later, if that's when you reconcile your bank statements or decide to enter your transactions.

Constructive receipt. Money you've received at a specific time, with the right to use it. (*See* Cash basis.) Usually this is important at year-end. A check was mailed to you by your customer in December, but you received it on January 2. Did you have constructive receipt of that check in December or January? Here are some common examples:

- If someone gives you a postdated check, you don't have the right to deposit that check until the date.
- On the other hand, let's say you own a controlling interest in another business. That business owes your company $5,000, but you tell the business to hold your money until next year. The IRS considers this as if you have constructive receipt of that money. You're the one who is in control of when that check is issued.
- A third case is where someone owes you money. You tell the person to pay that money to a third party to whom you owe money. Even though that check never hit your books, the IRS treats that as if you had constructive receipt of the money. You controlled how that money was spent.

Credit. In accounting, a credit is the negative half of an accounting entry (debits and credits). It reduces the balance of the account it's posted to. On the asset section of a balance sheet, it reduces the asset. A credit to the bottom of the balance sheet increases liabilities or equity. On the profit and loss statement (P&L), a credit increases income and decreases expenses. A credit balance on the P&L means you have a profit. (*See* Debit.)

Debit. The reverse of a credit. (*See* Credit.) A debit balance on the P&L means you have a loss—you're in the red. When you debit your bank account on your books, it means you've made a deposit. When the bank debits your bank account on *its* books, it means you have drawn money from it. Debits and credits are a confusing concept if you can't visualize both sides of the transaction.

Depreciation. The act of writing off the cost of an asset over a specific period of time, as designated by the tax code. (See Chapter 6.)

Double-entry bookkeeping. A balanced system in which each transaction has two sides, e.g., when you write a check for office supplies, you reduce the balance in your checking account and increase the balance in an account called office expenses.

Draws. In partnerships or pass-through entities, funds paid to partners or members. Draws are considered advances against income; they are not income. Draws are reported on the books as a negative amount under capital. At the end of the business year, they are netted against retained earnings—or the owner's capital account. (*See* Capital.)

Expense report. A worksheet submitted by employees wanting reimbursements for out-of-pocket expenses. It may also be an accounting for monies advanced before a business trip or shopping trip was made. Generally, receipts are attached to substantiate the expenses.

Fair market value (FMV). The price a stranger would pay for your asset in an arm's-length transaction. If you put it up for sale, what would someone pay for it? Try to avoid using sample prices you find on eBay as your source for FMV because you'll end up with a lower value.

General journal. Within the bookkeeping system, this is where adjustments are entered.

Global Intangible Low Tax Income (GILTI). A new tax enacted by the Tax Cuts and Jobs Act (TCJA) to tax the worldwide income of companies who have moved their intellectual properties overseas. Use Form 8992 to report this additional tax, which can range from 10 to 13.125 percent of the income.

Guaranteed payments. Guaranteed payments are required when most income comes from services. The IRS requires that if one partner performs most of the services, then he or she gets a reasonable amount of income before the profits are split. This reduces the income that can be moved to children or other nonparticipating partners, who are apt to be in lower tax brackets.

Journal entry. An accounting entry posted to the general journal. Most entries come into the books via money transactions—deposits or purchases. They are entered in the cash receipts journal or cash disbursements journal. However, corrections, depreciation, amortization, the splitting of payments between loans, and interest—all those noncash or correcting transactions—are entered in the general journal. Year-end adjustments are entered on the books using journal entries.

Liabilities. These represent money the business owes, including unpaid payroll and sales taxes accrued at the end of the year, credit card debt, loans, and monies owed to employees or officers. Accrual basis companies will include their accounts payable here.

Nexus. This is a business presence in a state or tax area. (See Chapter 12.)

Offshore income. Income held in accounts outside the United States. *Offshore* doesn't necessarily mean "on an island." It could just as easily be in an account right across the border in Mexico or Canada. There are some heavy-duty reporting requirements when you have bank accounts with a total of $10,000 or more in them in any year. Look up FBAR and FATCA on the IRS website.

Owner's capital account. An account in the equity or capital section of the balance sheet that tracks the partner's, shareholder's, or member's ownership interest in the business. When the investor contributed very little money but has received a lot of draws or losses, his or her capital account may be negative. When capital is negative, an investor is usually not permitted to deduct any more losses.

Owner's equity. *See* Capital.

Pass-through entities. Business entities that do not pay federal taxes. They pass through their profits and losses to owners, who report the amounts on their personal tax returns. (See Chapter 3.)

Payroll. Wages and salaries. Payroll is not just any money you hand to the workers. Payroll has a specific meaning. If you use *payroll* to refer to the compensation you're paying your freelancers within earshot of an auditor, you've just turned them into employees. (See Chapters 9 and 10.)

Percentage of completion. Another accounting method. It is a way of reporting income when you're on a long-term project and receive progress payments. This is used in construction and engineering projects, among others.

Profit and Loss Statement (P&L). A financial report summarizing a business's income and expenses, resulting in either a profit or loss on the bottom line. (*See* Balance Sheet.)

Purchase order (PO). A written document letting a company know that someone in authority approved a particular order. It also defines what was ordered and usually includes a promise to pay for a specific number of units at a specific price.

Qualified Small Business Stock (QSBS). In December 2015, Congress passed the PATH Act of 2015 excluding 100 percent of the profits from the sale of certain QSBS permanently. This article by Latham and Watkins LLP explains it well: http://iTax Mama.com/qsbs_100.

Quarter. When used in financial reporting, generally a three-month period. There are four quarters each year. You'll often see quarters noted as Q1, Q2, and so on. They usually run as follows—Q1 January–March; Q2 April–June; Q3 July–September; Q4 October–December. This schedule for quarters is particularly important for payroll, sales taxes, and estimated taxes. The IRS, of course, has a whole different schedule for quarters when it comes to estimated tax payments. (See Chapter 11.) In the financial world, publicly traded corporations release their profit and loss statements each quarter—to the acclaim or jeers of analysts.

Retained earnings. Profits the business has earned that have not been distributed to owners or shareholders. (*See* Balance sheet, Draws.)

Section 199A—Qualified Business Income Deduction (Section 199A). This is the new 20 percent deduction available to individuals and pass-through entities— *not* to corporations. This is a deduction from taxable income, after taking into account the standard or itemized deduction on Form 1040. (See Chapter 6.)

Specified Service Trade or Business (SSTB). This term defines occupations and services in the fields of health, law, accounting, actuarial science, performing arts, consulting, athletics, financial services, investing and investment management, trading, dealing in certain assets, or any trade or business where the principal asset is the reputation or skill of one or more of its employees or owners. Excluded are architects and engineers. SSTBs have limits on the amount of income that is qualified for the Section 199A deduction.

Tax Cuts and Jobs Act (TCJA). A sweeping tax law passed in December 2017 that made many permanent changes to business tax law, and temporary changes to individual tax law, many of which will expire by December 31, 2025—unless Congress extends those laws before that. (See the Prologue.) We will be using the abbreviation "TCJA" throughout the book.

Tax year (*also* fiscal year). The accounting year established by your business. In general, it should start on January 1 and end on December 31. However, corporations have the option of selecting their own year-end, to simplify accounting. If taxes will be deferred (delayed) more than three months, the IRS may require the company to pay the difference earlier as estimated tax payments.

Terms. The period of time by which an invoice must be paid; may also include a discount code. For instance, 2/10 means if you pay the invoice within 10 days, you're welcome to deduct 2 percent of the invoice.

Trades. An advertising industry term that describes formalized barter transactions.

Transposition of numbers (*also called* "transpo"). A mistake that occurs when writing numbers or keying them into your accounting program—when your fingers get dyslexic and two numbers switch places. Instead of typing "976," you type "796." The difference is 180. You can always recognize a "transpo" because the digits in your out-of-balance number will add up to a multiple of three. (For instance, $1 + 8 + 0 = 9$, which is 3×3.)

Trial balance. A list of all the accounts your company uses in its accounting system, with a balance in each account. When you total up the balances in all the accounts, you should get zero.

Wages. *See* Payroll.

Resources

In this chapter, you saw a variety of resources. Here's a summary of them, so you can find them quickly and easily. The resources are not necessarily in alphabetical order in each category. They are in order of their importance or usefulness, in TaxMama's opinion.

Online Glossaries

- **The AICPA (American Institute of Certified Public Accountants).** http://iTaxMama.com/AICPA_Glossary. Has a glossary of terms, acronyms, and abbreviations.
- **NYSSCPA (New York State Society of CPAs).** http://iTaxMama.com/NYS _CPA_Terminology. Has an accounting and financial glossary.

IRS Publications

- **Publication 583, *Starting a Business and Keeping Records.*** https://www .irs.gov/publications/p583
- **IRS Publication 334, Tax Guide for Small Business.** https://www.irs.gov /publications/p334/

Basic Bookkeeping and Record-Keeping Resources

- **FreshBooks.** http://iTaxMama.com/FreshBooks. Basic bookkeeping. A simple, online way to track your time and your income, do your billing, and get paid quickly. It integrates with many apps to make your life easier. The site has a community forum where you can learn—and even meet new clients, perhaps.

- **Outright.** http://iTaxMama.com/Outright. Bookkeeping designed for sole proprietors. It's now called GoDaddy Bookkeeping. Why? It's a good story. Kevin Reeth and Ben Curren used to work for the QuickBooks folks. They realized how excessively complex the software had become for the really small business owner who simply wants to keep track of records. They did such a great job with the system that GoDaddy bought the company. It lets you import information from your online bank accounts, credit cards, and other applications, such as Shoeboxed, PayPal, eBay, and FreshBooks.

Bookkeeping Resources

- **One-Write.** http://www.one-write.com (double-entry cash journals). This is one of the older manual systems for small businesses. Basically, it's designed so when you write your checks, the information is duplicated directly into the cash disbursements journal. At the end of each day, week, or month—depending on how many transactions you have—you simply total up each page. Just follow the formula at the bottom of the page to see if you're in balance. It's a little old-fashioned, but I remember having more free time when we used this system. You will still need to enter the data into a general ledger. Or have your tax pro do that for you. One-Write also offers a software system.
- **Dome.** It produces a variety of record books and bookkeeping systems that are inexpensive, including a 13-column pad in a three-ring binder, with tabs for cash receipts pages, cash disbursements pages, payroll journal, and general journal. You can find the products at all office supply stores and at online bookstores, and your tax professional can show you how to set things up.
- **Tax MiniMiser.** Tax MiniMiser allows you to log the usage of vehicles or mixed-use assets. You can use it to track income and expense as a complete, stand-alone, accounting system—on paper. Available at various office supply stores.
- **TaxPal.** http://www.taxpal.net/. A software tool to build IRS-compliant records. It lets you enter mileage and expense data by hand or import it from various apps. It's still growing and developing and welcoming input from users. The unique thing about this is, it's built around the questions the IRS asks about each meal or entertainment, trip, or deduction. It's designed to protect you in audits.

- **MileIQ.** http://iTaxMama.com/MileIQ. A versatile app you can use to track all your different types of travel—business, personal, medical, volunteering, etc.
- **Quicken.** http://iTaxMama.com/Quicken. This is a single-entry system with lots of bells and whistles. With its banking and investment tools, it has terrific value for personal use. But don't use it for business. Buy its big sister, QuickBooks, instead.
- **Sage 50c.** http://iTaxMama.com/Sage50. This is very popular with larger businesses and accountants but is more complex than QuickBooks. It's easier to use if you have some accounting or bookkeeping background. Generally, users set it up to work with account numbers, which are harder to use when trying to make entries quickly. The software is slow. I have tried it with various systems, and it is always slow.
- **QuickBooks.** http://iTaxMama.com/QuickBooks. A full double-entry system for small businesses, QuickBooks is available in many versions, including customized versions for various industries and point-of-sale systems for retail shops. This program can work with online banking systems. Add-on payroll systems are available. When buying the box, instead of using the online version, you may track many companies. It's one of the most popular systems. Intuit is buying up smaller companies, so a few years from now, it may be the only one left standing. But as improvements are made, it gets more and more confusing to users. Newer versions are not backward-compatible. So to enable your tax pro to review your work, or for you to see your tax pro's changes, you both have to constantly buy updates, which can be very frustrating. *TaxMama recommendation:* To avoid the compatibility problem, consider the online version, http://iTaxMama.com/QB_Online. You, or your accountant, can access it from anywhere and make entries even when you're on the road. QuickBooks does the backups for you. Mac and PC versions are available.
- **Xero.** http://iTaxMama.com/Xero. A relative newcomer to the scene. But they get it when it comes to technology. They can make your business life super-easy, with lots of drag and drop tools. You can attach documents to your entries for your checks or income. It can make business decisions and audits really easy.
- **Acclivity's AccountEdge** (formerly MYOB). http://www.accountedge.com. This system offers software for both Windows and Mac systems, with accounting software for several countries and currencies. It's a more sophisticated system, allowing you to add more modules as your business expands to include manufacturing, payroll, and other accounting functions. The company offers free conversions from QuickBooks.

- **Sage 300c** (formerly ACCPAC). http://www.sage.com/us/erp/sage-300. Another step up, this system works best for larger organizations needing a more formal accounting environment. The company offers free conversions from QuickBooks and Acclivity.
- **Shoeboxed.** http://iTaxMama.com/ShoeBoxed. For those who don't have the time to record all their invoices, receipts, etc., this is a terrific service. It is especially good for folks who experience total resistance to bookkeeping. Shoeboxed integrates with Outright.com, FreshBooks, and more—and is adding features all the time. In fact, you can even scan receipts directly from your phone.

Tax Resources—Calculators and At-a-Glance Summaries

- **Bankrate.com's loan calculators.** http://www.bankrate.com/calculators/mortgages/loan-calculator.aspx
- **CFS Tax Software.** https://www.taxtools.com/Home/Index/. This site has an excellent, inexpensive array of tax tools and special calculation tools, including payroll tools, you won't find anywhere else. Use discount code TaxMama239 to get 50 percent off their TaxTools software the first time you buy it.
- **Thomson-Reuters Quickfinders Handbooks.** http://iTaxMama.com/QuickFinder. Good for daily look-ups on how to handle issues, this book contains worksheets and basic explanations, with index versions for individuals and businesses. Great for at-a-glance information.
- **The TaxBook.** http://www.thetaxbook.com. TaxMama's favorite look-up resource. Similar to the *Quickfinders Handbook*—but better and cheaper. I use the Online WebLibrary in the TaxMama's Enrolled Agent Exam Review Courses because the subscription includes three years data on individuals, partnerships, corporations, and more. (Actually, older years are available, if you scroll down to the bottom of the home page.) Use code #817 to get a small discount.

Tax Resources—Research and Academia

The following publishers provide tax updates and resources to accounting firms and colleges—and to small businesses. You can get a copy of the tax code, regulations, or analyses on any tax issue. They have books for specific industries and entities. Teaching tools and study guides are available, too:

- **BeanCounter.com.** http://iTaxMama.com/BeanCounter. A fun way to learn the fundamentals of bookkeeping. Easy to understand *and* it's free. Of course, there are additional resources and a "practice set" you can buy for a small fee, so you can learn more about how bookkeeping really works.
- **AccountingCoach.com.** http://iTaxMama.com/Accounting_Course. An in-depth series of courses on all topics of accounting. The entire course is free. For a fee, you can get additional learning tools, with lifetime access.
- **Bureau of National Affairs (Bloomberg BNA).** https://bloombergindustry.com/, (800) 372-1033. It provides folios and in-depth analyses of tax issues.
- **Wolters Kluwer's Commerce Clearing House.** https://www.cchgroup.com/, (800) 248-3248
- **Lexis Nexis Matthew Bender.** http://bender.lexisnexis.com, (800) 227-4908. The original in-depth legal database teamed up with a major analytical publisher (super expensive).
- **Thompson-RIA.** http://store.tax.thomsonreuters.com/accounting, (800) 950-1216. Publishes in-depth analyses of tax and accounting issues.

TaxMama Resources

- **TaxMama's Quick Look-Ups.** http://iTaxMama.com/TM_QuickLookUp. You will find all kinds of useful reference materials, webinars you can replay, e-books, and more.
- **Your Business Bible.** http://www.yourbusinessbible.com. Look for worksheets, printable checklists, and other goodies and resources.

To-Do List and Questionnaire

☐ 1. What are your business's sources of income? Which can you increase? By what percent?
- Sales of products _____ _____
- Sales of services _____ _____
- Consulting fees _____ _____
- Contracts _____ _____
- Commissions or referrals _____ _____
- Registrations _____ _____
- Rents (inc. self-rental) _____ _____
- Royalties _____ _____
- Other _____ _____

☐ 2. Is your industry changing? Are any of those income sources about to start declining? If yes, which ones, and by how much?

_____ _____ _____
_____ _____ _____
_____ _____ _____

☐ 3. What can you do to replace those sources of income? With what cost?
Increase advertising? _____
Eliminate that revenue source? _____
Concentrate more energy on other existing revenue streams? _____
Close the business and seek employment? _____

Remember to put a copy of each document behind this page, folded in half.

5

INCOME

It's just as easy to love a rich man as a poor man.

—Your Mother

Money In, Money Out, Wave Your Hands All About

You'd think income would be the easiest concept for a business owner to grasp. It seems completely obvious to you, right? Income is the money that came into the business. Clearly, it's all the money that was deposited into your account.

But what if you don't have a business account? Or you use your personal account most of the time instead? Then, how much is income?

Naturally, this concept applies to new, or small businesses. Not Congress's definition of a small business, which is a business with average annual income of $25 million, during the past three years, increased annually by inflation. But the average business with net profits of well under half a million dollars. Older, more sophisticated businesses, with accounting staffs, employees, and well-organized operations—well, they know what is and isn't income. However, . . .

The following question is typical of a new business owner without any administrative experience:

> *I am self-employed as a carpenter. When someone pays me for a job I've done, and he pays me by check, how can I keep "supply" costs separate from "labor" costs? For example, if I charge $500 to do a job and spend $800 in supplies, I'll get a check for $1,300 in payment. I don't want the IRS to think I've earned $1,300 when in fact I've only earned $500. Help!*

Other troubling concepts involve understanding the difference between income and deposits to the business account. They're not necessarily the same thing. Let's take a little test. All the following are examples of items deposited in your business account. Can you tell which ones are income?

- Client reimbursement of your out-of-pocket expenses
- Customer's payment for completed work
- Your money, deposited to prevent an overdraft
- Cash advance from a credit card or your home equity
- Royalty for the oil under your home
- Money from investors or partners
- Money you borrow from Mom (Shhh. Don't tell Dad.)
- Insurance settlement for your pain and suffering arising from a work-related auto accident
- Money you took from your IRA to cover payroll
- Repayments of advances you took earlier

Which ones are business income? Only the first two. All the rest are often deposited into business bank accounts, but they have nothing to do with the income from your business.

It's really important to get this right because most small business owners don't bring their bookkeeping with them to their tax appointments. Instead, many only bring their profit and loss statements, some neat printouts on a spreadsheet, or a couple of scribbled pages of data. Your tax professional generally never gets to see your income records. So when you overstate your income, he or she has no way of knowing. The good news is that if you've reported these deposits as income, your audits will result in refunds.

A Capital Idea

If eight of these sample transactions aren't income, then what are they? Most of them are capital transactions. The rest are strictly personal and never belong in a business account at all. Money you receive for personal reasons, such as the royalties related to your residence and personal injury settlements, should be deposited into your personal bank accounts. That income is taxable on your personal tax return—probably on Schedule E. If your business really needs that money, fine—write a check and *lend* it to the business. Then you'll have an audit trail of a loan transaction.

Capital transactions belong on the balance sheet side of your financial statements. They include loans, credit card debt, investment, and assets bought or sold for business use.

Investor's Money

What about money you receive from investors? It depends on the nature of the investment. If an investor lent you money, which your business must repay, it's a loan. Sometimes the money an investor lends you is a hybrid of a loan and profit sharing: You're going to pay the money back to the investor, plus 6 percent interest, plus 10 percent of profits. It's still a loan. Report the funds as a debit to the bank account and a credit to a loan account. Be smart. Use the name of the person as the name on the account, for example, Loan from Rich Guy Malone.

To make it an investment, as opposed to a loan, the investor must have bought a percentage of your business—not just a percentage of your profits. We discussed the nuances of this in Chapter 3. Record this as a debit to the bank account where the money was deposited. The credit will go to stock if it's a corporation. It will go to owner's equity—George Generous—if it's a partnership.

What if you're a sole proprietor? Well, if you sold part of your business, you're no longer alone. If you file no formal paperwork, you're automatically a partnership. Remember to get your federal identification number for the new entity.

Did I tell you the best thing about investor's money? If everything falls apart, you don't have to repay it. That's the big difference between a loan and an investment. Lenders avoid risks. Investors share the risk with you. You succeed—the investors get a windfall. You fail, and so do they.

Of course, there are all kinds of additional nuances to loans and investments. Some loans might not charge just interest. Some loans might include a share of the profit on a property or a project. It's still a loan, not an investment. It all depends on the details spelled out in the loan contract.

So if these eight transactions weren't income, what is?

What *Is* Income?

Income is all the compensation you receive for your goods or services. Note the word *compensation*, as opposed to *money*. Sometimes you don't get money—you get stock or a share in a partnership or limited liability corporation (LLC). Perhaps you trade your expertise for services or two chickens or a pig (remember Doc Hollywood?), or you get a painting or your lawn mowed.

To determine whether an unfamiliar transaction is income, ask yourself: "Would the person have given this to me if I didn't provide them with a product or service?" If the answer is no, you have income.

If the answer is yes, you probably have a gift. Of course, what if your family and friends are using your services just to help you out? Well, even if it's a pity sale, it's still a sale.

To learn more about how the IRS defines income, read Chapter 5 of IRS Publication 334. It includes four pages describing various kinds of income.

Look back to Chapter 3 to review which IRS forms to use to report your income.

Timing of Income

Chapter 4 explained the difference between accounting on a cash basis and accounting on an accrual basis. Most small businesses are on a cash basis. Essentially, you report your income when you get the money. But even for cash basis businesses, there are times when money received is not income, such as the following:

- **As a landlord, you receive a security deposit; that's not income.** It's not your money. You must return that money to the tenants if they leave the premises in good condition when they move out. But last month's rent is rent. So that *is* income.
- **You're an attorney and receive a settlement from an insurance company for your client.** That's not your money. It belongs in your trust account until you pay all the costs and all the parties. Once the case is settled, the fee is income. When you draw money from the trust account specifically as fees, it's income. *Note:* If you don't draw the money, but could have drawn it—it's income when the money was available to you. The IRS audits attorneys regularly, examining the transactions in their trust accounts. The IRS knows attorneys often delay taking their fees from the trust account until after the beginning of the following year. It's seems like a nice way to control how much income you report on your tax return—but watch out. The IRS is very aware of this strategy.
- **You're a contractor and receive a third of the project cost from your client for the building you're erecting.** That money might be required to last several months as the construction progresses. You're only entitled to draw money for yourself at certain stages of completion. Often, the money is placed into a bank account by the client. Contractors must provide receipts to the bank to receive the funds—or to have the funds sent to vendors and

employee bank accounts. This process protects the client from liens by suppliers and employees who might otherwise not get paid. You'll be reporting that income on a "percentage of completion" basis. However, if you have been reporting all your income using the "cash basis" as your accounting method, you will need to file a Form 3115 to request IRS approval before switching to "percentage of completion." Try to file that request early in the year so the IRS has time to respond before you file your next tax return. This does not come with automatic approval—and may require some other adjustments to your accounting system. Work with a tax professional who has experience getting these accounting method changes approved.

- **You're a retailer, and someone buys something on layaway.** The money isn't yours until the person finishes paying for the merchandise and picks it up. If the person never does, how much of that money are you entitled to keep before you refund the difference? There may be a processing fee at the time the transaction is canceled. The fees will depend on your layaway contract. Until then, the money is a deposit. Deposits are liabilities.
- **You put on seminars or workshops for which people must pay in advance.** People pay an attendance fee weeks or months ahead of time. They are entitled to a refund, less a cancellation charge, at any time before the event. Before the event, the only part of the money you've received that is considered income is the cancellation charge. Once the event takes place, naturally, the rest of it is realized as income. (In tax lingo, "realized" means the event has now taken place or the income is now earned.)

You're getting the idea. Money isn't treated as income until you earn it.

TaxMama Tip

The abbreviated explanation of income: when there are strings attached to money, it becomes income when the strings are gone.

A Brief Explanation About "Accrual Basis"

Before I explain how this works, let me just say that you don't have to use the accrual basis if you don't want to do it. People believe that if your business has an inventory, you're required to use accrual as your accounting method. That used to be true. But the past few major tax law changes redefined small businesses as having an annual income of $25 million dollars or less, over the past three years. And this $25 million amount is increased by inflation each year. So, it's quite likely, that your business is exempt from the mandatory accrual rule.

What Is Accrual Accounting?

Small businesses that report their taxable income on the accrual basis report the income when they issue the invoice. (Using the accrual basis means that you report income when you send out the invoice. You report expenses when you receive the invoice or when the merchandise you bought is received into your office, shop, or warehouse.) You only send invoices when you've earned the money. So when people pay you a retainer or advance for services to be rendered, you record the money received as a debit to cash and a credit to accounts receivable instead of as a credit to income. It gets treated as income when you work off your obligation. When you issue your invoices for this work, you'll be crediting income and debiting accounts receivable.

Incidentally, since you control when you send out your invoices, if you don't want to pick up income in this year, you can wait to issue the invoice in January. This is a solid strategy —unless you wait several months to issue the invoice. How is this different from the attorney who has the money sitting in a trust account? In this case, you don't have constructive receipt of the money from your client. It's always a good idea to keep your books on an accrual basis, so you can see how much is owed to you —and how much you owe to your vendors. As we mentioned in Chapter 4, you are still allowed to report your taxable income on a cash basis, even when using accrual accounting for your operations.

Sales Taxes Received—Are They Your Money?

Bookkeeping can frequently be a messed-up area, but it's actually much simpler than it looks. You want your books and your deposits to balance to the income reported on your tax return. To do that, you must include the sales tax you collect as part of your income. Simple. Yes, include it.

Then, see the line of your tax return that asks about tax expenses? Deduct the sales taxes you paid to your state on that line. In fact, this is one of those expenses you get to deduct even before you pay it. Since you received all the sales taxes with your sales by December 31 (or your fiscal year-end), you deduct it in the year the taxes were collected. You'll be paying it by January 31, or the alternate due date if January 31 falls on a weekend. This is true even if you operate on a cash basis.

Most CPAs I know contend that you should not include the sales taxes as part of your total sales. It should be picked up on the books, from the outset, as a liability account. (Debit—Cash; Credit—Sales Taxes Due.) Why am I recommending a different approach? CPAs are trained to do financial accounting. For the purposes of financial analyses, they are correct. Sales taxes are not income. My focus is on income tax audits—and how to avoid them. If there is an IRS or state audit, the examiner will look at the business's total deposits. Let's say your business collected $25,000 worth of sales taxes during the year. That will be included in the total funds you deposited in the bank. If you haven't added this amount to your total taxable income, they will think you have unreported income. This strategy avoids having to convince the examiner that your books are truthful.

We will be talking more about sales taxes in Chapter 12, when we discuss nexus, and shipping products or selling products to customers in other states. As you may have heard, since the Supreme Court issued its Wayfair decision, every state is jumping on the out-of-state sales tax bandwagon.

Income Rarely Reported

There are three kinds of transactions most people either forget to report or don't bother to—illegal income, offshore income, and barter. I'll cover each of these briefly, just so you know the issues associated with these types of income.

Illegal Income—Can't Report It?

If you're engaged in criminal activities, the last thing you want to do is report your income to the IRS and turn yourself in. You're not an idiot. Well . . . you are a criminal, so there's room for doubt.

Remember, the arm of the IRS is all-powerful. Before Homeland Security was created, the IRS was the only agency of the US government that operated on the Napoleonic Code—guilty until proven innocent. The IRS has the distinction of catching Al Capone, where the relentless pursuit of the FBI brought no results. In fact, the documents related to his case are one of the most frequent requests to the IRS under the Freedom of Information Act (FOIA).

So, yes, if you're a drug lord, a thief, an illegal prostitute (it's legal in some states), an embezzler, whatever—report the income. You're welcome to call it "other" income. But report the income. Since being a criminal is a business, report it on Schedule C and pay the self-employment taxes on it. Enter 999999 as the activity code on Schedule C—it stands for unclassified establishments, or unable to classify. If you consider yourself a professional in your field, use 541990—all other professional, scientific, and technical services.

So, go ahead, pay the tax. Just because you're a criminal doesn't mean you can't be a good citizen, too. Or . . . consider switching to a legal business—then all your costs will be deductible.

Semi-legal income—the marijuana paradox—legal in states—not for the IRS. Unfortunately, although you must report the income from cannabis sales, you are not allowed to take any deductions for business expenses. The only costs you can actually deduct are those for costs of goods sold. This is particularly touchy in a certain semi-legal industry—marijuana (especially as related to medical marijuana). Most of the states in the United States have now legalized some form of marijuana use. It's only totally illegal in nine states. But the Drug Enforcement Agency (DEA) still classifies it as a Section I substance. If this is your business focus, consider taking TaxMama's course on the business of marijuana—"Marijuana's Tax Paradox (or the Uncanny Cannabis Controversy)."

Essentially, you will learn that you are entitled to claim your costs of good sold in your cannabis business. That means inventory costs and directly related costs, or the costs of production (farming, packaging, etc.). Unlike a regular business, your indirect costs are not deductible. Indirect costs include the "burden" or "burdened costs," explained in the Glossary in Chapter 4.

In order to take any deductions at all, the business must be legal in the state of operation. It must be licensed by the state. It seems obvious, doesn't it? But, believe it or not, even in states where it is legal to grow and sell cannabis and related products, there are still unregistered and illegal operations.

Internal Revenue Code (IRC) Section 280E does not allow the cannabis businesses to take any deductions for the ordinary and necessary business expenses (IRC Section 162) that most businesses get to deduct. On the profit and loss statement, these are often categorized as administration or operating expenses.

However, there is a way to deduct some of those expenses, but it involves a sophisticated and detailed accounting system. You need to work with an accountant or tax professional who understands how to set up a complex accounting system. It will include separate tracking of the labor and operating expenses for all the costs directly associated with the cannabis products—and those costs not associated with cannabis at all. For instance, in a retail operation, the store would not just be selling products containing cannabis. They would also be selling books, software, bongs, incense, papers, apparel, and vaping products. They might offer services, like counseling, therapeutic massage, classes, and more. All of these things have nothing to do with the actual sale of a cannabis product. So, all the costs associated with that part of the operation are fully deductible.

By setting up a good point of sale system to track the inventory, sales taxes, and employee activity, it's easy to keep the accounting separated for the different operations. This strategy has been proven in Tax Court. You can read the details in the case of *Californians Helping to Alleviate Medical Problems, Inc (CHAMP) v. Commissioner*.

Don't forget, though, if your business is legal in your state, all your Section 162 expenses are deductible on your state income tax return.

Incidentally, businesses that are only dealing in cannabinoids (CBDs) are legal on the federal level (IRS). But check with your state to see what the rules are for CBDs in your state. Generally, CBDs are legal, with a "but" in some states.

Offshore Income and Abusive Tax Schemes

Offshore income means income generated outside the United States. Sometimes you have transactions with businesses outside the United States. Most likely, your transactions are legitimate and reasonable. As a US citizen or resident, your business is taxed on its worldwide income, not just on its domestic revenues. With the Internet, it's easy to open a bank account in another country without ever setting foot there. You can deposit your offshore sales into that account and keep it as a secret nest egg until you're ready to retire. Or just have the bank issue you a debit card, and you can spend the money here at home. Most people think that the IRS will never see a record of that money, but those people aren't thinking straight.

The world is getting smaller and smaller. The IRS already has arrangements with Visa and MasterCard (your debit cards) to audit their offshore accounts. The unprecedented arrangement with the Swiss government shocked the world. Small countries often rely on US financial assistance or tourism. When the US government starts threatening to withhold those benefits, countries often elect to enter into treaties that effectively rat you out. In fact, Americans who had been living in some other countries for years started facing closure of their bank accounts as far back as 2008, according the Association of American Residents Overseas (AARO).Those banks don't want to have to deal with American scrutiny and reporting to the US Treasury, as required by the Foreign Account Tax Compliance Act (FATCA).

There are some very heavy fines, penalties, and even jail time if you're caught not reporting the funds in your foreign bank accounts, or your assets overseas. Read more about the rules on the IRS website or http://iTaxMama.com/FBAR_FATCA. These fines apply even if you reside in another country, permanently. Innocent people have gotten caught by these penalties. Although the penalties were designed to catch tax criminals, folks who live overseas and never even think about their finances sometimes don't realize they should be filing these reports. Or Americans living here, who cosign on their parents' or grandparents' account, just in case they get sick—those Americans are required to report the existence and location of those bank accounts. This also affects American children here, whose grandparents or relatives opened bank accounts for them, which have been growing since birth. Who even thinks about having to report these kinds of account? That's why I say, many innocent people have gotten caught up in the $10,000+ fines—because they didn't realize they had accounts subject to reporting.

The IRS is making a powerful effort to make the public aware of this—and paying rewards for information. So beware. Your friends who don't have money offshore might just get irked enough that you're flaunting your wealth. That reward is really nice.

Seriously, don't go there. It's not worth the price.

For those folks actually doing business outside the United States, there are legitimate ways to legally set up businesses and partnerships with people or businesses in other countries. If your business is heading that way, go for it. Be sure to report all your earnings when you do. It's done all the time. You've seen Coca-Cola, Motorola, McDonald's, Apple, FedEx, and many other very successful international businesses do it. When you reach this point in your business, add an expert in international taxation to your advisory team. Otherwise, you're bound to step on the toes of other countries' tax systems, too. If you don't know where to find an international tax expert, Team TaxMama may be able to help.

Being GILTI—Global Intangible Low Tax Income

The Tax Cuts and Jobs Act (TCJA) introduced another new tax on businesses with income or operations outside the United States. Too much money was being siphoned overseas by the large corporations, or clever tax planners by licensing their intellectual property to be produced and sold overseas. Essentially, the tax is designed to be assessed on earnings that exceed a 10 percent return on a company's invested foreign assets. The tax ranges between 10 percent and 13.125 percent of worldwide profits. The IRS issued a new form, Form 8992. You can read the instructions at http://iTaxMama.com/Form8992-GILTI_Inst. This doesn't just apply to business with operations outside the United States, it applies to any US shareholder that owns 10 percent or more of the total combined voting power of all the classes of voting stock of a controlled foreign corporation (CFC). If you're affected by this tax, you definitely need a tax pro to help you. And let me tell you ahead of time, most of us don't fully understand this tax quite yet.

Bartering—You May Not Even Know You're Doing It

Barter happens more often than you realize. It's not just a function of formal barter clubs or exchanges.

You do it without even thinking. Barter is older than speech. It's the foundation of civilization. Barter made it possible for people to specialize since they no longer had to do everything themselves. I cook and feed you. You weave and clothe me. I farm and give you food. You shoe my plow horse and make my tools.

How does this translate into today's world? You have skills and trade your services for someone else's products. When each side of the transaction has equal value, and both sides are providing something related to business, it's not nearly such a problem when you don't report it. There would be no net tax effect.

The advertising industry commonly gets columns, space, or airtime in "trade." Instead of paying for the ads, the client provides goods or services. When I was working for a radio station, in exchange for ads, FTD delivered flowers to each office every Monday. On Fridays, we'd all get Winchell's doughnuts. Licorice Pizza provided records (what, you were expecting pizza pie?). When the Shubert Theatre opened in Century City, we were all invited to a private, press-only performance of *Grease*. For the most part, both sides of the transactions were business oriented. Even though it may look personal, the station received certain merchandise and used it in the course of business. Staff benefited from all the goodies we were given, so we could spread word-of-mouth recommendations.

However, barter isn't usually done by contract. It's usually a casual exchange of a business product or service for a personal one. For instance, you're a plumber with a shop on Main Street. You provide $1,200 of plumbing services to your gardener at his home. In exchange, your gardener mows your home's lawn and maintains your landscaping for a year. You must record the value of your plumbing services as a sale. You have $1,200 in income.

Since the gardener is providing you with a personal service, you don't get to deduct the cost of the gardening. The gardener must report the $1,200 he would have been paid for his services as income. May the gardener deduct your plumbing bill? Perhaps a part of it. If the gardener has an office using 33.3 percent of his home, he'll be able to deduct one-third of the expense. As a result, the gardener has net income of $800 from this transaction.

When you add them together, that's $2,000 worth of income never reported to the IRS. The IRS understands this. Wherever the IRS stumbles across barter during an audit, it assesses taxes. Your innocent remarks may incriminate you, even when you didn't realize you'd done anything wrong.

So please be careful. When trading with people, be sure to think through the details of the tax implications of your transaction.

The IRS Has a Cash Audit Guide

Since there is such a healthy, abundant cash-based economy prospering in the United States, the IRS decided to develop an audit guide to train its examiners to "cherchez le cash." It targets specific industries and ways cash is transferred—digitally and in person. It addresses online businesses, as well as Laundromats, bail bonds, car washes, salons, head shops, and so on. Is your business income mostly via cash, or do you cash your clients' checks at their bank or check-cashing establishments? It is in your best interest to read the IRS Cash Audit Guide at http://iTaxMama.com/IRS_Cash_ATG.

Some 1099s Your Business Receives

1099-MISC forms are sent only to sole proprietors and partnerships. Corporations don't generally get them at all, except for medical and legal practices. All businesses must be issued 1099s when they are paid $600 or more. While a business might get an assortment of 1099s, here are the principal kinds to expect, in order of frequency:

- **1099-MISC.** Your company provides $600 or more worth of services to another company or person in a given year.
- **1099-INT.** Your company lent money to another company or person. You are receiving $10 or more in interest income. (Or your business bank account earns interest income.)
- **1099-DIV.** Your company used some excess cash to invest in stocks. This might also come when you receive income from a corporation whose stock your company owns. *Note:* If your business is a C corporation, the corporation might be entitled to exclude 50 percent of those dividends from the corporation's income if the corporation owns less than 20 percent of the stock in the company. (Which would be typical for investment in a publicly traded corporation.) The corporation would be able to exclude 65 percent of those dividends if the corporation owns 20 percent or more of the stock in the corporation issuing those dividends. That would often apply if the corporation had a subsidiary, or owned shares in a related business. This

is called a dividends received deduction or DRD (IRC 243). (These percentages were reduced by the TCJA.) *Note:* If two corporations are owned by the same shareholder, this deduction would not apply. The corporation must own the stock of the other corporation to get this deduction.

- **1099-B.** Your company sold stock or engaged in barter transactions.

The IRS's computer receives millions of 1099s from all over the country and matches up the amounts with everyone's tax returns. If a 1099 was issued to you, the IRS is going to be looking for that number on your tax return. You'd be wise to include the full amount shown on that 1099—even if it's wrong. Chapter 13 explains what happens when the numbers don't match. Read on for some tips to ensure you don't get those nasty notices.

What If a Company Sent You a 1099 for More Money Than You Received?

Of course, a person would be daft to pay tax on money he or she has never received. How can you fix the problem without getting yourself into trouble? You have two choices—contact or correction.

Contact the company that issued the 1099 and ask it to issue a correction. Or, as I always like to do, ask the company to pay you the difference. (Pity, it rarely does.)

If the company is smart enough to hold off filing the 1099s with the IRS until it has received feedback from recipients, the company will be most agreeable. Simply provide some proof or documentation explaining why the 1099 is too high. The company will be happy to help—or it will show you why you're wrong. See how easy that is?

I wish it were so. Unfortunately, this avenue usually results in an argument with some closed-minded bureaucrats who stubbornly refuse to help. They get defensive because they didn't have the foresight to wait for feedback from the recipients. They've already submitted the 1099s and don't want to file amended forms. Amending them attracts attention. The 1099s also are used in audits or court cases when examiners are looking for evidence of fraud. One of my longest, nastiest audits started when a corporation was audited and the examiner happened across an amended 1099 with my client's name on it. He jumped on that amended 1099, deciding he'd found fraud. (We had asked the company to void the 1099-MISC and include his bonus in payroll, where it belonged.) In fact, the auditor was so aggressive, he was shooting for a RICO audit. (RICO is the acronym for the Racketeer Influenced and Corrupt Organizations Act—we're talking about organized crime here!) But . . . that's a story for another day . . . perhaps another book.

What If the Money Is from Last Year?

Be aware that sometimes the 1099 will be right—as far as the sender is concerned. It's a timing difference. Take the example of my client, Eddie the Entertainer. Eddie is on the road most of the year. He does his darnedest to keep up with his bookkeeping, but it's tough when you're rarely home. As a result, my office always calls Eddie's agent to verify his earnings for the year. In 2018, the agent reported $20,000 more than Eddie had on his books. That's a large sum. Eddie couldn't really account for the difference. Tracking down the payments, we learned the agency issued some checks at the end of 2018 that Eddie didn't receive until 2019. That accounted for the difference. As far as the agency was concerned, it paid the bill in December 2018—it wanted the deduction. There was no error.

How can you fix this when it happens to you? When the money was sent out in one year, but you received it the next, report the full income, but adjust your expenses to account for the difference in income. The tax code, when it comes to cash basis taxpayers, operates on the doctrine of "constructive receipt." You don't report the income until you receive the money in such a way that you can actually use it. (For example, a postdated check received on December 20 that is dated January 15 is considered received in January. The bank won't accept the deposit until January 15.)

As far as I am concerned, this is the easiest and fastest course of action. If the amount in dispute is really large or if it's a substantial part of your overall income for the year, it would be wise to attach proof with your deduction.

To prove you received the money in the following year, here are some things you can use:

- **A copy of the postmarked envelope the check arrived in will help.** If the envelope was postmarked on December 31, no matter where you are, you didn't get it until the following year. If it was postmarked earlier, maybe the 28th or 29th, it will depend on how far you are from the sender. So be prepared to describe the normal travel time for letters between your locations. If the envelope has stamps or notations about being misdelivered, that will also help demonstrate that you got it later.
- **A copy of the check and the deposit slip can also prove your case.** In Chapter 4 you were advised to make copies of all deposits, with the deposit slips. Here's a perfect example of an instance when you'll need it.
- **A signed statement from your bookkeeper or accountant that states you didn't receive the check until the following year can help.** If the person doesn't really have firsthand knowledge, don't put him or her on the spot. Be kind to your staff.

- **When all else fails, you can use your bank statement.** Circle or highlight the deposit in the following year. I don't like providing bank statements if I don't have to. It gives the IRS too much information about your bank account. And there might be some innocent deposit of a loan or something that the IRS will jump on as unreported income. So use this as a last resort.

There's one timing issue that may be a gray area with respect to constructive receipt. Suppose the check was sent so that it arrived at your business before December 31, but you were out of town or the office was closed. There was no one to receive or deposit the check until January. When do you report it?

Use your best judgment. The answer to this question will depend on how well you can support your position that you didn't have constructive receipt.

Incidentally, if you don't include that income on your tax return in the year shown on the 1099-MISC, make sure that you do report that income in the year you did receive it. Remember, it won't be included on that year's 1099-MISC. Omitting a significant amount on the following year's tax return could generate more than additional taxes, if you're audited. Understatement penalties of 25 percent or more, plus interest, could be assessed, so be conscientious. And worse! If there is a significant amount of income not reported (25 percent or more), the IRS can audit up to six tax years, instead of only three years. So, it's really important to include all income that is reported to the IRS—even if you do have to deduct it back out.

When the Issue Is Not a Timing Difference

Suppose you flat-out disagree with the amount on the 1099. You know you keep good records, and you know you never got that money. What do you do?

First, let's examine why the 1099 is wrong. Did the company you worked with report that it paid your whole invoice, but didn't really pay you? Check with the company's accounting department. It may have a check that never cleared, got lost in the mail, or is sitting in someone's drawer, forgotten. All these scenarios are common. Who knows, perhaps you just found some money. Collect the money—and include the adjustment to your tax return. Regardless, ask the accounting department to give you a printout of checks it paid to you. Sometimes you'll catch a posting error. Perhaps the department posted someone else's payment to your name.

If the company you are working with refuses to cooperate and the difference is substantial, you may want to pursue the issue. After all, the company might owe you money. Most likely, you're no longer working with that company.

At the very least, you should look into why the company is so insistent on reporting a larger amount. Does the company do this to others, too? What other fraud is going on? Send a letter via certified mail, return receipt requested, asking for the detail on all the payments to you. Give the company 10 business days to respond. If it doesn't, be prepared to go to small claims court, or superior court depending on the amount, to collect the difference. Clearly, if the company says it paid you that much money, but you didn't get it—the company owes it to you. You'd be surprised how quickly a company will cooperate with you once it's been served with a lawsuit. You'll either get your information—or get your money.

If it's not a lost check and not unpaid bills but simply a completely wrong number, it will be up to you to convince the IRS you're telling the truth. In this case, be very sure that all your bookkeeping is up to date and that you've identified all your mystery deposits. (Yes, even I have those—when my filing hasn't been done for a while and I can't find my copies of the deposits where they should be.) Attach a statement to your tax return, containing a list of the checks you did receive from that company, with the dates and check numbers. Include some words about the steps you took to straighten out the problem and the company's lack of cooperation.

Then there are those cases where the amounts reported are flat-out lies. Unfortunately, we do get complaints about this happening from people writing to TaxMama. There may be several reasons for those lies:

- Identity theft—someone is using your Social Security number on the job:
  - This could be a total stranger.
  - Family members use a relative's Social Security number without permission or notification. (Yeah, this really does happen!)
- An error in the Social Security number on the company's books. Perhaps someone typed in the wrong number. Or there is just some other innocent error.
- Theft. Someone in the company is stealing money by creating payroll checks in the name of real people—often people who no longer work there but whose identity information is in the payroll department's database.
- Someone vindictive in the company simply wants to cause you trouble.

To What Do You Attach All These Statements?

The tax return you use will depend on the business format you've chosen. Chapter 3 gives the details and the forms. For our purpose, you need to know where on those forms to put your adjustments. Bear in mind, you will probably not be e-filing. Your best bet is to file a paper tax return.

Frankly, the easiest way to deal with incorrect 1099-MISC forms is to report the income they show on your tax return exactly as each Form 1099-MISC shows.

Why? Because the IRS computer will be looking for that number on your tax return. So whichever box is shown on that 1099-MISC, report it where the IRS computer expects to see it.

Does that mean you're going to pay taxes on income you never received—or that is flat-out fraudulent? Heck no!

Sure, you're going to appease the IRS computers—then you're going to deduct the erroneous amount from your tax return. How do you do that without getting into trouble? Simple. *Disclose, disclose, disclose!*

How do you disclose? Follow these two simple steps:

Step 1. You will include a Form 8275 Disclosure Statement with your tax return. You will include a detailed explanation of why that Form 1099-MISC is incorrect. Include as much detail as necessary so someone reading your explanation can understand the situation. Do not rant. Explain concisely. If there are only one or two documents that can clear this up, include copies. Never send originals.

Step 2. Make the adjustment on the appropriate form. This is where you will be deducting the erroneous amount:

- **Sole proprietorships.** Look at page 2 of your Schedule C. There are empty lines in "Part V Other Expenses." On one of those lines, enter "1099 income in error. See Form 8275 and Statement XXX attached." Replace the XXX with the heading you put on the statement. Incidentally, if you run out of lines on Part V, you're welcome to attach a list of expenses. Simply save one line for this purpose and on it write "See additional expenses on Schedule XXX attached." After you've listed the overflow of expenses, put the total on the line you saved for this schedule.
- **Partnerships or LLCs filing as partnerships and corporations.** There is a line on Form 1065 and on Forms 1120 and 1120S for "Other deductions (attach schedule)." Most business expenses end up on that attached schedule. On one line of that list of other deductions, simply enter "1099 income in error. See Form 8275 and Statement XXX attached."

You can add the statements even when you file electronically. Simply be sure to check the box on your software that says the note or statement is to be printed or included with the tax return. All the major software providers give you this option.

If you're worried about this getting you audited, don't be. I'm going to give you some really great news. The IRS hardly ever reads these statements—especially not when you file electronically. Your electronically filed return is rarely touched by human hands.

What about that difference you just adjusted? The IRS's computers only match up to the income reported on line 1 of your Schedule C and line 1a of your Form 1065. So be sure to include the full amount of the 1099 on those lines. The computers doing the matching have no way of cross-referencing your miscellaneous expenses.

What Should You Do If the 1099 Never Showed Up?

The purpose of the 1099 system is for the IRS to catch cheaters. It's not designed for you to have someone else do your bookkeeping, though many small business owners rely on 1099s for just that purpose. If you're already doing everything right by keeping proper books, the way you were taught in Chapter 4, you already know your income. Don't wait for the 1099s to come in. Use your own records. For you, the only purpose of the Forms 1099 is to ensure that your business's gross income is as high as, or higher than, the 1099s you receive. That might be the only reason to hold off filing your tax return until they all come in—to make sure there are no errors on those forms.

Generally, when companies send out 1099s, they tend to be correct. If you get one later and it's wrong, be prepared to amend your tax return solely to report the additional income and deduct it back out at the bottom. (See the two steps earlier.) Usually, that's not a problem. Then again, if you're working with a spouse, partner, or boss who doesn't remember to tell you everything, here's what might happen to you.

One of my clients, the Big Macher, is the embodiment of the entrepreneurial spirit. He's the golden boy everyone trusts and loves. You probably know someone like him—or are like him yourself. Family and friends gave him lots of money to invest in real estate. In the 1980s, Big Macher was the limited partnership king. He was the general partner in dozens of partnerships, owning millions of dollars of property across the country. His management company wasn't incorporated—he filed on a Schedule C. He operated his business on a handshake. While emotionally satisfying for him, it was a nightmare to his accountant—me! Trying to get the details of agreements and contracts was harder than holding on to a snowflake. Not surprisingly, Big Macher received an audit notice. The IRS was concerned about him because he never reported $33,000 of interest income from a company in Long Beach, California. That made no sense. I logged in each 1099 meticulously. And since I kept his books and records, and reconciled his bank accounts, I certainly recorded every check and source of income received. If it wasn't reported on Big Macher's tax return, we never received that 1099. Besides, if we'd received $33,000, I'd know about it. It never happened.

The auditor faxed me a copy of the incriminating document. I asked Big Macher if he knew anything about this. He just shrugged it off, saying, "I don't think so." Furious, I called the company that had issued the Form 1099-INT. Bob, the company's owner, explained what it was—Macher was a partner in one of Bob's partnerships. The venture came up short, and it had to borrow money. Big Macher was responsible for his share of the interest payments. However, Bob happened to owe Big Macher a chunk of money. So Bob wrote a check to Big Macher for the $33,000 interest. Big Macher endorsed the check back to Bob to pay his own obligation. That's why I had never seen the income. Bob sent me a copy of the front and back of the check Big Macher had received and endorsed. He also sent me paperwork on the interest Big Macher was paying. (He never explained why he didn't send *us* a copy of the 1099 in the first place.)

Net tax effect? There was $33,000 interest income received and $33,000 interest expense paid. Taxable total: 0!

Cost to Big Macher? Plenty! Lots of fees. Despite the fact that there was clearly no taxable error, the auditor insisted on auditing three years' worth of tax returns. He felt this was a big enough omission that he wanted to see what else was missing. After months of work, he found—ta-daaaa!—a couple of thousand dollars of expenses he disallowed. There was no tax due—just a minor reduction of the net operating loss carryforward.

The key points of this story are:

1. No matter how careful you are, there's always something outside your control.
2. For heaven's sake, if you're the Big Macher, have pity on your support staff and debrief them at the end of each day. If you're not a report-and-staff-meetings kind of person, set up a voice mailbox you can call, using your voice-activated, hands-free cell phone (no accidents or distractions, please). You can tell the story of your last meeting. Be sure to brag and include all the details and nuances you're so proud of. Your assistant will be able to check the messages throughout the day. One of those offhand remarks will alert your assistant to ask you about a contract, order, or whatever.

So What the Heck *Is* Income?

And you thought this was easy. Income is more complex than you think it is. Some funds you intuitively consider income aren't. Other things you'd never dream of as income really are. If you're not sure, call your tax advisor—especially to learn if there any more changes to the tax rules. The good news is, the SECURE Act didn't include any new laws affecting how your business income is reported.

The best thing to do to keep yourself on track is to have your accountant or tax professional review your books each quarter. Errors will be caught before they cost you money or penalties.

Resources

In this chapter, you saw a variety of resources. Here's a summary of them, so you can find them quickly and easily. The resources are not necessarily in alphabetical order in each category. They are in order of their importance or usefulness, in TaxMama's opinion.

IRS Resources

- **IRS Publication 334, *Tax Guide for Small Business*.** https://www.irs.gov /publications/p334/, (800) 829-3676. Order this book; it is a must-have reference source, covering all the tax-related aspects of your business. (You can remember the phone number more easily if you see the letters: TAX FORM = 829-3676.)
- **IRS Form 3115—Application for Change in Accounting Method.** https://www.irs.gov/pub/irs-pdf/f3115.pdf
- **IRS Form 8275—Disclosure Statement.** https://www.irs.gov/forms-pubs /about-form-8275
- **IRS Abusive Tax Schemes information and IRS warnings.** http://iTaxMama .com/IRS_Abusive
- **IRS on Barter.** https://www.irs.gov/taxtopics/tc420.html
- **IRS on Barter Clubs and Exchanges.** http://iTaxMama.com/IRS_Barter
- **IRS Cash Audit Guide.** http://iTaxMama.com/IRS_Cash_ATG
- **Al Capone and the IRS.** http://iTaxMama.com/IRS_Capone. The relentless pursuit of Elliot Ness and the FBI ("The Untouchables") brought no results. The IRS documents related to his case are one of the most frequent requests to the IRS under the Freedom of Information Act (FOIA). You can read all about it on the Freedom of Information Act site.

Other Resources

- **Association of American Residents Overseas (AARO).** http://iTaxMama .com/Overseas_Bank_Closure. Information on overseas banks closed to Americans.
- **Dividends Received Deduction (DRD).** https://www.law.cornell.edu /uscode/text/26/243. Internal Revenue Code Section 243. See the details in the Prologue.
- **FreshBooks.com.** http://iTaxMama.com/FreshBooks. Collect your accounts receivable more quickly by emailing a more professional-looking invoice with a variety of payment options.
- **Marijuana by State.** http://iTaxMama.com/Pot_By_State. It's totally illegal in only a few states.
- **Tax Court Ruling—Californians Helping to Alleviate Medical Problems, Inc.** http://iTaxMama.com/Cannabis_CHAMP
- **US Supreme Court Ruling: The Wayfair Decision.** https://www .supremecourt.gov/opinions/17pdf/17-494_j4el.pdf

TaxMama Resources

- **TaxMama on Barter.** http://iTaxMama.com/Unreported_Barter. An overview of how and why barter is taxable using a real case that the IRS took to court.
- **Chapter 2 of this book—"Business Plans You Know and Trust."** Devote some time to understanding your income and how to increase it.
- **Marijuana's Tax Paradox (or the Uncanny Cannabis Controversy).** http:// iTaxMama.com/Pot. TaxMama's course on the tax issues faced by the marijuana industry.
- **TaxMama's Quick Look-Ups.** http://iTaxMama.com/TM_QuickLookUp. You will find all kinds of useful reference materials, webinars you can replay, e-books, and more.
- **Your Business Bible.** http://www.yourbusinessbible.com. Look for worksheets, printable checklists, and other goodies and resources.

To-Do List and Questionnaire

☐ 1. What "listed property" do you use? And how many of each?

_____Vehicle _____Camera _____Video equipment
_____Cell phone _____ Other

What kind of a log have you decided to use for each "listed" asset? Enter the date you have created it (or bought it), implemented it, and updated it through the current date, for this year, for each asset (use another sheet).

_____ Excel spreadsheet   _____ Favorite app   _____ Calendar
_____ Appointment book   _____ Smartphone   _____ Software/Other

☐ 2. Are you logging both personal and business use? _____ Yes _____ No

☐ 3. Is each user logging his or her personal and business use?
_____ Yes _____ No

☐ 4. Start tracking your mileage—business and personal, *right now.*

☐ 5. If you carry inventory, when do you take your year-end count?
Date: _____

☐ 6. Collect copies of the written contracts for your facilities and equipment into one file.

☐ 7. What expenses are specific to your industry? List them on another sheet.

☐ 8. What questions do you have to ask your advisory team or tax professional?

_____

Remember to put a copy of each document behind this page, folded in half.

6

COMMON DEDUCTIONS

Time is worth more than money. You can always earn more money.

Can you replace lost time?

—TaxMama

The best part about being in business for yourself is all those luscious deductions. You can't go to a cocktail party, networking meeting, or anyplace people gather without hearing how someone deducted a cruise, a party, a luxurious car, a home—in fact, most kinds of living expenses. Owning your own business is great, they say, because most of your living expenses are deductible.

Listening to what other people say, you might as well get the best of everything—the most expensive briefcase, watch, PDA, computer, and cell phones for everyone! After all, it's practically free. It's all tax deductible.

Please curb your euphoria for just a moment.

Even if all those things are acceptable as deductible business expenses in your particular business, your tax savings is only a percentage of the amount you spend. It's not more than 50 percent of the price. You're still spending $100 for every $50 you save.

No, you can't make it up in volume.

How do you know what you can deduct and what you can't? This chapter explains it all for you.

Rule of Thumb

Actually, you're really rather right to rejoice in your expenses. Let's face it; if you must spend the money, you might as well enjoy what you've bought. In most cases, the IRS doesn't really have the right to dictate how much you spend on any given item. Would you like to have your business carry you around first class? If you can afford it, go for it—as long as it makes sense in the context of your business, your business budget, or your target client or marketplace. After all, traveling first class, you get to meet people who can afford to pay top rates for your products or services. You won't meet them in steerage.

Looking at the cost of something I want to use for business, this is my rule of thumb: How many hours will it take me to pay for this thing or this experience? Do I want to devote that many hours after I've consumed this trip or bought this device? Or . . . will this expense or extravagance pay for itself—and soon?

Think about it. Once you develop a solid business, the money will come. On the other hand, time is not a renewable resource. Think about that when you pull out that credit card to pay for a needless extravagance or excessive expense.

Universally Deductible

As long as we're in a spending frame of mind, what shall we spend money on that we know the IRS is used to seeing on business tax returns? The following sections describe some of the items you can deduct.

Mixed-Use Assets

Car, computers, cameras, cell phones, and even other things that don't start with a *c* are mixed-use assets—things you use both personally and for business. We'll talk more about them later in this chapter because you need to keep detailed records about your personal and business usage.

Office Expenses

Especially when working at home—out of your back pocket, so to speak—you overlook a substantial part of your office costs. You may pick up supplies while you're out running around, shopping for the family, but you often forget to split the receipts you've collected. Some of those family supplies were used in the business office. This category is often used as a catchall for all general business expenses. Don't dump everything in here—or in office supplies. Look at each purchase and put it in the category where it belongs. Stamps and postal supplies belong in postage or in postage and shipping. Software, if it's renewed annually, should be considered computer supplies. Software that has a long-term life is capitalized. It's an asset that gets depreciated.

Auto expenses, including gasoline and parking, don't belong in office expenses. They belong in auto expenses and parking, respectively. The $1,000 down payment on the copy machine doesn't belong here either. That's an asset. Here's how you enter the copier purchase on your books.

When you take out a loan to buy an asset, such as a copier, you must put the full cost of the copier on the books, as well as the loan. Here are the entries you'll be making when you purchase the copier (journal entry #1) and when you make payments (journal entry #2):

Account Name (Description)	Debit	Credit
Copy Machine (cost of asset)	$5,000	
Bank Account (wrote check)		$1,000
Loan Payable (borrowed money)		$4,000
(Journal Entry #1) Record the purchase of the copier		
Interest Expense (make loan payment)	$25	
Loan Payable (principal part of payment)	$75	
Bank Account (wrote check for payment)		$100
(Journal Entry #2) Record monthly loan payment		

Cost of Goods Sold (COGS)

This deduction is generally for merchandise or inventory. When you're selling a product, wholesale or retail, your merchandise is considered your cost of goods sold.[1] That cost gets reported on the second page of the Schedule C for proprietorships and on a separate form, Form 1125-A, when you file a 1065 or 1120 for other entities. Other costs of goods sold include the product's packaging and the labor to make it, to get it ready for sale, or to install it. Freight to ship it to your facility is also a cost of goods sold. The freight to ship it to customers, however, is part of the sales costs.

For personal injury attorneys, your cost of goods sold would be the clients' costs on a specific case, such as the filing fees for the case, the doctors' bills, investigators' costs, witness fees, and things like that. For someone putting on seminars, the cost of goods sold would include the fees paid to instructors or speakers, the cost of the facility and the refreshments, and the costs of the handouts or books.

When you're involved in manufacturing, there is a raft of direct and indirect costs that may end up in this part of the tax return. It's much more complicated. Be

---

1 Cost of goods sold is the hard costs involved with producing your product or delivering your service.

sure to have your tax professional set up your accounting system so you get it right. Better yet, ensure that you get the highest possible deductions and tax credits available in your industry.

Advertising, Marketing, and Publicity

The IRS clearly has no trouble with these obvious expenses. For some reason, though, people don't deduct these correctly. When I see a business growing that doesn't show anything on the advertising line, I wonder where the business misposted those costs. On the "Advertising" line, you may include trade shows where you exhibit your company's products or services. Include print, radio, television, or Internet advertisements; open houses, if you're a real estate agent; and mailers, brochures, and flyers. Other things that might find their way into this category include business cards, magnetic signs for your business's window or your vehicle, or T-shirts with the company logo that staff must wear at work and give to clients to wear so your company gets more visibility. Certainly all the social media expenditures and freelancers who help build your company's brand or image would fall in this category too. Don't forget to include the cost of your website and cloud spaces for all your articles, art, and mailing lists. Again, those are routine parts of a marketing plan.

Commissions and Fees

Be sure to issue 1099-MISC forms to everyone you pay $600 or more in a year. Chapter 9 tells you how to make the experience painless. I have seen people lose these deductions because the 1099-MISC forms were not issued. Be careful in this category. If your professional code of ethics doesn't permit commissions to be paid to anyone who isn't licensed in your field, you may not want to report illegal commissions. (Those are also known as bribes.) On the other hand, even during an audit, I haven't seen examiners question the legality of commission paid by real estate agents to unlicensed individuals.

Interest Expense

Most businesses borrow money. In fact, it's a good idea to establish a business line of credit now, when you don't need it. Your bank will give you a better rate of interest now—when you're flush with cash—than when you're broke and begging.

Do you understand how lines of credit work? The money is available for your use whenever you need it. You pay no interest unless you use the money. And if you're really sweet, your banker will waive the annual fees.

So what interest expenses *are* deductible?

- If it's a business loan, deduct the interest.
- If it's a personal loan, the interest deduction does not belong on your business books. Period.
- If it is a personal loan, but you used all the money for the business, put the proof into a file with each year's tax return. (You don't need to mail or transmit the proof when you send in your tax return.) Your business may deduct the interest.
- Credit card interest is easy to deduct if you use a separate card for all your business purchases. *Personal interest expenses are not deductible.* So if your funds are limited and you have to choose between paying off the balance on a personal credit card and paying off the business one—pay off the personal card first. *Let the business card earn the interest fees. Those are deductible.* When using the same card for both personal and business use, you'll have to do some computations, each month, to see what percentage of the interest on that card can be treated as a business deduction. For the future, set aside one card just for business use. It will make your life much easier, and your record keeping, too.
- For vehicle loans, if you use the car for personal purposes, be sure to deduct only the business percentage of the auto interest. For example, if you use the car personally 15 percent of the time, deduct only 85 percent of the vehicle loan interest. *Note:* When you use the car as an employee (even as an employee of your own corporation), you may not deduct any of the interest. In fact, as a result of the Tax Cuts and Jobs Act (TCJA), you won't be allowed to deduct any employee business expenses—at least through December 31, 2025.
- Be careful with loans from owners. Write up a loan contract for each loan, with an interest rate. Even if you don't pay the interest, compute it for the year and accrue it. (Journal entry: Debit to interest expense. Credit to interest payable [or to loan from officer].) For corporations, be sure to put the decision to borrow this money from the officer or shareholder into your minutes. Have all the officers or members of the board of directors sign the minutes to approve them. Not paying off the loan will have other tax and financial consequences. Since we are presenting information for successful businesses, we're not going to cover that here.

What about the interest on your home? Can you take that deduction for your business? Yes, if you are using the office in home deduction (Form 8829) and the actual expenses. This can be a tempting consideration now that mortgage interest deductions are limited to mortgages with balances of $750,000 (or $1,000,000 if the loan originated before December 15, 2017). Let's say you're using 20 percent of the house for business. If your mortgage loan is above those limits, can you move 20 percent of the mortgage to Form 8829 and increase your overall mortgage interest deduction? I thought that might be a worthwhile option and explored it. It turns out that the limit on the loan is absolute. Moving part of the debt to office in home means you need to reduce the allowable deduction on Schedule A.

A new provision in the TCJA limits business interest deductions (Section 163(j)).[2] You may have heard of that provision. Good news. It doesn't apply to small businesses. Remember the very liberal definition of a small business? A business with average income of $25 million or more in the past three years. If your business is doing *that* well—you have graduated past this book.

Rent and Utilities

The IRS expects going concerns to rent office or manufacturing or storage space. That won't attract any attention. But if you're trying to deduct your home office expenses, please read Chapter 7 for instructions. Please read it carefully because the TCJA allows a Section 199A deduction for self-rentals. (More about Section 199A later in this chapter.)

Insurance

Business insurance premiums, including workers' compensation, business liability, malpractice, and facility and equipment coverage, are all deductible. When it comes to health insurance or life insurance, Chapters 9 and 10 explain what you may and may not deduct. Health insurance issues are complicated for planning purposes. Take the time to learn the tricks. Health credits and deductions are available to those who make the effort to invest the time. Also, read our discussion in Chapter 10, if you are taking advantage of the Premium Tax Credit for advance payments on your health insurance premiums. Monitor your profits and income during the year. If you see your adjusted gross income (AGI) rising to more than 400 percent of the posted poverty level, start taking steps to reduce your AGI. You can do that by making contributions to an IRA or a retirement plan (if the retirement plan is opened in time). Or you can pay bills before the end of the year—or hold off on generating some income until next January. Sometimes, just a few dollars will get you below that 400 percent and save you $5,000 or so of repayments. If you cannot run the numbers yourself, this one issue is worth a annual consultation with your tax professional.

---

2 https://www.irs.gov/newsroom/basic-questions-and-answers-about-the-limitation-on-the-deduction-for-business-interest-expense

Taxes and Licenses

One of the things I always find in this account is estimated payments on the owner's personal income tax. Sorry, my friend, those are not a business expense. Deductible taxes include the employer's share of the payroll taxes, personal property taxes on your business assets, real estate taxes on your office (in home), excise taxes, fees paid to your secretary of state, the fee for your city business license, the cost of your professional license, sales taxes you collect from your customers (if the sales tax was included in your gross income), and if you're a corporation, the state taxes your business pays. *Note:* The state income taxes or franchise taxes are generally not deductible on your state corporation tax returns. Some people advise you to pay them in December of the year before they are due so you can take the deduction early. That's great for one year. The next year, if you don't also do that, you won't have a state tax deduction at all. See how that works?

Remember, if you've been accustomed to using Schedule A to itemize your deductions, the deduction for all taxes on Schedule A is limited to $10,000. Besides, with the standard deduction being so high, you might not even be able to itemize at all. So, it's time to see if you can use the office in home deduction, and claim the property taxes and mortgage interest on that form, instead of using the safe harbor home office computation (see Chapter 7).

Education

It doesn't matter what industry you're in—whether you're a professional, tradesperson, or truck driver, you must keep up with the latest news, information, and technology relating to your business. Classes, seminars, workshops, books, and magazines—all these are acceptable—and expected. You're entitled to deduct travel costs. So why not look for courses in places you'd like to visit? Combine your personal and business interests. Who knows; if you're having fun, you may even attract other people who are apt to become future clients or customers.

You may not deduct courses taken toward your degree if having that degree is a minimum requirement of the job. Nor may you deduct the cost of education to learn a new career. These sound like foolish rules, but that's the law. You would think our legislators would do everything in their power to encourage Americans to have the best education and skills in the world. We have all seen major shifts in the workforce several times through the years. You've seen times when entire professions or trades were put out of work—engineers in the 1970s, teachers in the 1980s, engineers in the 1990s, data entry folks in the 1990s, just to name a few. (Telephone customer service folks' jobs have been outsourced for at least 20 years.) It's important that people and businesses look toward the future and learn skills to fall back on if things go poorly in their present industry. That can cut social welfare costs way down. Even if no deduction is available, have the good sense to keep learning new ways to support yourself. It may also provide new, lucrative directions for your business. Besides, learning can be very satisfying!

Incidentally, some taxpayers get really aggressive about their education deductions—and stubbornly take their case all the way to Tax Court on their own. Lori Singleton-Clarke[3] beat the IRS and got to deduct the full amount of her MBA degree. She's not the only one. There are more cases hitting the courts where taxpayers are winning on these higher education deductions. It's not an accident. The taxpayers who win, did their due diligence and kept excellent records about their activities and how their education related to their jobs or careers.

Gifts

Gifts are limited to no more than $25 for business gifts given *directly or indirectly* to any one person during the tax year. (Yes, this is archaic! The amount hasn't risen in over 40 years.) A gift to a company that is intended for the eventual personal use or benefit of a particular person or a limited class of people will be considered an indirect gift to that particular person or to the individuals within that class of people who receive the gift. (*Note:* That awkward wording is from the IRS.) Promotional items (pens, keychains, etc.) imprinted with a name or logo are fully deductible if the item costs less than $4. Separately track costs of wrapping, shipping, engraving, and anything else that will make it possible to deduct the full cost of a gift that exceeds $25.

Travel and Transportation

General business travel is deductible, and so is travel to attend trade shows and courses. However, if your spouse or family members come along just for fun, you don't get to deduct their expenses. You may only deduct their travel expenses if they are an integral part of the business.

You have a choice of keeping careful receipts and deducting the actual cost of your lodging or using rates set by the IRS. If you're frugal, the IRS's standards, called per diem rates, may be higher. Look up current, or prior, per diem rates for travel in the continental United States (CONUS) at the General Services Administration (GSA) website (available at http://iTaxMama.com/PerDiem). When you're traveling

3 *Lori A. Singleton-Clarke v. Commissioner of Internal Revenue*, http://iTaxMama.com/Singleton_Nurse _v_IRS.

off the continental United States (OCONUS), to places like Alaska, Hawaii, Guam, and US territories, use the Department of Defense per diem rates (available at http:// iTaxMama.com/PerDiem_OCONUS). And when you travel internationally, you can find the rates on the secretary of state's website at http://iTaxMama.com/PerDiem _Foreign. Incidentally, the GSA has a nifty, free mobile app to help you track your travels and per diem rates (check out http://iTaxMama.com/GSA_Moble_PerDiem).

Before you use per diem rates at all, please do your research or consult with a tax professional on how to use per diems correctly. It's a complicated subject. In fact, if I were to do a webinar on this topic, I could probably fill at least four hours—or a whole separate book. (And heck, I might just do that soon, so stay tuned.) In the meantime, please read some of the discussions we've had about the issues in the TaxMama .com forums at http://iTaxMama.com/TM_PerDiem.

Something new you need to know. Employees may no longer take a deduction for travel expenses—or any employee business expenses. So, why should they track their travels? It's time for employers to step up and provide reimbursements for the travel and other expenses and to work out accountable plan. (See Chapter 4.) If they do, employees will be able to use these rates for their expense reports—and the app, to track their travel nights, meals, etc.

Just one other note. Owners of companies (Schedule C, partnerships, corporations) may not use the lodging per diem rates as a deduction. They may only use the meals rates. But, they can get reimbursed from their businesses using the lodging rates!

Entertainment

Entertainment expenses are no longer deductible by anyone. Period.

There is one thing you can deduct when it comes to entertainment events— that is food and drink. But only if you get a totally separate invoice from the venue. Someone asked, what's if it's spelled out as a line item on the overall invoice? *No.* If your company is holding an event and wants to be able to get any deduction at all for this—be absolutely clear with the caterer, event organizer, or location that you want a stand-alone, separate invoice for all the food and beverages.

Also, be sure to differentiate between an entertainment event as opposed to a sales presentation or an educational event. Those events are still deductible. So once again, how you document your marketing, invitations, brochures, etc., becomes critical. If you want the deduction.

The company may certainly continue to spend money on entertaining clients, employees, or prospects. But there will be no deduction on the tax return. These expenses will go to the bottom of the profit and loss statement, as "Nondeductible

Expenses." On partnership and corporate tax returns, these amounts will go in the same place as you've been putting that 50 percent meal deduction you haven't been able to use on the tax return—Schedule M-1. For instance, see Figure 6.1:

FIGURE 6.1 Adjustment for Nondeductible Expenses, Line 4

Schedule M-1	**Reconciliation of Income (Loss) per Books With Income (Loss) per Return**					
	Note: The partnership may be required to file Schedule M-3. See instructions.					
1	Net income (loss) per books			6	Income recorded on books this year not included on Schedule K, lines 1 through 11 (itemize):	
2	Income included on Schedule K, lines 1, 2, 3c, 5, 6a, 7, 8, 9a, 10, and 11, not recorded on books this year (itemize):			a	Tax-exempt interest $	
3	Guaranteed payments (other than health insurance)			7	Deductions included on Schedule K, lines 1 through 13d, and 16p, not charged against book income this year (itemize):	
4	Expenses recorded on books this year not included on Schedule K, lines 1 through 13d, and 16p (itemize):			a	Depreciation $	
a	Depreciation $			8	Add lines 6 and 7	
b	Travel and entertainment $			9	Income (loss) (Analysis of Net Income (Loss), line 1). Subtract line 8 from line 5	
5	Add lines 1 through 4					

Meals

Except for places in the business of serving food (like restaurants and daycare centers), you generally only get to deduct 50 percent of this expense. That's why it's so important that you post your travel expenses properly. You don't want to find yourself in shock right before an audit, when you pull out those credit card receipts and see that a hefty part of your travel deduction was really meals.

When you travel, you may use the per diem rates for meals instead of your actual expenses. They are often higher than what you normally spend. Look up current, or prior, meal per diem rates at the websites we listed for the lodging per diems. (*Note:* When clients come to tax professionals and have not split out their travel meals, we will generally reduce the cost of travel by 25 to 40 percent, based on your spending patterns, and move those costs to meals expenses. The percentage will depend on the spending habits of the client. If you separate your own meals and travel costs, you might get to keep a higher travel deduction.)

Uniforms

Aside from the tax deduction, there are other advantages to having uniforms. You know exactly what you're going to wear each day, and your wardrobe costs drop. Uniforms create brand awareness, spreading your company name wherever you go. They also can give you and your staff a sense of pride. *And* they're deductible. You can turn anything into a uniform. Simply sew your logo onto your jackets, shirts, or other garments. Establish a particular look to enhance your image and to be remembered. (Don't look—there's a guy wearing a brown shirt and shorts, with heavy shoes. Who is he? We all know it's the UPS guy.) Create your own look so that people seeing you will instantly associate you with your business.

As far as the IRS is concerned, uniforms are something you only wear for work. If you can wear those clothes in places not related to work, I have seen the IRS disallow them as a uniform cost. In fact, one taxpayer went to his audit in his uniform to prove that he wore uniforms. The auditor took one look at him and said, "Clearly, this is street wear. No deduction!" Nasty!

Special TaxMama Tip

How do you overcome this? Treat these costs as advertising costs, not uniforms. You are proudly wearing your logo to create brand awareness. In fact, those clothes are a conversation starter—and they do attract clients or customers.

New Deduction—20 Percent Qualified Business Income Deduction

Everyone is talking about this new deduction. It's meant to help level the playing field (as far as deductions go) for companies that are not C corporations. C corporations got a new flat tax rate of 21 percent on all profits. So this is meant to provide an extra deduction for individuals, partnerships, and S corporations—essentially, pass-through entities where the tax on income is paid on the individual taxpayer's tax return.

What is this new deduction and how does it work? (Notice I didn't say "what exactly.") It's complicated. The IRS spent over a year trying to define various provisions of this new deduction. They are still issuing more guidance and interpretations. When it comes to the subject of real estate rentals, the IRS has issued nearly 250 pages of clarification.

So, let's see if I can just give you some of the important fundaments:

- What is the Section 199A deduction?
    It's a deduction from income, not a tax credit. It's worth up to 20 percent of qualified business income. The deduction is taken right after the itemized deductions or standard deduction has reduced taxable income. The qualified income can come from a variety of different kinds of businesses. The

deduction is computed separately for each business, as well as taking the overall adjusted gross income into account.

- Which taxpayers can use Section 199A?

    Sole proprietorships, S corporations, partnerships, trusts, and estates—including publicly traded partnerships and REITS—can use it.

- What are Specified (or Specific) Service Trades or Businesses (SSTBs)?

    They are similar to the definition of personal service corporations (PSCs). Though architects and engineers have been removed from the definition and a few other services have been added (everything on the list after "consulting"). The services are in the fields of health, law, accounting, actuarial science, performing arts, consulting, athletics, financial services, investing and investment management, trading, dealing in certain assets, or any trade or business where the principal asset is the reputation or skill of one or more of its employees or owners.

    People who meet this definition only qualify for the Section 199A deduction if their income is below certain limits.

- What is the income limit for SSTBs to be able to claim the Section 199A deduction?

    The income is increased for inflation each year. And there is a phase-out range of $50,000 for individuals and $100,000 for couples filing jointly. For 2020, individuals may earn $163,300–$213,300; married couples filing jointly may earn $321,400–$421,400. You can find the most current amounts on the Form 8995A (available at http://iTaxMama.com/Form 8995A-Sec199A).

- What is the other computation—when income exceeds the SSTB limits?

    You pick up one of these amounts:
    - 20 percent of Qualified Business Income (QBI)
    - *or* the greater of 50 percent of the W-2 wages paid by the business
    - *or* the sum of: 25 percent of the W-2 wages paid by the business plus 2.5 percent of the unadjusted basis immediately after acquisition of depreciable property

- What does the phrase "unadjusted basis immediately after acquisition of depreciable property" mean?

    Essentially, it means the business's total assets—without deducting any depreciation. So it's a good idea not to remove depreciated assets from the business's books and depreciation schedules if the business is still using the asset. The IRS is maintaining an extensive resource on their website about Section 199A, including webinars and videos. Look there for more guidance at http://iTaxMama.com/IRS_FAQs_199A.

Now that you know different specific items you can deduct, let's look at expenses specific to some industries.

It's All About You

Each industry has certain characteristic deductions to consider. These deductions won't apply to all members of the industry, but they apply to enough to make them worth knowing. To find out the deductions unique to your industry, the best place to start is with your industry association. Often, national trade and professional associations hear from their members when they face audits relating to the industry. The better associations track the information about what was handled incorrectly by members. Either they will educate members to avoid that accounting practice, or they will lobby to change the law so that it coincides with industry practices.

While there's no room to cover all industries, here are some tips on a few industries. Use a search engine on the Internet and look for your own trade or profession to find tax issues relative to your business. That's how I find my best resources.

Beauty Salons, Barbershops, and Other Salons

For beauty salons, barbershops, massage salons, and so on, your biggest issue is determining whether the people working at your shop are employees or independent contractors. Chapter 9 describes the results of a barber's audit. To avoid paying employment taxes on your tenants (or people renting out chairs in your shop), get rental contracts signed with your operators. They must be responsible for rents, even on weeks they are not using their stations. When renting out space in your salon, don't deduct the money from customers' payments. Have the operators write you monthly or weekly checks.

If you are processing customers' credit card payments, the contracts should include a provision allowing you to do that, spelling out the fees or percentage you will charge the operators for this service.

Remember to include laundry costs for the towels and robes you clean at home each day. The following are some sites you will find useful:

- **The Cosmetology Fairness and Compliance Act of 2001.** https://www .govtrack.us/congress/bills/107/s879. This is the salon industry's reply to provisions affecting it in the 2001 Tax Act. This law did not pass, but it gives you an idea of some of the issues involved.
- **Beauty Salon Defined.** http://iTaxMama.com/IRS_Barber_Beauty. This beauty salon guide provides information about many aspects of the

cosmetology industry, including business structure, tips, estimated taxes, and more. You will also find links to videos. This guide is intended to provide an overview of the industry.

- **IRS's Salon Industry Audit Procedures, Including Allowable Expenses.** The IRS replaced their audit guide for this industry, with an overall audit tax guide (ATG) for cash-intensive businesses—http://iTaxMama.com/IRS _Cash_ATG. See Chapter 10 in this ATG.

Childcare Providers

Many childcare businesses are operated in the owner's home. IRS Form 8829 has a special computation for your office in home. Rather than basing your business use on square footage, it is based on the percentage of hours your facility is in operation. It's imperative that you keep daily logs. Often, you have parents coming very late to pick up their children—that's still business time. The IRS has standard per diem–per student rates for the food you provide. The amounts appear to be low, to my eyes, so track your actual food costs. At the end of the year, see which is higher—your actual costs or the IRS's rates. When buying groceries and class supplies, get separate receipts for your school purchases and household purchases. If you don't, keep the receipt in your business and circle the business purchases.

The IRS regularly audits such businesses, since so much cash changes hands. You can read the audit guide that IRS auditors use—the IRS's Child Care Provider Audit Technique Guide—available at http://iTaxMama.com/ATG_ChildCare.

Construction Industry

Many states have rules requiring construction businesses to pay their workers as employees if they are not licensed contractors. While you may not have specific uniforms, for many trades, you can only wear your jeans or shirts once. After that, they are too caked with cement or other dirt to be washed. Since those items of clothing are disposable and definitely cannot be used on the street in that condition, pick up the costs. Keep receipts for all your tools, gloves, boots, safety equipment, and the toolbox on the back of your truck. Your in-home office (see Chapter 7) probably includes the whole garage and additional storage units you've built. Taking that into consideration, your ratios of business use may change. On some projects, using percentage of completion costing will let you delay paying taxes on some of the money you've received. Sometimes, the completed contract method will work better for you. Check with your tax professional for some tricks of the trade.

An excellent resource for the construction industry is the website http://www .construction.com. During the years I spent working in this field, the *Dodge Reports* were an excellent source of bidding opportunities for larger projects we would never have known about on our own.

Protect yourself from audits by understanding the IRS's Construction Industry Audit Procedures, Including Allowable Expenses. This guide, which the IRS auditors use, is available at http://iTaxMama.com/ATG_Construction.

Multilevel Marketing Industry (MLM)

Surprisingly, the IRS does not list an audit guide for MLM companies, yet the IRS has instituted an aggressive push to shut down abusive MLM schemes, such as the Tax People prosecution in Kansas. (*Note:* Not all MLM companies or activities are abusive. But when these people approached me to refer their products, it felt so wrong that I asked my contacts at the IRS to look over their claims. The IRS confirmed my suspicions.) Think carefully before treating this as a business. If you're only buying the products or services for personal use, then all your expenses are personal. If you get a 1099 for your sales to yourself, report the income, and on page 2 of Schedule C, on the "Other expenses" line, enter "Not income—personal use discount only," and deduct the same amount. If you're getting a discount on merchandise you purchase for use in your business, your commissions are income. Add the commissions to your business income. However, if you are actively and aggressively building your downlines, selling products, and generating revenues, then you should take all the deductions you're entitled to use. (In multilevel marketing terminology, downlines are the members that you have recruited to the company. These are the people whose sales [or purchases] earn you a commission.)

In case your income never builds up enough to show a profit, keep a log of all your marketing activities and marketing expenses. You'll need them to fight the IRS in the event of a hobby loss or fraud audit.

Truckers

If you're a trucker, you're subject to a variety of gasoline, road, and vehicle taxes; tolls; and weight charges. Keep all the receipts for those fees in a safe place for each year. Even as an owner-operator, you've contracted with one or two companies that give you the majority of your runs. Have you ever looked at the pay stubs they give you? They have deducted for at least two kinds of insurance and several fees they share with you. Usually, the 1099-MISC they issue to you is for the *gross* amount of your income or the contracted fee. Yet the check you actually get might be at least

10 percent less. Ask the accounting department if this is the case. Or hold on to every single check from that company and add them all up. Odds are, you haven't been taking a deduction for this 10 percent or so worth of fees. There's also an annual heavy vehicle use tax due, $550 minimum (Form 2290). It is due on the anniversary date of your vehicle purchase plus one month. The IRS includes a chart in the instructions to Form 2290, in case the due date confuses you—see https://www.irs .gov/pub/irs-pdf/f2290.pdf.

The IRS's per diem rates allow truckers to get a standard daily meal allowance, just like other business travelers. There's a special rate for transportation workers, like truckers, railroad personnel, etc.—see http://iTaxMama.com/Trucker_Per _Diem. The rate changes every year. In 2020 it is $66 per day ($71 OCONUS). Please note, if you are subject to "hours of service limits" by the Department of Transportation, you may only use 80 percent of the per diem amount. Keep an eye on this at http://iTaxMama.com/Hours_Service. It may rise to 100 percent someday.

Bad news for employee truckers. You can no longer take any of your employee business expenses as deductions on your tax return. It's time to renegotiate your contract with your employer. See some tips in Chapter 9.

Bad news for owner-operators in California. The recent Dynamex decision by the California Supreme Court may redefine you as an employee, That means that all those expenses you're carrying, including the cost of your rig—you might lose the right to claim those deductions. Read the article on Trucks.com about your industry at https://www.trucks.com/2019/05/15/trucker-labor-rulings-california-dynamex/. At a recent meeting of the California Society of Enrolled Agents State Tax Liaison Committee, this issue was hotly argued. The state officials suggested that they might be proposing revisions to the new legislation (California AB5) that was issued as a result of the Dynamex decision. The Truckers have filed suit against California.

Why I am telling you about California? It's only one, minor state. Well, once California starts passing laws, other states watch the results—and often pass similar laws. Hopefully, your state will wait until California cleans up the legislation. Clearly, this law was meant to address the Ubers and Lyfts of the world—not long-haul truckers with massive investments in their rigs!

Since you're usually on the road, your administrative time is limited. Here are some resources to cut your time and costs of tax administration:

- **Truckers Helper Online.** http://www.truckershelper.com/. Trucking business software and tools.
- **Drivers' Daily Log.** http://www.driversdailylog.com. A software tool to help you maintain daily logs and hours of service. It's not fancy, but certainly seems functional.

- **Form 2290, Heavy Highway Vehicle Use Tax Return.** https://www.irs.gov /pub/irs-pdf/f2290.pdf. You must file Form 2290 within the first month that you put any heavy highway vehicle, with a taxable gross weight of 55,000 pounds or more, into use.

Cash-Intensive Businesses

One of the wonderful things about a business that collects cash from its customers is that there is little or no accounts receivable. The big drawbacks are that you are a frequent target for thieves—and for IRS audits. After all, since all the revenue is cash, it's easy to skim off some money each day without paying taxes. The IRS has a special audit guide (available at http://iTaxMama.com/ATG_Cash) to help close that insidious tax gap. Read it carefully if you own a restaurant or a grocery or convenience store—in other words, an establishment that handles a high volume of small-dollar transactions. The IRS also uses the audit guide for industries that engage in services, such as construction or trucking, where independent contract workers are generally paid in cash.

These days, there is another growing industry that is quite a target for federal scrutiny—on many levels. The state-legal marijuana industry has rapidly grown to a multibillion-dollar level. The federal government has made it a semiofficial policy to leave the medical marijuana businesses alone. But the feds are still raiding and auditing recreational marijuana businesses. For more in-depth information about the special tax and business issues involved, watch the video of my annual course— Marijuana's Tax Paradox (or the Uncanny Cannabis Controversy)—http://iTax Mama.com/CPE_Pot. (See also Chapter 5.)

Mixed-Use Assets

Mixed-use assets were introduced earlier. Now is the time to look at them in depth. Cars, computers, cell phones, cameras, and other property used for entertainment, recreation, or amusement are called "listed property" and have the honor of occupying their own special place, taking up most of the second page of Form 4562. (Internal Revenue Code §280F(b) applies to assets being used for less than 50 percent of the time for business purposes.)

Computers, video equipment, cameras, monitors, and beepers—you can't run a business today without them. They're no longer a luxury. Parents and their businesses no longer share the home computer. As it happens, Congress removed computers and peripheral equipment from the "listed property" category as part of the TCJA.

These days, all of these other devices are now so reasonably priced that many children have their own electronics. Since the initial public offerings (IPOs) of the 1990s, everyone is trying so hard to re-create the phenomenon, who has time for a personal life anymore? Besides, with digital cameras and reality television, everyone's family and home are going online.

Let's talk about how you can make the most of your deductions with each of these mixed-use assets.

Cars, aside from real estate or a complete manufacturing plant, are likely to be the biggest one-shot expense to a small business. In the American economy, your car is the key to your image. Chapter 8 tells you all of the most effective ways to squeeze deductions out of it—whether you lease or buy.

Would you like to get even more money out of your car dollars and be able to get something better than you thought you could afford? Go to the dealer selling the model of your dreams—and buy a used model. New luxury cars lose value instantly when taken off the lot. That's not just a myth. So let someone else pay for that quick devaluation. Instead, you can buy the completely refurbished one- or two-year-old dream machine with most of the warranty left, and have the dealer detail it for you before you pick it up. If you don't squeal, people will think you bought the car new.

The listed property rules with respect to just about everything except cars, televisions, and stereos are obsolete. They should be removed from the tax code. Even the IRS isn't paying attention. The IRS used to target the split usages of listed property. Aside from personal use of cars, I haven't seen an auditor ask about personal use of property (except for television or cable) since the early 1990s. Congress removed cell phones from "listed property" permanently in the Small Business Jobs Act of 2010. And now, they have removed computers, as we mentioned, in the TCJA of 2017.

What Do the Listed Property Rules Mean to You?

For all listed property you want to deduct, you must track the business and personal usage so you know what percentage of that usage is for business. If you want to treat your camera, stereo, DVD player, and television as business property, you have to keep logs of all the usage with a separate column for business. That's right. Can you just see yourself sitting down to watch television and making a notation in your log with the date, starting time, and list of the programs you're watching? Be sure to include a few lines about how you're using the time or the programming for business purposes. If other family members use the TV, they have to make log entries, too. After all, your family's time counts toward total use of the asset. At the end of the year, you'll be able to deduct about 20 percent of the expenses, based on the few business hours you actually logged. Yes, it's a pain—that's the point. Congress wants to discourage you from deducting personal assets. Many entertainment industry folks set up their equipment in a separate screening room, even if it's just a separate bedroom, to use for business viewing.

The main thing you need to know is that when business use of the asset falls to less than 50 percent, you can't take a depreciation deduction for the asset—or you have to switch your depreciation to a straight line method. If you've been depreciating over several years and business use falls below 50 percent, you may have to recapture, or pay back, some of the depreciation that exceeds 50 percent of the basis of the asset. This is what you have a tax professional for—to help you in times like that.

As for the special rules for cars—and there are many—we've devoted an entire chapter (see Chapter 8) to this subject. But we didn't explain what depreciation is all about—that comes next.

Depreciation

Back in the good old days, a depreciation deduction was provided so companies could write off a portion of the cost of their large capital expenses (buildings, equipment, fixtures, and so on) over the item's useful life. This was to provide them with the incentive to put that money aside, into a reserve fund, so they could afford to replace items as they wore out. Back then, depreciation life was related to how long a piece of equipment or building would last without substantial repairs or improvements.

Depreciation was also easy to figure out back then. Using a simple mathematical formula or two, you could determine depreciation without a scientific calculator or slide rule—just a pencil and paper . . . and perhaps an extra finger or toe. We used nifty worksheets, which you can use too. (See Table 6.1.) Really, depreciation was logical: you could use straight line, declining balance (DB), or sum-of-the-years digits.

Straight line was the easiest type of depreciation. For this, you just had to divide the cost of the asset by the number of months in its useful life. Then all you had to do was multiply that result by the number of months the asset would be in use during the year:

Cost ÷ useful life in months × months used this year

Straight Line

Trixie bought a computer for $1,200 on September 5. It had a five-year useful life: 5 years × 12 = 60 months. Dividing $1,200 by 60 = $20 per month. She used the computer for four months this year. The deduction is 4 × $20 = $80.

TABLE 6.1 Form 4562, Depreciation Worksheet

Depreciation Worksheet (Keep for your records.)

Description of Property	Date Placed in Service	Cost or Other Basis	Business/ Investment Use %	Section 179 and Special Allowance	Depreciation Prior Years	Basis for Depreciation	Method/ Convention	Recovery Period	Rate or Table %	Depreciation Deduction

Next year, Trixie will depreciate it for a whole year: $20 × 12 = $240, or 20 percent per year.

In a double-declining balance (DDB) or a 1.5 declining balance (1.5 DB), you simply took the first formula and multiplied it by 2 or 1.5:

(Cost ÷ useful life × months used this year) × 2

or

(Cost ÷ useful life × months used this year) × 1.5

The only difference in the declining balance method is that you multiply your resulting percentage against the undepreciated balance of the asset. Let's go back to Trixie, shall we?

Double-Declining Balance

Divide the number of months the asset was in business use this year by the total life. Trixie had 4 months of use, divided by 60 months' life. Her straight-line depreciation rate would be 6.67 percent. Using DDB, she would multiply that rate by 2 = 13.33 percent. Trixie's first-year depreciation would be $160 (13.33 percent × $1,200).

The following year, Trixie deducts the $160 already written off from the full purchase price of $1,200 to equal $1,040. She would multiply this reduced asset cost by the second year's depreciation. In Trixie's second year, she used it 12 months out of a total of 60. That's 20 percent. Remember, we multiply that number by 2 to equal 40 percent. So the second year, Trixie's depreciation is $416 ($1,040 × 40 percent). From then on, Trixie's rate would be 40 percent, but the balance will keep decreasing. In the third year, the asset cost is $624 ($1,040 − $416). Multiplying $624 by 40 percent gives Trixie a smaller deduction than last year, equal to $250. And so forth.

The formula is:

(Cost ÷ useful life × months used this year) × 2 × (cost − previous depreciation)

or

(Cost ÷ useful life × months used this year) × 1.5 × (cost − previous depreciation)

Halfway through the useful life, you'd switch back over to straight line.

I know, this is a lot more detail than you really wanted to know. And you know what? You don't need to know it. The IRS has tables in their publication on depreciation where you can look things up. And your software has the numbers built in. All you have to do is select the correct type of asset and the correct asset life. Let me explain some of the other things you still do need to understand.

Depreciation in Today's World

Aside from mere historical value, there's a reason for explaining the old way of determining depreciation to you. The present depreciation system still has a little resemblance to these two computation methods.

The IRS changed its depreciation rules in 1986. It introduced concepts such as the accelerated cost recovery system (ACRS) and modified accelerated cost recovery system (MACRS). For the present, you'll be using MACRS, which is based on the two systems described earlier. (See Table 6.2.)

Depreciable assets are categorized in groups called classes. You can look them up in IRS Publication 946, *How to Depreciate Property* (available at https://www.irs .gov/publications/p946) or read IRC §168. Most businesses only need to know about these four classes. The life is called a recovery period.

- **Three-year property.** This property includes manufacturing equipment, certain racehorses, tractor units, and rent-to-own property.
- **Five-year property.** This category includes autos, taxis, small aircraft, trailers, computers and peripherals, office equipment, apparel manufacturing equipment, certain construction equipment, and fixtures and appliances used in rental properties.
- **Seven-year property.** Office furniture; manufacturing equipment (not already included in the first two classes); oil, gas, and mining equipment; agricultural buildings or structures; and anything that isn't classified anywhere else fit here.
- **Real estate (buildings only, not land).** Commercial real estate is depreciated over 39 years using a straight-line method. Residential real estate is depreciated over 27.5 years, straight line. The TCJA added another element to real estate depreciation. Residential property placed in service after 2017 may use straight line depreciation with a life of 30 years.

Don't worry; as I mentioned earlier, you won't have to do the calculations. You'll be able to look up depreciation in the tables. Table 6.3 gives you the most commonly used depreciation table for small businesses. Tables 6.4 and 6.5 cover residential real estate (apartments and homes rented out) and commercial and business property. This also includes your home office. Although you're living in the house, the office part makes it subject to the 39-year rules.

TABLE 6.2 MACRS Percentage Table Guide

Appendix A
MACRS Percentage Table Guide
General Depreciation System (GDS)
Alternative Depreciation System (ADS)

Chart 1. *Use this chart to find the correct percentage table to use for any property other than residential rental and nonresidential real property. Use Chart 2 for residential rental and nonresidential real property.*

MACRS System	Depreciation Method	Recovery Period	Convention	Class	Month or Quarter Placed in Service	Table
GDS	200%	GDS/3, 5, 7, 10 (Nonfarm)	Half-Year	3, 5, 7, 10	Any	A-1
GDS	200%	GDS/3, 5, 7, 10 (Nonfarm)	Mid-Quarter	3, 5, 7, 10	1st Qtr 2nd Qtr 3rd Qtr 4th Qtr	A-2 A-3 A-4 A-5
GDS	150%	GDS/3, 5, 7, 10	Half-Year	3, 5, 7, 10	Any	A-14
GDS	150%	GDS/3, 5, 7, 10	Mid-Quarter	3, 5, 7, 10	1st Qtr 2nd Qtr 3rd Qtr 4th Qtr	A-15 A-16 A-17 A-18
GDS	150%	GDS/15, 20	Half-Year	15 & 20	Any	A-1
GDS	150%	GDS/15, 20	Mid-Quarter	15 & 20	1st Qtr 2nd Qtr 3rd Qtr 4th Qtr	A-2 A-3 A-4 A-5
GDS ADS	SL	GDS ADS	Half-Year	Any	Any	A-8
GDS ADS	SL	GDS ADS	Mid-Quarter	Any	1st Qtr 2nd Qtr 3rd Qtr 4th Qtr	A-9 A-10 A-11 A-12
ADS	150%	ADS	Half-Year	Any	Any	A-14
ADS	150%	ADS	Mid-Quarter	Any	1st Qtr 2nd Qtr 3rd Qtr 4th Qtr	A-15 A-16 A-17 A-18

Chart 2. *Use this chart to find the correct percentage table to use for residential rental and nonresidential real property. Use Chart 1 for all other property.*

MACRS System	Depreciation Method	Recovery Period	Convention	Class	Month or Quarter Placed in Service	Table
GDS	SL	GDS/27.5	Mid-Month	Residential Rental	Any	A-6
GDS	SL SL	GDS/31.5 GDS/39	Mid-Month	Nonresidential Real	Any	A-7 A-7a
ADS	SL	ADS/30	Mid-Month	Residential Rental	Any	A-13
	SL	ADS/40	Mid-Month	Residential Rental and Nonresidential Real	Any	A-13a

Chart 3. **Income Inclusion Amount Rates for MACRS Leased Listed Property**

	Table
Amount A Percentages	A-19
Amount B Percentages	A-20

TABLE 6.3 MACRS Depreciation: 3-, 5-, 7-, 10-, 15-, and 20-Year Property; Half-Year Convention

Year	Depreciation Rate for Recovery Period					
	3-Year	5-Year	7-Year	10-Year	15-Year	20-Year
01	33.33%	20.00%	14.29%	10.00%	5.00%	3.750%
02	44.45	32.00	24.49	18.00	9.50	7.219
03	14.81	19.20	17.49	14.40	8.55	6.677
04	7.41	11.52	12.49	11.52	7.70	6.177
05		11.52	8.93	9.22	6.93	5.713
06		5.76	8.92	7.37	6.23	5.285
07			8.93	6.55	5.90	4.888
08			4.46	6.55	5.90	4.522
09				6.56	5.91	4.462
10				6.55	5.90	4.461
11				3.28	5.91	4.462
12					5.90	4.461
13					5.91	4.462
14					5.90	4.461
15					5.91	4.462
16					2.95	4.461
17						4.462
18						4.461
19						4.462
20						4.461
21						2.231

In addition to recovery periods, you have "conventions" that dictate adjustments in the MACRS tables. Did you notice that "half-year" designation in the title of Table 6.3 (MACRS Depreciation: 3-, 5-, 7-, 10-, 15-, and 20-Year Property; *Half-Year Convention*)? It refers to the date you bought your assets:

- The half-year convention treats all your property as if you bought it in the middle of the year.

TABLE 6.4 Residential Rental Property Mid-Month Convention Straight Line—27.5 Years

Year	Month Property Placed in Service											
	1	2	3	4	5	6	7	8	9	10	11	12
1	3.485%	3.182%	2.879%	2.576%	2.273%	1.970%	1.667%	1.364%	1.061%	0.758%	0.455%	0.152%
2–9	3.636	3.636	3.636	3.636	3.636	3.636	3.636	3.636	3.636	3.636	3.636	3.636
10	3.637	3.637	3.637	3.637	3.637	3.637	3.636	3.636	3.636	3.636	3.636	3.636
11	3.636	3.636	3.636	3.636	3.636	3.636	3.637	3.637	3.637	3.637	3.637	3.637
12	3.637	3.637	3.637	3.637	3.637	3.637	3.636	3.636	3.636	3.636	3.636	3.636
13	3.636	3.636	3.636	3.636	3.636	3.636	3.637	3.637	3.637	3.637	3.637	3.637
14	3.637	3.637	3.637	3.637	3.637	3.637	3.636	3.636	3.636	3.636	3.636	3.636
15	3.636	3.636	3.636	3.636	3.636	3.636	3.637	3.637	3.637	3.637	3.637	3.637
16	3.637	3.637	3.637	3.637	3.637	3.637	3.636	3.636	3.636	3.636	3.636	3.636
17	3.636	3.636	3.636	3.636	3.636	3.636	3.637	3.637	3.637	3.637	3.637	3.637
18	3.637	3.637	3.637	3.637	3.637	3.637	3.636	3.636	3.636	3.636	3.636	3.636
19	3.636	3.636	3.636	3.636	3.636	3.636	3.637	3.637	3.637	3.637	3.637	3.637
20	3.637	3.637	3.637	3.637	3.637	3.637	3.636	3.636	3.636	3.636	3.636	3.636
21	3.636	3.636	3.636	3.636	3.636	3.636	3.637	3.637	3.637	3.637	3.637	3.637
22	3.637	3.637	3.637	3.637	3.637	3.637	3.636	3.636	3.636	3.636	3.636	3.636
23	3.636	3.636	3.636	3.636	3.636	3.636	3.637	3.637	3.637	3.637	3.637	3.637
24	3.637	3.637	3.637	3.637	3.637	3.637	3.636	3.636	3.636	3.636	3.636	3.636
25	3.636	3.636	3.636	3.636	3.636	3.636	3.637	3.637	3.637	3.637	3.637	3.637
26	3.637	3.637	3.637	3.637	3.637	3.637	3.636	3.636	3.636	3.636	3.636	3.636
27	3.636	3.636	3.636	3.636	3.636	3.636	3.637	3.637	3.637	3.637	3.637	3.637
28	1.97	2.273	2.576	2.879	3.182	3.485	3.636	3.636	3.636	3.636	3.636	3.636
29							0.152	0.455	0.758	1.061	1.364	1.667

TABLE 6.5 Residential Rental Property Depreciation Schedules

Table A-13. **Residential Rental Property Placed in Service After 2017**
Straight Line—30 Years
Mid-Month Convention

Year	Month property placed in service											
	1	2	3	4	5	6	7	8	9	10	11	12
1	3.204%	2.926%	2.649%	2.371%	2.093%	1.815%	1.528%	1.250%	0.972%	0.694%	0.417%	0.139%
2–30	3.333	3.333	3.333	3.333	3.333	3.333	3.333	3.333	3.333	3.333	3.333	3.333
31	0.139	0.417	0.694	0.972	1.250	1.528	1.815	2.093	2.371	2.649	2.926	3.204

Table A-13a. **Straight Line—40 Years**
Mid-Month Convention

Year	Month property placed in service											
	1	2	3	4	5	6	7	8	9	10	11	12
1	2.396%	2.188%	1.979%	1.771%	1.563%	1.354%	1.146%	0.938%	0.729%	0.521%	0.313%	0.104%
2–40	2.500	2.500	2.500	2.500	2.500	2.500	2.500	2.500	2.500	2.500	2.500	2.500
41	0.104	0.312	0.521	0.729	0.937	1.146	1.354	1.562	1.771	1.979	2.187	2.396

- The mid-month convention applies to real estate. It treats all buildings as if they had been bought in the middle of the month.
- The mid-quarter convention comes into play if more than 40 percent of your assets (based on cost) were bought in the last three months of your tax year.

I'm sorry; despite the title of this book, there is no way to make depreciation easy. All this, and we haven't even talked about the part you're most excited about— bonus depreciation.

Bonus Depreciation or Special Depreciation

This is like a yo-yo. Some years, we have bonus depreciation. Others we don't. Lawmakers use this provision as a political toy. You will have to read the "What's New" section of IRS Publication 946 each year to see if you are entitled to any bonus depreciation. In the past, if there is bonus depreciation, it only applied to the purchase of new, not used, assets. The TCJA changed that law to include used assets, as well. Sometimes, the bonus depreciation will only be available in designated disaster areas. Sometimes, it will be universally available. For now, bonus depreciation will continue to be available for 100 percent of the purchase of qualified assets until 2022. Then the percentage will decline—until it finally phases out in 2027. (See Table 6.6.)

TABLE 6.6 Bonus Depreciation Rates 2017–2028

Placed in Service Year[500]	Bonus Depreciation Percentage	
	Qualified Property in General/Specified Plants	Longer Production Period Property and Certain Aircraft
Portion of Basis of Qualified Property Acquired before Sept. 28, 2017		
Sept. 28, 2017 – Dec. 31, 2017	50 percent	50 percent
2018	40 percent	50 percent
2019	30 percent	40 percent
2020	None	30 percent[501]
2021 and thereafter	None	None
Portion of Basis of Qualified Property Acquired after Sept. 27, 2017		
Sept. 28, 2017 – Dec. 31, 2022	100 percent	100 percent
2023	80 percent	100 percent
2024	60 percent	80 percent
2025	40 percent	60 percent
2026	20 percent	40 percent
2027	None	20 percent[502]
2028 and thereafter	None	None

One other note about bonus depreciation. If you don't want to write off 100 percent of your asset purchases in any class of assets for the year, you must specifically include a statement on your tax return about that. If you elect out of 100 percent bonus depreciation for one asset in any class, you cannot use 100 percent depreciation for any asset in that class for the year. The election must be made each year for any asset purchases. I will admit that I was surprised to learn about this backward election. How did I find out about it? Through an IRS announcement in October of 2018—with just days to alert people to file amended returns for 2017 to correct this oversight (http://iTaxMama.com/IRS_Bonus_Elect_Out).

Section 179 Depreciation

It is called Section 179 depreciation because that is the Internal Revenue Code section that covers this. Section 179 depreciation may be used for new or used property. This limit changes constantly with the political wind. The Protecting Americans from Tax Hikes (PATH) Act of 2015 finally locked in some permanent amounts for Section 179 depreciation. However, due to the TCJA, starting in 2019, you may now deduct up to $1,020,000 in business assets purchases each year. The Section 179 numbers increase with inflation each year.

There are strings attached to the Section 179 deduction:

- If more than $2,550,000 worth of property is placed in service during the year, the allowable Section 179 expense must be reduced by the amount in excess of the limit.
- The Section 179 election can't cause income from all trades or businesses to be reduced below zero.
- Any amounts expensed under this provision reduce the depreciable basis of the assets placed in service during the year. In other words, you can't expense part or all of the cost of an asset and also depreciate the same costs.
- If the property is disposed of prior to the end of its useful life, you will be required to recapture some of the Section 179 deduction previously taken. *Recapture* means that a portion of your Section 179 deduction must be included as taxable income on your tax return.
- You can use Section 179 on vehicles more than 6,000 pounds. But the deduction is limited to $25,500 (see Chapter 8).

Large corporations have entire departments devoted to tracking assets and recording their disposal. Take the cost of administration into account when you discuss the value of depreciation deductions.

If the Section 179 deduction will take your business income to zero, cut back on how much of it you use. As previously mentioned, you cannot use Section 179 to take your business profit below zero. However, regular depreciation may be used to generate a loss. A good tax professional will play with the numbers to give you the highest deduction you can get without throwing you into alternative minimum taxes, or having you waste the deduction. When the Section 179 depreciation you take is too high, the rest of it gets carried forward to the next year, while regular depreciation might have given you a deduction. I've seen people totally waste this deduction, year after year. Remember, you may have to pay back the deduction if you stop using the asset for business, trade it in, or sell it. So do a careful analysis before using Section 179.

Affecting Pass-Through Entities

When using bonus depreciation and Section 179 depreciation for partnerships, LLCs, S corporations, or other pass-through entities, talk to the partners, members, or shareholders first. If you use the Section 179 deduction on the business return, but they can't use it, they'll be forced to carry it forward. It might be wasted.

Depreciation is one of the most complex tax computations. So many forms, schedules, and limits are affected that it's like playing multidimensional chess. Even the best tax software doesn't always get this right. If you talk to your tax advisors, they'll admit they check their software's depreciation calculations to make sure all affected forms and limits are taken into account on your tax returns.

And let's add one more twist. The more depreciation you deduct, the lower your profits are, right? That's generally a good goal to reduce your income taxes and other related taxes. But, now you have that Section 199A deduction. The lower your profits, the lower your Section 199A deduction is. You may be tempted to aim for a higher Section 199 deduction.

Don't be too tempted to do that. There are some major advantages to using depreciation to reduce profits. It's much more straightforward and less apt to face the intense scrutiny that the IRS will be giving the new deduction. In addition, depreciation reduces your AGI. Which allows you to claim more tax credits, or higher IRA and other deductions limited by AGI.

More Deductions Than You Can Imagine

We've just scratched the surface of how to use expenses, and we haven't delved deeply into the expenses you can't use. Some businesses are subject to passive loss limitations or alternative minimum taxes and the intricacies of net operating losses. These are things you'll need to have your tax professional explain if they pertain to you. After all, you need to have something to call your tax person about now that you've learned all you need to know to run your business.

You will find a lot more information on the IRS's website, where there is a pretty good summary of the overall depreciation rules. And if you can't get an answer there . . . just ask TaxMama. Really. All you have to do is visit www.TaxMama.com and click on Ask a Free Question. You will get an answer, usually within 24 hours, on a business day.

Incidentally, a word to the wise—don't spend *all* your time learning to run the business. At some point, you have to take action—and start working.

Resources

In this chapter, you saw a variety of resources. Most of them have been left in the text, because they are so relevant. But here's a summary of some of the primary resources, so you can find them quickly and easily. The resources are not necessarily in alphabetical order in each category. They are in order of their importance or usefulness, in TaxMama's opinion.

IRS Forms, Publications, and Resources

- **Form 1125-A, Cost of Goods Sold.** https://www.irs.gov/pub/irs-pdf/f1125a.pdf
- **Form 4562, Depreciation.** https://www.irs.gov/pub/irs-pdf/f4562.pdf
- **IRS Publication 946, *How to Depreciate*.** https://www.irs.gov/publications/p946
- **IRS—Real Estate Rentals and Section 199A.** https://www.irs.gov/pub/irs-drop/td-reg-107892-18.pdf. The IRS issued nearly 250 pages of clarification on the subject of real estate rentals and Section 199A.
- **The IRS's New and Improved Gig Economy Resource.** https://www.irs.gov/businesses/gig-economy-tax-center

Per Diem Rates

- **CONUS—Continental United States.** http://iTaxMama.com/PerDiem
- **GSA Mobile app for CONUS per diems.** http://iTaxMama.com/GSA_Moble_PerDiem
- **OCONUS—Outside the Continental United States.** http://iTaxMama.com/PerDiem_OCONUS
- **International.** http://iTaxMama.com/PerDiem_Foreign
- **Meal per Diems for Transportation Workers** subject to Department of Transportation (DOT) rules. http://iTaxMama.com/Trucker_Per_Diem
- **Questions and Answers About per Diems in the TaxMama forums.** http://iTaxMama.com/TM_PerDiem
- **IRS Audit Guides for Specific Industries.** http://iTaxMama.com/IRS_ATG

Mileage Tracking Resources

- **TaxPal.** http://www.taxpal.net/. A software tool to use to build IRS-compliant records. It lets you enter mileage and expense data by hand or import the data from various apps. It's still growing and developing and welcoming input from users. The unique thing about this is, it's built around the questions the IRS asks about each meal or entertainment, trip, or deduction. It's designed to protect you in audits.

- **MileIQ.** http://iTaxMama.com/MileIQ. A versatile app you can use to track all your different types of travel—business, personal, medical, volunteering, and so on.

Other Resources

- **Construction Industry Resources.** http://www.construction.com
- **Marijuana's Tax Paradox (or the Uncanny Cannabis Controversy).** http://iTaxMama.com/CPE_Pot. TaxMama's recorded webinar about the tax issues of the marijuana industry.
- **Open, by American Express.** http://open.americanexpress.com. Here you'll find discounts on business supplies and services.
- **Slide Rule.** http://www.hpmuseum.org/srinst.htm. In case you don't know what a slide rule is, it's a classic geek tool. These instructions on how to use one are provided by the Museum of HP Calculators.
- **Small Business Taxes and Management.** http://www.smbiz.com. Tax updates, summaries, and news for small businesses.
- **The Tax People Prosecution in Kansas.** http://www.mlmlegal.com/taxpeople .html. Analysis by attorney Jeffrey A. Babener of the 2001 prosecution of Kansas-based company Renaissance, The Tax People.

TaxMama Resources

- **TaxMama's Quick Look-Ups.** http://iTaxMama.com/TM_QuickLookUp. You will find all kinds of useful reference materials, webinars you can replay, e-books, and more.
- **Your Business Bible.** http://www.yourbusinessbible.com. Look for worksheets, printable checklists, and other goodies and resources.

To-Do List and Questionnaire

☐ 1. Do you have an office in home? _____ Yes _____ No
   If not, and you are not planning to have one, skip this chapter.
   If yes, continue.

☐ 2. Do you have a distinct and separate area you are using for your
   business? _____ Yes _____ No
   If not, you will probably lose your deduction, unless you operate a day-care
   center, you store inventory, or your entire home *is* your business.

☐ 3. For a day-care center, etc., keep a log of the days and hours the house is
   used for business. Note the date that the log was created and updated with
   year-to-date information: _____

☐ 4. Create the schematic of your home or property, showing the distinct areas
   you use for business. Enter the total square footage: _____
   Business square footage: _____ Date: _____

☐ 5. Take photographs or video of each area, labeling what it is used for.
   Date: _____

☐ 6. Do this again each year; keep a copy in your tax file for that year.

☐ 7. Homeowners, get the cost split between land and building for depreciation
   purposes. What is your source (attach a copy)? What is the split
   percentage?
   • Property tax assessment: _____
   • Written appraisal by: _____
   • Other: _____

Remember to put a copy of each document behind this page, folded in half.

7

OFFICE IN HOME

Wherever you wander, there's no place like home.

—SONG LYRICS BY JOHN HOWARD PAYNE

The Song Is Right! Let's Stay Home

In 2016, the latest year for which IRS statistics are published at the time I am writing this, more than 150 million individual tax returns were filed. Of these businesses, about 25 million were "nonfarm sole proprietorships." In other words, they were businesses like yours and mine. Businesses like ours produced $1,422,204,586,000 in revenues for this country—that's more than $1.4 trillion! In total, those small businesses also reported a little more than $1 trillion in expenses, leaving about $400 billion in profits. The IRS statistics report for fiscal year 2016 shows nearly $10 billion in deductions for "business use of home."

For a new business, having your office at home is an excellent idea because it keeps your overhead low. You can get away with earning less, so you can concentrate on building the business instead of paying the bills. Not only do you save money on renting an office space, but you also save precious time by not having the distractions and office politics of a shared suite.

For me, moving out of the penthouse suite on Ventura Boulevard meant a savings in tangible dollars of more than $1,000 per month. I no longer paid rent, additional annual common-area costs, parking for staff and myself, parking validations for clients, tips to the valets, or utilities. I saved at least another $1,000 per month in my staff's increased productivity because they didn't have all the distractions that came with managing a suite with several tenants. Many tenants had too much free time and liked to hang around chatting with my charming staff.

Another advantage to working from home is that when your family needs you, you're there. Once all the interruptions end, or the family time is over, you can slip back into your office, perhaps late at night, without having to dress up and drive across town. You can step in for just a minute, even on days off, to take care of something quickly and conveniently.

Besides, you can take expenditures you're already making and use them to help reduce your business profit and the related self-employment taxes. Which expenses do double duty like this? Your rent. Or if you own a home, your mortgage and property taxes. You're already paying those bills, right? With an office in the home, a percentage of those costs will move to your Schedule C.

Of course, working at home may have some drawbacks.

It's a Red Flag; It's Just Asking for an Audit

Sure it's a red flag! So what? If you are operating a real business out of your house, shouldn't you be entitled to take legitimate deductions for it? True, having an office-in-home deduction and using Form 8829 will definitely increase your chances of an audit. Actually, it's not as much of a concern as it used to be. So many companies operate remotely, or reduce office rent by having staff work from home—including the IRS. Folks who keep good records have nothing to worry about. You'll need to be able to prove exactly what part of your home you used for business. It's also important to define what the business use was for each area you're claiming as business space. But with the instructions that follow, you'll be able to prove to the IRS that you're entitled to the deduction. And if you're ever audited again, you'll have proof that the IRS accepted your evidence in the past.

Why does having a home office seem risky to many small businesses? Here's the court-related background on the issue. It relates to the Pomarantz case and the Soliman case. I'll tell you about them in a moment.

Until 1998, the IRS knew an office-in-home audit was one easy way to generate money for Uncle Sam's coffers.

Why? Until the end of 1998, the rules for in-home offices were dictated by the results of the court ruling against Dr. Pomarantz. He was a physician whose work took place in a hospital. But he did have a legitimate office at home where he took care of all his business transactions, planning, and calling and where he maintained his records. Since he didn't meet with patients at home, under a strict definition of the Tax Code, he was not permitted a deduction for an office at home.

Pathetic, isn't it?

Here's some history on the Pomarantz and Soliman cases:

- *Pomarantz v. Commissioner*, **867 F.2d 495 (9th Cir. 1988).** The Ninth Circuit Court concluded that an emergency care physician's home office was not his "principal place of business" under § 280A. The Ninth Circuit ruled that Pomarantz could not deduct home office expenses because he consistently spent more time on duty at the hospital than he did at home. The essence of his profession was the hands-on treatment of patients, which he did only at the hospital and never at home. Finally, he generated income only by seeing patients at the hospital, not by studying or writing at home.
- *Commissioner v. Soliman*, **506 US 168—Supreme Court 1993.** In this case, an anesthesiologist spent 30 to 35 hours per week working in the hospital. He performed his billing, management, and administrative functions at home. The US Tax Court supported him. So did the Fourth Circuit Court of Appeals. The IRS took the case to the Supreme Court, which supported the IRS—there was no office at home since Dr. Soliman derived his income from the practice of anesthesiology.

The same treatment applied to such people as plumbers (they didn't fix their customers' pipes by bringing them to their own home and working on them there), Laundromat owners, traveling salespeople (a whole other problem), actors, and . . . you're getting the idea.

Looking at these businesses' returns, odds were in the IRS's favor to score some good money by auditing office-in-home returns. But no more.

Finally! Under the rules that took effect January 1, 1999 (based on a law that passed two years earlier . . . why it took so long to take effect, I have no idea!), you no longer have to meet customers in your home to qualify for the office-in-home deduction.

IRS Publication 587 outlines the present requirements:

1. Your use of the business part of your home must be:

   a. Exclusive
   b. Regular
   c. For your trade or business

and

2. The business part of your home must be one of the following:

   a. Your principal place of business

    b. A place where you meet or deal with patients, clients, or customers in the normal course of your trade or business

or

    c. A separate structure (not attached to your home) you use in connection with your trade or business

That little item you see in 2a opened up the door to you if your office in home is only used for administrative purposes, even if you generally work at customers' locations. But this must be the *only* business office you have. The office in home doesn't have to be a whole room; it may be part of a room. It doesn't have to be just a room; it may also include closet space, garage space, carport, or parking pad for your primary business vehicle or tools (tractors, cement mixers, clown cars, drill presses, whatever you use or store).

Under the present rules, pretty much everyone who operates a business from home will have a legitimate claim to an office in the home. Since 1999, the odds of the IRS finding fault with the office-in-home deduction on a tax return have decreased dramatically.

Oh, there's no doubt that many people who are taking the deduction are not really entitled to it. But it's no longer a sure thing that you'll get audited. These days, to get the IRS's attention, you need to have both an office in home and a loss on Schedule C. (See Chapters 5 and 6.)

Frustrating Change to the Law Affecting Employees

The Tax Cuts and Jobs Act (TCJA) of 2017 took away the right for employees to get a deduction for their office-in-home use, along with all other employee business expenses. (See Chapter 6 for more details.) So our discussion in this chapter is only for business owners.

New Benefit for Self-Rentals

While the TCJA took a benefit away, it also gives us a new benefit. You learned about the new Section 199A 20 percent qualified business income deduction in Chapter 6. The good news is, if your business (corporation or partnership) pays you rent for the use of your home, that self-rental income might be taken into account when you compute your total qualified income. It's a little complicated. The IRS only issued about 500 pages worth of explanations on how Section 199A affects real estate income. I just wanted to give you a heads-up to go back and read Chapter 6.

An Attractive Change to the Law Affecting Homeowners Only

Before May 6, 1990, there was a consideration even more daunting than IRS audits for people who planned to sell their homes within a few years. You would lose the $250,000 ($500,000 for couples) personal residence exclusion on the business portion of your home. As a result, when you had a large gain on the sale, you would have to pay tax on the business percentage of that gain. For instance, let's say you used 15 percent of your home as your office. Your home was worth $200,000, but you bought it for $100,000 several years ago. In the past, when you sold the house, $170,000 would have been treated as sale of your personal residence. The gain would not have been taxable since it's less than the $250,000 exclusion per person. But $30,000 ($200,000 × 15 percent) would have been treated as the sale of business property. Without going through all the numbers, essentially, you would have had to pay $3,000 to $5,000 in IRS and state taxes on the sale, depending on how much depreciation you had taken.

That additional tax is no longer an issue. Under the present law, you get to treat the whole house as your personal residence when you sell it. You only have to pay tax on the depreciation you've deducted. Since most people don't get to deduct more than $500 per year of depreciation, the tax doesn't usually amount to much. (See http://iTaxMama.com/Sale_Home_Ofc.)

New computation complexities have arisen as a result of the Housing and Economic Recovery Act of 2008. They affect second homes used as rentals. They won't affect your office in home. So relax. It's all right to use office-in-home deductions if they apply to your business.

Simplify, Simplify

In 2013 the IRS came up with a new twist on the home office deduction. Believe it or not, it made it easier for you. You have the option of deducting $5 per square foot times up to 300 square feet of home office space, instead of going through most of the complex steps I am about to present to you. Although this only gives you a maximum deduction of $1,500 if you use 300 square feet or more to work in, it has a lot of benefits:

- You don't have to take depreciation on your home:
  - Which means you don't have to pay tax on the depreciation deduction when you sell the house.
  - However, you still have to pay tax on the depreciation deductions you took before switching to the simplified method.
- You get your full mortgage interest and property tax deductions on Schedule A. Before, you moved part of that to your office-in-home schedule.
- You don't need to keep records on all your utilities, insurance, and other expenses for business purposes, since you won't be using them.
- Best of all, you reduce your audit risk.

There are quite a few drawbacks to this arrangement, too. The worst is for you folks who haven't been able to use all your home office deductions in the past. You've been carrying those deductions forward into a year when you expect to show a sizable profit. And you know that year is coming, right? Well, when you switch to the simplified method, you lose all those unused deductions. You're saying, "Aw, what the heck! It's been a pain to keep track of all those records anyway. What do I have to lose?"

That's what I thought, too. At the end of this chapter, read the story about Erica. That will help you understand why you might not want to give up those carryforwards. Figure out how much you really will lose by being too lazy to keep records on the allowable home office deductions. Hmmm . . . the recordkeeping is suddenly looking more attractive, isn't it?

Take a look at the pros and cons of the IRS's new simplified home office deduction versus the detailed deduction in Table 7.1.

Inner Space

If you decide to opt for regular deduction, great. Let's get into the details. Now that you're comfortable taking the deduction, just how much of the home's area can you deduct?

Carefully measure out the square footage of the space(s) you use. You'll find you use substantially more of your home for business than you realize. After all, most businesspeople use their car for business more than 40 percent of the time. Have you ever noticed how much space your garage takes up? While you may have a 1,400-square-foot home, your two-car garage may add 800 square feet (about 20 feet × 40 feet). If half that garage is used for your 75 percent business-use car—that

TABLE 7.1 Comparison of Methods

Simplified Option	Regular Method
Deduction for home office use of a portion of a residence allowed only if that portion is **exclusively** used on a **regular basis** for business purposes	Same
Allowable square footage of home used for business (not to exceed 300 square feet)	Percentage of home used for business
Standard $5 per square foot used to determine home business deduction	Actual expenses determined and records maintained
Home-related itemized deductions claimed in full on Schedule A	Home-related itemized deductions apportioned between Schedule A and business schedule (Schedule C or Schedule F)
No depreciation deduction	Depreciation deduction for portion of home used for business
No recapture of depreciation upon sale of home	Recapture of depreciation on gain upon sale of home
Deduction cannot exceed gross income from business use of home less business expenses	Same
Amount in excess of gross income limitation may **not** be carried over	Amount in excess of gross income limitation may be carried over
Loss carryover from use of regular method in prior year may **not** be claimed	Loss carryover from use of regular method in prior year may be claimed if gross income test is met in current year

amounts to 300 square feet (800 × 50 percent × 75 percent). Add in the storage for your files, inventory, tools, and records (about 10 × 20 square feet), and that's another 200 square feet. You've just found 500 square feet in the garage alone!

Look at the space you're using in the house. You have that area at the back half of the living room. You have a desk (or two to make an L-shape), a bookcase or three, a cabinet for your printer, several upright or lateral files. You're talking about 12 feet × 15 feet = 180 square feet. Don't forget the closet filled with office supplies—another 6 feet × 4 feet = 24 square feet. So far we have 704 square feet! (24 + 180 + 500). Dividing that by the total square footage of the house and the garage (1,400 + 800), which is 2,200 square feet, results in a business use of 32 percent of your home. You can use the worksheet in Table 7.2 to help you.

TABLE 7.2 The Home Office Spaces

Total Business Square Footage		
Area of your desk and main files		_____
Primary supply closet		_____
Additional in-house storage		_____
Office lavatory		_____
Vehicle parking area		_____
Garage or carport storage area		_____
Additional structures		_____
Total Business Square Footage	(A)	_____
Total Home Square Footage		
Area of primary residence		_____
Area of garage or carport		_____
Area of additional structures, if used in the business		_____
Total Home Square Footage	(B)	_____
Percentage of Business Use		
(A) ÷ (B) = (C)	(C)	_____%

Just using your unimaginative desk area, you'd have had 180 ÷ 1,400 = 12.9 percent.

As long as the areas you're taking for the deduction are really used for business, you will have no problem in an audit.

Just remember one thing—you can't add in space that is not exclusively used for business. If you do your work on the kitchen counter and then clear it all away to make and serve family meals, that's *not* office space. On the other hand, if you use the dining room as your office and never use it for family meals—that is office space.

Isn't this exciting?

Two Critical Reminders

Let's pause for just a second here. Please do be careful about two things when claiming this deduction:

1. You really do have a business with a profit motive.
2. You really are using your home as your principal place of business.

While the IRS isn't chasing after office-in-home deductions per se, it is looking for fraud. So please don't be frivolous about this because the IRS really doesn't have a sense of humor in this area.

Incidentally, having gone through this exercise to see how much of your home you're using for business may get you to do some thinking about your business space. Is there really enough space to run your business the way you'd like? Would you be better off in a traditional business facility? Or would you be better off in a bigger house? Perhaps, looking all this over will help you realize not only that you need more space but also that your business can afford to pay for it.

Prove It, Baby!

OK, you're comfortable using the home office. You've learned how to determine how much of the home is a business. Now, how do we prove it to the IRS in the event of an audit?

After all, if the IRS does audit you, it will be about two or three years after the year you used the area. You might have remodeled that area by now—or moved away. How do you protect your deduction? Simple: take photographs. Take lots of pictures of the office spaces in the house and remember to include the closets and storage areas. Take photos of the garage area and any business space out there.

I know you love your digital camera. It makes life so easy. But print those snapshots. Keep a hard copy in your permanent file for the house and another copy in your tax file. Who knows if you'll still be able to read the same digital medium in 2025?

Make a schematic drawing of the home. It doesn't need to be fancy. Just make an outline of the house, garage, and storage areas, putting lines in to separate each room. (Remember those old-fashioned things called rulers? They come in really handy for making neat, straight lines. If you don't have a ruler handy, use the edge of a book or your L.L. Bean catalog.) Write in the lengths and widths of each room. Then add up the total square footage and list it neatly in a corner of the page. Next, identify all the areas you use for business and add up their measurements. Enter the total business square footage on the page. Finally, show the computation of the business percentage (business square feet divided by total square feet). If you're not comfortable drawing this up yourself, take a look at SmartDraw (https://

www.smartdraw.com/floor-plan/home-design-software.htm). Or here's a resource with five free online room design applications: https://www.thebalance.com/free -online-room-design-applications-1357750.

Do not use the number of rooms used for business divided by the total rooms in the house. It doesn't work that way. You must use square footage.

Set up a permanent office-in-home file. Put a copy of your photos and this schematic into that file and another copy in your tax file for each year that you operate from this home. That way, in case of an audit, you won't have to scramble to find a copy.

Now that you have the measurements, what can you deduct?

What Are Office-in-Home Expenses?

Don't get too carried away here. I've seen people drag in everything they spend money on and try to turn it into a business expense. Don't get greedy. If you don't have clients coming to your home, don't deduct things like your gardener, pool guy, or other outside maintenance expense. When it comes to your housekeeper, if you don't even let her set foot in your office, don't take that deduction. I'm not trying to spoil your fun—just trying to keep you looking good.

Rent Is Easy

If you don't own your home, multiply the business percentage (you've already computed it) times your total rent. For example, let's say you pay $12,000 per year for rent plus $500 for renter's insurance. Earlier, you computed your business use as 32 percent. Your net deduction then is $4,000 (12,500 × 32 percent). That's it. On Form 8829, use column (b) "Indirect Expenses." Enter the full $500 of insurance on line 18 and the full $12,000 of rent on line 19. (These line numbers are subject to change as the IRS revises forms annually.) Your software will compute the 32 percent.

If You Own, You Depreciate

Since the home office area is being used for business, you'll need to use the nonresidential real property tables to look up your depreciation. Business property is depreciated over 39 years. If you can't get your hands on a depreciation table, just do the computation yourself. There are 468 months in 39 years (12 × 39). Divide your depreciable cost by 468. That gives you the depreciation per month. Then multiply the monthly amount by the number of months you used the space for business this year. For instance, if you started the business in August, you used the home office for five months.

It's important to figure out the value or cost of your office in home. It's not quite as easy as it looks. The number might start with your purchase price of the home. Or if the current market value of the home is lower than your purchase price plus improvements, then the lower number is your starting point. That will give you a basis (tax cost) for the home. You can't depreciate land. To determine the cost of the land, look at your appraisal, if you have a copy. Most professional appraisers include that information. If you're in the process of buying the home, or refinancing, ask for a copy of the appraisal. Be sure to ask the appraiser to define the land value. You can't get your hands on an appraisal? Use a copy of your property tax assessor's statement or annual invoice. It shows land and building value. Don't use the value shown. Use the percentage (divide the land value by the total value of the property shown on the property tax invoice). Apply that percentage to your basis to get the cost of the business portion of your home. Use the worksheet in Table 7.3 for guidance.

TABLE 7.3 Depreciation of Home

Lower of cost of home or fair market value		_____
Improvements to home before becoming office		_____
Less:		
Cost of land		_____
Casualty loss used		_____
Total Adjusted Basis	(D)	_____
Multiply (D) by business percentage (C) in Table 7.2	(E)	_____
Divide (E) by 468 (months)	(F)	_____
Multiply (F) by months of business use in current year		
Total Depreciation	(G)	_____

Add in any major improvements that weren't previously depreciated or expensed. Have you ever taken a casualty loss deduction on your home? If you live in a flood, tornado, or earthquake zone, you might have. Be sure to reduce your basis by the amount of the casualty losses you deducted. Line (D) in Table 7.3 will give you the adjusted basis. Table 7.4 will guide you on the rest of the depreciation calculation.

TABLE 7.4 Home Office Deduction Overview

Total Business Profit from Schedule C	**(H)**	_____
Indirect Expenses: Shared with Home		
Rent or mortgage interest	_____	
Property taxes	_____	
Home insurance	_____	
Utilities	_____	
Repair and maintenance	_____	
Other	_____	
Total Indirect Expenses	**(I)**	_____
Multiply this by the percentage in Table 7.2 (C)	**(J)**	_____
Direct Expenses: Business-Related Only		
Insurance	_____	
Repair and maintenance	_____	
Other	_____	
Other	_____	
Total Direct Expenses	**(K)**	_____
Depreciation from Table 7.3	**(G)**	_____
Prior year carryforward from Form 8829		_____
Total Office-in-Home Expenses		
(J) + (K) + (G)		_____
Deduct profit from	**(L)**	(_____)
Deductible Office-in-Home Expenses This Year	**(M)**	_____
If the result is negative, you have a carryover to next year.		

Honestly, though, the first time you do this, it's a good idea to have a tax professional set this up for you. Ask the tax professional to give you all the details and a copy of the depreciation schedule. Once you have that, you can take it from there. It's well worth the expense for your first year.

There are still more expenses you may take.

Utilities (gas, electric, sewage, trash, water). Rather than using the square-foot method, what I like to do is this:

- Start with your utility bills from before the office was in your home, if you can get your hands on them. Add up a year's worth. Take the average (divide by 12). That number is your average monthly personal utility charge. Deduct this amount from your present monthly utility total. The difference is your business expense. For instance, before working from home, your electricity bill was $50. Now that you're working from home, with all the computers and air conditioning, your bill is $150. The $100 increase is your business expense. Do this every year. Keep a copy of these records and computation in your permanent office-in-home file, as well as the file for each tax year.
- If your office was always at home, you're stuck using the same percentage as your square footage of business use. If you have a way of proving that your home office uses more power or water than is needed for regular living, use it. One way would be to get copies of a neighbor's utility bills for a year. Even three months would be great. Find someone who works outside of the home, has a similar number of people living in the home, and won't mind letting you use his or her utility invoices for your audit. Follow the instructions earlier.
- Generally, doing the calculation this way will result in a higher and more reasonable deduction.

Keep logs for the following expenses! Even the courts are disallowing deductions when you don't maintain logs.

- **Internet access.** If your family is using the same lines, you'll have a hard time justifying the deduction. You might get away with deducting the difference between a lower-speed and a high-speed line, using the logic that you wouldn't have gotten the high-speed line if not for the business. However, if you are paying a flat fee for all Internet access, and the business doesn't cost you anything extra—you don't really have a business deduction, do you?
- **Cable TV.** To get this deduction, you'll need to keep a log of the shows watched and which were for business purposes. Keep a notebook outlining how that program related to your business. Deduct only the business use. When I take this deduction, even for my entertainment folks, I know it's usually a giveaway—one of those things you're prepared to give up during

an audit. But, I have prevailed in audits when my director client did keep detailed records about his viewing and he kept a notebook showing what information he was gleaning from each show he watched.

- **Repairs and maintenance.** If you repaint or repair any part of your business space, naturally, 100 percent of those costs are deductible. For instance, if you install an additional bathroom just for your office, you can deduct all those expenses. However, if you make repairs or improvements to the whole house, such that it also benefits your business space, you'll only be able to deduct the business percentage we arrived at earlier. An example of such an improvement would be installing a central air-conditioning system in the whole house.
- **Property tax and interest.** Deduct the business percentage on Form 8829. Use the rest on Schedule A.
- **Insurance.** Business liability insurance or business insurance just on your office space is fully deductible. You may use the business percentage of whatever you pay for homeowner's insurance, earthquake or flood insurance, or renter's insurance.
- **Household supplies.** You'll buy certain things at the supermarket or discount store for household cleaning or beverages or coffee. Some of those things may look like personal groceries. But if you are using them strictly for your clients or staff, they may be business expenses. Think about the expenses from this perspective: If you were in an outside office, you would have a "kitchen" area containing a coffeemaker, microwave, and refrigerator, and you would stock it with coffee, tea, cocoa, popcorn, and other supplies for visitors and staff. Are you doing the same thing at home? At the store, I like to separate out the groceries that are for the office from the ones for the house. The store doesn't mind ringing it up as two sales. If you keep separate receipts, it's easier to support your deduction. Better yet, use a business credit card to pay for the business purchases. Be careful not to abuse this.

When You Can't Use Office-in-Home Deductions

If your business shows a loss, your office-in-home deductions are suspended. Or, suppose your business shows a profit before the office-in-home deduction. Then, when you use the office-in-home expenses, your profit turns into a loss. You may only deduct enough home office expenses to zero out your profit. The unused expenses don't entirely go away. You carry them forward to next year's tax return. There's a line at the bottom of Form 8829 for carryovers. Remember, I told you how valuable these carryovers can actually be—when your business becomes more profitable.

Evaluate Your Options

You understand how to use the office in home. Now, the question arises, should you use it? There may be times when it's wise to just skip it.

These are some of the considerations I look at for my clients:

- Do you own or rent your home?
- If you own, will you still be living there two years from now?
- How soon *do* you plan to sell it?
- Will you have a gain or a loss if you sell it?
- Do you expect your business to show a profit after using these deductions?

If you are renting the residence, there are no long-term repercussions from using this deduction.

When you own your home, it has most likely appreciated since you bought it. You will have to pay taxes on the depreciation you've taken. Is it worth it for the small amount of depreciation deduction you get anyway? It may be worth using the full-blown office-in-home deduction if all the other office-in-home expenses really help reduce your taxable business profit. You don't get to use all the other office-in-home expenses without also using the depreciation. The Tax Code has a special rule about depreciation. It's called the "allowed or allowable" rule. That means if you should have taken depreciation, but didn't, the IRS will treat your tax return as if you had—especially when you sell the property. It's complicated and nasty—and if you were in business for more than three years and didn't take the depreciation, but should have, it could cost you. This is definitely one of those areas that you want to discuss face-to-face with a good tax professional. Why? Because we have a way to fix this for you.

One of the questions earlier asks whether your business is profitable. I ask that for two reasons:

1. When your business shows a loss, your office-in-home deduction cannot be used. (Sure, it will carry over to the next year, but it's useless until the year[s] in which you show profits.)

2. If you expect to be showing losses for several years, you may never get the advantage of the office-in-home deduction, but you will attract an audit for a hobby loss. (See Chapter 2.)

Generally, seeing a pattern like that, I avoid the office-in-home deduction altogether. If you can stand the scrutiny and have a solid business plan that shows how and why your business will start being profitable five years from now, go ahead and use the office-in-home deductions.

Then there are times when you just want to throw out the whole deduction altogether. Which is what I did for one client, until I went all the way. Erica hadn't filed tax returns for a long time. I prepared seven years' returns for her, including her office-in-home deduction. It wasn't that hard because she was renting an apartment. As a self-employed publisher, she worked from home. You can just bet that a substantial portion of her home really was devoted to her business.

Erica had losses for the first six years. She could prove how deeply in the red she was by the very high balances on her credit card and bank loans. Seeing all those losses during the first years' returns and thinking of the added scrutiny the IRS gives to nonfilers, I went back and removed the office-in-home deduction. (I kept a printed copy of those pages in case I needed them again.)

Good thing I did! When I prepared the seventh year, she had a profit of $50,000. Suddenly, all those years with losses became very attractive. Putting the office-in-home deduction back in and carrying it forward each year wiped out most of Erica's $50,000 profit, including her self-employment taxes, saving her thousands of dollars in taxes. In the end, Erica only owed a few hundred dollars for all seven years. (I love it when I can see the future like this, don't you?)

When I first removed the Form 8829, it was because she already had such high losses that it was clear her net operating losses (NOLs) would wipe out income for years to come. The trouble with NOLs is that they don't wipe out self-employment taxes. The self-employment tax is 15.3 percent of your business's current-year profit. Some people don't mind paying that money because it goes into their own Social Security and Medicare coverage. Others are so broke or operating on such a tight budget that they can't look toward the future—only to keeping the lights on. The problem with this shortsighted view is, when you are ready to retire but you haven't built up investments or savings, your Social Security benefits will be $300 or less. What will you live on? (I've listened to many people in frightening situations like this who wish they had done things differently earlier.) So, please, try to plan and budget to build up savings and Social Security benefits.

Working on this series of tax returns for Erica helped remind me that NOLs only have a limited use. It was also a defining moment for me. Preparing Erica's tax returns was how I came to understand that the office-in-home carryforwards are one of the few deductions that *will* reduce self-employment tax.

All the reading and education in the world doesn't help. You've got to be hands-on to understand the tax system.

A Final Note—and a Final Story

Working at home can be really grand. You are free to indulge yourself when you simply need a break. You can spend time with friends, children, and lovers. Or you can be interrupted constantly. How you separate work space and time from personal space and time is strictly up to you. But you will reduce your stress levels if you establish specific boundaries for your family, friends, and clients—and stick with them. When you work at home, people tend to treat you as if you're not really working. Or they will call you to service them at all hours of the day or night.

Personally, I set time boundaries. TaxMama's telephone hours are Monday through Thursday from 8 a.m. to noon. Outside of those hours, even if I am here, I will rarely ever pick up the phone. That is my time to write, teach, or get other work done, without interruptions—or to give myself some *me* time. We all need time that we control. So remember, budget time for your own relaxation. Whether it's five minutes of meditation each hour or a half-hour nap each afternoon or a once-a-week bubble bath, you need time to recharge yourself. Or you will collapse.

Alex's Productivity Hat

Alex Mandossian is best known for his TeleSeminar Secrets course, which is, naturally, a course conducted as a teleseminar. Mandossian works from home, surrounded by a young, bright, inquisitive, and active family. How does he get anything done with small children around? He turns it into a game. When Alex is wearing his Productivity Hat, he can work unmolested. Alex can even wander into the kitchen to pick up a sandwich or go out to the yard. His children might come running to him, but then they stop. They see Daddy's Productivity Hat, put their fingers over their lips, and tell themselves to shhh . . . Daddy's working. Try your own version of a Productivity Hat or scarf or sock or sash, . . . or whatever turns you on. It really works.

Resources

In this chapter, you saw a variety of resources. Here's a summary of them, so you can find them quickly and easily. The resources are not necessarily in alphabetical order in each category. They are in order of their importance or usefulness, in TaxMama's opinion.

You can get some help and support with the issues you're facing from an assortment of online resources. Many have articles and tools to help. Some also have forums where you'll find it a relief to talk to other people dealing with the same issues as you. The good news is, the SECURE Act didn't do anything to change your office in-home deductions.

IRS Forms

- **Form 8829, Expenses for Business Use of Your Home.** https://www.irs.gov/pub/irs-pdf/f8829.pdf
- **IRS Publication 587,** *Business Use of Your Home.* https://www.irs.gov/publications/p587/index.html

Books

- *The Home Daycare Complete Recordkeeping System* by Brigitte A. Thompson. http://iTaxMama.com/DayCare1. The SimplyDayCare.com website offers free guidance, forms and worksheets you can use in your day care business.
- *Family Child Care Record-Keeping Guide*, by Tom Copeland, JD, ninth edition (Redleaf Business Series). http://iTaxMama.com/DayCare2. Lots of information on how to run a daycare business.

Online Support for Home-Based Businesses

- **Work at Home Moms** by Cheryl Demas. http://www.wahm.com. Resources, tools, message boards, a way to find local moms. There's also a forum for work-at-home dads at http://stayathomedads.about.com.
- **WomanOwned.com** by Christina Blenk. http://www.womanowned.com. Articles, resources, forum, networking.
- **Alex Mandossian's TeleSeminar Secrets.** http://iTaxMama.com/Mandossian. Eye-opening information about how to run your business

from home, with sensible and practical ways to turn your own education and expertise into a variety of online or tangible products.

TaxMama Resources

- **TaxMama's Quick Look-Ups.** http://iTaxMama.com/TM_QuickLookUp. You will find all kinds of useful reference materials, webinars you can replay, e-books, and more.
- **Your Business Bible.** http://www.yourbusinessbible.com. Look for worksheets, printable checklists, and other goodies and resources.

CHAPTER 8: **VEHICLES: EVERYONE'S FAVORITE DEDUCTION**

To-Do List and Questionnaire

☐ 1. List all the vehicles you use for business:

Primary business vehicle—license and make: _____

Part-time business vehicle—license and make: _____

☐ 2. What is the odometer reading today on each vehicle?

Primary business vehicle: _____

Part-time business vehicle: _____

☐ 3. Find the earliest repair or service receipt this year.

What is the odometer reading on that receipt? _____

Follow instructions in this chapter to reconstruct year-to-date mileage.

☐ 4. What are you using to keep a mileage log?
_____ Spreadsheet software
_____ Appointment book
_____ Mileage app

☐ 5. How much have you already depreciated your vehicle?
• Actual depreciation on Form 4562: _____
• Depreciation component of mileage: _____

☐ 6. In whose name is the title to each vehicle?
• List for each vehicle.
• Does title need to be changed?
• Make a copy of the "pink slips" and keep them with this checklist.

Remember to put a copy of each document behind this page, folded in half.

8

VEHICLES: EVERYONE'S FAVORITE DEDUCTION

Leasing means never having to say you're debt-free.

—Eva Rosenberg

Autos, trucks, vans, minivans, trailers, SUVs—whatever you're using—it's probably one of your most costly assets. It's also your best source of business deductions since you've got to have a set of wheels for personal use.

Vehicles are essential to your life and your business. Practically everyone has at least one car at home these days. You may have several, depending on your family size, hobbies, interests, and business requirements.

When it comes to using cars for business, select just one of those vehicles as the business vehicle. When more than one family member is involved in the business, assign one business vehicle to each person as a business vehicle, or have several family members or staff use one vehicle. Try not to keep switching around. Consistency of use makes it simpler to track business mileage. If you must use more than one vehicle, keep logs in each car to track total mileage and business mileage. Being able to track the actual miles may be more important for a "fleet" than for a single car.

When your business requires the use of a single-purpose truck or van, such as an outfitted plumbing truck or delivery van, you shouldn't have problems establishing that you used it 100 percent for business. That vehicle is not fit for personal use. Take a photo of the vehicle full of your usual equipment or inventory and put it in your tax file. Do this every year.

Clearly, certain vehicles are used 100 percent for business by their very nature. But for regular vehicles, don't expect the IRS to allow you 100 percent business use. The IRS realizes that even if you have several cars, sometimes you're going to use your business car to shop for groceries, pick up your children, or run some personal errands. The IRS expects that you will record a reasonable amount of personal use.

Some of my clients have a separate business vehicle, or they work from home and practically all of their driving is business. For them, it's easier to track the personal miles than the business miles. While they may not drive many miles during the year, the larger percentage of the miles they do drive will be business.

Deducting Auto Expenses for Employees

As you learned in Chapter 6, employees no longer get to deduct any of their out-of-pocket expenses. So the only way to get any kind of tax benefit for those costs is for the employer to pay the expenses, or to reimburse the employee, or to provide a vehicle cost allowance.

Naturally, if the boss pays all the expenses directly, the business gets the full deduction. The business also gets the full deduction if it reimburses the employee. The employee must submit detailed expense reports showing the mileage, with receipts for out-of-pocket expenses (parking, valet, tolls, etc.)—or notes about cash-paid expenses. The third option—the vehicle allowance—has two ways for the employer and employee to handle this:

1. Flat fee monthly allowance to the employee *with no* proof of expenses
   a. The employer gets the full deduction.
   b. The employee gets this added to his or her wages, in full, subject to all employment taxes (not a great alternative for the employee). It will be included in the W-2.
2. Flat fee monthly allowance to the employee *with* proof of expenses
   a. The employer gets the full deduction.
   b. Nothing is added to the employee's wages,
      i. unless the expenses that are submitted are less than the allowance;
      ii. in that case, the difference can either be returned to the employer or added to the employee's wages.

In some cases, the employer may provide a company-owned vehicle for the employee's use. (Remember, when you have a C corporation or S corporation, you are an employee.) If there is no personal use at all, the employer gets a full deduction for the vehicle; the employee has no taxable income. But if personal use is permitted, then you will need to add the personal-use value to the employee's paycheck and W-2. You can do this by either adding a percentage of the vehicle allowance to wages each month (say, 10 percent personal use) or by tracking the personal mileage and using this table, http://www.smbiz.com/sbrl003.html#cmv.

Deducting Auto Expenses for Business Owners

Table 8.1 shows you three ways to report auto expenses—the mileage method, actual expenses for owned vehicles, and actual expenses for leased vehicles. Actual expense rules are different for owned and leased vehicles. Please note that the mileage method isn't nearly as easy as you may have thought. You have four different rates, depending on how you use your car. (We'll show you rates in a moment in Table 8.2.) In addition, there's also a depreciation component built into each mile.

TABLE 8.1 How to Deduct Auto Expenses and Mileage Rates

Mileage Method	Actual Expenses for Leased Vehicles	Actual Expenses for Purchased Vehicles
• _____ cents per mile	• Lease payments	• Interest on auto loan
• Parking/valet	• Parking/valet	• Parking/valet
• Tolls	• Tolls	• Tolls
• Garage rent	• Gasoline	• Gasoline
	• Repairs and maintenance	• Repairs and maintenance
	• Parts, washes	• Parts, washes
	• Insurance	• Insurance
	• License and registration	• License and registration
	• Parking/valet	• Parking/valet
	• Garage rent	• Garage rent
	Minus	• Depreciation
	The lease inclusion amount	

Actual expenses used to be simpler before depreciation got so complicated. Now you have such a varied menu of depreciation options that it does take a computer to find the best treatment.

Regardless of which method you use to write off your auto expenses, you will need to know two mileage numbers for each car you use—total miles and business miles. The second page of Form 4562 still asks for the mileage breakdown. To make this as correct as possible, on January 1 of each year, write down your vehicle's odometer reading on your calendar. If you didn't record your odometer reading in January, that's OK. You can do it right now.

For those people who didn't make any notes during the year about your total miles, you can reconstruct the total miles. Find a repair or service or smog test invoice from early in the year and one from later in the year. Find the box showing the mileage when you brought the vehicle in for service. Deduct the miles shown on the earlier invoice from the miles on the later invoice (e.g., the February 16 invoice shows 14,500 miles and the June 8 invoice shows 19,600 miles). Divide the difference by the number of days in between invoices (in our example, 5,100 miles ÷ 112 days = 45.54 miles driven per day). Multiply the result by 30 to get the number of miles per month (returning to our example, 45.54 miles × 30 days = 1,366 miles per month). Then multiply by 12 to get the total miles for the year (1,366 miles × 12 months = 16,392 miles driven this year).

If you tracked the business miles, you'll easily be able to figure out your business use of your vehicle. If you only tracked your personal miles, deduct the personal miles from the total miles you drove to get your business miles (continuing our example, 16,392 total miles − 2,634 personal miles = 13,758 business miles). Divide your business use by the total miles to arrive at the percentage of actual expenses you're entitled to deduct (13,758 business miles ÷ 16,392 total miles = 83.9 percent business use of the vehicle).

Using the Standard Mileage Rate

Once you have the total miles and the business miles, enter them on the second page of Form 4562. If you're using the mileage rate, multiply the current year's rate by the total business miles (for 2019 using our example, 13,758 × 58 cents = $7,980), and pop it onto the "Car and Truck expenses" line of your personal tax return's Schedule C or onto a schedule on your business return. Steve Hopfenmuller, CPA, at the Small Business Taxes and Management website, maintains a list of mileage rates, generally for the past six years to the present. You'll find the link in this chapter's Resources. Visit that site if you need the most current rates. Or log in to TaxMama.com's Quick Look-Ups resource.

You can see the mileage rates for the most recent five years in Table 8.2. Built into the standard mileage is a certain amount of depreciation per mile. Don't worry about the number until you sell the car. Then add up the miles you've deducted each year and multiply the sum by the depreciation rate for each year. Often, though, if you've used the vehicle extensively for business, the depreciation amount will add up to more than the vehicle's basis. You can find the annual depreciation component at http://www.smbiz.com/sbrl003.html#dsm. Don't worry if your mileage depreciation is higher than your car's purchase price. You don't need to use a negative basis. Just take the basis to zero, and you'll be fine.

TABLE 8.2 Standard Mileage Rates

Cents per Mile	2020	2019	2018	2017	2016
Business	57.5	58	54.5	53.5	54
Charitable	14	14	14	14	14
Medical	17	20	18	17	19
Moving	17	20	18	17	19
Depreciation	27	26	25	24	24

Just a little note that no one seems to tell you—if you take advantage of any of the depreciation methods in the year you put the car into service, you may not use the mileage method to deduct your car expenses for the life of the vehicle. That includes the special (bonus) depreciation, Section 179, and regular depreciation. Your only option is to use the actual expenses for the life of the vehicle—and that means you must keep excellent records of all your operating costs.

When using actual expenses, follow the guide in Table 8.1 to see what you can deduct for owned and leased vehicles. We'll examine the special vehicle depreciation rules later in this chapter.

Should I Lease or Buy?

Car ads make automobile leases sound awfully tempting. Before getting seduced by the thought of driving a sleek Lexus for a low monthly payment, know that there are big-dollar tax ramifications lurking behind the small-dollar dealer hype.

The most frequent call I get is from business clients trying to decide whether to buy or lease a car. Being a number cruncher, I computed several test scenarios, concluding that there are too many variables to generate general answers. Instead, let's highlight the questions you need to ask yourself when facing this decision.

Thoughts to Ponder

All of these issues will affect your long- and short-term operating costs and tax benefits:

- Do you plan to drive more than 12,000 miles per year?
- How many miles do you drive for business?
- How many commuting miles do you drive? (Commuting is not deductible.)
- What percentage of the total use of that vehicle will be for business?
- Do you have a second car for personal use?
- How long do you normally keep your vehicles?
- Do you mind having payments for the rest of your life?
- How frequently do you service your vehicles?
- How much money can you afford to put down on a vehicle?
- If you lease, how much of a "deposit" does the leasing company require?
- How good are you at keeping detailed records?

Aside from my being nosy, how do my clients' responses affect my recommendation? Let's examine each topic more carefully.

Driving Issues

Most leases penalize you for driving more than 12,000 miles per year. Consider the additional costs for the excess mileage. This is usually prohibitive. Some people, though, don't mind.

If you live in your car, getting your wheels serviced can be a problem. Look for a lease or purchase that includes free loaner cars. I discovered that whether buying or leasing an Infiniti from the dealer (even a used one), free loaner cars during scheduled service are included as a matter of company policy. For me, that's one of the most valuable accessories any car can offer. To be competitive, other car companies or dealers may offer the same deal if pressed—so ask. It never hurts to negotiate. Have you ever noticed that if you don't ask for something, you're not apt to get it? But if you do ask, the worst they can do is say no.

Presently leases are advertised at very low, very tempting prices. But when you can buy a car with 0.0 percent interest and no down payment, buying may be better. Look closely at your options and compare them carefully.

To negotiate the best price, whether you lease or buy, you must be an informed shopper. Remember, lease payments include a built-in interest rate that is usually higher than the interest rate for buying a car. Besides, you can often get good vehicle loan rates from your own bank or credit union. Make the arrangements before car shopping. You will find detailed instructions on how to buy a used car in an article on Edmunds.com by senior consumer advice editor Philip Reed and automotive editor John DiPietro (http://iTaxMama.com/Edmunds_Used). In another article, Ronald Montoya, senior consumer advice editor, provides eight steps to buying a new car (http://iTaxMama.com/Edmunds_New).

The lease down payment is often almost as much as (or sometimes more than) the down payment to buy the car. That makes the total cost over the life of the lease less attractive—especially since you must turn your vehicles over every two to three years under most lease agreements. That's a lot of "down payment" money for something you'll never own!

Tax Issues

When deducting the lease expenses on your tax return, even if you use the car 100 percent for business, there is a mandatory "lease inclusion cost," described later in this chapter.

Whether you lease or buy, you still must maintain mileage logs to track what percentage of the actual expenses to deduct. The best way to keep track of mileage is to keep a daily log in your car. Most people find that too onerous. I've found it's a good habit to record your mileage in your appointment book when you get into your car. Just put it at the top of the page or in your smartphone calendar for that date. Even more convenient is a mileage app, like MileIQ, or your favorite app. Use the record-keeping tips you learned in Chapter 4 to track all your time and expenses. Or keep a monthly envelope handy. Not only can you record your mileage, but you can also toss in receipts and make notes about cash payments (such as valets tips, parking meters, etc.).

You computed your business use percentage earlier in this chapter. In our example, it was 83.9 percent. Multiply your total expenses by that business percentage. Assuming you spent $5,400 on the lease, $250 for registration and license fees, $1,200 for insurance, $600 on gasoline, and $600 on car washes and routine service, the total expenses equal $8,050. Your lease inclusion cost was $120. Subtract that. Then net expenses are $7,930. Multiply that by 83.9 percent. Your total deductible auto expenses are $6,653, plus parking and tolls.

The only expense that doesn't get hit by the percentage is parking. After all, you're only including your business parking receipts.

TaxMama's First Rule of Thumb

If you drive very few miles each year (10,000 or less) and more than 80 percent of that mileage is directly business related, I recommend that you *buy the vehicle*, deducting the actual expenses.

Why? The numbers say it all.

The lease deduction based on a $450-per-month lease would be *more than $6,600*:

+ $1,200 insurance
+ $350 license
+ $800 fuel
+ $500 repairs and maintenance
+ $60 washes
× 80 percent business use
− $18 lease inclusion on a $25,000 car
= $2,310 + $4,320 (lease $450 × 12 × 80 percent) = $6,630

After taking the tax benefit into account, how much cash have you spent for the year? Let's see:

$450 × 12 = $5,400 (lease) + $2,910 (operating costs) = $8,310

$8,310 cash spent − $2,400 tax benefit (24 percent IRS and 5 percent state) = $5,910 spent for the year

Using the actual cost method, the total first-year cost for a similar car that you have purchased would only be around $4,900, plus your down payment of $5,000:

$0 interest on a $25,000 loan (dealers offer 0 percent rates all the time)
+ $1,200 insurance
+ $350 license
+ $800 fuel
+ $500 repair and maintenance
+ $60 washes
+ $10,000 depreciation (approximately—first year only, without bonus depreciation)
Add up the numbers—they equal $12,910
× 80 percent business use = $10,328

After taking the tax benefit into account, how much cash have you spent for the year? Let's see:

$5,000 (loan payments) + $2,910 (operating costs) = $7,910

$7,910 cash spent − $2,995 tax benefit (24 percent IRS and 5 percent state) = $4,915 spent for the year

Over five years, that adds up to a net after-tax expense of $24,575 plus the $5,000 down payment. That's a total cost of just under $30,000.

At the end of five years, you will have spent around $33,000 for the leased car (including the down payment), after taxes. At the end of five years, you will have spent around $30,000 for the owned vehicle. Owning the vehicle costs less over a five-year period—even with a heft down payment.

At the end of five years, you still have annual lease payments of $5,400 or something similar for the replacement leased car. When you own the car, at the end of five years, your annual payments are—*zero! (Or maybe you have just one more year of payments.)*

Oh sure, you might have some repairs. But if you paid for an extended warranty on your car, you may not have to pay for anything but oil changes, tires, and brakes for the first 7 to 10 years. That means at least two years without a car payment or significant repair bills.

My Second Rule of Thumb

If you drive 20,000 miles per year for business, I usually recommend that you *buy*.

Why?

The deduction based on buying the car and using the actual expense method would be *nearly $6,200.*

Because you need to pay the cost for excess mileage, which is generally charged at $0.15 × miles over 12,000 = 8,000 × $0.15 = $1,200.

Your tax savings are about $650 higher if you own the vehicle. And if you take good care of it, it can look and run like new for about a decade. (Just be sure to get the extended warranty.)

Hmmm—I think you are coming to the conclusion that leasing is not the best tax alternative for moderately priced vehicles. You're right! Frankly, I just can't figure out why people would lease a car and saddle themselves with payments forever.

The only time you really get a tax advantage from leasing is when you lease a hyper-expensive motorcar. Assuming monthly lease fees of $750 or more, plug your costs into the examples earlier.

Since the depreciation deduction is limited, the tax benefits are far higher when you lease a BMW, Eldorado, Mercedes Benz, or other high-ticket car. Although, with the new special depreciation rules (Chapter 6), you could conceivably write off the entire purchase price in the first year—then have no depreciation deductions at all in future years.

On the other hand, wouldn't it be nice to have three to five years without a car payment? Buy it!

Lease Inclusion Cost—It Reduces Your Expenses

When you lease a vehicle, unless it is a commercial vehicle like a Mack truck, the IRS knows you will have some personal use. There is no 100 percent business use for leased personal vehicles. The IRS has established a formula to use, which reduces your allowable lease expenses, based on the value of the car. The agency publishes new tables each year. In fact, it has now added tables for trucks, due to the new rates. You can look them up in IRS Publications 463 and 946 or at the IRS website. Or you can do it more quickly and easily by using the online tables provided by the folks at Small Business Taxes and Management (http://www.smbiz.com/sbrl003.html). That site typically has lease inclusion tables for the past six years.

The Cons of Depreciation

Chapter 6 outlined how depreciation works. Now that you understand the principle, let me tell you how it's different for vehicles.

First of all, be aware that the rules for autos change slightly almost every year. Next, be aware that this aspect of taxes is a political football and gets changed dramatically whenever Congress feels like it.

It's a really confusing area of tax law. It's not enough to know the numbers. You need to know when to use which numbers. Please have a tax professional set up depreciation for your vehicle(s)—at least for the year of purchase. You may also want to have your tax pro review the depreciation again in the fourth year when the limit drops to $5,760 to see what your options are at that point.

Special depreciation is a political football. Some years it's there; some years it's not. It often becomes available for residents of disaster areas. In the past, when bonus depreciation was available, we were only allowed to use it on the purchase of new vehicles. The Tax Cuts and Jobs Act (TCJA) redefined special depreciation to include new or used assets. You may only use special depreciation (if it is available in a current year) and Section 179 depreciation if your business use of the vehicle is more than 50 percent.

The good news is, the SECURE Act didn't do anything to change these rules.

Once you've used up as much of the special depreciation and Section 179 as you can, it's time to take regular depreciation on your vehicle. Unless you have fully depreciated the asset. *Note:* Under the new rules, if you are not using 100 percent special depreciation, you must make an election on your tax return to opt out of the 100 percent rules.

When it comes to cars, you can forget everything you learned in Chapter 6 about depreciation methods. For vehicles, there are luxury auto limits, which brings us to special limits on how much depreciation you may use each year.

Luxury Auto Limits

Congress has finally acknowledged that "luxury vehicles" cost more than $15,000. The TCJA changed the vehicle depreciation schedule to allow the taxpayer to write off about $47,000 ($55,000 if using special depreciation) within the first five years, instead of the previous $15,000 ($23,000 if using special depreciation). So, for now, depreciation numbers actually make sense.

Most cars you use for business will be subject to the luxury auto deduction limits—unless they weigh more than 6,000 pounds gross. That means, regardless of what your total depreciation should be for the vehicle, you may deduct no more than the amounts shown in Chapter 5 of IRS Publication 946. The good news is, with the TCJA depreciation increases, you might actually be able to write off the cost of your car in five years.

There are different rates for autos, trucks, and electric vehicles, so be sure to look up the rates for your type of vehicle. The rules were originally written to penalize owners of high-cost vehicles such as Mercedes, Jaguars, or Rolls-Royces. Back then, in 1984, an average person could actually buy a fully loaded car for about $5,000. Not anymore!

The SUV Craze

Despite the push to cut back on emissions and to discourage gas-guzzlers, there is a little loophole in the depreciation rules that rewards you for buying a gas hog. Intended to exempt trucks and commercial vehicles from the luxury auto rules, this loophole has been snapped up by clever planners to subsidize the cost of expensive cars.

Buying vehicles weighing more than 6,000 pounds provides dramatically better tax benefits. They are not subject to the luxury vehicle rules. You may be able to deduct as much as $25,500 for 2019 plus regular depreciation costs in one year, using the Section 179 depreciation. Or you can use the 100 percent special depreciation to write off the entire cost of the vehicle in the first year, as we mentioned earlier. (See Chapter 6 for more information about depreciation.)

Give Yourself Credit

When considering buying a vehicle, there is one more tax benefit to explore: tax credits for "green" vehicles—electric and hybrid cars. Form 8834 allows you a variety of credits for golf cart–type vehicles, hybrid cars, and a variety of other engines that use little or no gasoline. The laws change regularly. And the credits need to be renewed by Congress, practically each year. The credits phase out as the manufacturers' sales hit certain limits. For electric vehicles, here are two IRS pages to use as a reference for the most recent information about credits:

- http://iTaxMama.com/Plug-In_Vehicle
- http://iTaxMama.com/IRS_PlugIn

Be sure to explore the IRS website before buying an alternative fuel cell vehicle if you are counting on a credit. As it happens, the credit for fuel cell vehicles expired at the end of 2017. The SECURE Act extended this credit to 2020, retroactive to 2018. (http://iTaxMama.com/IRS_FuelCell). Under no circumstances should you believe what a salesperson tells you without looking it up yourself. The credit might have expired or phased out just when you are ready to buy. Isn't that always the case? Sigh.

Driving Home Conclusions

Remember, if you sell the car or stop using it for business within five years, you will have to pay back some of that depreciation. So don't get too greedy.

If you're going for the moneybags image—such as a Mercedes or Rolls-Royce—lease the car.

If you want a good value, give yourself a break from payments and buy the vehicle! At least you'll have something to sell when the payments stop. Or better yet, breathe easy for a couple of years with no payments at all. (I kept my Infiniti for more than 20 years—no payments for at least 15 years.) What a concept!

Does all this confuse you? Me, too. Please, as I said earlier, don't try to figure this out alone. There are so many nuances to vehicles and depreciation. This is one of the easiest parts of your tax return to get wrong. To make the vehicle deductions on your business tax return work out correctly, here's what you need to do.

Give your tax professional a good summary of each of your auto expenses. Provide the total mileage and business mileage for the year. Provide a copy of the purchase or lease contracts if you got a new car during the year. Be sure to provide copies of the sales documents if you sold the car.

With that information in hand, a good tax pro can get you the maximum deductions with the lowest audit risk.

Resources

In this chapter, you saw a variety of resources. Here's a summary of them, so you can find them quickly and easily. The resources are not necessarily in alphabetical order in each category. They are in order of their importance or usefulness, in TaxMama's opinion.

- **Bankrate.com. Lease-versus-buy calculator.**
  http://iTaxMama.com/Bankrate_Lease_Buy
- **"How to Get a Used Car Bargain," Edmunds.com.**
  http://iTaxMama.com/Edmunds_Used
- **"Eight Steps to Buying a New Car," Edmunds.com.**
  http://iTaxMama.com/Edmunds_New

Mileage Tracking Resources

- **MileIQ.** https://www.mileiq.com/howitworks. This app works with Android or iPhones. It has lots of practical features. Turn on the location function and it can track your driving.
- **Other Mileage Apps.** Do a Google search on "best mileage apps."
- **Standard Mileage Rates.** http://www.smbiz.com/sbrl003.html#smr. For the current year and several prior years.
- **Cents per Mile Valuation for Use of Company Vehicle.** http://www.smbiz.com/sbrl003.html#cmv. The amount added to an employee's wages when employees are given a company car for their personal and business use.
- **Amount of Depreciation Included in Each Year's Standard Mileage Rates.** http://www.smbiz.com/sbrl003.html#dsm

- **All Other Vehicle Rates.** http://www.smbiz.com/sbrl003.html. Depreciation and lease inclusions.
- **IRS Publication 463, *Travel, Entertainment, Gift, and Car Expenses.*** http://iTaxMama.com/Pub463_Vehicles
- **IRS Publication 946, *How to Depreciate Property.*** http://iTaxMama.com/Pub946_Deprec
- **Form 4562, Depreciation.** http://iTaxMama.com/Form4652
- **Form 1040, Schedule C.** http://www.irs.gov/pub/irs-pdf/f1040sc.pdf
- **Form 8834, Qualified Plug-in Electric and Electric Vehicle Credit.** http://iTaxMama.com/Form8834
- **IRS Plug in Vehicle Information.** http://iTaxMama.com/IRS_PlugIn
- **IRS Qualified Fuel Cell Motor Vehicle Credit.** http://iTaxMama.com/IRS_FuelCell

TaxMama Resources

- **TaxMama's Quick Look-Ups.** http://iTaxMama.com/TM_QuickLookUp. You will find all kinds of useful reference materials, webinars you can replay, e-books, and more.
- **Your Business Bible.** http://www.yourbusinessbible.com. Look for worksheets, printable checklists, and other goodies and resources.

CHAPTER 9: **EMPLOYEES AND INDEPENDENT CONTRACTORS**

To-Do List and Questionnaire

☐ 1. Review your staff:
- Does anyone work at your office who is not on payroll?
- Does anyone work outside your office who is not on payroll?
- If any of them should be employees, set them up on payroll ASAP.

☐ 2. Have you been issuing nonemployees 1099-MISCs? _____ Yes _____ No

☐ 3. Get a Form W-9 from each nonemployee worker—*now*. Date: _____

☐ 4. Get all documents on the Independent Contractor Checklist—*now*.
Date: _____

☐ 5. Get your employer ID # from the IRS. EIN: _____
Date: _____

☐ 6. Get your employer ID # from the state. EIN: _____
Date: _____

☐ 7. Have each employee fill out a Form W-4 and a Form I-9.
- Get copies of the identity documents required by Form I-9.

☐ 8. Have you hired members of your family?
- Be sure they fill out time cards or keep accurate records of the basis of their compensation (time vs. commission).

☐ 9. What employee benefits do you offer? _____
_____ _____ _____

☐ 10. Meet with your tax pro and insurance broker to see what your tax savings would be for employee benefits. Date: _____

☐ 11. Meet with your staff to discuss which benefits they can use.
Date: _____
Consider restructuring compensation to provide tax-free benefits for things they are already spending money on—or need:
☐ Health care   ☐ Childcare   ☐ Education   ☐ Retirement

Remember to put a copy of each document behind this page, folded in half.

9

EMPLOYEES AND INDEPENDENT CONTRACTORS

It's always easier to do it yourself. You do a much better job.

—TaxMama's Mother (or Yours?)

Just a quick note: This chapter, by its very nature, is totally full of links and references. To make the information flow more smoothly, especially for electronic and audio editions, I have moved most of the links to the Resources area of this chapter. That way, whatever you need is all in one place.

Back to our topic!

On your last job, you came to realize you did all the work but got paid only a fraction of what you're worth. You quit and ranged out on your own. Now, with your own business, you get to keep all the money. You're better off, it's true; only now you have to do all the work yourself.

You may decide that you need help; if so, it's time to hire your own staff. Excellent idea—many companies can grow to great heights with the right employees, and there are tax benefits to hiring employees. This chapter covers the primary things you need to know about categorizing employees, hiring family members, setting up payrolls, paying employee taxes, and much more.

Who Is an Employee?

Often, new small business owners are apt to think of people who work for them as temporaries or as freelancers. You may feel that since you haven't had employees until now, you don't want to go through the hassle of setting up a formal payroll until you absolutely must.

You've got my sympathy—but not the IRS's.

Knowing the legal difference between an official employee and an independent contractor can be challenging. This is even more challenging since states have started to pass laws that define "employee" differently than the IRS does—often, more stringently. The following examples show just a small sampling of the wide range of possible employment situations:

- Nancy comes to Jackie's home to open mail, do filing, and pay bills. Nancy picks up a big stack of files and works on them at her own home. Is Nancy an employee?
- Joe hires Dan as his webmaster and site developer. Joe is gearing up for a big marketing push, making it clear that Dan must devote all his time to the project. Dan agrees to work for Joe exclusively for 2019. Dan works from his home in another state. Is Dan an employee?
- Perry is self-employed as a journalist. During the school yearbook season, Perry works for PhotoKiddie, snapping shots of schoolchildren for the yearbooks the company creates. Perry uses PhotoKiddie's film, contracts, and forms and also collects all the payments, which are made out to Photo-Kiddie. Is Perry an employee of PhotoKiddie?
- You do work for your own corporation, but you also have a full-time job. You're only working on your own corporate matters 10 hours a week. Are you an employee of your own corporation?

All right, which of these people are considered legal employees, and how can you tell?

In actuality, the descriptions of those activities don't provide enough information to make a decision. To determine if someone counts as an employee, you must ask more questions about each person you pay. As the positions are described, it could go either way. With more information, however, there is an answer.

The IRS used to use 20 common-law factors to determine a person's employment status, and the factors don't all carry the same weight. (IRS has refined those factors a bit. But the basic concepts have not changed.) Without having experience facing employment audits, you won't know which factors matter. To make things more challenging, your state might have its own factors that don't match up to the IRS's. A tax professional whose practice specializes in small businesses and freelance work can evaluate the relative importance of each of the following factors for your business and industry.

The Original 20 Common-Law Factors the IRS Uses to Define Independent Contractors

1. Instructions are generally not given by the company that hires you.
2. Training is not essential and is not given by the company.
3. Your personal services are not required; you can assign the work to anyone.
4. The work you are performing is not essential to the company.
5. You set your own hours.
6. You have no continuing relationship with the company.
7. You control and hire your own assistants.
8. You are free to pursue other work.
9. Where you work is your choice.
10. You set your own work priorities.
11. No interim reports are required of you.
12. You work for more than one firm.
13. You pay your own business expenses.
14. You use your own tools and equipment.
15. You bear a risk of loss.
16. Your services are available to the general public (or industry).
17. You have a significant capital investment.
18. Right of discharge is limited by contract.
19. You are not compensated for incomplete work.
20. Timing of payment coincides with completion of the job, rather than in regular intervals.

Consider those 20 factors whenever you need to decide if someone you hire should be on payroll or not.

Or take a shortcut and look at the IRS's three "Common Law Rules":

1. Behavioral: Does the company control or have the right to control what the worker does and how the worker does his or her job?

2. Financial: Are the business aspects of the worker's job controlled by the payer (these include things like how worker is paid, whether expenses are reimbursed, who provides tools/supplies, etc.)?

3. Type of Relationship: Are there written contracts or employee type benefits (i.e., pension plan, insurance, vacation pay, etc.)? Will the relationship continue and is the work performed a key aspect of the business?

Do They Act Like a Business?

If you're unsure how the IRS definition of *contractors* applies to your situation, consider this when looking at someone you want to treat as an independent contractor—people in business must look and act like a business. They must have all the licenses and certifications standard for their profession and their city, county, state, province, or other government division. They don't need to have a business name, but if your contractor uses Susan Johnson Consulting instead of plain old Susan Johnson, she'd have to get a fictitious name filing, otherwise known as "doing business as" or a DBA.

People you consider freelancers who are working for you, on your premises, using your equipment, and following your instructions are typically employees. Did you give them a key? Or access to one, to get in when you're away? That sounds like an employee relationship. If they feel like taking off, going down to the beach for the day, and sending a colleague to do the work, may they? If not and you require that only the person you hired do the work, on your schedule—you have an employer-employee relationship. Essentially, it means that you control the person's work, hours, and staffing decisions. If people were in business for themselves, you couldn't do that, could you?

Now, if your new hire does fit the definition of an *independent contractor*, what should you do to prove it to the IRS just in case the agency ever asks?

Protecting Yourself from Independent Contractor Claims

Whenever the IRS audits a business return that shows independent contractors, the first thing it checks is whether the 1099-MISCs are filed. (You'll learn about them later in this chapter.) The second thing the examiner looks at is the worker's job duties. If the IRS decides you have an employee, not an independent contractor, it will create a payroll and assess you for payroll taxes you should have paid, plus penalties and interest.

To legitimize your claim of the independent relationship, use a checklist when hiring new vendors who provide rent or services of any kind (see Table 9.1). Simply hand the list to all new hires, along with a copy of IRS Form W-9.

TABLE 9.1 Independent Contractor Hiring Checklist

Obtain These Original Documents from Independent Contractor
☐ Form W-9—Request for Taxpayer Identification Number—signed
☐ Business card
☐ Flyer, advertisement, brochure
☐ Contract or proposal—signed
Obtain a Copy of These Documents from Independent Contractor
☐ Current business license(s)
☐ Professional license number, if applicable
☐ Sales tax certificate or license, if applicable
☐ Link to their website and a printout of the home page or "about" page

Alert: If needy friends beg you to hire them without putting them on the payroll, be wary. The biggest cause of employer audits is a nonemployee who is let go (even voluntarily) or gets sick. Suddenly, people in this situation realize they can't collect unemployment or disability insurance, but they file anyway—and turn you in. Yes, this could even be your best friend—someone who was really in need and begged you to hire him or her under the table. Here is a horror story from one of my clients.

Bennie the Barber

Bennie the Barber had a modest shop in Santa Monica that supported his family. Carlos came to him, begging for work. Bennie really couldn't afford it, but Carlos kept calling and coming by, telling Bennie how desperate he was for work. Relenting, Bennie gave him the second chair and turned customers over to Carlos. Bennie cut his own income because Carlos didn't bring in a single customer of his own. Then Carlos started coming in late. Some days, he just didn't feel like coming in—no explanations and no notice. After two years of being treated rudely, Bennie finally got smart and let Carlos go.

What did Carlos do? You guessed it. He filed for disability. Carlos claimed he didn't know why he wasn't an employee. Carlos accused Bennie of cheating him. The state disability auditor was no dummy. But under the circumstances she had no choice. She audited Bennie. Digging deeply and looking at the whole situation, the auditor was sympathetic and limited her assessment for unpaid state of California payroll taxes to only one year. This consisted primarily of state disability costs and state unemployment costs. With penalties and interest, the bill was less than $1,000. It could have been double, without her sympathy. Once the state is done with their audit, the results go to the IRS. The IRS then issues assessments on the employer's share of FICA, Medicare, and federal unemployment taxes, plus penalties and interest. This added another $2,500 to Bennie's bill. All because he helped out a "friend."

TaxMama Tip

Insist that all independent contractors provide all the information on the checklist in Table 9.1 before issuing the *first* check. Make this a part of all contracts. It's easier to compel people to provide an address and identification number when they want their check than it is in the following January when you want to file 1099-MISCs—and they weren't expecting to get one.

Incidentally, this avoids hostility, anger, and even violence (yes, that has happened). In addition, since freelancers know they are going to pay taxes on this income, they can charge their fees accordingly.

If you encounter a situation similar to Bennie the Barber's case, there's a way to reduce the IRS assessments when it decides your independent contractor is really an employee. You can use a safe harbor, which we'll discuss in the next section.

Before moving on, though, there's one very important thing you need to remember about independent contractors. Don't call them employees when talking about them, describing them, or speaking to them. Especially, do not use the word *employee* during an audit. You'd be surprised how many people trip themselves up that way. It's important that you change the word you use to think of these people. Get your mind around a new word, depending on what they do. Some options are *consultant*, *expert*, *contractor*, or *advisor*.

Also, they are not your associates or your partners—that's a different relationship. How you think of the person will determine what you instinctively say. At least, if the terminology is common in your industry, the safe harbors covered next may help reduce the damages.

Safe Harbor Rules

Section 530 of the Revenue Act of 1978 provides a safe harbor with special leniency toward certain employers. Barbers and beauty salons are among those protected by Section 530.

Congress decreed that you have a reasonable basis for treating your staff as independent contractors if you can pass a test. You pass the test if you relied on:

- Judicial precedent, published rulings, technical advice, or letter ruling to the employer
- A past IRS audit in which no assessment was made on account of improper treatment of workers (even if the audit was not related to employee issues)
- A longstanding recognized practice of a significant segment of the industry in which the individual worked (The IRS used to require the practice to span more than 10 years, before 1979, or more than 50 percent of the industry. Current law requires no fixed amount of time and no more than 25 percent of the industry.)

Earlier, we posed some situations. The PhotoKiddie example would fit the safe harbor rules. Why? When an industry (photographers) treats its freelance workers as contractors, it can get the penalty reduction.

When the IRS decides you should have had an employee, the agency charges you for both halves of the Social Security and Medicare taxes that should have been withheld from the worker's wages. It may also charge you for a certain amount of the withholding. Then the IRS adds various penalties and finally tops off the whole thing with interest on the combined total. The final balance due may be hefty enough to shut down or bankrupt your business.

When facing an employment tax audit, be sure to ask your tax pro to invoke the Section 530 safe harbor rules, if they apply to your business. You'll be relieved of a substantial part of the Social Security taxes and IRS withholding you should have taken. Hopefully, you'll never need this rule.

What Are 1099-MISCs?

You're familiar with W-2s. Think of 1099-MISCs as the same thing—but for people who are not employees. Form 1099-MISC is also the IRS's way of catching tax cheaters. Before the program started in 1980, there was a huge under-the-table economy.

It's still large, but getting smaller as enforcement improves. Using 1099-MISCs, the IRS can ensure that freelancers report all their income. Knowing you'll be reporting their earnings to the IRS, freelancers have two choices:

1. They can refuse to work for you, which has happened. If someone refuses to provide the requisite information, you're better off knowing this when the project starts while you have time to find someone else. You don't want to find out that this person may not be ethical after giving him or her access to sensitive information or to your clients or customers.
2. They can do as everyone else does—earn the money and pay taxes on it.

OK, there's always a third option—where they collect the fees and don't file. When they do that, the IRS sends out notices to companies that filed 1099-MISCs, insisting that the companies withhold 24 percent of all checks to those individuals as backup withholding. You'll rarely face this issue. If it comes up for you, you'll find instructions and explanations in IRS Publication 1281, A Guide to Backup Withholding on Missing and Incorrect Name/TINs.

Some states realized that waiting until 1099s are filed and processed means the tax evader can stay on the job before being caught until July or August of the following year. To shorten the time, many states are coming up with solutions. California created Form 542, which companies must file with the state as soon as they pay anyone $600 or more. Since this is working for California, expect other states to request it, too. Since the state garnishes the wages of "deadbeat dads or moms," this is one way to help locate deadbeats when they keep switching jobs to avoid supporting their children.

Who Gets 1099s?

IRS instructions on the 1099 forms require you to send them out to people you've paid for services rendered in the course of your trade or business, as well as rents to unincorporated landlords. 1099s are issued to individuals and to limited liability corporations (LLCs) that report their businesses on their personal income tax returns or on partnership returns. Generally, corporations are exempt, with the exception of legal and medical practices operating as a corporation. When your business pays these types of corporations, you must issue 1099s to them.

Note: If you are paying people for nonbusiness services, you don't need to issue a 1099-MISC to them, unless you plan to (and are able to) take a deduction or credit on your personal income tax return for their work. Of course, if they work for you regularly as household employees (think of daily housekeeper, or the gardener living in the carriage house), then you need to put them on payroll and file a Schedule H. But that's a whole other issue.

When your own corporation pays you for your work, without putting you on payroll, the corporation should issue 1099s to you. However, the truth is—the corporation should really put you on payroll. Getting paid by your own corporation as a freelancer could generate an audit with costly results. And if you ask IRS audit managers about issuing 1099s to corporate officers, you will find them shaking their heads. Partnerships should not be putting their working partners on payroll, though some do. Partnerships should report your compensation as "Guaranteed Payments" on page 1 of the Form 1065 and also on line 4 of the partnership Schedule K-1.

TaxMama Tip

Here's a 1099 and W-2 secret. Hardly anyone knows this, but if you need extra time to file those 1099s or W-2s, you can get another 30 days using Form 8809. *Note:* The 1099 forms are now due on January 31 of each year.

Looking at the boxes on the 1099-MISC form, even without reading the Tax Code or the instructions, you can readily get an idea of who gets 1099s. Let's review only the boxes that are apt to affect your business.

- **Box 1: Rents.** This is for payments to your landlord. Also, use it for equipment leases from private parties. If you pay for storage and the company is a partnership, it gets one, too. If your business pays you rent, you get one.
- **Box 2: Royalties.** This applies if you have a graphic artist, you're licensing technology, you have a coauthor or ghostwriter, or you're a publisher. If you are licensing something to your entity, issue this to yourself.
- **Box 3: Other income.** Be generous with this. If you're paying someone for something that clearly is not self-employment, use this box instead of Box 7. Anytime you're not sure how to categorize payments to people and have no one to ask, use Box 3. For 2020, the IRS has completely eliminated a box for nonemployee compensation (NEC) on the Form 1099-MISC. Instead, the IRS has resurrected the Form 1099-NEC (Nonemployee Compensation) to report that kind of freelance income.
- **Box 4: Federal income tax withheld.** Some of your vendors may want withholding (rarely). Usually you will withhold taxes when the IRS garnishes their incomes. You may hear from the IRS if people give you a phony Social

Security number on the Form W-9 they give you or if they are in arrears on their tax payments. When you do hear from the IRS, it's bad news. You must withhold 24 percent from all monies you pay these folks—or pay it yourself. So don't be softhearted. Incidentally, having the company take withholding from their compensation is a convenient way for partners or LLC members to avoid making quarterly estimated tax payments (more on this in Chapter 11). When you do withhold, be sure to issue the 1099s early so recipients can file their tax returns on time.

- **Box 6: Medical and health care payments.** When individuals are not your employees—when they are independent contractors—if your company has paid their medical or health care, this is self-employment income to them. They will report this on their Schedule Cs.
- **Box 7 (2019): Nonemployee compensation.** All remuneration to anyone performing a service to your business gets reported here, including your tax pro, consultants, freelancers, web designers, outside services, virtual assistants, trainers, advertising agency, and public relations firm. Believe it or not, you also need to issue the Form 1099-MISC to landlords and for equipment rentals (see Box 1). *Attorney fees go into Box 14.*
- **Box 7 (2020): Payer made direct sales of $5,000 or more of consumer products to a buyer (recipient) for resale.** This is for network marketers and multilevel marketing (MLM) or direct selling participants. The company you represent will report the gross sales you've made. Remember, the IRS knows you also use the products. So when receiving a 1099 in this case, be sure to deduct your personal usage of the purchases and any returns.
- **Boxes 15 through 17: State income tax withheld and state/payer's state number.** When you have withheld money for state taxes, remember to fill this in. See the notes for Box 4 for instances where this might be necessary.

The other boxes won't affect the average small business. If they do, you need to have an accountant on staff to help you.

When Are 1099s Issued?

1099-MISC forms must be issued when paying $600 per year or more to anyone for services rendered or rents. The forms must be distributed to payees by January 31. Due to the PATH Act of 2015, we have tighter rules.

I recommend that you mail out all the forms as early as possible in January. Then hold off filing them until the last minute, giving you time to get the address corrections back from the post office or the payees. During this time, you'll probably hear from people if their earnings records are different from your records. This will give you the time to reconcile the amounts before you send in the final 1099s.

When you find errors, naturally, you may send in corrected 1099s, but those attract attention. Try to get it right the first time.

What If You Don't Issue 1099s at All?

Not issuing 1099s is a common oversight. And I have seen auditors disallow all non-employee compensation deductions when 1099s were not issued. One day, someone asked me where the IRS gets the authority to disallow these deductions. So I started researching the issue. The truth is, I couldn't find any law or IRS procedure that gives them this right. So I asked my contacts at the IRS. They couldn't find a citation either. So, here's a tip. If you're ever audited, and they try to disallow the deduction, ask them to give you a citation that allows them to do this. They won't be able to. What they do have the right to do is to issue a penalty of $50 for each 1099-MISC that wasn't issued.

Later in this chapter I will tell you about a special amnesty for employers who should have put their employees on payroll, but didn't. To qualify for that amnesty (VCSP), you need to have issued 1099-MISCs to your workers.

Payroll and Payroll Taxes

To avoid complications and painful audits, once you start using regular help, go ahead and put them on payroll. In the short run, this may cost you a little more than using contractors. In the long run, though, you'll be better off. Depending on the form your business takes, you may even end up putting yourself, your spouse, or your children on payroll.

Payroll Across Entities

Before we get into the mechanics of payrolls, you'll need to know whether or not you're required to be paid wages. Let's look at a quick outline of personal and family compensation for the different forms of businesses you learned about in Chapter 3.

- **Sole proprietorships.** The owner may never be on payroll. After all, all the money simply belongs to the owner. The spouse and children may be—if they perform services for the company and are not owners of the company.

Watch out for community property states with laws that say each spouse owns whatever the other spouse owns. You can overcome community property rules with contracts. Be careful; make sure you have a solid marriage. Otherwise, in the event of a divorce, one spouse will have signed away valuable ownership rights just to gain some short-term tax benefits. When you hire your children you must put them on payroll. If the child is under age 18 (under age 21 if performing domestic services), it's not necessary to withhold FICA (Social Security) and Medicare taxes from the child's paycheck. The parent doesn't need to pay the employer's share of those taxes either, or the Federal Unemployment Taxes (FUTA). (IRS Publication 15 contains all the rules and the withholding tables for payrolls.)

- **Partnerships, limited liability partnerships (LLPs), and limited liability companies (LLCs) taxed as partnerships.** The rules are the same as for sole proprietorships. However, partners may receive "guaranteed payments." These are specific allocations, such as a monthly stipend. Partners may receive different amounts, based on the time or resources they contribute to the business. Be sure to allocate reasonable guaranteed payments to working partners. Define the compensation arrangement in the partnership or entity document. You can add addendums to the documents each year, as conditions change. If you don't, as explained in Chapter 3, the IRS will assign a compensation level to you. When you want to hire your children in an entity that files taxes as a partnership, you must put them on payroll. When both partners are the parents of the child, the payroll tax rules are the same as the rule as for sole proprietors.

- **Corporations and LLCs taxed as corporations.** The shareholders and officers must be on the payroll, and reasonable compensation must be paid based on profits, time devoted to the business, and industry standards. Family members may be hired. Children's payroll is fully taxed. Officers are entitled to receive benefits like any employee. When it comes to profit-sharing and retirement plans, there are special rules to avoid discriminating in favor of highly compensated employees. Those rules won't affect you if you have no employees outside your family. If you have employees outside your family, this is where your advisory board will become really helpful. We won't be covering the details in this book—that's advanced tax planning. I just wanted you to be aware of the issue.

- **S corporations.** Working shareholders must receive wages. The IRS is running an audit campaign to catch omissions in this area. People who own more than 2 percent of the company are excluded from benefits. Legislation has been proposed to require 100 percent of profits be treated as wages for S corporations where the income is generated primarily from the services of three or fewer shareholders. Although this legislation did not pass, it's wise to show reasonable, market-level salaries for the owners. And no, taking the compensation in the form of fees instead of wages will not allow the shareholders to escape IRS penalties for lack of payroll. (This is an area of discussion with the IRS and tax professionals lately. The IRS has come down solidly on this issue.)

- **On the issue of what is "adequate compensation."** The following resource, introduced in Chapter 3, can provide definitive reports to use to back up your decisions for wages or guaranteed payments: http://www.rcreports.com/.

With these points in mind, let's start with the very touchy issue of hiring family members.

Hiring Family Members

Your email is likely full of messages from scamsters wanting to sell you tax-cutting kits. One of the tax loopholes they push most aggressively is the practice of hiring family members. The IRS has shut down a number of operations whose primary focus is encouraging people to take fraudulent deductions for home and family expenses, including The Tax People and Tax Toolbox. The IRS has filed civil and criminal charges against tax professionals promoting this practice fraudulently.

Does that mean you should completely avoid hiring your spouse and children? Nonsense! There would be no Rothschild dynasty, Ford Motor Company, Disney, Walmart, Harry & David, or any number of great companies if people had been afraid to build family businesses. To the contrary, many founders nurture dreams of having their children take over the family business. Some of today's major corporations started out as family businesses. Many publicly traded companies still have significant family leadership and ownership.

So please, don't let fear of the IRS prevent you from establishing your own dynasty. Besides, so much good comes from getting your family involved—and some of the benefits have nothing to do with taxes.

Intangible Benefits of Hiring Family

Among the benefits of hiring your family are:

- Your spouse and children understand the time requirements and pressures you face. This reduces familial conflict.

- You see your children more often. You don't just see them rushing out in the morning or wolfing down dinner on the way out to the library or to meet friends.
- You have things to talk about together, rather than the vacuous, "So how was your day?"
- Being in the same office or business location, you're apt to overhear your children's conversations with their friends and be more tuned in to the good and bad things in their lives. (Avoid deliberate eavesdropping, though.)
- Working with you, your family members have less time to get into the kind of trouble that comes from boredom or from too much time and money.
- Your children actually earn their "allowances." This is so important in eliminating that attitude of entitlement. You see other people's children growing up rude and demanding, without consideration for their parents. Your children won't act this way if they work for their spending money.
- When you are your family's employer, you know how much money your children have available to spend. If they suddenly come home with something unreasonably expensive, you won't fall for "I got a bonus at work." You'll know it's a warning sign.
- Your family knows the details of your business and where the important files and documents are. If anything happens to you, they can carry on.
- Each of your family members develops marketable skills. If your business fails, your spouse and kids will be able to get jobs and earn decent money. When your children head off to college, they'll be able to score higher-paying jobs because of their skills and experience.
- Maintaining all the records and time sheets needed to prove your family members are working in the business develops discipline, organization skills, and reporting skills—all of which will be important in the business world.
- Finally, growing up together in the business, your children may become passionate about getting an education they can bring back home to enhance the family's business.

Oddly enough, doing everything right, doing things just the way the IRS demands, could be the glue that holds your family together. After all, your family can join the group of top 500 family businesses worldwide. Some of the most recently established businesses are the wealthiest.

See, it *is* in your best interest to avoid the temptation to take shortcuts and to pay your family members from the business without their earning the money. Think about the kind of message you will be sending them if you cheat. You would be telling them it's all right to lie; to operate outside the rules; to avoid your responsibility to your community; to shrug off authority. Teaching them to lie or cheat will tell your children they may behave that way toward you, too. Children do not see the difference.

Sure, we could get into long arguments about what your tax money pays for and how often it's wasted. And it *is* wasted! The bottom line: your taxes do go toward maintaining a measure of sanity, safety, comfort, and predictability in a community of millions of passionate individualists.

Tax Benefits of Hiring Family

In Chapter 10 you'll learn all about the health care, insurance, and retirement benefits available to small business owners and their families. Right now, we're going to cover the payroll tax and compensation benefits available to you.

Special Tax Benefits of Hiring Your Child(ren) for Proprietorships and Partnerships

- Wages paid to your children are fully deductible to your business. Allowances are not. You can give your children more money than you give them now—but have them earn it. All of it will be deductible to you.
- If you are a sole proprietorship or partnership, the wages you pay your children who are under 18 are not subject to Social Security, Medicare, or federal unemployment taxes. Most states also waive payroll taxes—but not all, so be sure to check with your state's payroll tax authority (you'll find the link in this chapter's Resources). On wages of $7,000, this strategy would save you nearly $1,100 (15.3 percent) worth of your self-employment taxes and $1,540 (22 percent) of federal and state income taxes. You've just cut nearly $2,650 off your tax bill.
- If you had hired a nonchild employee, you'd be paying half the Social Security and Medicare taxes, all the federal and state unemployment taxes, workers' compensation insurance, holidays, sick days, and, possibly, benefits. Those additional expenses would add more than $1,000 to your business overhead. Paying your child, you're just converting money you'd give to your child anyway into a deduction. Even when you spend twice as much on your child as before (through allowances), the government pays for nearly half the money you give him or her.
- The SECURE Act is encouraging part-time employees to participate in the company's retirement plan. In fact, the IRS will give you a tax credit for making the enrollment in the retirement plan automatic. Employees must opt out if they don't want to participate. So, not only can you provide

compensation, you can also contribute to your child's retirement and get a deduction for the contributions made by the business.

Tax Benefits of Hiring Family in General

- For jobs requiring the use of cars, you may pay your spouse, your child, or yourself a mileage allowance or auto expenses. Be sure to get a mileage report and a copy of auto expenses to support your checks. The US Tax Court just issued a ruling in support of the IRS's position. The IRS determined that payments that Continental Express, Inc., made to its drivers were subject to the meals and entertainment rules. Continental Express didn't require substantiation of the expenses from its drivers. That ruling cut the company's deduction by 50 percent. Expect this same logic to be applied to other businesses. Warnings aside, paying your child $100 per month for deliveries and errands cuts your taxes by about $550 per year (15.3 percent self-employment taxes and 30 percent federal and state taxes). If your child submits expense reports, he or she doesn't report this income at all. You don't have to pay your spouse or child's auto upkeep from your own pocket. Remember, though, you have to provide the same kind of reimbursement benefits to all employees performing the same kind of functions. And yes, they also need to submit expense reports.
- The money you pay your spouse and child doesn't need to go into their pockets. Arrange to set up IRAs, Roth IRAs, or other retirement plans (remember the new SECURE Act rules), to save $3,000 to $5,000 of those wages each year. They will get a deduction for the contribution to a regular IRA—but not the Roth IRA. Your child may end up paying no tax at all on that money, and your personal taxes are reduced. Chapter 10 describes the types of plans available. Just one thing—be sure to actually issue real paychecks with paystubs, real checks, or electronic transfers to the relevant accounts. The IRS has disallowed payroll deductions when the parents just pocketed the money or handed the child cash. Sweat the details!
- Chapter 10 also explains how medical expenses may be deducted by small businesses. This could convert $5,000 to $10,000 of unusable deductions into business deductions.

The financial and emotional rewards of hiring family members are substantial. Only don't push it. If they resist, don't force the issue relentlessly. You'll only take a good thing and turn it into something nasty. Knowing that you're doing it for their own good won't make them resent you less. Know when not to push. Just leave the door open for whenever they're ready to join you.

Better yet, sucker them into it. Just ask for a little help with some minor thing. Be sure to thank them and praise them. Once they get used to doing that, add one more little thing. As they do the small things automatically, and well . . . gradually add a few more tasks. In fact, they might have ideas about things they'd like to improve in your business. Pretty soon, they'll be working by your side—and loving it! Shhh, don't tell them I told you.

Now it's time to work on the payroll.

Paying Payroll

First of all, whenever you hire someone, have the person fill out two forms *before he or she starts working*. The first is Form W-4, Employee's Withholding Allowance Certificate. You've seen W-4s before—get a new one filled out by each employee every January. The second form is the I-9, which you can access at https://www .uscis.gov/i-9. It's important that all of your employees fill out this form for the benefit of the immigration department (currently known as US Citizenship and Immigration Services—USCIS, now a part of Homeland Security), even if they are citizens. Make a copy of each identification document used by the employee to substantiate his or her right to work. Keep it with the signed I-9 in the person's permanent employee file.

Compensation Methods

You may pay your employees in a variety of ways. Each one is acceptable, as long as you're consistent, using the same method for all people in the same position. If you pay people doing the same job at different rates, or using different methods, it won't be the IRS you'll have to face. Most likely it will be the wrath of the employee, in front of a labor judge. So if you're going to discriminate in favor of friends or family members, give them a higher title or additional duties to justify the higher pay rate.

Note: Be sure to look up the latest rules relating to hiring employees on the US Department of Labor's website. Look up minimum wage rules, overtime rules, and so on. Also, check with your state to see if it has specific rules and rules for your industry.

These are common compensation methods:

- **Hourly.** Your employees keep a time sheet or punch a time card. Multiply their hours worked by their hourly pay rate. If they work overtime, multiply the pay rate by 1.5 to get the overtime rate. For example, if the base hourly rate is $15, overtime is paid at 22.50 (22.50 × 1.5). A weekly payroll for 50 hours of work including 10 hours of overtime would look like this:

Base pay: $600 = 40 hours × $15

Overtime pay: $225 = 10 hours × $22.50

Total wages: $825

- **Salary.** Your employee gets paid the same amount each pay period, regardless of the hours worked. For instance, Nancy gets $50,000 per year, paid every two weeks. (*Note:* That does not mean twice a month. Twice a month is 24 pay periods.) Divide 52 weeks by 2 weeks, and the result is 26 pay periods. Now divide $50,000 by 26 weeks. That gives Nancy $1,923 per pay period. Often, people who are paid salaries get no overtime.

   Note: There are new federal Department of Labor overtime compensation rules that apply to employees that have traditionally been classified as exempt. Read those rules carefully, or consult with a human resources expert for guidance specific to your business. Always look for someone familiar with your state's unique rules, as well as any special rules that relate to your industry.

- **Commission.** Employees are paid on a percentage of their sales or unit's revenues. Often, to equalize the compensation, they are paid some fixed rate against commission. That means they get a base pay of, let's say, $1,000 per month, before they earn commissions. That $1,000 per month should be treated as wages, with all the usual withholding. When they earn the commissions, their advance payments get deducted from their commission checks. For example, Josey had her first big sale at the end of December. It netted her a commission of $25,000. She had been with the company since May and had received $8,000 in advances. When she gets paid her commission in December, her employer will deduct the $8,000 from her net check, before taxes are taken out—since she has already paid taxes on the first $8,000. The payroll taxes will be computed on the remaining $17,000 ($25,000 − $8,000). Some employers have the habit of putting commissions on the Form 1099-MISC. This is not correct. Doing this puts the employee in the position of having to pay the employer's half of the Social Security and Medicare taxes—which does not make them happy at all. They have recourse to avoid these extra taxes, and that recourse can cause your business to be audited. So just include all the commissions on the W-2, please. (Sorry, tax professionals are always asking me how to fix this problem. The easiest way? Not to create the problem in the first place.)

- **Bonus.** Regardless of the other compensation methods, there is nothing to prevent you from giving your employees bonuses at any time you choose. Bonuses may be rewards for individuals or teams hitting targets or goals. They may simply be split among all employees because you had a great month. Even small bonuses, given to everyone to celebrate, can really boost morale and build team spirit. The bonus is fully taxable, just like payroll— and is part of their payroll. Bonuses should be reported on the W-2. This applies even if the bonus was issued at the end of the year. Employers often forget to include this on the final payroll. Don't forget!
- **Employee gifts.** Except for minor gifts worth $25 or less for the whole year, the value of a gift is fully taxable. Include the value of all gifts in excess of $25 in the employee's wages.
- **Employee achievement awards.** When the award is part of a written plan with defined targets, you may give an employee an award worth up to $1,600, without including it in the employee's income. Unfortunately, the award must be a thing (tangible personal property), not money or anything like money. There are very specific rules about who qualifies. Read Chapter 2 of IRS Publication 15-B for more details.

Payroll Taxes

Along with a payroll come payroll taxes. When you cut the check to the IRS at the end of each payroll period, it looks like you're paying the IRS a ton of money. Actually, your payroll taxes are lower than you think. Most of the money you're sending to the IRS is the employees' own money, deducted from their paychecks. The only things the employer pays are:

Social Security, up to an annual wage limit (which changes each year):	6.2 percent
Medicare, no wage limit:	1.45 percent
Federal unemployment, up to $7,000 in wages:	0.6 percent
Total federal employer taxes:	8.25 percent

Add in your state unemployment taxes and other minor local taxes as well as mandatory workers' compensation, and you're paying about 10 percent of the employees' wages.

Alert: If your state gets behind on paying its share of the unemployment fund, your federal unemployment rate might go up. Your payroll tax software will know the correct rate for your state.

Note: While the percentages haven't changed in decades, the limits on Social Security wages increase each year. See the "What's New" section of IRS Publication 15 for the new Social Security limits each year.

Preparing Payroll: Checks, Journals, Reports

You have several options when it comes to the accounting involved with payroll. You can do it the old-fashioned way, by hand, on paper, on columnar pads, or by using journals. You can do it by hand using preprinted manual systems. One-Write is a very popular manual system. You also can use software that either integrates into your accounting system or stands alone, like QuickBooks. Or you can do the really smart thing—*turn it all over to a professional!*

Payroll record keeping is fraught with danger. There are so many little things that go wrong all the time, due to errors on your part, program glitches, or tax law changes you didn't get. Messing up on payroll tax forms unleashes a gusher of notices. Your time is worth more than that. Worse, most really small businesses end up with huge IRS payroll tax debt because they don't do their payroll reporting properly and don't pay their payroll tax deposits.

Make all the problems go away. Turn over your payroll processing to a tax professional or a professional payroll service. It will cost $50 to $100 per month for a small company, but it's really worth it. A good payroll processing house will make your life so easy. Once you set up your employees, all you have to do is call in with their hours or enter the hours online. All the major companies have toll-free customer service centers.

They prepare your payroll, cut payroll checks on your account, file all the tax returns, issue the W-2s, and—for a small extra fee—arrange to make your tax agency payments directly from your account. This will give you proof your payments were made on time. If they make an error, the payroll services must pay any penalties incurred, not you. (But if you don't have funds in your bank account on payroll day— that's your error, not theirs.) The best thing about payroll services is that if the IRS sends correspondence, they will handle all the responses. You don't need to be bothered. If you're the kind of person who cringes every time you see one of those white envelopes with the IRS eagle . . . a payroll service is for you.

Below, you will find two of the more reliable companies in the industry. There are bigger companies—but their systems are often filled with errors. Though, if you can find a good, local company, that might be your best bet:

- **Intuit's QuickBooks Payroll.** If you request the Complete Payroll Service, you can get additional services, including background checks before hiring, integration into QuickBooks, cafeteria plans, and retirement plans. Reach the company at http://iTaxMama.com/Intuit_Payroll.

- **Paychex.** Though geared toward companies with 50 employees or more, it will still work with mom-and-pop businesses. The service representatives are a joy to work with. Check out the company at http://www.paychex.com/.

For more options, visit the IRS's list of payroll providers, available at http://iTax Mama.com/IRS_Payroll.

Tips on Using Payroll Service Bureaus

- Be sure to get yourself assigned to a local personal account manager. He or she will be a big help to you anytime there is a problem or you have a question. It really helps to be able to work with the same person all the time— someone who is familiar with your company.
- Give your tax professionals online access so they can look up information and print out forms and reports when working on your business return, without ever bothering you.
- Some payroll services, or your bank, will enable you to offer direct deposit to your employees' bank accounts, so you never have to cut checks or mail them.
- With some services, your employees will be able to see their own payroll accounts online and can look things up without bothering you or your tax professionals.
- You will be able to offer employee benefits economically, even if you're a small company.

Alert: You must set up an IRS electronic federal tax payment system (EFTPS; see https://www.eftps.gov/eftps/) account and a similar state account, if available, so your payroll tax deposits can go directly from your own bank account to the IRS and your state (see Chapter 1). That way, your payroll service will not be holding your funds. Unfortunately, there have been instances of payroll companies going bankrupt while holding client funds—or worse—absconding with your funds. You don't want that to happen.

Regardless of who prepares your payroll, it pays for you to get educated about it. After all, you are ultimately responsible. The IRS provides detailed information on its Employment Taxes for Small Business website, available at http://iTaxMama .com/IRS_Employment_Tax.

The IRS, SCORE, and your state government frequently offer free workshops on how to handle payroll and employee issues. Take advantage of the free information if you're not already intimately familiar with the reporting and depositing requirements. It's important that you understand what your responsibilities are and how things work. It also will help you catch errors or oversights on the part of your staff, service bureau, or tax preparer. It's important that you know what forms must be filed and when.

Reporting Payroll

Payroll tax returns are filed quarterly and annually. Table 9.2 provides the due dates and lists the specific forms that are due. For the final quarter of the year, you must file both the fourth quarter reports and the annual summaries, for both the IRS and state, along with the W-2s and 1099s. These days, as much as possible, the IRS wants to see payroll tax forms filed electronically. That's another benefit of payroll services.

TABLE 9.2 Quarterly Payroll Tax Return Due Dates

When the last day of the month falls on a weekend or holiday, the forms and payments are due on the following business day.

Quarter	Due Date	Forms Due
1st (Q1)	April 30	941 and state
2nd (Q2)	July 31	941 and state
3rd (Q3)	October 31	941 and state
4th (Q4)	January 31 of following year	940, 941, 1099s, W-2s, and state

Form 941 is the quarterly report. You can generally find the most current version of this form on the IRS's website.

On Form 941, do you see that box on line 4, where it says if no wages or compensation are subject to Social Security or Medicare tax? If you've hired your children who are under age 18 and they are your only employees, check that box. That alerts the IRS that you didn't omit the Social Security and Medicare wages by accident. Remember, your children's wages are *not* subject to those taxes. If you have other employees who are subject to Social Security and Medicare, leave that box empty. You will be using lines 6a–6e to enter your children's and other exempt payroll. Be prepared to get a flurry of mail from the IRS. It usually takes the agency three letters before it accepts your explanation about having hired your child. But keep replying to the letters. In time, you will get the IRS to accept it—and next quarter the letters will start again. Though, hopefully, not.

You must send in your payroll tax payments within three business days after each payroll. (Some people have more time, but it's a good habit to get into.) When you file the returns at the end of the quarter, you should owe no more than $2,500. If you do owe more than that, you will be required to establish that EFTPS account I mentioned. The IRS has phased out the Form 8109 vouchers in that thin yellow book the IRS used to send you when you got your employer identification number. (Only old-timers remember that booklet.)

Form 941-V is the payment coupon for Form 941. If you are making payment by check, fill in the coupon and send the check with it. Be sure to include FYTIN (Form number, Year, and Taxpayer ID number). You must deposit all payroll taxes electronically or you will face a 10 percent penalty. If the balance due is more than $2,500, pay it online via the EFTPS.

There are special rules for marijuana and associated businesses that cannot get bank accounts. We discussed the income and expense issues in Chapter 5. But when it comes to payroll, there is a special code section you need to know from the IRS's own Internal Revenue Manual. *IRM 20.1.4.26.1.1, Unbanked Taxpayers*, (2015). If the IRS assesses any penalties to your pot business because you're paying payroll taxes in cash, just ask for a penalty waiver and cite the Internal Revenue Manual Code section referenced earlier. If you have already paid these penalties, use Form 843 to get a refund. If you need guidance on how to do this, just drop by ask TaxMama on the website. The link is at the end of each chapter.

Form 940 is the annual unemployment tax return. The final tax rate only ends up being 0.6 percent if you file the return on time and pay your state unemployment taxes on time. (See this chapter's Resources for states in default of their FUTA obligations.) If you default on the state tax, you end up paying 6.2 percent for federal unemployment. So make sure you always pay the state unemployment taxes first.

W-2s must be mailed out to employees by January 31. No payment goes with these forms. They must also be mailed to the Social Security Administration by January 31. Due to the millions of dollars of fraudulent tax refunds, Congress changed the filing date in the PATH Act of 2015.

Form W-3 is the summary of all the W-2s. Be sure all the boxes on the W-2s add up to the totals on the W-3. Included on the W-2 is the information about employee benefits, which we'll discuss in the next section.

Shoulda Had a Payroll—But Didn't

Reading all of this, it may have dawned on you that you should have been running a payroll all along. Now, you're afraid that you're going to face some horrendous penalties for not putting your employees on payroll. Right? Well, I have good news for you. The IRS has a permanent amnesty program that will give you a huge break—and help you avoid audits. It only works if you have been issuing 1099-MISCs to your workers who should have been employees. It's called the Voluntary Classification Settlement Program (VCSP). If the IRS accepts you into the program, you will pay about one-tenth of one year's payroll taxes for the past. That's it.

Normally, the IRS can audit a company for every year in which a relevant tax return has not been filed. When it comes to payroll, if a company has been in business for 10 years and has never filed a payroll tax return, there is no time limit on the IRS's right to audit and to create a payroll, along with taxes, penalties, and interest. Businesses that are accepted into the VCSP can avoid that problem. Yes, they really can! You see, the IRS will agree not to audit any of your prior years for unreported payroll. It's a really good deal. The bad news? The IRS didn't coordinate this with the states. So when you come in out of the cold, so to speak, you may still face state audits and penalties.

Employee Benefits

Companies may offer their employees an array of benefits. Owners can only participate if they are incorporated. On the other hand, S corporation shareholders who own 2 percent or more of the company are excluded from most benefits.

Two of the common benefits employees receive are sick pay and vacations. Were you aware that these benefits are not a legal requirement in all states—particularly for small companies? Paying for these for employees is more of a custom than law. Check with your own state's labor commission to learn the standards in your state.

You can offer some fringe benefit plans for employees that they pay for themselves—and would gladly. When it comes to medical and insurance plans, even if you don't pay the premiums, your employees could get some terrific tax savings. You pay a small administrative fee, offset by the tax savings from the plan, and for your employees it's like a small raise. They save nearly 35 percent of the amount of money on things they pay for anyway, on things such as medical insurance, medical costs, or dependent care (7.65 percent Social Security and Medicare, 22 percent federal tax, 5 percent state tax). For the average family of four, paying $17,000 in medical premiums, that's nearly $500 per month into the family's pockets, perhaps double if the plan has dependent care. As the employer, you save about 12 percent of the cost of those premiums because the employer's taxes and workers' compensation insurance fees don't apply to that money either. That savings will more than cover your administrative costs for the plan.

Plans Where Employees' Money Is Spent

Here are two popular fringe benefit plans employees pay for:

- **Premium-only plans (POPs).** The employees pay their medical insurance premiums. Premiums are deducted from their wages before taxes are computed.
- **Flexible spending accounts (FSAs).** These accounts let your staff deduct their medical, dental, optical, and therapy costs, up to $2,650 per employer for each spouse. Dependent care expenses (child or elder care) are limited to $5,000 per year, but may increase with inflation. Employers, or your payroll service, set up limits on the medical spending. The FAQs page on the HealthCare.gov site provides a comprehensive set of answers to most FSA questions. And IRS Publication 15-B has a nice chart with a summary of all the fringe benefits and limits in their Table 2.1.

Plans Where Your (Employer) Money Is Spent

Setting up employee plans for small companies has been complicated and expensive. Now that the payroll services are offering complete administration packages, even a small employer can offer these benefits. It only costs a few extra dollars per employee per month for the administration:

- **Group term life insurance.** Employee benefits up to $50,000 are free to the employee. The premiums for coverage exceeding $50,000 are added back to their wages. Have the insurance expert on your advisory team help you find the right plan.
- **Education benefits.** You may reimburse employees for up to $5,250 per year. It's tax-free to them and a full deduction to you.
- **Employee death benefits.** Employee death benefits may be paid to the employee's family to help out with the funeral and other related costs. It would be a deduction to the employer. And it would be income to the employee if the benefit is based on the employee's past service or other economic benefit due to the employee.
- **Meals and lodging.** Some companies set up a cafeteria offering free meals to all employees to save time off from work or to ensure they get some nutritious meals. When you offer it to all employees, the company used to be able to deduct 100 percent of the costs without charging the employees. The Tax Cuts and Jobs Act (TCJA) changed that rule to limit the employer's deduction

to only 50 percent, like all meal deductions. (The employees can still get the meals for free.) I'd be careful about this if you're working from home and it's just you and your family. Lodging is a bit more interesting. When your employee (such as an apartment manager) must live on the premises for the benefit of the employer, so he or she is available full-time, the lodging is free, without tax consequences to the employee.

Companies providing fringe benefits to qualified employees may deduct the costs of the benefits and administration. You'll want to think carefully about setting up these plans, because once you start, employees expect them. To keep employees for the long term, you need to be generous. But it's worth it to keep terrific employees. After all, recruiting and training new employees can be very expensive. Then, consider how long it takes to train them in your business's processes and systems—even when they have the expertise you need. Add in the additional supervision time—and you can see why it's in your best interests to keep your present, competent, loyal employees happy. Be sure to build the costs of the perquisites into your product or service costs. On the other hand, many of these benefits reduce your tax and insurance costs, and you can use that savings to pay for the benefits.

There are a variety of retirement plans and profit-sharing plans you can offer your employees. Chapter 10 describes most of them as they apply to business owners and related parties. The various tables in Chapter 10 will give you an overview of each plan, with the limits, setup dates, and funding dates as well as the pros and cons of each plan.

Employee Ownership and Stock Options

Whether for tax planning or retention, employee ownership is an appealing option. Since the initial public offering (IPO) craze of the 1990s, highly skilled employees are starting to expect a share of the equity and growth of a company.

Using stock is an excellent lure to hire an employee whose price you couldn't otherwise afford. Giving up stock, you can offer a salary you can presently afford, with a promise of riches as the company grows. The right highly talented employee, who isn't also highly strung, will make the difference between growing slowly or explosively. Which is better, giving up 5 percent of a company worth $10 million or owning 100 percent of a company worth $250,000? That's the kind of difference the right employee(s) can make.

You can also use employee stock ownership plans (ESOPs) to avoid paying taxes. The National Center for Employee Ownership (NCEO) has an extensive ESOP resource section. When you turn over 100 percent of the company's stock to an ESOP, the ESOP pays no taxes on the company's profits. It does mean giving up stock to each employee as he or she becomes eligible, and so you will own less of the company. But you will also own a share of the ESOP. However, with all the tax money available to the company for growth, what you've given up may earn you a greater reward—allowing you to build a bigger company.

Companies such as Janus Global Operations and Armstrong Garden Centers have substantial employee ownership. You don't have to be a large company to do this. Kinko's started out quite small and was entirely employee-owned. With great employee training and participation, the company grew dramatically. In February 2004, Federal Express paid $2.4 billion for the company. You can just bet those Kinko's employees' retirement plans look healthy. All the profit went into their ESOP accounts, ready to be withdrawn whenever they want to retire.

You can also offer stock options. The rules on when the options are taxable, when the employee can exercise them, and what taxes get paid when are very complex. I prefer to leave all that in the hands of the tax and labor attorneys. If you want to study this in depth, you'll find a feast at the National Center for Employee Ownership's website at http://www.nceo.org.

Summing up Employees

Overall, you and your family can gain great benefits by having eligible family members go on the payroll. The trick is to pay wages only for valuable services performed on behalf of the business. Do what the IRS asks of you—your family will be closer knit, and your business will grow in leaps and bounds.

Just as the benefits are good for your family, think of how treating your employees well affects them. Seeing you extend yourself to provide them with ways to make their money go further will increase their loyalty to you.

At tax educational seminars I often hear the presenters speak about how to devise retirement and benefit plans that cut out the employees. Isn't that the silliest thing you've ever heard? Why would you not want to give your employees benefits? Cost? Sure, cost is a factor. But think of the cost of hiring, training, and teaching a new employee because you didn't value the previous employee enough. Cheap labor is not cheap! New hires make mistakes—sometimes mistakes big enough to cost you important clients.

So as you prosper, see to it that your employees do, too. Get some good planning with the help of the employee benefit specialist on your advisory team—and you'll ensure being able to retire in style.

Resources

In this chapter, you saw a variety of resources. Here's a summary of them, so you can find them quickly and easily. The resources are not necessarily in alphabetical order in each category. They are in order of their importance or usefulness, in TaxMama's opinion.

IRS Forms and Publications

- **Form I-9, Employment Eligibility Verification.** https://www.uscis.gov/i-9. Although this is an immigration form, not an IRS form, it's an important part of new hiring rules.
- **Form SS-8, Determination of Worker Status.** https://www.irs.gov/pub/irs-pdf/fss8.pdf
- **Form W-4, Employee's Withholding Allowance Certificate.** https://www.irs.gov/pub/irs-pdf/fw4.pdf. Get an advance look at the 2020 Form W-4 at https://www.irs.gov/pub/irs-dft/fw4--dft.pdf. The IRS thinks this version is an improvement. Time will tell.
- **Form W-9, Request for Taxpayer Identification Number and Certification.** https://www.irs.gov/pub/irs-pdf/fw9.pdf
- **Form 940, Employer's Annual Federal Unemployment (FUTA) Tax Return and Form 940-V Payment Voucher.** https://www.irs.gov/pub/irs-pdf/f940.pdf
- **Form 941, Employer's Quarterly Federal Tax Return and Form 941-V Payment Voucher.** https://www.irs.gov/pub/irs-pdf/f941.pdf
- **Form 1099-MISC.** https://www.irs.gov/pub/irs-pdf/i1099msc.pdf
- **Form 8809, Application for Extension of Time to File Information Returns.** http://iTaxMama.com/IRS_Form8809
- **W-2 Filing Deadlines.** https://www.ssa.gov/employer/filingDeadlines.htm
- **IRS Publication 1281, A Guide to Backup Withholding on Missing and Incorrect Name/TINs.** http://iTaxMama.com/IRS_1281
- **IRS Employee vs. Independent Contractor Rules.** http://iTaxMama.com/IRS_Emp_v_IC. The IRS's three "Common Law Rules."
- **IRS Employment Tax Issues.** http://iTaxMama.com/IRS_Employment_Tax
- **IRS Publication 15 Series:**
  - **https://www.irs.gov/publications/p15a.** The basic payroll rules and payroll tax tables.

- **https://www.irs.gov/publications/p15#en_US_2020_pub link1000202301.** Hiring your children.
- **https://www.irs.gov/publications/p15b.** Guide to fringe benefits—see Chapter 2 to learn about gifts and other fringe benefits
- **Section 530, Safe Harbor Information.** http://iTaxMama.com/IRS_530. See the article "Section 530: Its History and Application in Light of the Federal Definition of the Employer-Employee Relationship for Federal Tax Purposes" (February 2009) by the National Association of Tax Reporting and Professional Management.
- **IRS EFTPS (Electronic Federal Tax Payment System).** https://www.eftps .gov/eftps/. Set it up for your payroll tax deposits.
- **IRS Internal Revenue Manual IRM 20.1.4.26.1.1, Unbanked Tax-payers, (2015).** https://www.irs.gov/irm/part20/irm_20-001-004r#idm 140629082271952
  - **If you have already paid penalties** to the IRS for paying payroll taxes in cash, use Form 843 to get a refund. https://www.irs.gov/pub/irs-pdf /f843.pdf
- **IRS Flexible Spending Accounts (FSAs).** http://iTaxMama.com/FSA
- **IRS Voluntary Classification Settlement Program (VCSP).** http://iTax Mama.com/TM_VCSP
- **TaxMama's Webinar on the VCSP.** http://iTaxMama.com/TM_VCSP
- **IRS's Resource on Employment Tax Fraud Investigation.** https://www .irs.gov/uac/ examples-of-employment-tax-fraud-investigations-fiscal-year -2016; https://www.irs.gov/compliance/criminal-investigation/examples -of-employment-tax-fraud-investigations-fiscal-year-2017 (Change the year to see more recent investigations—if the IRS has posted them.)

Other Resources

- **US Department of Labor's Website.** http://webapps.dol.gov/elaws/flsa.htm
  - **Department of Labor Overtime rules.** https://www.dol.gov/whd/over time_pay.htm
- **Links to State Tax Agencies.** http://www.taxadmin.org/state-tax-forms. Look up your state's payroll tax authority.
- **Intuit's Complete Payroll.** http://iTaxMama.com/Intuit_Payroll
- **Paychex.** http://www.paychex.com/
- **CFS Tax Tools and Payroll Systems.** http://iTaxMama.com/TaxTools _Payroll. Easy to use, includes direct deposit for employees.

- **IRS's List of Payroll Providers.** http://iTaxMama.com/IRS_Payroll
- **Overtime Rules.** https://www.dol.gov/whd/overtime_pay.htm. Defining and Delimiting the Exemptions for Executive, Administrative, Professional, Outside Sales and Computer Employees under the Fair Labor Standards Act.
- **FUTA Credit Adjustment.** http://iTaxMama.com/FUTA_State_Penalty. If your state gets behind on paying their share of the unemployment fund, your federal unemployment rate might go up. Look up your state here.
- **Service Corps of Retired Executives (SCORE).** https://www.score.org/
- **The Global Family Business Index.** http://familybusinessindex.com/. Lists the top 500 family-owned businesses in the world—dating back to 1610. This is a fun chart to explore!
- *Family Business Magazine.* http://www.familybusinessmagazine.com. An excellent collection of articles, resources, and information for small family businesses intending to become major businesses.
- **National Center for Employee Ownership (NCEO).** http://www.nceo .org/. A private, nonprofit membership and research organization providing unbiased information on employee stock ownership plans, broadly granted employee stock options and related programs, and ownership culture.
  - ○ **See the thorough ESOP resource section** at http://www.nceo.org /main/publications.php.
  - ○ **There is an extensive stock options resource** at https://www.nceo.org /articles/employee-stock-options-factsheet.
  - ○ **Find the top 100 employee-owned companies** at https://www.nceo .org/articles/employee-ownership-100.
- **What Is "Adequate Compensation"?** http://www.rcreports.com/. This website can provide definitive reports to use to back up your decisions for wages or guaranteed payments.
- *Boyd v. Commissioner, 122 T.C. No. 18 (4/24/04).* https://www.leagle.com /decision/2004427122rtc3051410. An S corporation's shareholders were not entitled to a 100 percent deduction for the portion of the per diem allowance paid to drivers for nonmeal expenses, including mileage. It all boils down to establishing clear accountability.

TaxMama Resources

- **TaxMama's Webinar on the VCSP.** http://iTaxMama.com/TM_VCSP
- **TaxMama's Quick Look-Ups.** http://iTaxMama.com/TM_QuickLookUp. You will find all kinds of useful reference materials, webinars you can replay, e-books, and more.
- **Your Business Bible.** http://www.yourbusinessbible.com. Look for worksheets, printable checklists, and other goodies and resources.

CHAPTER 10: **OWNERS' FRINGE BENEFITS, RETIREMENT, AND TAX DEFERMENT**

To-Do List and Questionnaire

☐ 1. What business entity are you using? _____

☐ 2. What are the legal limits to your deductible benefits, if any?
_____ _____ _____

☐ 3. Do you have children under age 13?
   • Do you pay for childcare?
   • Do you have an employer-provided childcare facility?

☐ 4. Do you have medical coverage? _____ Yourself _____ Family
_____ Employees
Is your employee medical coverage in compliance with your state's rules?
_____ Yes _____ No
What tax-deductible methods are you using for medical coverage?
_____ Section 105 plan
_____ Section 125 plan
_____ HSA
_____ Small business health care tax credit
_____ Other: _____

☐ 5. Do you have a retirement plan? _____ Yes _____ No

☐ 6. Does it cover your employees? _____ Yes _____ No

☐ 7. Are you funding it regularly and properly? _____ Yes _____ No

☐ 8. Are you filing the annual Form 5500, if applicable? _____ Yes _____ No

☐ 9. Schedule a meeting with your tax pro and retirement administrator to review the plan for compliance. Date: _____

☐ 10. Schedule a meeting with your tax pro to see if there are any owner benefits you have overlooked. Date: _____

Remember to put a copy of each document behind this page, folded in half.

OWNERS' FRINGE BENEFITS, RETIREMENT, AND TAX DEFERMENT

Income tax is the fine you pay for thriving so fast.

—Tom Antion

There are wonderful benefits to being in business for yourself. You may spend as much as you like to improve yourself, educate yourself, care for your health, and plan for your ultimate triumphant retirement. While I won't cover all the potential benefits here, I will include some options you won't find anywhere else. For the ones everyone covers—you know the usual suspects—simply go to an Internet search engine and type in "fringe benefits" or read IRS Publication 15-B, which is all about fringe benefits and available on the IRS website.

Fringe Benefits and Reimbursements

When you're an employee in a in a large corporation, you are always offered an array of fringe benefits to induce you to take the job—or to stay on the job. You get vacation, sick time, bonuses, stock options, medical plans, and various reimbursement plans for things like childcare, education, auto, and meals. Your employer pays for all that.

Having your own company means you may offer those things to your employees. (See Chapter 9.) But if you get them, the cost for all the benefits comes out of your own pocket. On the other hand, if you handle the benefits properly, Uncle Sam will pick up a nice part of the freight.

Health Insurance

Sigh of relief! The Obamacare penalties are over if you don't have health insurance coverage. That doesn't mean you shouldn't get health insurance. (Beware! Some states have enacted their own laws about mandatory insurance coverage.) If your employer doesn't provide health insurance coverage, employees may be able to find coverage on the Marketplace website at https://www.healthcare.gov/. You might even qualify for government subsidies for your premiums. Employers are able to get health care coverage for their employees from the federal Marketplace—and possibly your state's system. But, if you have nonfamily employees, I urge you to sit down with an expert in this area because there's a lot to know, way more than I can possibly fit into a single chapter. (Besides, I am still learning new nuances and pitfalls every day.)

The form of business you've chosen (see Chapter 3) will govern whether or not your insurance expenses are deductible in your business. C corporations get to deduct all employee fringe benefits, and as an employee of your own C corporation, you're treated the same way as other employees. On the other hand, when you're self-employed, in a partnership, or in an S corporation, you don't get a business deduction. You may have seen a company pay the officers' medical insurance or expenses in an S corporation. The money must be added to the wages as additional compensation. Or it is treated as dividends or as repayments of loans to the officers.

You may deduct your family's health insurance costs on page 1 of your tax return, as an adjustment to income. If you have an S corporation, this doesn't matter as much because you're not paying self-employment taxes on your profits. But when your income is on your Schedule C or through a partnership (or LLC filing as a partnership), all your profit is subject to an extra 15.3 percent assessment for Social Security and Medicare taxes.

Not being able to deduct your family's medical insurance costs of $650 per month from your Schedule C business or partnership may cost you more than $1,200 extra in taxes each year. Toss in the cost of routine out-of-pocket medical expenses (braces, contacts, eyeglasses, annual checkups, copays, etc.), which might average another $1,500 for a family of three. Your overall extra taxes are nearly $1,500 per year from self-employment taxes alone.

You may provide insurance coverage for your dependents until they reach age 26, as a result of the Affordable Care Act of 2010. More about that in a moment. (And you'll find a link in this chapter's Resources.)

Health Savings Accounts

Congress voted health savings accounts (HSAs) into law on December 8, 2003. By now, coverage is easy to find. To help you find insurance carriers for these plans in your state, HealthCare.gov put up a special section on its website.

What's so special about these accounts? Several things. First of all, you get an adjustment to income (remember above-the-line expenses?) for your costs. For a self-only plan, the adjustment is $3,500 ($3,550 for 2020). For a family plan, your adjustment is $7,000 ($7,100 for 2020). Your medical insurance costs are lower because your deductible must be at least $1,350 ($1,400 in 2020) for an individual or $2,700 ($2,800 in 2020) for a family (revised annually for inflation). See Table 10.1 for an overview of the numbers.

TABLE 10.1 Health Savings Arrangements and Accounts (HSAs)

Description	2019	2020
High Deductible—Self-Only	$1,350	$1,400
High Deductible—Family	$2,700	$2,800
Deduction—Self-Only	$3,500	$3,500
Deduction—Family	$7,000	$7,100
Maximum Out of Pocket—Self-Only	$6,750	$6,900
Maximum Out of Pocket—Family	$13,500	$13,800
Additional over 55 contribution	$1,000	$1,000

Your medical expenses drop for two reasons:

1. Premiums decrease when your deductible increases.
2. There are limits to your out-of-pocket expenses. Your annual maximum out-of-pocket expenses are limited to $6,750 ($6,900 for 2020) for an individual or $13,500 ($13,800 for 2020) for a family.

A health savings account is something like an individual retirement account (IRA). The money you deposit is deductible in the current year. You can draw out that money to pay for medical expenses, tax-free. Or if you and your family are generally healthy, you can leave the money invested for years. Draw it when you really need the money to cover medical expenses, or wait until you get old and infirm and need to spend money on in-home care or long-term care. Or just draw it out and pay taxes on it, like an IRA.

Be very careful about the funds you draw from your HSA. Your administrator will give you a credit card that allows you to pay your medical care providers and pharmacist. Please don't think that everything you buy at the pharmacy qualifies as an allowable medical expense. After all, in my pharmacy, I can buy gifts, makeup, potato chips, and lots of other nonmedical junk. Whenever you spend money from that account during the year, you will have to report how that money was used on Form 8889. Save all the receipts. One of my clients was recently audited. It turned out fine, but we had a few panicky moments there for a while. Her therapeutic masseuse, prescribed by her physician, had changed the name of her business to something very New-Agey (actually, the name sounded provocative, sensual). As a result, we had to get proof that the masseuse really was licensed as a physical therapist.

Code Section 105 Medical Reimbursement Plans

Created for farming families whose lives are closely tied to their businesses, this is a special provision of the Tax Code. It provides a way for family businesses to deduct all the medical insurance and medical expenses for family members from their business returns, just the way you can for your employees. The plan is based on the premise that you can hire your spouse, paying him or her a salary. The family medical plan is part of the compensation. There are stringent rules to follow, including having a plan document and keeping records of all the expenses and reimbursements. You could do it yourself or with the help of your tax professional. You can also contact the Agri-BizPlanNOW folks at TASC. You can reach them at (888) 595-2661, extension 17732. They pretty much own this niche, so they are quite efficient and reasonably priced. So rather than trying to re-create the wheel, don't do it yourself and get it wrong. Contact them. For more information, go to https://www.tasconline.com/products/bizplan/section-105-plan/.

If you prefer to do it yourself, you will need a plan document. You will find a link to a template you can use in this chapter's Resources. Update it to comply with current rules. Make sure you don't issue reimbursement checks to your spouse or your employees unless you have a copy of the medical receipt in your hands—and it qualifies as a medical deduction. Keep separate files for each employee and separate files for each year—either with tabs or using different folders for each year.

However, I strongly advise you to turn over the administration of your plan to someone experienced with the details of compliance. Avoid this extra stress. You're much better off using your time to generate income in your business.

Since Section 105 lets your business deduct all the family medical expenses, not just the insurance premiums, the savings are substantial.

The Section 105 Plan in Action

Ward Carver is self-employed by his California business. He hires his wife, June, to answer his phones at his office. He pays her a modest salary, so she has some spending money—$500 per month. In addition to the salary, he sets up a Section 105 plan, giving his entire family full medical coverage. The insurance premiums are $1,200 per month for the family of four ($14,400 per year). Ward and June pay another $125 per family member for dental and visual insurance ($500 per year). Even with the dental insurance providing $1,500 toward Bobby's braces, the Carvers are still paying $3,000 out of their pockets. Bobby's scrapes and Wally's sports activities usually result in a few hospital visits, generally at least $500 per year. Ward's and June's annual checkups and co-pays usually add up to $500 per year. And they spend an additional $500 on Ward's eyeglasses and prescription sunglasses and June's contacts each year. The medical benefits added $19,400 to June's compensation. Since the $19,400 was not subject to employment tax or income tax, it saves the Carver family over $9,000 in taxes (15.3 percent self-employment tax, 22 percent IRS tax, 9.3 percent state tax = 46.6 percent).

Without the Section 105 plan, they would only have been able to deduct the medical insurance, on page 1 of Form 1040. This reduces the Carvers' taxes by about $4,500 ($14,400 × 31.3 percent, rounded). As for the other $5,000 of medical expenses, it would have to exceed 7.5 percent of Ward's adjusted gross income (AGI) to be used at all. With the lower threshold under the SECURE Act (it was 10 per cent beforehand), the Carvers might be able to get a medical deduction of $1,250—but only if their overall itemized deductions were to exceed the standard deduction of over $24,800 (in 2020). These days, the average family doesn't have enough itemized deductions to bother.

So, back to the value of the Section 105 plan. The Section 105 plan saved the Carvers more than $4,500 ($9,000 savings less the $4,500 deduction they could have had)—and only cost about $500 to administer.

I know, there are a lot of numbers in that example. Are your eyes glazed over yet? Don't worry. Test out the numbers in your own life with a tax professional who understands fringe benefits and various medical and retirement plans.

The Affordable Care Act of 2010

Ever since 2010, as a small employer, you may take a tax credit if you are paying at least 50 percent of your employees' health insurance costs. The credit is as high as 50 percent (35 percent for exempt organizations). If your spouse or children are your employees—or if you are employed by your corporation—this may apply to you. Watch out, though; the average annual wages of your employees, including yourself, must be under $54,000 ($55,000 in 2020). The IRS provides details and information on how this works in the instructions to Form 8941.

Adoption Credits and Benefits

As an employer, you may pay all or most of the adoption expenses of your addition to your family, as a nontaxable employee benefit. The limits change each year. For 2019, the amount is $14,080. There is both an adoption credit and an adoption expense. The expense allows employers to pay this benefit to their employees. So it can be an employee benefit for a spouse in a sole proprietorship or partnership, if a spouse is an employee. Or it may be an employee benefit to a shareholder-owner in a corporation. In addition to employer-provided benefit, if the adoption costs exceed $14,080, the new parent may get a tax credit for up to $14,080 on Form 8839 Adoption Credits. For more information, visit IRS Topic 607.

The SECURE Act added a new twist to adoption benefits. Taxpayers may withdraw up to $5,000 from their IRAs or retirement accounts without penalty after December 31, 2019. How does that work? Parents who adopt a child, or give birth to a child, may withdraw that $5,000, penalty-free, as long as the withdrawal is within 12 months of the date of birth or adoption. They don't have to prove the money was used for the birth or adoption costs. The taxes on those distributions will still be due—but not the 10 percent early withdrawal penalty.

Employer-Provided Childcare Facilities Credit

Hardly any small businesses even know about this excellent way to reduce your taxes if you have a child. The IRS will give you up to 25 percent of the cost of a qualified childcare facility for your children—or your employees' children—to a maximum of $150,000 per year. Unused credits may be carried to the future for up to 20 years. That doesn't mean you have to set up your own childcare facility. You can get the credit for paying an existing facility for childcare, as long as it's licensed and meets all the IRS's rules for such facilities. The employer must pay the facility directly; reimbursements are not permitted. Use Form 8882, available at https://www.irs.gov/pub/irs-pdf/f8882.pdf.

You can get another 10 percent credit for the cost of having your child evaluated by an expert to help determine the appropriate childcare facility for your child. This need will usually come into play if your child seems to have trouble learning or adapting to other children.

Your state might have similar credits. For instance, California used to have a 30 percent credit. Although it's no longer available here, something like this might be available in your state. Ask! Just think, if you lived in a state with this credit, and paid $300 per month for your child's care, your tax credit would be $1,080. In addition, the business gets the deduction of $2,520 (total cost of $3,600 reduced by the credit of $1,080). That deduction is worth about $1,100 more (15.3 percent self-employment tax, 24 percent IRS tax, and 5 percent state tax). You've just saved more than $3,000 of the $3,600 costs of your child's daycare ($900 IRS credit, $1,100 deduction, plus $1,080 state credit).

Employer Credit for Paid Family and Medical Leave

This benefit only applies to leave granted to employees—not family members. But it can be an important benefit if you have valuable employees you want to keep. When they have to take time off for personal or medical reasons, you can get a tax credit of 12.5 to 25 percent of the compensation you pay them. You must provide at least 2 weeks of leave time, up to 12 weeks. You must pay them at least 50 percent of their regular wages to get the minimum credit of 12.5 percent. If you pay them 100 percent of their wages, the credit is worth 25 percent of their wages. You can prorate the credit for part-time employees. Family leave is not the same as sick pay. This is for time off for these kinds of things:

- Birth of an employee's child
- Care for the child
- Placement of a child with the employee for adoption or foster care
- Time to care for the employee's spouse, child, or parent who has a serious health condition
- A serious health condition that makes the employee unable to perform the functions of his or her position
- Any qualifying exigency due to an employee's spouse, child, or parent being on covered active duty—or having been notified of an impending call or order to covered active duty—in the Armed Forces
- To care for a service member who is the employee's spouse, child, parent, or next of kin

The form to use is Form 8994 Credit for Paid Family and Medical Leave. The bad news is, this credit expires on December 31, 2020. (Note: The SECURE Act extended it for one year. It was set to expire on December 31, 2019.)

Work Opportunity Tax Credit

Community-minded business owners can pick up a tax credit for hiring people from certain disadvantaged categories. That can include veterans, qualified summer youths, ex-felons, disabled persons, welfare (SNAP) recipients, etc. The credits are taken over the first two years of their employment, as a certain percentage of the employees' wages. Each category of employee comes with a different amount of the credit. You have to hire the individuals through local government agencies to get them certified for the credit. You just might end up with some of the best workers you could ever imagine. (Or not—so screen employees carefully.) For more details, visit the IRS website—especially because this credit keeps expiring and needs to be renewed. The upcoming expiration date was December 31, 2019. But don't worry, Congress usually does renew this credit. And they did. The SECURE Act extended the deadline to December 31, 2020.

Life Insurance

Typically, life insurance is not a deductible expense—certainly not when it is for the benefit of the owner of the business. In a C corporation, though, you may deduct the cost of up to $50,000 coverage for each employee, including the shareholders and officers working for the corporation. Check with your tax professional to see if there are other ways to include life insurance in your business and make it deductible. The corporation may pay for much more coverage, if it chooses, but the additional premiums are added to employees' wages.

Employee Leasing and Trusts

There are ways to use trusts and employee leasing arrangements to generate substantial deductions—and to avoid time-consuming administration issues. This is also a way to move employees out of your pension plan and into one of their own, requiring lower contributions by you. For companies with high profits where the owners are trying to put maximum contributions into their own retirement plans, using an employee leasing service gets around the ERISA rules. That's advanced tax planning, with both benefits and pitfalls, often requiring the services of a sophisticated tax attorney.

Education

Naturally, your business may deduct the cost of all courses you or your staff take to increase your professional or trade expertise related to your business or industry.

Management and business courses and seminars are deductible. When it comes to courses taken in order to get a college degree, you may have to fight to win those deductions. Individual courses related directly to what you need to know for your business can probably be deducted. But those anthropology courses? For a plumber . . . well, I don't think so. You get the idea.

In Chapter 6, we pointed to a Tax Court case in 2010 that clarified some of the issues that determine whether or not you can deduct your education. Lori Singleton-Clarke, a nurse, objected to the IRS's decision in her audit and presented her own case to the Tax Court—and won an impressive decision.

Your company may offer an education assistance plan, reimbursing employees for up to $5,250 of annual education expenses. See IRS Publication 970 for more education fringe benefits. Even graduate-level courses qualify. Before 2002, only courses up to a bachelor's degree or a certificate program were allowable. If you are a C corporation, the cost of your education expenses for a degree may be reimbursed, along with those taken by other employees. However, in an S corporation or other entity does not qualify. You may, of course, deduct the cost of specific seminars or workshops for your industry—just not the cost of the rest of the courses leading to a degree. Unless, of course, you can prove that your degree, like Ms. Singleton-Clarke's, qualifies for the education deduction. (Please note: Employees can no longer deduct their education costs at all. So if the employer can provide the benefits and/or reimburse employee costs, it would be a very valuable perk.) You may hire your spouse or children. If they legitimately work for the business, like any other arm's-length employee, you may be able to reimburse their education expenses as part of their employee compensation. This may be iffy in an S corporation. Since your family members are related parties, the IRS treats them as owning the business, too. Definitely clear this with your tax professional before including it in your business plan, especially because this is an area of tax law that may change soon.

What expenses are deductible when it comes to education? The cost of books, tuition, fees, tools, and supplies related to the course. Sometimes, even computers are deductible. Travel to the course or seminar is also included as well as meals, if you are gone overnight. There's a broad definition for *tools*. But if you're studying construction and your class project is to build a house and you build one for yourself . . . I don't think you'll be able to deduct the costs as education expenses. So be reasonable when you take deductions on your tax return.

Courses to qualify you for a new business or a new profession aren't deductible. For instance, if I were working for a certified public accounting firm and wanted to take a CPA review course, that wouldn't be deductible for me. Even if I took the course and passed, and I continued to do exactly the same job as before, as if nothing had changed, it would *not* be deductible. The IRS considers CPAs a different profession than simply a degreed accountant. However, individual courses relating to accounting and tax topics would be deductible. Look at your industry and see how that relates.

In addition to being able to provide up to $5,250 worth of reimbursements to your employees (including family employees), as an employer, you may pay for courses directly related to your business. For instance, I pay for continuing education courses for my long-term staff. When appropriate, I also pay for their travel and lodging. For instance, you will find us in Las Vegas or Reno each year at the IRS Tax Forums or the NAEA or NATP or CSTC Seminars.

Education deductions can be lucrative—or they can be dangerous. However, for the next few years, even if you can't use the deductions as business expenses, you have education credits and above-the-line deductions available to use. The American Opportunity Credit is worth up to $2,500 per eligible student; the Lifetime Learning Credit is worth up to $1,000 per person for up to two people per tax return. Publication 970 provides current information.

Don't forget about the working benefit fringe—that's a nice little secret allowing you, the employer, to pay more than just $5,250 toward your employees' education (think—your spouse or child working for your business). When the education payments qualify as a working benefit fringe, none of the payments are taxable to the employee—even if the employer pays out $30,000 or more. How do you get that? Well, there must be a written plan, the benefit must be available to all employees, without favoring "highly compensated employees," and it must cover practically all costs, except for tools and supplies that employees get to keep after the course ends. Alas, it cannot cover the owners of the business. But even small businesses can offer this benefit, say, to family members who don't meet the definition of "related parties" when it comes to ownership of the business.

Retirement Plans

The good news is, if your business follows your business plan, you'll be making lots of money and living well. The bad news is, you won't die young. At least, so says the Centers for Disease Control and Prevention (CDC). The CDC's 2017 projections say you'll live until age 78.6. That looks like a long time from now, doesn't it?

News flash. It sneaks up on you faster than you can imagine. I was just 24 last week. Or so it seems. I blinked and (many) more than two decades passed. Looking around at friends, family, and clients, many are living well into their eighties and nineties. In fact, have you seen Raquel Welch lately? (Google her pictures online.) She is still looking stunning! May we all look that good and be that healthy at her age. If we're going to live a long, healthy life, we'd better look toward saving for our own longevity.

Retirement Basics You Must Know

Each investment vehicle has contribution limits based on your income, except the SIMPLE-IRA. In general, if you (or your spouse) have a job with a retirement plan, your contribution to any plans related to an IRA will be limited.

You may contribute $1,000 to $6,000 extra per year if you're age 50 or over, depending on the plan retirement plan you establish for your business. These contributions are called catch-up contributions. All contribution amounts, catch-ups, and income limits change based on inflation or congressional rules.

You may not put money into all these retirement vehicles at once. Putting money into one will generally conflict with your right to fund one of the other retirement options—so pick the optimum retirement plan(s) for your business.

A common misconception is that these plans are investments. The plans themselves are not. They are vehicles (or buckets) into which you put money. You may open these plans with banks, brokerages, or perhaps even with insurance companies. Once you open the account, the brokerages and mutual fund companies let you diversify and manage your investments. You control the rate of the return by watching the appropriate market. You may move the funds from one company to another—as long as they stay within the same investment vehicle.

All the plan descriptions assume you have no employees. If you have any, please see a good local tax professional who understands qualified and nonqualified plans. And if that person doesn't know what those terms mean, go somewhere else.

Tax-Free Retirement

Tax-free means you'll never have to pay tax on the money when you take it out. You also don't generally get a deduction for your deposits when you make them, though. Table 10.2 provides an overview of the tax-free plans. Here are the details of some plans available to small business owners.

Roth IRAs. For any year, contributions to Roth IRAs must be deposited by April 15 of the following year (or the first business day after April 15, if it falls on a weekend or holiday). For 2019 and 2020 contributions, for example, you may contribute up to $6,000, plus a catch-up of $1,000 by April 15, 2020 or 2021.

There is no deduction for the amount you contribute to a Roth IRA. Obey the rules—you'll get all the money out tax-free when you retire. You may only draw

TABLE 10.2 Tax-Free Retirement and Savings Plans Available in 2019 (2020 if different)

Tax-Free	Roth IRA	Municipal Bonds in Your State	Section 529 College Plans	Employee 401(k)s 403(b), 457, SAR-SEP
Basic contribution 2019 and 2020	$6,000	No limit	$15,000 —tied to the current year gift tax exclusion limit	$19.000 ($19,500)
Age 50 catch-up	$1,000	N/A	N/A	$6,000
Income limits— single	$122,000–$137,000 ($124.000–$139,000)	No limit	No limit	
Income limits— joint	$183,000–$193,000 $193,000–$203,000 ($196,000–$206,000)	No limit	No limit	
Date account must be opened	April 15 of following year	N/A	December 31 of plan year	December 31 of plan year
Date contribution is due	April 15 of following year	N/A	December 31 of plan year	October 15 or tax return filing date
Pros	Qualified withdrawals are not taxable.	Earnings are not taxable. Draw money anytime.	Earnings are not taxable if funds are spent on courses, supplies, or room and board, including travel or hobbies.	
Cons	People who deposit early may face penalties if they don't remove the funds by April 15, when they prepare their tax returns and don't qualify. Requires planning. May not withdraw for five years.	Low interest rate. Tax-free interest may be subject to alternative minimum tax and other modified adjusted gross income (MAGI) computations.	This isn't really a retirement fund. It's an education fund. It can affect financial aid considerations. Disclose on the FAFSA application.	
Age to draw	59½	Anytime	Anytime	

the money out of your own account when you or your spouse are over age 59½ and you've left the money in the account for five years. In times when investments do well, this is a very appealing investment. For young people, whose money will grow in these IRA accounts for 15 or 20 years, this option can yield a generous source of tax-free money in the future.

Why doesn't everyone use it? Several reasons:

- The contribution allowed is low.
- The income limits to qualify are low.
- Roths are a nuisance to fix if you contribute when your income is too high.

Section 529 College Education Plans. For 2019 and 2020, you may contribute up to $15,000 per beneficiary, per year. Or in the first year, you may deposit up to $75,000, using up five years' contributions at once. Contributions must be made by December 31 of the plan's year. Section 529 plans are unique because, although you are gifting a fortune to your child, relative, or friend, you still have control of this asset. At any time you choose, you may pull it back into your own estate and keep the money. Or if your beneficiary doesn't use up all the money, you may either transfer it to another student or take it back. The money may be spent on tuition, fees, books, supplies, room, and board—as long as the school is on the approved list. As a result of the PATH Act of 2015, you may also use the money for computer equipment and technology.

Here are the eligible beneficiaries to whom you can transfer the funds from IRS Publication 970:

Members of the Beneficiary's Family

For these purposes, the beneficiary's family includes the beneficiary's spouse and the following other relatives of the beneficiary:

1. Son, daughter, stepchild, foster child, adopted child, or a descendant of any of them
2. Brother, sister, stepbrother, or stepsister
3. Father or mother or ancestor of either
4. Stepfather or stepmother
5. Son or daughter of a brother or sister
6. Brother or sister of father or mother
7. Son-in-law, daughter-in-law, father-in-law, mother-in-law, brother-in-law, or sister-in-law
8. The spouse of any individual listed in this list
9. First cousin

You're saying 529s are not really retirement plans? My approach is perhaps novel. No one else has written about this—but it was cleared with the IRS on May 13, 2004. The IRS agrees it's legal. If you are related to the beneficiary, you may transfer the money to yourself as the new beneficiary, even if you're a senior citizen (note the reference to "ancestors"). Once in your name, you're free to use that money to get educated—taking courses on cruise ships, traveling across Europe or wherever, including most expenses and course supplies for accredited schools. Just think—gourmet cooking school, scuba training, professional golf college . . . what have you always wanted to learn? Just make sure the schools are accredited.

New—Some Changes to Section 529 Plans

First, let's discuss qualified elementary and secondary education expenses. For distributions made from qualified tuition programs (QTPs) after 2017, qualified education expenses may include no more than $10,000 paid for elementary or secondary school tuition. That includes certain qualified home schooling expenses.

Second, you can roll money over to ABLE accounts. ABLE accounts are special accounts for persons with disabilities. An amount distributed from a QTP after December 22, 2017, isn't taxable if it's rolled over to an ABLE account for the benefit of the same beneficiary or for the benefit of a member of the beneficiary's family (including the beneficiary's spouse).

The SECURE Act added two new provisions for Section 529 plans:

- Costs related to registered apprenticeships qualify as educational costs.
- Up to $10,000 may be withdrawn from a Section 529 plan to pay student loans. That total may be applied to principal or interest. And it's only a once-in-a-lifetime limit. In other words, if you use $5,000 to pay toward a student loan in 2020, you still have up to $5,000 to use in the future. Incidentally, if any Section 529 funds are used to pay the student loan interest, the taxpayer cannot deduct that interest on their tax return.

Your Home: A Tax-Free Strategy. Buy a home and build equity. You may sell a home every two years and keep up to $250,000 ($500,000 for couples) tax-free. Use the proceeds to buy the next home in a rapidly appreciating area. Repeat every few years. Ten years before you plan to retire, accelerate the mortgage payments so you pay off the loan entirely. If your profits look as if they'll be more than $500,000, add your children, living at home, to the title. Each owner, who resides in the house, gets that $250,000 exclusion. Along the way, you collected lots of money to use either toward a better house or toward funding your retirement plans, or both. Once retired, you'll have no mortgage payments, so if anything goes wrong with your retirement accounts (as happened to many in April 2000, and again in 2009 and 2010), you'll still be fine. If you ever need money, simply make sure to establish a home equity line of credit (HELOC). A home equity line costs little or nothing to have if you are not tapping into the money. You only pay interest on any money you borrow—usually at favorable rates. Set up the HELOC when you don't need it, that ensures you can access cash quickly when you have an emergency—like needing a roof, or fixing things after a storm, fire, or flood.

Tax-Deferred Opportunities

Tax-deferred means you get a deduction or credit for your contributions now, when you deposit the money. But you'll pay tax on all the money when you take it out.

There is a whole menu of retirement savings opportunities, but they're deceptively complicated. Many have income limits and strings attached. Use Table 10.3 as a starting point. Discuss the options with your own tax pro. Table 10.3 provides an overview of tax-deferred plans. Here are the details of some plans available to small business owners.

TABLE 10.3 Tax-Deferred Retirement and Savings Plans Available in 2019 (2020 if different)

Tax-Deferred	IRAs	SEPs	Simple IRAs	Solo 401(k)s
Basic contribution	$6,000	25% of income up to $56,000 ($57,000)	$13,000	Up to $56,000 ($57,000)
Age 50 catch-up	$1,000		$3,000	$6,000
Income limits— single	$61,000–$71,000 $64,000–-$74,000 ($65,000–$75,000)	$280,000		
Income limits— joint	$98,000–$118,000 $103,000–$123,000 ($104,000–$124,000)	$280,000		
Defined plan limits		$280,000		
Date account must be opened	April 15 of following year	SEP—Due date of your tax return	September 30 of plan year	December 31
Date contribution is due	April 15 of following year	Due date of your tax return, including extensions	30 days after the end of the month for which you're making contributions	Due date of your tax return, including extensions

Tax-Deferred	IRAs	SEPs	Simple IRAs	Solo 401(k)s
Types of Plans Available		Money purchase, profit-sharing, defined benefit		
Pros	Contributions are deductible.	Contributions are deductible. Employer may match with profit-sharing contributions.	1% or 3% matching may be paid on due date of return, including extensions. Employees may contribute up to 100% of compensation.	You may transfer over your IRA balances and borrow up to 50% or $50,000. Employees may also borrow from their 401(k)s if set up to allow that.
Cons	Withdrawals are taxable.	Withdrawals are taxable. Employee salary reduction contributions cannot be made under a SEP.	Withdrawals are taxable.	If you close the business or the plan, you must pay back the loans or pay early withdrawal penalties and taxes.
Special Rules Phase-out	Applies only if covered by qualified plan at work or from your own business.	Income is net business profit or wages per person.		
Special Rules		Lets you contribute up to 100% of business earnings or up to 25% of all employees' earnings.	Employer must also match 1% or 3% of employee's wages, if employee participates, and/or owner's profits—for Schedule C.	Employees with outstanding loans from 401(k) have additional time to repay the loan— until tax return due date, including extension, due to TCJA.

Savings Incentive Match Plan for Employees (SIMPLE IRAs)

You may contribute up to $13,000 for 2019 or 2020 plus $3,000 catch-up. You may contribute your entire profit, or wages from your own corporation or limited liability corporation (LLC), up to those limits. The employees' contributions must be deposited by December 31, or immediately after the last payroll in December. As your own employer, you must also make a matching contribution of 1 or 3 percent of your wages or profits. The matching contribution may be funded when you file your tax return, including extension. So be sure to put your personal or business tax return on extension. The plan must be opened by September 30 in the same year that you plan to use it. For example, for 2020, you must open the SIMPLE IRA by September 30, 2020, to be able to deduct contributions on your 2020 tax return. This applies even if the owner is the only participant.

Simplified Employee Pension (SEP-IRA)

You may fund 25 percent of your net profits or wages from your own business, up to $56,000 ($57,000 for 2020), into an SEP-IRA. You may set up and fund SEP-IRAs until the due date of your tax return, including extensions—another reason to go on extension. This is the only retirement plan that allows you to open it *and* fund it that late into the following year. For folks with large profits, this is the best way to reduce some of the tax hit for the previous year.

Special strategy tip: If you don't really have the spare cash to fund the SEP-IRA, here's how you can get around it if you don't have employees who qualify for a pension contribution. Open a solo 401(k), effective for the current tax year, as we will discuss soon. Open and fund the SEP-IRA for the *previous* year. Give it a few weeks. Then roll the funds into the new solo 401(k). You may borrow up to 50 percent of the account balance up to $50,000 from your solo 401(k). So you can fund your SEP-IRA for 2020 in 2021, but get the money right back if you need it for operations in 2021.

Solo 401(k)s

These are like the regular 401(k)s you might get from an employer—only much better. You have the same contribution limits as the SEP-IRA—$56,000 ($57,000 for 2020) (plus the $6,000 catch-up). But the percentages are more generous. At lower levels of income, you may contribute 100 percent of your wages. The best part about these plans is that you may roll over your funds from your existing IRA into a solo 401(k) account. Then, as mentioned immediately before, you may borrow up to 50 percent of the account balance, or up to $50,000. You will be paying yourself back over five years. If the loan is used to buy your primary residence and secured against the residence, you have a longer payback period. You will have a relatively favorable interest rate. So whatever you borrow will still be repaid toward your retirement. This is the only account that lets you and your spouse (and even your children if they are employees) get the maximum tax benefit—but still gives you access to your money. If each family member works for you, legitimately, and owns shares in the company, they may each have their own plan. That means, in a couple of years, you could have access to $100,000 or more easy capital (your account and your spouse's). You may borrow the money without penalties or taxes, as long as you honor the payment plan—and don't shut down the business. Otherwise, you will face early withdrawal penalties and taxes if you close the business and the 401(k) plan, don't pay it back.

Great news! The Tax Cuts and Jobs Act (TCJA) made repayment terms more lenient. This applies to all employees who have borrowed from their 401(k) accounts. In the past, when you left your job (or closed the business and/or the 401(k) plan), you had to pay the money back—or roll it over into an IRA—within a short period of time—generally 60 days or so. The TCJA extended the repayment or rollover period. Now you can replace those funds until you file your tax return for the final year of employment (or the plan), including extensions. In other words, speaking to business owners, if you shut down your plan in 2020, you have until October 15, 2021, to repay any outstanding 401(k) loans. But, you must be sure to put your tax return on extension—otherwise your repayment deadline is April 15, 2021. If the plan account is still open, you can deposit all the funds (loan plus interest) into that account. Or you can open an IRA and deposit the full amount due into the IRA. Remember to watch this deadline. If you don't repay all the funds into the 40(k) account or an IRA, you will face taxes and potential early withdrawal penalties.

Defined Benefit Plans

Defined benefit plans are a different animal and require some long-term planning. The concept is to provide you with a specific monthly payout when you retire. To get that payout later, how much do you have to put away now? The older you are, the more you get to put away. The computation is predicated on the three highest consecutive earnings years based on income or wages from your business. The annual benefit limit for 2019 and 2020 is $280,000. You may contribute as much as 100 percent of those wages to achieve the benefit limit. The plan must be opened before December 31 of the year for which you want to contribute, but it may be funded until you file your tax return, including extensions.

This is an excellent option for anyone wanting to build up plan assets quickly and get immediate deductions for the contributions. This is especially valuable for folks closer to retirement age. The biggest objection to these plans is that once you set them up, you are obligated to make the annual payment to cover the defined benefit, even if your business doesn't show any profits or doesn't have the money to cover the costs. So what do you do in lean years? Suspend the plan. But be very careful how you handle this. If you get your timing wrong, the whole plan is invalid and may be subject to penalties. Work with a tax planning professional who really understands this area well. Not all do. And stay with that tax professional, when it comes to dealing with this plan, until you retire. So be very discerning about whom you choose.

A good tax professional, whether it's an attorney, enrolled agent, or certified public accountant, can help you devise the best way to set aside money for the future by letting Uncle Sam give you tax breaks. This will cut the financial pinch so you can live well now—and when you're age 77 and beyond.

One last caveat: limits and benefits change all the time. So if you build a retirement plan, be sure to get your professional or trade organization, friends, contacts, chamber colleagues, and family to lobby Congress to keep the provisions intact.

Using the IRS to Your Advantage

Clearly, with the right kind of planning, you can practically wipe out your present tax obligation or at least move much of it to your retirement years, when your earnings are likely to be lower; although I'm finding that many of my clients' earnings are higher during their nonworking years than they were when they were struggling. A nice surprise.

One of the nice surprises they've gotten is Social Security. They didn't really expect it to still be there for them. So let's just address that for a moment. In all our efforts, we've done our best to reduce or eliminate the self-employment taxes paid in. You may want to rethink that strategy.

For those of you who have not built up your Social Security account, you may want to pay in for a while. This may be especially important to immigrants who don't have their 40 quarters paid in through jobs. Have your tax professional help you develop a balanced strategy that cuts your taxes, increases your retirement income— and also ensures that you get the most out of Social Security when you retire.

Resources

In this chapter, you saw a variety of resources. Here's a summary of them, so you can find them quickly and easily. The resources are not necessarily in alphabetical order in each category. They are in order of their importance or usefulness, in TaxMama's opinion.

Resources

- **HealthCare.gov Federal Health Insurance Marketplace.** https://www
  .healthcare.gov/small-businesses/
  - ○ **HSA Resource.** http://iTaxMama.com/HSA_Info. All about health
    savings accounts.
  - ○ **Health Insurance for Dependents Under Age 26.** https://www.hhs
    .gov/healthcare/about-the-aca/young-adult-coverage/index.html
  - ○ **Explanation of Health Savings Accounts (HSAs).** http://TaxMama
    .com/insurance/hsa
  - ○ **HealthCare.Gov.** HSA information. _Info, http://iTaxMama.com/HSA.
    Look at the links to all the related resources. They are generally
    up-to-date.
- **Section 105 Medical Reimbursement Plan Document.** You can use this as
  a basic template. http://www.smbiz.com/sbfrm002.html
- **TASC's Agri-BizPlanNOW.** https://www.tasconline.com/products/bizplan
  /section-105-plan/, (888) 595-2661, extension 17732. Rather than a
  do-it-yourself Section 105 plan, call these folks. They have a long history
  of experience.
- **IRS information on S Corporations and Health Insurance.** http://iTax
  Mama.com/S-Corp_Health
- **IRS Information About the Small Business Health Care Tax Credit and
  the SHOP Marketplace.** http://iTaxMama.com/Employer_HealthCareCredit
  - ○ Unfortunately, as I write this, the IRS numbers only go through 2017.
    For the most current annual wage limits, look at Form 8941 for the year
    in which you provide the benefits at http://iTaxMama.com/F8941
    _EmployerHealthCr.
- **IRS Form 8889 Health Savings Accounts (HSAs).** https://www.irs.gov
  /pub/irs-pdf/f8889.pdf
- **IRS Publication 502 Medical Expenses.** https://www.irs.gov/forms-pubs
  /about-publication-502

Other Benefit and Tax Break Resources

- **ABLE Accounts and Section 529 Rollovers.** http://iTaxMama.com/529
  _ABLE
- **Adoption—IRS Topic 607.** https://www.irs.gov/taxtopics/tc607.html
- **Adoption Credit.** https://www.irs.gov/pub/irs-pdf/f8839.pdf

- **TaxMama's AccountingWeb.com Blog Article About How the Nurse Won the Right to Deduct Her MBA.** http://iTaxMama.com/Deduct_MBA
- **Employer-Provided Childcare Facilities and Services.** https://www.irs.gov /pub/irs-pdf/f8882.pdf
- **IRS Publication 15-B,** *Employer's Tax Guide to Fringe Benefits.* https://www.irs.gov/pub/irs-pdf/p15b.pdf
- **IRS Publication 970,** *Tax Benefits for Education.* https://www.irs.gov /publications/p970/. For education fringe benefits.
    - ○ **Accredited school information.** https://www.irs.gov/pub/irs-pdf/p970 .pdf#page=52
- **Form 8994 Credit for Paid Family and Medical Leave.** https://www.irs .gov/forms-pubs/about-form-8994
- **Information About the Credit for Paid Family and Medical Leave.** http://iTaxMama.com/Form8994-Family-Leave.
- **SEP Retirement Plans for Small Businesses.** https://www.dol.gov/sites /default/files/ebsa/about-ebsa/our-activities/resource-center/publications /sep.pdf
- **The 401k Help Center.** http://iTaxMama.com/401k_HelpCenter. The 401k Help Center's chart compares contribution limits to various plans for self-employed and incorporated businesses. They provide several years' limits, side by side.
- **CNNMoney.com Retirement Calculator.** http://money.cnn.com/retirement /tools/index.html
- **Centers for Disease Control and Prevention (CDC) Fast Stats on Average Life Expectancy.** https://www.cdc.gov/nchs/fastats/life-expectancy.htm
- **Work Opportunity Tax Credit.** http://iTaxMama.com/Work_Opportunity _Credit

TaxMama Resources

- **TaxMama's Quick Look-Ups.** http://iTaxMama.com/TM_QuickLookUp. You will find all kinds of useful reference materials, webinars you can replay, e-books, and more.
- **Your Business Bible.** http://www.yourbusinessbible.com. Look for worksheets, printable checklists, and other goodies and resources.

To-Do List and Questionnaire

☐ 1. Is your business profit over $5,000? _____ Yes _____ No

☐ 2. Are you making estimated tax payments? _____ Yes _____ No
Or have you adjusted your or your spouse's payroll withholding?

☐ 3. For ES tax payments, input date you set up EFTPS account: _____

☐ 4. Date you set up your state e-pay account (if applicable): _____

☐ 5. List your estimated tax payments for the year:
Refund applied: IRS amt. _____ State amt. _____ Local amt. _____
Date: _____ IRS amt. _____ State amt. _____ Local amt. _____
Date: _____ IRS amt. _____ State amt. _____ Local amt. _____
Date: _____ IRS amt. _____ State amt. _____ Local amt. _____
Date: _____ IRS amt. _____ State amt. _____ Local amt. _____

Remember to put a copy of each document behind this page, folded in half.

11

ESTIMATED PAYMENTS

*I love giving the IRS lots of money. It means I have made
a huge fortune!*

—TaxMama

Estimated Payments Overview

You're in business now. Cool, isn't it? But your safety net is gone. If you're not on payroll, you don't get any W-2s. For the first time, you have to make your own tax deposits. Your mind is filled with questions:

- When do you make them?
- What forms do you use?
- Where do you send them?
- How much should you pay?
- What's the big deal if you don't make the payments?

Not making payments can cost you big-time! That's one of the two ways to destroy your business and drain your cash flow. (The other way is to skip paying payroll taxes. See Chapter 9 to learn about this important topic.) While it may hurt your wallet a little to make the payments each quarter, it might wipe you out, or worse, to try to pay all the taxes on April 15.

If you want to succeed in business, set the money aside and pay the tax throughout the year.

What's in It for You?

When you have a system to guide you, life is much less stressful. There's a comfort to knowing how much to budget each month for each of your expenses. Taxes are no different.

If you're a numbers freak, like me, you like to see a nice, steady monthly cash flow statement, with all the numbers being consistent. Knowing how much you'll need to pay the IRS each quarter, you can put a fixed-dollar amount aside each month. You won't have to panic, wondering if you must make up for last quarter and pay a large amount all at once.

Best of all, if you do come up short, the IRS will go out of its way to help you because you've established a consistent history with the agency. It's like a credit history. The IRS is used to dealing with people who are contentious and belligerent. You'll be a breath of fresh air.

Think how easy it will be to get bank or venture capital financing once people see how responsibly you've handled your tax obligations. Lenders and investors get skittish when business owners come to them after having gotten themselves into tax trouble. Naturally, if you're totally brilliant and have a killer product, the "angels" might overlook your financial failings. Of course, they'll charge you more for the money—or demand a bigger share of your company due to the financial risk you create, needlessly.

Then again, not everyone needs to be paying estimated taxes. After all, if you don't have a profit, you don't need to pay taxes, estimated or otherwise.

Who Should Be Making Estimated Payments?

There are four categories of people who should be paying estimated payments:

1. People who are self-employed
2. People whose nonwage income is increasing (or expected to increase) in the current year
3. People who have done well on the stock market
4. People who have gotten a healthy inheritance (or other windfall), with assets that produce income

Anyone else? For business owners receiving wages, if you expect to owe extra taxes, simply have your tax professional manipulate your payroll tax withholding before year-end. That way, you never have to make estimated payments.

There is one other category, which is hitting the news a lot these days. And that's collecting and paying sales taxes. Not an IRS issue—but it affects your relationships with your state, and other states. We'll talk more about this in Chapter 12, For now, please understand that if you are selling things and collecting sales taxes, be sure to submit your payments according the schedule your state established for your volume of sales.

When Should You Be Making Those Payments?

When we talked about payroll quarterlies in Chapter 9, you learned that "quarterly" means every three months, right? Not when it comes to estimated payments. We're dealing with the tax code here. Some extremely clever lawmakers decided that *quarterly*, for tax purposes, breaks down as indicated in Table 11.1. Notice that sometimes you've got to pay within two months; other times, the quarter is four months long.

TABLE 11.1 Estimated Payment Schedule

When the 15th falls on a weekend or holiday, it's due on the following business day.			
Quarter	**Earnings Period**	**Due Date**	**Number of Months**
1st (Q1)	January 1–March 31	April 15	3
2nd (Q2)	April 1–May 31	June 15	2
3rd (Q3)	June 1–August 31	September 15	3
4th (Q4)	September 1–December 31	January 15 of following year	4

How Much Must You Pay?

Before we get into any payment specifics, let's start with some fundamental tips about making estimated tax payments. You will find a handy link at the end of this chapter to the online version of IRS Publication 505, which is about withholding and estimated tax payments. Changes in the rules will appear there.

You will be using Form 1040-ES, and your state's equivalent. For the current year, look up the instructions to Form 1040-ES.

Typically, you must only pay estimates *if*:

1. You expect to owe $1,000 or more beyond any payroll withholding.

and

2. Your withholding or other tax credits (education, children, and so on) will be less than 90 percent of the tax you expect to owe on your current year tax return. (If your income falls into the "wealthy" or "high-income" levels for the year, you must pay 100 percent of what you expect to owe.)

or

3. Your withholding or other tax credits (education, children, etc.) will be less than 100 percent of the tax shown on your prior year's tax return. If you expect to have losses from the business, don't worry about making estimated tax payments on the business.

Wise heads feel that it is best to pay the minimum required taxes in advance. You can put your money to better uses than the IRS can.

My Short Method

Use this shortcut if your expected taxable income will be the same as or higher than it was last year. It's so simple. Everyone loves using it.

Start with your last year's return:

Look at page 2 of your 1040, where it says—total tax. Let's say it was:	$10,000
From that, deduct any withholding you have from any sources (wages, interest, dividends, unemployment). Let's say:	$3,000
Deduct the withholding you expect to have for this year from last year's taxes:	$7,000
Divide the result by four quarters ($7,000 ÷ 4):	$1,750

Ta-daaa! That's how much you should be paying each quarter. That's it. That's all there is to it. Read no further.

That Makes You Nervous? You Want to Pay More?

You'd rather pay just enough to owe nothing next April? OK, increase each of those payments by a couple of hundred dollars.

You don't have to. All you have to do to avoid the penalties is to pay the minimums. Some people prefer to have a small refund. That's fine. Uncle Sam can surely use your money.

You're well within your rights to open a savings account or investment account to hold those funds until it's time to pay. But in today's economic climate it may not be worth going to all that trouble. Earning less than 0.5 percent interest on my money doesn't excite me. On $5,000, that's less than $25 of interest for the whole year. Of course, when interest rates rise—or if your additional tax due is much larger—you may have an incentive to hold on to that money.

Cash Flow Strategy: Yes or No?

Some businesses feel they can make better use of this money to grow their operations, so not making estimated payments is part of their strategy. This is not a good idea.

Take the example of the Klaus Company (not the real name), which had a steady stream of work. Klaus's bids were generally accepted for large-ticket jobs. He was able to subcontract some of the work, so he didn't need a payroll. He worked more than 15-hour days on the jobs, usually hundreds or thousands of miles from home. He'd be gone for months at a time. It's not that he didn't want to make the estimated payments, he wasn't home long enough to take care of bookkeeping or administration or to cut the checks. Besides, every time he'd get a job, little disasters beyond his control would occur, wiping out most of the profit on the job. (In one case, he and his crew were not permitted to work during office hours. No one mentioned that when he bid the job.) Often, he'd be working for nothing, due to not including provisions in his contract about specification changes, when he bid the job. While he felt there was no profit at all, he actually made enough of a profit so the household rent and family expenses were being paid. That means he always had lots of self-employment taxes due. Since he didn't set any money aside each quarter, in April there'd be no money. And so he didn't pay the estimates, and he didn't get the bookkeeping done—and he hasn't filed tax returns. He's frequently behind several years, and the IRS is often on the verge of attaching his bank accounts, or home.

In another example, Matt and Jamie Garrison of Aluria Software LLC, considering what it would cost them to borrow money, decided to hold back much of the money from their estimated taxes as their business grew. That money could be better used for payroll, payroll taxes, or advertising. As part of their strategy, they knew at the end of each year they had to save money, quickly, to cover the tax debt by April. They didn't always make it. By filing an extension, the Garrisons were able to keep the late-payment penalties to 0.5 percent per month. With IRS interest rates at the lowest in my lifetime, the penalties and interest paid to the IRS were lower than interest rates charged by traditional lenders.

I bring you the story of Aluria Software LLC because Matt and Jamie successfully built it into a million-dollar business. Their strategy did not get them into big trouble. Aluria is one of the few companies that managed its funds successfully using this strategy, until it got bought out—for millions of dollars.

Generally, when companies start tapping into the tax coffers, they're signing the death knell for their business. They end up like Klaus, whose business and marriage were both in jeopardy.

Worst-Case Scenario

Did I forget to tell you? Getting behind on your estimated taxes may destroy your marriage.

There's this whole snowball effect. First it's last year's estimates; then this year's taxes. Then the IRS is attaching your bank account or levying your spouse's wages. Then your children start noticing that you're afraid to answer the phone or get the mail. You start losing sleep. Then you start quarreling with your spouse—usually over nothing. I cringe when I get calls from certain clients. I know they're into this loop. They're depressed. They can't work through their problem. They won't follow my advice, and their business starts going down the tubes. Then the spouse calls.

While people are most afraid of going to jail over their tax troubles, that's not the worst thing that can happen to you. After all, in jail you get room and board, plenty of exercise, and a library to use. You won't work any harder than you do now—probably fewer hours, even. The worst thing isn't going to jail. No, the worst thing is staying home—watching your home, family, and reputation fall apart.

Am I scaring you? Well, I'm trying to.

Sorry, my friends, but I've been doing this for a long time, working with people who think the rules don't apply to them. Your tax professional probably isn't dealing with this—he or she is sending those failures to people like me. There are a few of us in each town who work with taxpayers in trouble. We're not the ones running those ads on the radio or television, collecting huge fees. But the pros know who we are. People only come to us by word of mouth. It's a gut-wrenching business. I hate this part of my practice, and all of us in it want to do less of it. The only way for that to happen is to convince you not to get into trouble. So . . . don't monkey with your tax obligations.

If you can't afford your estimated payments now, what makes you think you'll be able to pay them in April? It's time to look at your budget and see what's wrong. Go back to Chapter 2 and review your business plan and budget to see what steps you need to take to be more profitable, or to improve your cash flow.

The only solid reason to delay those payments is when your business is cyclical. If much of your income comes in over the Christmas shopping season, for instance, or during the first quarter—you know you'll have the money in time.

Computing Your Estimated Installment Payments

Ideally, at this point in the book, you should sit down with the tax advisor on your team. (See Chapter 1 to review.) Figure out your payments, project your income, and estimate your profits, from all sources. Prepare for the meeting by making a list of your investments and how much income you expect. Do a realistic projection of your business profits. Your business plan from Chapter 2 and your accounting records from Chapter 4 should come in handy now. Run those numbers through one of the free handy online income tax estimator tools, if you're trying to do this yourself. Use the tax estimator calculators at TurboTax.com, H&R Block, or 1040.com.

Better yet, have your tax professional review the results to determine whether to revise your tax projections.

The main reason to use electronic brains like the online calculators is to compute self-employment taxes, Schedule SE (which you learned about in Chapter 9), and alternative minimum taxes, Form 6251. Whenever I see people guesstimating their tax liability, those are the two big surprises they get on April 15. You think you have no taxable income because your mortgage, property taxes, and child tax credit swallowed up your income. Then these two taxes rear their ugly heads.

Self-employment taxes amount to 15.3 percent of your business profits from Schedule C or your Schedule 1065 K-1.

The alternative minimum tax limits and rules have changed several times during each presidential administration, and Congress is always talking about changing them. All you need to know is that if your itemized deductions are too high or your income reaches certain levels, you will owe taxes you didn't anticipate. You can easily look up the alternative minimum tax levels at the Small Business Taxes and Management website.

The original concept of the alternative minimum tax was to ensure rich people didn't get away without paying taxes. Instead, it's hitting the folks struggling to make ends meet.

There is one bright note about the alternative minimum tax. If you pay it this year for certain kinds of income, next year it generates an alternative minimum tax *credit* (Form 8801). That might reduce next year's tax—unless you have another alternative minimum tax. Chapter 32 of IRS Publication 17 can tell you more.

These are the kinds of questions and issues to submit to the National Taxpayer Advocate. If you have a solution or a viable suggestion, the Advocate is open to your input. The Advocate writes an annual report to Congress, outlining problems taxpayers have had with the IRS and the tax system. The Advocate proposes fixes, which sometimes become legislation. The submission form is on the IRS website.

Incidentally, the IRS also has a program called the Issue Management Resolution System (IMRS), where current systemic problems are reported, investigated, and fixed. This team is part of the IRS Stakeholder Liaison department. Aside from general submissions, they also have a monthly phone call for stakeholders, to give us updates. If you see a systemic problem and cannot figure out how to report it to the IRS, drop by TaxMama.com and tell me about it using the AskTaxMama link in each chapter's Resources. Please give me enough detail so I can pass it on to the IRS. Do *not* include personal information or ID numbers. *Note:* This is not for your personal frustrations, which are probably many. The IMRS is for things like computation errors in forms, printing errors, or other parts of the IRS system and communications pipelines that are broken. For errors on IRS webpages (and there are many—the site is huge), you can personally tell them. You will find the link in this chapter's Resources.

Paying the Tax

Naturally, if you have the money, make the payment. Always put the form number, the tax year, and your Social Security number (and your spouse's) on each check. (See the section on FYTIN in Chapter 13.)

The IRS is pushing its electronic federal tax payment system (EFTPS). Once registered, you can make all your estimated payments online. Please set up your account now. It takes about 5–10 business days to activate the account. Aside from the fact that paying via EFTPS is required for certain kinds of taxes, like payroll taxes, certain exempt organization taxes, and high payments, it's actually a great idea to use an EFTPS account. You can make your payment at the last minute, and you'll get proof that you paid it. The input form asks you all the pertinent questions. You're likely to get the payment applied for the correct tax year and to the correct account.

Is that important? You bet. If you don't put the correct information on the check, the IRS doesn't know to which form or year to credit the payment. This comes back to haunt you. It's such fun having the IRS locate your payment and apply it to the right account and year. You'll learn the IRS coded it wrong when you get a CP23 notice of underpayment (discussed in Chapter 13) for a year you thought you'd paid. So, yes, if you have access—pay online.

If you didn't set up an EFTPS, you may pay by credit card. Chapter 13 tells you how. Since the information about how and where to pay changes so rapidly, it needs to be maintained online.

Tips to Reduce Penalties for Underpayment of Estimated Tax

The IRS bases its penalty computation on the date and amount of your payments. Here's a way to make a December payment look like it was paid on time. Change it from an estimated payment to withholding.

Withholding

Did you know that when your taxes are taken out of your paycheck, the IRS treats all the withholding as if it had been paid in evenly throughout the year? Even if you had a total of $1,000 withheld from January through November and then paid $20,000 in December, the IRS doesn't blink. This is something doctors and lawyers have been doing for decades. But it's not the greatest idea. It means scrambling during the most expensive gift-giving time of the year to come up with big chunks of cash to cover taxes.

While I really don't recommend that you handle your payments that way, it does give you a way to avoid late-payment penalties when you get behind in your estimated payment schedule. After all, if you're reading this book late in the year, there's a chance you haven't kept up with estimated payments until now. You didn't realize how important they were. Now you want to catch up and avoid the penalties.

How does this help when you're in business? If you have a spouse with a job, arrange to increase the withholding for his or her last paychecks of the year. You may even need to deduct everything except $1, so your spouse still gets a check. Will he or she be angry? Not if you hand over the money you would have mailed in for withholding.

When your spouse has a job, it's much easier just to increase his or her withholding all year long. We did that with my husband's paycheck when I operated as a partnership. I didn't need to pay as much each quarter. Now that I am an S corporation, I am on payroll—and taking withholding out.

Another Withholding Option

When being paid as an independent contractor by your own company or a customer's, you have the option of requesting withholding from your fee. There's even a box on the Form 1099-MISC to allow for this. (See Chapter 9.) Take advantage of this option and deduct withholding from each remittance, if it can make your life easier.

Note: Beware! If you have a tendency to be behind on your tax payments, the IRS can mandate that your clients and customers take withholding from your fees and checks.

Annualized Payments Method

When you file your tax return, use the worksheet on page 4 of Form 2210, Underpayment of Estimated Taxes by Individuals. With good bookkeeping software, getting the information you need is easy. You must be able to compute your net profits from January through the end of these months: April, June, September, and December. Armed with this information, you or your tax pro will have to allocate your deductions to each period. You'll need to know when you paid big medical bills, made large charitable donations, or bought the expensive employee tool. Apply all the deductions to the appropriate time frame. Then follow the computations. Better yet, have a computer do it.

I'll tell you right now, unless you owe tens of thousands of dollars' worth of tax, the time investment to fill in this page is prohibitive. Remember, you might save $100 in penalties and pay your tax pro $150 to work out the numbers. (It's not that bad, but it should be.)

This is only worth doing if the substantial part of your income was received in the last three months of the year—or your big expenses happened in the beginning of the year. Otherwise, it won't save you much.

Don't Overpay Your Estimates If You're in Trouble

Perhaps in the past you got into trouble with the IRS or a state. Perhaps you have a former spouse chasing after you for support. Or suppose you've defaulted on your student loan or ignored traffic tickets. Until you clear up those problems, the IRS will be grabbing your refunds. (These are called "offsets.") In your case, you're better off owing a little bit in April, rather than shooting for a big refund. You won't get it.

The best idea, however, is to clear up those old debts or get on a payment plan (which we'll discuss in Chapter 13) so the IRS doesn't embarrass you in your business. The last thing you need is for your employees or vendors to get wind of your tax woes.

Basically, though, if you just follow the guidelines at the beginning of this chapter, the whole process is easy.

Resources

In this chapter, you saw a variety of resources. Here's a summary of them, so you can find them quickly and easily. The resources are not necessarily in alphabetical order in each category. They are in order of their importance or usefulness, in TaxMama's opinion.

Estimated Payment Forms and Tools

- **IRS Tax Withholding Estimator.** https://www.irs.gov/individuals/tax-withholding-estimator
- **Form 1040-ES, Estimated Tax for Individuals.** https://www.irs.gov/pub/irs-pdf/f1040es.pdf
- **Form 2210, Underpayment of Estimated Taxes by Individuals.** https://www.irs.gov/pub/irs-pdf/f2210.pdf

- **Form 6251, Alternative Minimum Tax—Individuals, Estates, and Trusts.** https://www.irs.gov/pub/irs-pdf/f6251.pdf
- **Form 8801, Credit for Prior Year Alternative Minimum Tax— Individuals.** https://www.irs.gov/pub/irs-pdf/f8801.pdf
- **IRS Publication 17, Chapter 32.** https://www.irs.gov/publications/p17/ch32.html
- **IRS Publication 505,** *Withholding and Estimated Payments.* https://www.irs.gov/publications/p505/ch02.html
- **Links to All States' Tax Forms.** http://www.taxadmin.org/state-tax-forms
- **TaxMama's Payment and Installment Agreement Information.** http://taxmama.com/category/installment-agreement/. Scroll down to see the articles and posts.
- **The Taxpayer Advocate's Suggestion Page.** http://taxpayeradvocate.irs.gov/submit-a-suggestion
- **The Taxpayer Advocate Service's—Systemic Advocacy Management System (SAMS).** https://apps.irs.gov/app/samsnet/IssueQualification.jsp. Submit information about problems with the IRS's system (not about your personal frustrations).
- **The Library of Congress's Searchable Legislation Database.** https://www.congress.gov/
- **TurboTax Income Tax Liability Estimator and Other Tools.** https://turbotax.intuit.com/tax-tools/
- **H&R Block Tax Liability Estimator and Other Calculators and Tools.** https://www.hrblock.com/tax-calculator/#/en/te/aboutYou
- **Small Business Taxes & Management Website Quick Look-Up for AMT and Other Annual Limits.** http://www.smbiz.com/sbrl001.html

TaxMama Resources

- **TaxMama's Payment and Installment Agreement Information.** http://taxmama.com/category/installment-agreement/. Scroll down to see the articles and posts.
- **TaxMama's Quick Look-Ups.** http://iTaxMama.com/TM_QuickLookUp. You will find all kinds of useful reference materials, webinars you can replay, e-books, and more.
- **Your Business Bible.** http://www.yourbusinessbible.com. Look for worksheets, printable checklists, and other goodies and resources.

CHAPTER 12: **SPECIAL CONSIDERATIONS FOR ONLINE BUSINESSES—AND BUSINESSES THAT SELL ACROSS STATE LINES**

To-Do List and Questionnaire

☐ 1. Do you have an online business? _____ Yes _____ No

☐ 2. Where is your nexus?
Home state: _____
Fulfillment state: _____
State incorporated: _____
Affiliate states: _____
States with virtual workers or consultants: _____

☐ 3. In which states must you register your business?
_____   _____   _____

☐ 4. With what agencies did you register in each state?
_____ Secretary of State (for LLC or Corporation)
_____ Sales tax department
_____ Employment tax department
_____ Income or franchise tax department
_____ City business license(s)

☐ 5. Do you need to revoke any affiliate relationships in states where laws are too stringent or expensive to comply with? _____ Yes _____ No

☐ 6. Dates notices went to affiliates—by state:
_____   _____   _____
_____   _____   _____

Remember to put a copy of each document behind this page, folded in half.

12

SPECIAL CONSIDERATIONS FOR ONLINE BUSINESSES— AND BUSINESSES THAT SELL ACROSS STATE LINES

Internet Riches Made Easy! How I made $30,000 in 42 days.

—Spam email

WWW = Who, What, Where

In 1996, when talking to radio and television talk show hosts about an Internet site I had created, I had to devote most of that precious on-air time to explaining what the Internet was, how to get on it, and how to use the site's address to find the site.

We've come a long way, baby! We've learned the jargon. We can find websites, with or without their www's. We can tweet, post on Facebook, IM our friends, or text all day.

Today, no business is complete without a website. Even if you sell nothing, it's vitally important to establish a web presence. You certainly want to secure ownership of the uniform resource locator (URL) that is your business's name. (Remember Chapter 1!)

Your website provides information about your business for your clients or customers to access when you're not available. We are all faced with questions our customers ask over and over again. You can easily provide the information online. With the right software and security, even a small company can arrange for clients, vendors, and customers to look up their own accounts, make corrections, and find information.

The web offers many time-saving tools. It's easy to set up an online database with your clients' contact information. In fact, many accounting programs integrate with MS Word or other customer relations management (CRM) software with your iPhone, Android, BlackBerry, or favorite portable communications device. You can email all your clients instantly when something important happens. Or you can target just a few—just those with children, for example. You simply write the message and click—and they have it. They can respond instantly.

Compare that to the time and cost of writing to a hundred people. You print out all the letters, stuff the envelopes, add postage, and get everything to the post office before the last pickup. The Internet offers so many time-saving applications that you can kill a lot of time, saving time. In fact, you can get lost for hours, can't you?

CRM software isn't just good for sending emails, messages, and newsletters. CRM software let's you keep track of all your communications with the client. You can keep notes on conversations—not just for business matter. Be sure to include personal issues. That way, months later, you will seem clairvoyant because you'll be able to bring up things they mentioned and forgot all about when you follow up with them. It can be very flattering when you remember their child's hockey triumph, or that their puppy had been to the vet.

All kidding aside, once you stick your toe into the Internet's web, you're stuck forever. And all kinds of new tax issues and questions surface.

What? I Thought There Was No Internet Tax

You're so right. For now, no one may assess you taxes for your use of the Internet. In fact, the Internet tax moratorium bill (HR 3678) passed in October 2007, extending the moratorium on Internet taxes for another seven years. And so on, and so on, and so on. Finally, in February 2016, President Obama signed the Permanent Internet Tax Freedom Act into law. (It was hidden in part of another bill. You will find the link in this chapter's Resources.)

> SEC. 922. PERMANENT MORATORIUM ON INTERNET ACCESS TAXES AND ON MULTIPLE AND DISCRIMINATORY TAXES ON ELECTRONIC COMMERCE.
>
> (a) PERMANENT MORATORIUM.—Section 1101(a) of the Internet Tax Freedom Act (47 U.S.C. 151 note) is amended by striking "during the period beginning November 1, 2003, and ending October 1, 2015"

(b) TEMPORARY EXTENSION.—Section 1104(a)(2)(A) of the Internet Tax Freedom Act (47 U.S.C. 151 note) is amended by striking "October 1, 2015" and inserting "June 30, 2020."

Subsection (b) means that those states that do tax the Internet have until June 30, 2020, to repeal their laws and come into line with the federal government. So it's all good, right?

Unfortunately, though, that doesn't mean you don't have to pay taxes on the Internet. The legislation only refers to communications activities—being connected to the Internet—access, online services, and hosting services. You can't pay a separate Internet tax for that. But you are paying taxes, nonetheless.

Have you looked at your phone bill lately? You know, the bill for the phone line you use to be connected—even if it's a DSL line or cable.

One of my recent phone bills shows:

Federal Subscriber Line Charge	$8.98	
911 Emergency System	.29	
CA High Cost Fund Surcharge—A	.08	
CA High Cost Fund Surcharge—B	.98	
Universal Lifeline Telephone Surcharge	.48	
Rate Surcharge Credit	2.54	(no explanation)
State Regulatory Fee	.05	
CA Relay Service and Communications Devices Fund	.13	(no one asked if I wanted to donate this!)
Federal Universal Services Fee	.78	
Federal Taxes at 3.00 percent	1.49	
Local Taxes at 10.00 percent	4.96	
Total Taxes and Surcharges	$20.76	

Holy baloney! That adds 20 percent to each of my phone bills. And your state may have other charges not listed here. Are you telling me there are no Internet taxes?

Also, nowhere does any federal law say anything about not taxing income earned online or prevent charging taxes on sales of products and services. Of course you're going to be taxed.

In fact, these days, we need to know about several different kinds of nexus, thanks to recent court cases, like the Wayfair case decided by the Supreme Court in 2018. It's just getting more and more and more complicated to do business and sell products or services to anyone outside your own state. Sometimes, you might not even think in terms of selling across state lines—especially if you sell electronic products that a buyer, somewhere, downloads. When you sell downloads and the buyer uses an Internet wallet or electronic payment system, like PayPal, Google Pay, Amazon Pay, etc., they will typically take care of collecting the taxes and sales tax reporting. They will generally issue you a Form 1099-K to report your sales. (Watch out, though. That report won't include refunds and returns and the fees you paid those companies. So remember to deduct those costs and expenses.)

So now it's not *if* you will be taxed, the real questions are, of course, *where* will you and/or your customers be taxed? To answer that, you must know your nexus.

Nexus

What an odd word—*nexus*. What is it? A car? A telephone company? A quickie photo shop? No! *Nexus* means a place where you have a business presence. It sounds pretty simple, doesn't it?

Not according to Diana DiBello, a senior sales tax architect at Wolters Kluwer. DiBello is one of the top people in the country who have seen the broad picture. She once used nearly 80 PowerPoint slides to explain the complexity of this question to an audience of tax professionals. While the average small business owner doesn't need to know *that* much information, he or she does need to understand the information that typically affects small businesses.

Start by answering these two questions correctly:

- Where is your business located?
- And, Where are your customers located?

First: Where Is Your Business Located?

Consider these questions:

- Is it in your home?
- Is it at your office?
- Is it where your website's server is located?
- Is it where your webmaster is located?
- Is it where your post office box is located?
- Is it where you've incorporated?
- Is it where you're drop-shipping your products?

- Is it where your salespeople are?
- Is it where your affiliates (commissioned sales force) are?
- Is it where your related companies are?
- Is it where your merchant account receives your money?
- Is it where your virtual assistant is located?
- Is it where your online shopping cart is hosted?
- Is it where your mailing list is hosted?
- Is it where your advertising agency or public relations agency is?
- Is it where you're running your ads?
- Is it where your shoppers or customers are located?

Next: Where Are Your Customers Located?

Think about these questions:

- Are they in your state?
  - What county or parish (or other governmental unit) do they live in?
- Are you shipping merchandise to another state?
- Are you selling electronic products that can be downloaded in another state?
- Are you providing services to people in another state?
- Are you providing the services *in* that state, or from your own state?
- How many days are you spending in the other state?
- Do you know if their state charges sales taxes for tangible and intangible products or services?

Are you starting to get the picture? A business's nexus can be widespread. But the good (or scary) news is that with the advent of the Internet, home-based businesses can have customers all over the globe. Literally.

For instance, in my current Enrolled Agent course and my Tax Roundtable meetings, there might be live attendance from Spain, England, Australia, Mexico, Hawaii, Texas, or even right here in California. Conferencing communications are so good that 100 or 10,000 people can tune in on a presentation without loss of visual or audio definition. No! No! I don't have thousands of people in attendance at my online courses. But the IRS does—often.

Why Do We Care About Nexus?

Nexus costs money. Even when you don't think you have a physical presence in a state, that state might believe it has the right to your money. State governments are hungry. With the slump in the economy after the wild ride in the 1990s and again in the early 2000s, state revenues have dropped dramatically. With more people shopping over the Internet, states are also losing the sales taxes they used to count on.

Having to make up the money somewhere, states have tapped into anyone they feel is operating within their reach. And they've won. There are solid legal precedents for states to assess income and sales taxes from people and companies that lightly brush the boundaries of their domain.

Perhaps you remember that infamous day in 1991 when Michael Jordan, playing for the Chicago Bulls, was hit by the state of California for a share of his earnings. David Hoffman, Tax Foundation economist and author of the "jock tax" report, explains: "The jock tax began with California trying to get back at Michael Jordan for beating the Lakers in 1991 and Illinois fought back with a retaliatory tax the next year. Ironically, if Jordan rejoined the Bulls in any capacity, he would find himself paying double taxes."[1]

Once other states learned that California had succeeded in taxing a transient, they too started to see this as a lucrative new means to replenish their depleted treasuries. The "jock tax" now affects all performers traveling across state lines, traveling sales folks, even Internet businesses. Many of my clients are affected. These days, their employers routinely provide W-2s with all the states' incomes and withholdings. Some of my film industry clients get three or four W-2s from the same employer for the same show.

As I predicted in the first edition of this book, this has become a major issue for online retailers. In particular, this is affecting the affiliate marketing community—companies that sell their products online with the help of people like you, who put links on your website to promote companies. You do this with Amazon.com, Vistaprint, the *Wall Street Journal*, and more. New York was the first state to get really aggressive about forcing online retailers based out of state to start charging sales tax if they had affiliates in New York. Now you have Colorado and California, too. Commission Junction is keeping tabs on the situation, since it is one of the major players in the affiliate marketplace. They have published a nexus tax map on their website.

And now that the Supreme Court issued their decision on Wayfair, many states have stepped up to establish sales tax collections requirements for out-of-state merchants. If only all states used the same set of rules. But they don't. Some tax services. Some don't. Some tax electronic downloads. Some don't. Some have modest limits before taxing incoming sales (like $100,000 per year or 200 transactions).

---

1 Tax Foundation report—Washington, D.C., July 14, 2003: "'Jock Taxes' Spread as State and City Governments Try to Maximize Revenue from Nonresidents," available at http://taxfoundation.org/tax-topics/jock taxes.

Others have really low limits (like Washington state's $10,000 or compliance with their overall rules). And a couple of states, like California and New York, give you a break for sales into their states of up to $500,000 before you have to register with their sales tax authorities.

Once you start making a lot of money online, if you're not aware of how the nexus rules and definitions affect your business, you might find yourself paying taxes to a state you've never visited. It's also extremely necessary to have a shopping cart system or order system that tracks the locations of your customers—and lets you differentiate between the tangible and intangible products. This resource at the Streamlined Sales Tax Initiative website allows you to look up the policies of all states in one place. You'll find the link in this chapter's Resources.

Another question that is raised (and I am truly not sure of the answer) is: If you're collecting sales taxes in another state, do you also have to file income tax returns in those states, based on your shipments to (or downloads in) those other states?

Where Is My Nexus?

I sit here in my living room; it is my principal office. I have several websites I don't even know where the servers are located. One of my mailing list servers is in Canada and another is in Georgia—or at least the company I pay is. The company may be hosting its server in China, for all I know. My freelance web designer is in Colorado. My corporation is in California. My partners or freelancers for various ventures are in South Africa, Pennsylvania, one of the Carolinas. Each person is in business for themselves and works with other clients. I have a mailing address in California, but my sites' shopping carts could be anywhere. In fact, I don't even know where many of my cloud-based services are sourced. Do you? My tax returns are electronically transmitted to the IRS from a company headquartered in California—but with locations all over the country. I don't know which location actually transmits my tax returns. My tax clients have been in Africa, Asia, South America, North America, Europe, Australia, New Zealand. . . . My affiliates, those people who get a commission for selling my products or referring clients to me, are all over the world.

With all this information, where is my nexus? And what part of it is affected by tax laws?

You're beginning to see how unclear this can be, even for a small home-based business, once you take it online.

Internet Sales Tax Issues

Internet commerce is no longer a new concept. Businesses are generating billions of dollars online. Even Black Friday and Cyber Monday have moved online. People don't have to queue up half the night to get deals. Still, more new ground will have to be broken to establish guidelines for when and how taxes are paid. We have seen the Supreme Court tackle this—and there will be more cases in the future.

Some of the sales tax issues involved with online transactions are the same ones the mail-order industry has been facing for decades. Currently, domestic sales tax issues are governed by your state's sales tax department. But what will happen in the long run? About 20 years ago, several states got together to create a system and software that collects sales tax from shoppers, remits it to the correct state automatically, and doesn't require the vendor to file forms in those other states. I don't think it ever worked out that way. But, they do have a way to let you volunteer for a free project to collect and report your sales taxes in multiple states. You'll find that link in this chapter's Resources.

What do you do now? DiBello recommends that you stay tuned in to the status of the legislation so that when it does affect you, you're prepared.

Before we leave nexus, it's important for you to understand that there are now several kinds of nexus. Yes, it has gotten more complicated. You can find detailed definitions at the Sales Tax Institute. The link to this detailed explanation is in this chapter's Resources. For now, let me give you brief, basic definitions:

- **Click-through nexus**—This nexus is created when you have someone in another state recommending your product on their website or email. Buyers click on the link and you pay that "agent" a commission.
- **Affiliate nexus**—You own a business or subsidiary, or part of a business in another state.
- **Economic nexus**—You sell enough product or service to someone in the other state(s) that you meet their minimum thresholds requiring you to collect sales taxes in that state(s).
- **Marketplace nexus**—You use a third party, like Amazon, iTunes, or another intermediary, to handle all your sales. They collect the money and deliver your electronic (or tangible) product—and they collect and pay the sales taxes in the appropriate state(s). This option lets you off the hook. It's becoming quite appealing for smaller businesses that don't want the reporting headaches.

The really, really bad news is, according to my contact at Wolters Kluwer, there are more than 50,000 sales tax reporting authorities just within the United States (states, counties, cities, parishes, other subdivisions).

In the meantime, should you simply ignore sales taxes for out-of-state shoppers?

Sales Tax Case Law

DiBello cited interesting situations where states went after companies that have no business presence in a state. Connecticut, for instance, sued Dell Computer for unpaid sales taxes because Dell contracted with a company to provide local service on customers' computers. The Connecticut Superior Court ruled against the state only because of the low volume of service calls. If the volume of repairs were higher, Dell would be paying sales tax in Connecticut.

Dell got hit because it simply had a contract with a local company.

What about your business?

Perhaps you're using an affiliate program or agents to sell your products on their own websites or in their own locales. You might just have created an "agency nexus" in their states. An agency nexus occurs when you have a representative in a state. Exactly what constitutes an agent depends on how aggressive the state is.

In another instance, the Scholastic Corporation was hit by California. You're familiar with Scholastic products. The *Junior Scholastic* magazines are in every dentist's office. We all got Scholastic books and publications in school, even preschool. That's how the publisher got into trouble. Scholastic sold books to students by having their teachers give them order forms and collecting the money. The California Supreme Court held that because the teachers in California schools sell Scholastic's products, Scholastic does have nexus.

Think about how your business and sales avenues are structured. Will agency nexus affect you?

Sales Tax Nexus and Your Business

Because online sales tax is such a hot issue, I want to make sure you receive the best information possible. Until speaking with DiBello, I took a conservative approach to sales tax collections. I had been advising clients and readers that if they started shipping a high volume of sales to a state, it would be wise to register with that state's sales tax authority.

After all, you don't really pay the sales taxes. You collect them from your customers and pass them along to the state. The money only comes out of your pocket if you don't collect but should.

As we pointed out, the old rules relating to collecting sales taxes no longer apply. Hiring a contractor or agent in another state to represent you, along with the agent's other companies, falls under the rules of affiliate nexus. Of course, if you place your own agent in a state and that person represents you exclusively, you've just established a physical presence in that state. For instance, the state of California has a tax collections office in Florida, where many former Californians have retired. California has nexus in Florida. Do you think the state of Florida should be taxing California on the taxes it collects?

You do have to comply with your own state's rules, but you already know that. You registered with your state's sales tax department for in-state sales when you went through your checklist in Chapter 1.

Recently, I spoke to a manager in an educational business based in California. Its employees work remotely—one in a distant city in California, another in Montana, and a project manager in South Africa. These first two people are not being treated as freelancers. They are full-fledged employees. So the company had to register its business in Montana in order to set up the payroll there, which means it also has to file business tax returns in Montana. It contracts with the South African company, so it doesn't have to file tax returns there. Or . . . does it?

Some resources you can use for your business if you're handling all the cross-state sales tax reporting:

- Avalera has a package to help small business owners integrate your accounting software with your sales tax system, http://iTaxMama.com/Avalera
- Wolters Kluwer had a sales tax system to help you integrate your software with the massive reporting requirements, https://taxna.wolterskluwer.com/sales-and-use-tax.

Rents and Services—Domestic and Abroad

Since I started operating on the Internet in early 1995, it became clear to me that federal tax issues were going to emerge. As early as 1998, IRS spokesman Ed Mieszerski ruefully admitted, "Some of these questions [dealing with online taxes] will only be dealt with when they come before us as a result of an examination or court case."[2]

To date, I haven't seen an IRS case addressing these issues head-on. After all, the nexus issues we have been discussing primarily affect states. However, Congress passed legislation, as part of the Tax Cuts and Jobs Act (TCJA), taxing companies that have sent their profits offshore. Remember the global intangible low-tax income (GILTI) taxes we discussed in the Prologue?

As a result, the IRS is in the game, too—on an international level. To avoid problems, you need to be aware of the issues. Following are some real-life scenarios and some points to ponder.

---

2 In a memo to the author, in response to Internet-related tax questions, for use in the 1998 Insiders Series Workshops for tax professionals in Burbank, California.

Incorporated in Nevada (no state income tax), Starry-Eyed, Inc., is based at home in California and receives money from product sales. The company's inventory is stored and shipped from a fulfillment house located in Pennsylvania. The website is hosted on a server in New York. Starry-Eyed encountered the following questions—the answers should help you stay legal, too:

Q: *As a corporation, can it deduct office-in-home costs? (As a proprietor it can, so . . .)*

A: Treat your office at home the way you would if you weren't doing business online. Chapter 7 explains the rules for office in home.

Q: *In which state is it conducting business? All work, including design, artwork, search engine placement, etc., is often done by people working from their homes, often across the country. Under what circumstances would those workers be employees? Will the company have to file income, sales, or property tax forms in each (or any) state?*

A: Consider your business nexus to be only those states where you have a physical presence or meet the affiliate nexus rules. Comply with all local rules. See Chapter 9.

Q: *Should the company be sending a 1099-MISC to the web hosts (those hosting the actual site) for rent?*

A: The web server rent is unclear. If you want to be safe, send the 1099-MISC for rent.

Q: *Some work is being done by foreign nationals in their own country. Since payment is being made for services rendered, how does the company "1099" a foreigner? Must it issue a 1099? Must the company take any backup withholding?*

A: Don't send 1099s to foreign individuals or companies outside the country that do work for you. If you knowingly hire a US citizen or someone who holds a green card who works overseas, issue the 1099-MISC. Don't withhold taxes unless the IRS sends you a withholding order on that person. Review the 1099 instructions in Chapter 9 for guidance. But do have the foreign national fill out and sign a Form W-8BEN for your records—https://www.irs.gov/pub /irs-pdf/fw8ben.pdf. This certifies that the individual is a foreign national, and will allow you to pay the foreign individual without having to deduct any withholding.

However, if no treaty exists between the United States and your affiliate in another country, you as "payor" must withhold 30 percent of the payment and send that off to the Treasury and the balance to the "payee." (This backup withholding also applies to American nationals who refuse to provide you with a signed Form W-9, providing their taxpayer ID number and address.)

To make things just a little more complicated, the foreign individual might have to get an individual taxpayer identification number (ITIN) to claim the treaty benefit. That is where the real problem will present itself, as this is no easy task for those abroad.

Let's look at another company with some different issues.

I Can Sell Anything to Anyone (ICSATA) is based in the United States, and its website also is hosted here. The company operates an associate or affiliate program that pays commissions to people with links on their website to ICSATA's products. Other websites link to ICSATA's site—and ICSATA pays the linked companies a commission on whatever sales arise from those links (this is similar to how Amazon.com operates). Many of the companies that are linked are overseas businesses. The questions to consider here include:

Q: *Is this a commission, referral fee, royalty . . . what?*

A: When someone is a contributor to the design, content, or substance of your product or services, and he or she is contractually entitled to a share of the sales, it's royalty. Otherwise, you're paying commissions. Chapter 5 explains why we care about the distinction.

Q: *Is any of this subject to self-employment tax?*

A: When regular salespeople receive commissions, it's self-employment income. Why shouldn't this be? Chapter 11 explains self-employment taxes.

Frequently, when you ask the IRS these types of questions, you'll receive a vague answer. The previous answers provide the most sensible approach for you to use until the IRS issues formal guidelines.

Legal Issues on the Internet

Once your business touches the Internet, you're going to be hit with some powerful legal issues, and you won't realize it until you get into trouble. Even though the book was written back in 2000, several Internet generations ago, the best guide to this topic is still attorney Jonathan I. Ezor's *Clicking Through: A Survival Guide for Bringing Your Company Online.*

So many things can affect you, even if you're just minding your own business:

- **You face copyright issues.** For instance, did your web or logo designer give you a written release for all the graphics and design? Or does he or she own your site?
- **You face liability issues.** You have affiliates marketing your product or service. They say something that isn't true, without your permission. You're the one getting sued.
- **You face spam issues.** You think you're sending out a simple newsletter. But one recipient becomes violently upset and decides he or she never subscribed. What do you do?
- **You have liability issues.** You are running someone's ads on your site. Perhaps you have banners through an affiliate program. You might be using Google's AdSense service. Someone clicks on an ad and is unhappy with the product, or the ad contains porn. Are you liable?
- **You face privacy issues.** Issues with privacy can become very nasty. Suppose someone hacks your site or telephone book and steals client information. Or suppose you do something with a sponsor that results in the sponsor gaining access to your clients' email. Your members can get really unpleasant if they feel invaded.

Overall, we're just scratching the surface of Internet issues. But don't let the worries get to you. Resources like Ezor's book will keep you safe. (If you can find the book in print.)

The World Wide Web is an exciting environment. It can make your dreams come true. It did for me and for many of the people I know. The streets are virtually paved with gold. As I've said before, the Internet has the pioneering spirit and excitement of the Old West—law just hasn't been established yet. Getting there is lots of fun.

In the End

Most issues related to Internet taxation are unclear and apt to change. You now know you don't have to worry about sales taxes across borders. For all the other areas, when questions arise, treat them the way you would if you were not doing business online. If you're not sure, check with your advisory team for guidance. And if your advisory team can't give you reliable guidance, you can always try TaxMama's TaxQuips Forum at http://iTaxMama.com/AskQuestion. One of our tax professional members will either have an answer or be able to point you to a resource that can help you.

Resources

In this chapter, you saw a variety of resources. Here's a summary of them, so you can find them quickly and easily. The resources are not necessarily in alphabetical order in each category. They are in order of their importance or usefulness, in TaxMama's opinion.

Online Business Resources

- **Wolters Kluwer Sales Tax Resources.** https://taxna.wolterskluwer.com /sales-tax-nexus. Lots of current information and resources, along with products to help your business integrate sales tax collection and reporting.
- **Avalara Inc.** http://iTaxMama.com/Avalera. Another terrific resource for various compliance software (sales taxes, excise taxes, hotel taxes, etc.), articles, white papers, and information.
- **Sales Tax Institute.** Good information about the sales tax issues and what nexus means, in current law.
   - For a detailed explanation of nexus, check out https://www.salestax institute.com/sales_tax_faqs/what_is_nexus.
- **Streamlined Sales Tax Project.** http://streamlinedsalestax.org. This is a cooperative effort by most US states to create a universal sales tax system to allow them to collect sales taxes on Internet sales. Here are some resources they provide:
   - Remote Seller Guidelines. http://iTaxMama.com/State_Nexus_Reporting
   - Do you qualify for free sales tax calculation and reporting services? https://www.streamlinedsalestax.org/certified-service-providers /freeservices
- **Senate Finance Committee.** http://finance.senate.gov. Watch laws being made.
- **The Tax Foundation.** http://www.taxfoundation.org. Find tax facts, statistics, and in-depth analyses of federal and state governments.
   - Their view on the Wayfair case. https://taxfoundation.org /supreme-court-decides-wayfair-online-sales-tax-case/
   - The Supreme Court decision on Wayfair (just as a reference). https:// www.supremecourt.gov/opinions/17pdf/17-494_j4el.pdf
- **Performance Marketing Association.** http://www.thepma.org/. This is a not-for-profit trade association founded in 2008 by the leaders of the performance marketing industry to connect, inform, and advocate on behalf of

this rapidly growing field. It is an excellent source of information about the sales tax issues related to nexus.

- **Commission Junction Internet Tax Map.** https://www.cj.com/nexus-tax
- **Kelly Phillips Erb's Tax Column on Forbes.com.** She has informative and entertaining articles on many subjects.
  - Congress Makes Internet Access Tax Ban Permanent. http://iTaxMama.com /TaxGirl_Internet_Tax_Ban. In particular, this column relates to this chapter.
  - A link to the relevant law mentioned in Kelly's article—The Trades Facilitation and Trade Enforcement Act. http://iTaxMama.com/Internet_Tax_Bill_2015
- **The Internet Tax Freedom Act.** http://en.wikipedia.org/wiki/Internet_Tax _Freedom Act. A summary of the act.
- **PC Magazine's Review of the Top CRM Software.** https://www.pcmag .com/roundup/253275/the-best-crm-software
- **Google's AdSense.** http://adsense.google.com. If your website provides useful information, Google can provide advertising revenues for your site. Once accepted, you simply paste Google's code on your site, and Google sells the advertising. The software reads the content on your page and serves advertisements related to the content. People are excited, saying it adds value to their articles or information. The income is terrific—and you never have to sell an ad or give out information about your demographics.
- **Google's AdWords.** https://www.google.com/adwords/. Use this to advertise and test your advertising campaigns by targeting your online audience.

TaxMama Resources

- **TaxMama's Ask a Question.** http://iTaxMama.com/AskQuestion. The Ask TaxMama feature is free. Pose your question. If it hasn't been asked dozens of times before, you'll get an answer.
- **TaxMama's Quick Look-Ups.** http://iTaxMama.com/TM_QuickLookUp. You will find all kinds of useful reference materials, webinars you can replay, e-books, and more.
- **Your Business Bible.** http://www.yourbusinessbible.com. Look for worksheets, printable checklists, and other goodies and resources.

CHAPTER 13: **TAX NOTICES, AUDITS, AND COLLECTION NOTES**

To-Do List and Questionnaire

☐ 1. Do you get IRS notices after you file your tax return? _____ Yes _____ No

☐ 2. To understand them, find your usual notices using the notice numbers in this chapter. (The notice number is at the top, right side of the letter.)

☐ 3. To avoid audits, take these steps—review your business now:

a. _____ Make sure your address is current. If not, file a change of address, Form 8822, and your state's form.
Date filed: _____

b. _____ Report *all* your income, even if you did not receive a Form 1099-MISC.
Note: You are responsible for your own bookkeeping.

c. _____ Remember to report all cash and barter income.
Date entered on books: _____

d. _____ Use a separate bank account and credit card for your business and personal activities.
Date accounts set up: _____
Bank Account #: _____
Credit Card Type: _____
Account #: _____

e. If this is your only source of income, review your PROFIT to see if it makes sense compared with your lifestyle. If not, explain why, when you file your tax return—what is your source of support? (Be prepared to prove it, if audited.)

- Credit cards and loans

- Savings and investment income

- Family and friends

Remember to put a copy of each document behind this page, folded in half.

TAX NOTICES, AUDITS, AND COLLECTION NOTES

Blood's not thicker than money.

—Groucho Marx

This chapter will walk you through some of the routine or terrifying interactions you will have with the IRS. Whenever you get notices about audits or owing money, don't just ignore the notices. Always address them. If you are afraid or uncomfortable about dealing with the IRS alone, engage the services of a good local tax professional who understands how to handle audit or collections issues. Not all tax pros do. Ask them to tell you how much experience they have—and if they've been successful. If they complain about all their problems with the IRS, move on. The real pros know how to get right to the key people who can help you. It's not because they have any personal connections or privileges. It's because they attend many professional tax conferences, seminars, courses, and events where they learn exactly how the tax laws are administered—and how to research IRS procedures. It's also because the best tax professionals are members of the top tax associations. As a result they also have access to IRS directories that provide the contact names and phone numbers of key IRS managers and supervisors in their territories.

Alert: The IRS just got one of the biggest budget increases in recent history as part of the SECURE Act—more than $400 million. They will be using quite a bit of that money to increase their collections activities. A lot of their focus is to send out more notices and make it possible for taxpayers to use online tools to pay the balances due on those notices. But what's if the notices are not correct? This chapter will help you with that.

Dealing with Basic Tax Notices
for Individual Returns

When you file a tax return—or don't file—sometimes, there may be errors or you will have a balance due. The IRS has a series of standard notices it sends you. Each notice has a little CP code on the top right-hand corner of the first page of the letter. *CP* stands for "computer paragraph."

The notices are issued in a particular timed sequence by the IRS computer. If you don't respond in time for someone to receive your response and key it into the computer, it will automatically spit out the next notice. If you are mailing a response right at the end of the response period, call the IRS immediately. Ask the agency to put a hold on any collections actions until it receives your information. Let me repeat—*call the IRS*. Don't just hope it will get your response in time. And when you call, always be sure to write down the name of the person you speak with, his or her IRS employee number, and the date and time of the conversation. (The person will give you that information at the beginning of each conversation. But he or she will say it quickly, so don't overlook it. If necessary, ask the person to repeat the name slowly—and to spell it for you.) Follow up with a written note to the IRS or that employee, summarizing your conversation.

Incidentally, if you reach the right person (or the right group), he or she may be able to accept your information over the phone and the fax. If a person has helped you, it's always nice if you send a thank-you letter. Remember, even though the agency is the big, bad IRS, you are dealing with real live people who have jobs and families. A nice letter in their file does two things. First, it could help them get a raise or a promotion. Second, a copy stays with your file, too, and alerts the IRS that you are a nice person. In the future, that could work in your favor.

The IRS has added many more notices to its repertoire. It has also been redesigning its notices. A *San Francisco Chronicle* journalist and I were puzzling over the changes. We weren't sure they were really improvements. But the IRS is trying. You might want to know that both the IRS and the Taxpayer Advocate Service is always trying to improve the notices and make them easier to understand. If you have specific suggestions on how to make a letter or notice easy to understand, let them (or me) know. (Review Chapter 11 for information on how to submit your suggestions.)

A Key to Certain IRS Notices

To look up your notice, look for the notice number or letter number (usually CP-[something] or LTR-[something]) in the top, right-hand corner of the letter.

Then visit this page on the IRS website and enter the notice or letter number—http://iTaxMama.com/IRS_Notices. Incidentally, some of these notice numbers come in a series, like CP12, CP12A, CP12E, etc. Below is a list of common notices you can expect to receive. There are lots more (and they change all the time)—and a whole set of notices just for businesses:

- **CP05–CP06 Series. Your income and Premium Tax Credits.** Your refund is being held up while the IRS verifies your income, and whether or not you qualify for the Premium Tax Credit—or have to pay it back. The IRS is cross-referencing databases to verify your earnings. Your refund might be held up for as many as two months (or more) due to the extensive fraud in the system.
- **CP08—Additional Child Tax Credit.** You may qualify for the additional child tax credit and may be entitled to some additional money.
- **CP11—Changes to Tax Return, Balance Due.** This is generally based on the math in your return. You probably owe this. Pay it.
- **CP11A—Changes to Tax Return and Earned Income Credit, Balance Due.** This is generally based on the math in your return and information the IRS has cross-referenced about your dependents. Or you have not provided information about the dates of birth of your dependents. Call the IRS to see if you can provide better information about your dependents to save your earned income credit.
- **CP12—Math Error—Overpayment of $1 or More.** You still have a refund coming, but it may be lower than you expected. Look for child tax credit adjustments or disallowed dependents because of a Social Security number (SSN) mismatch. *You have 60 days to respond or pay.* Compare the numbers on the notice with those on your tax return. The IRS's adjustment may be wrong. Or you may never have gotten a check from the IRS. Respond in writing before the deadline, with your explanation.
- **CP14—Balance Due, No Math Error.** This is the computation of the underpayment penalties and interest to your tax return. It may also include late filing or payment penalties. *You have 21 days to respond or pay.* You can reduce the underpayment of estimated tax penalty if most of your income was received toward the end of the year. Use the annualized income installment method of computing your penalties, found on page 4 of Form 2210, Underpayment of Estimated Tax by Individuals, Estates, and Trusts.
- **CP23—We Changed Your Estimated Tax Total, You Have an Amount Due.** Perhaps one or more of the checks you thought were estimated

payments were something else (perhaps payments for last year's tax). It's also possible that you sent a check (or made an electronic payment) but didn't provide the correct year, form number, or Social Security number on it. The IRS may have your money but hasn't applied it to any specific year. Find your canceled check (or electronic receipt) and make very clean photocopies of both the front and back (or provide a copy of your electronic receipt). Send the proof of payment to the IRS with the notice and your explanation. *You have 21 days to respond or pay.*

- **CP24—We Changed Your Estimated Tax Total, You Are Due a Refund.** Quite often, you either haven't recorded a payment to the IRS or didn't remember that you applied last year's refund to this return. The second page of the notice will show a list of the payments and dates the checks were received by the IRS. *There is no need to reply.* By the time you get the notice, the IRS will already have sent the check. However, it may be giving you credit for a payment you intended for a different year. Since you're getting the money back, you might not care. But it may involve an estimated payment that you had made on time for the current year—and now you'll get hit with underpayment of estimated penalties. To avoid this problem in the future, make sure you always write the following three pieces of information on each check or electronic payment you send to any government agency. TaxMama's acronym **FYTIN** may help you remember:
  - ◦ *F.* The form number.
  - ◦ *Y.* The tax year you're paying (use a separate check for each year).
  - ◦ *TIN.* The taxpayer identification number (TIN)—your Social Security number (SSN) or employer identification number (EIN)—to credit with this payment. If you are paying money in toward a married filing joint return, list both SSNs.

  If the IRS sends you a refund for a payment that was intended as an estimate and you shouldn't have gotten the refund, do this: (1) Write "VOID" on it. (2) Make a copy. (3) Send it back to the IRS, via Certified Mail with proof of delivery, with a letter explaining that you want that money applied to your account. Specify the tax form and year. This may prevent penalties for a tax you did mean to pay. Better yet, stop mailing in your estimated tax payments. Use the IRS's Direct Pay system at https://www.irs.gov/payments/direct-pay.

- **CP 45—Unable to Apply Your Overpayment to Your Estimated Taxes.** The IRS found math errors in your tax return; or you included withholding or estimated tax payments that were not on record. That means your estimated taxes will be underpaid. Check your records to see if you made a payment last year that the IRS does not show. If so, contact the IRS and send copies of the canceled check or other proof of payment. If it is not an IRS error, make additional payments using Form 1040-ES. Be sure to give your tax professional a copy of this notice. This will ensure that they reduce the refund carryover to your subsequent year's tax return. If you don't remember to alert them that the IRS has not applied this year's refund to the next year, you're going to have an unpleasant surprise next year. Why? Your tax return will show higher estimated tax payments than were actually paid.

- **CP 49—Overpaid Tax Applied to Other Taxes You Owe.** The IRS will send you this notice if you owe money for prior years. You might also get one of these if you owe back child or spousal support, state income taxes, or motor vehicle fines. These are called offsets. The IRS will also grab your refund if you've defaulted on student loans or owe money to the Social Security Administration. The notice will spell out which years or debts are being paid. Often, the money isn't staying with the IRS. When the money is sent to another agency, you'll have to get a release from that agency. When that's the case, don't even waste your time trying to get more information about the outstanding debt from the IRS. It won't have it. You'll have to go to the source, for instance, the motor vehicle department, the district attorney's office, and so on. You'll need to contact the agency that initiated the lien on your refund. Sometimes you get an unpleasant surprise, learning about an old IRS balance you didn't know about or forgot. Track down the details. While the IRS may have only grabbed $39 this year, don't just shrug it off as being too small to matter. It might take $3,000 next year.
- **CP53**—The IRS can't provide your refund through direct deposit, so they are sending you a refund check by mail.
- **CP90—Final Notice—Notice of Intent to Levy and Notice of Your Right to a Hearing.** You will only get this notice if you have ignored all the other notices. *You have 30 days to respond or pay.* If you know you owe the money, call the IRS to work out a payment plan or an offer in compromise (OIC). Ask the IRS to put a hold on the collections activity until you either file the OIC or start the payment plan. Once you're on the plan, the IRS will hold off as long as you're current on your payments.
- **CP91—Final Notice Before Levy on Social Security Benefits.** See CP90. The IRS will grab up to 15 percent of your Social Security benefits if you don't communicate with them and start dealing with your outstanding taxes.
- **CP161—No Math Error—Balance Due.** This is the business version of CP14.

- **CP501—Reminder Notice—Balance Due.** *You have 10 days to respond or pay.*
- **CP504—Urgent Notice—We Intend to Levy on Certain Assets.** Respond within 10 days or lose your state tax refund. The IRS will also start locating and levying bank accounts, wages, or other funds it knows where to find. (If you have a government contract or 1099s have been filed under your SSN—watch out.) *Note:* If your bank or employer calls to tell you your wages or bank account has been levied or garnished, don't panic. The bank and your employer must hold those funds for 20 days to give you time to fix the problem. How can you solve the problem? First get a copy of the levy notice they received. Then call the IRS *immediately*. If you can set up a payment plan or get the agency to agree to give you some time (typically 30 to 45 days), you'll be able to get the IRS to release the levy.
  - ° **Good news.** The bank levy only lets the IRS grab the money in the account on the day it receives the levy. Any money deposited afterward is safe—until the next levy.
  - ° **Bad news.** Since most banking is electronic, you're not likely to learn, from the bank, about the bank levy until after the bank has sent the money to the IRS. So be absolutely sure you open all your IRS notices on a timely basis.
  - ° **Bad news.** If wages are garnished, that deduction continues until you get the IRS to release the garnishment or until you pay the balance in full.
- **CP523—Notice of Default on Installment Agreement (IA).** When you signed the IA, you gave the IRS your bank account numbers and the permission to levy if you didn't make your payments. Now it will. *Call immediately.* (See CP90.) You have 30 days to sort this out. If you have a problem, the IRS is willing to help you modify your IA or put it on hold if you are unemployed or disabled.
- **CP2000—Notice of Proposed Adjustment for Underpayment/Over-payment.** This notice results from the IRS's computers matching up all the W-2s, 1099s, 1098s, and K-1s issued under your Social Security number. Quite often, the notices are wrong. Or they are reporting stock sales on which you had losses anyway. The information is reported somewhere on your tax return. Review the notice carefully. If the IRS is wrong, call the phone number on the form immediately and ask for another 30 days to respond. That way, if it takes a while for your response to reach the IRS, it won't already be billing you. When the IRS is right, it's because you left off employment income (perhaps a brief job early in the year) or dividends you forgot about. If the IRS is correct, just pay the bill. You don't need to file an

amended return. *You have 30 days to respond or pay.* However, if there was an error, you must file an amended return with your state. Sure, your state will get notified about the error from the IRS. But some states will waive the penalties if you file the amended return yourself within six months of the IRS revision.

- **LT18—Reminder—We Have Not Received Your Tax Return.** The IRS's records show that you have income and should have filed a tax return for the year. Prepare and file the return. Or if you have already filed it, clearly, the IRS doesn't have it. So send it again. Be sure to stamp it as a copy (or write "Copy" over it). Sign it, dating it the same date that you originally filed it. If you never filed a return—prepare one and file it now.

More Notices

We don't have room to list all the notices. You will find the current list on the IRS website. The link to that page is in this chapter's Resources.

Anytime you get a notice, the IRS recommends you call the phone number listed on the letter within the deadline shown on the letter. Yes, sometimes you only have a few days because the notice was mailed late. The IRS computer doesn't know when it was mailed, so it will take the next action on schedule. Don't argue with the IRS staff person who answers the phone. He or she isn't at fault. Be pleasant and polite, and the person will be more apt to help you.

News Flash! **We just learned about this new issue affecting people who don't respond to IRS notices. This is very important. So please don't skim the next paragraphs.**

As you may have heard, the IRS is extremely concerned about tax identity theft and data security. The first week of December is generally National Tax Security Awareness Week. Due to the IRS's increased security protocols, they have dramatically reduced incidences of fraudulent refunds. But there is a price for this kind of vigilance. Refunds are delayed. Often for months. It's probably happened to you. Generally, the tax returns that are affected are those with refunds from using a head of household filing and status and claiming one, or all, of these credits (adjusted annually):

- The Child Tax Credit and the Additional Child Tax Credit (up to $1,400 per child is refundable)
- The Earned Income Credit (potentially more than $6,500 with three children)
- The American Opportunity Credit (up to $1,000 per eligible student)

Since these are "refundable credits," funds that are released to taxpayers who have not paid any money into the system, they are a major target of tax fraud. As you can see, if tax criminals create phony W-2s and add several dependents, they can try to scam the US Treasury out of $10,000 or more per tax return. Why does this affect you? Because they might have stolen your SSN and used it to file their fraudulent returns. As a result, most tax returns with these credits will be sidetracked by a special team at the IRS. The IRS might send out a notice asking for more information. **What we have just learned is**—if you don't respond to those IRS notices, your account is flagged. Since you didn't answer, the IRS is concerned that you were not the one who filed the tax return. Aside from not getting your refund, you may face an IRS criminal investigation.

Advice: Respond to the notices right away. Or turn them over to your tax preparer to respond for you. And don't do it at the last minute. Too often tax pros are getting emergency calls from clients about notices they have had for weeks.

IRS Audits

Sooner or later, just about all businesses get audited. Not that often, though. The IRS does happen to be behind on its audits. Current IRS audits are much more targeted than they ever used to be. Perhaps you've heard of "Big Data Analytics"? (You'll find a link to that information in this chapter's Resources.) Using Big Data, the IRS is able to target specific kinds of information to pinpoint taxpayers who are most likely to have unreported income or excessive deductions or credits.

During the IRS's fiscal year 2018 (covering your 2017 tax return and prior), the IRS audited a little more than half a percent of all tax returns filed (0.59 percent). That makes you feel great, right? Think again. As a result of those examinations, the IRS assessed more than $10 billion dollars in additional taxes. The good news? Only about $3 billion was assessed against individuals who were audited. The rest against corporations.

Nearly 2 percent of tax returns with an adjusted gross income of zero or less were audited. More than 13 percent of tax returns showing over $1 million in income were examined (nearly 7 percent of returns with more than $10 million in income). In between? Less than 2 percent of tax returns with incomes in the $200,000 to $1 million range. The average tax return, between $1 and $200,000, was hit about 0.5 percent of the time.

For folks who like to play with statistics, we have posted the links to these IRS statistics tables in this chapter's Resources. It's kind of fun to explore these numbers. But, boy does it eat up time!

With the tax gap being in the hundreds of billions of dollars, the IRS believes that a large part of the unreported income, or underpaid taxes, is coming from small businesses. In fiscal year 2018, the small business audits on both individuals and S corporations have been ever more focused because the IRS knows it can assess taxes due to the many failings of small businesses and their accounting practices. In particular, the IRS is increasing their attention on payroll tax audits and delinquencies.

Why am I boring you with these statistics? Because it will help you with two areas of your business. First of all, it will help you determine what business format you want to adopt. Second, it will help you understand just how much risk there is of your transactions being scrutinized. So if you're thinking of doing something questionable—you know the risk.

What Is Most Apt to Attract the IRS's Attention?

As a small business, inconsistent information on your tax return will generate an audit. For instance:

- You have an office in home, but you are also taking a deduction for rent. You can't have both. At least not without an explanation. (See Chapter 7.)
- You are an S corporation with a profit, but no officer wages. Major red flag! (See Chapters 3 and 9.)
- You are a partnership, showing substantial profits, but show no guaranteed payments to partners. Another big red flag! (Again, see Chapters 3 and 9.)
- Your adjusted gross income is very low, but you are able to afford to live in a high-rent district (zip code), with expenses that substantially exceed your reported income. In other words, if your profits don't support your lifestyle, expect the IRS to notice. (See this item on the checklist—it's of paramount importance.)

Anticipating an Audit: Laying the Groundwork

Knowing you're being audited is usually simple. You get an audit notice. If you've moved frequently and haven't updated your address with the IRS by filing Form 8822, you might not have gotten the notices. If this happens, some nice Fed in a dark suit might come knocking on your front door. You'll go running out the back door to call your tax professional. (Yes, one client of mine really did that. It's not a good idea.)

Whether you deal with the audit yourself or turn it over to a pro, you need to understand the process. After all, you'll be gathering all the documents. Following the guidelines here will save you hundreds of dollars off your professional's invoice.

Your Return Is About to Be Scrutinized

What will the IRS want to know? The primary goal is not to see if you have receipts for the expenses you reported on your tax return. What the agency is really looking for is unreported income. You're about to get some insider information on how to handle audits.

Unless you have a simple tax return, don't handle the audit yourself. Send a seasoned tax professional to the audit instead. In addition to the paperwork, if you are there, the auditor will be looking you over during the audit. Avoid that part of the scrutiny. Let them look you over on paper, instead. The examiner will focus on five fundamental audit issues, and one new issue:

1. Your financial lifestyle
2. Your standard of living and reasonableness of business operations costs
3. Your spending habits and new purchases (conspicuous consumption)
4. All your bank deposits
5. Whether you reported all income from 1099 or W-2 reports
6. Whether or not you have any cryptocurrency transactions or accounts

If these factors don't match your tax return (or industry practices), the IRS will suspect unreported income, inflated expenses, or worse, though your source of funds may simply be nontaxable income or savings. When you've done nothing wrong, you don't want your intermingled accounts to get you into trouble.

When it comes to cryptocurrency, please don't think that the IRS is behind the times. While you may keep hearing about the outdated IRS computer systems . . . their techs are highly sophisticated. At a recent IRS Stakeholder Liaison meeting, the collections manager told us about finding one person's unreported cryptocurrency account worth six figures. At the UCLA Tax Controversy Institute, IRS Commissioner Chuck Rettig told us about the IRS having broken up a major, international child video pornography ring operating on the dark web. Of course, it involved the help of officials in the UK and Korea (where the servers were based). Dozens of children were rescued. The images are currently being analyzed by the National Center for Missing and Exploited Children (NCMEC). The point is, this was initiated and investigated by the IRS. So, the time to be complacent about cryptocurrency and hiding activities on the dark web is over.

Remember, the IRS is the nation's tax collector. It knows that people will do anything to reduce their taxes, or to hide income—even something illegal. The IRS's main focus is no longer on substantiating expenses—although it will still make sure your expenses are legitimate. The IRS is serious about identifying unreported income and making the audits profitable.

With so many electronic tools and so much information-sorting technology, it has become easy to pinpoint the right tax returns for audit. Before it sees you, or your representative, the IRS can run a search of your name or your company name on the Internet.

The IRS can find your press releases or newsletters, puffing your company's successes. It can find your marriage, engagement, birth, and death notices. If you throw a really big confirmation, bar mitzvah, or wedding, chances are your pictures and announcements are online. You may even have a website. Consider this: you're probably giving the IRS the information yourself. So make sure that the information you've put into the public arena matches what the IRS sees on your tax return.

Don't believe me? Google your name. Now Google your business name. See?

Where Else Will the IRS Look for Information About You?

Take a look at Table 13.1. You'll find a whole list of sources the IRS can use to find out about you and your industry if the agency is uncomfortable with your audit. Typically, before an audit, the examiner will pull all the information the IRS has on you internally. (See the first section of Table 13.1.) Sometimes, the examiner doesn't have time to get everything, so he or she asks you to bring things—like prior-year returns. If you notice errors on prior-year returns, don't fix them. Sooner or later the examiner will pull the actual return that was filed—and you want them to match. Right?

Incidentally, most tax professionals will tell you that we rarely bring a prior-year tax return to a client's audit. Generally, we are able to handle the average (very) small business audit in one meeting and settle it—if we have done our homework.

The IRS will only dig into the sources in the second section of Table 13.1 if it feels you're holding back information. If the examiner doesn't believe your story about that $10,000 deposit being a loan from Dad, he or she will start digging into city, state, or credit resources to see if there is evidence of business income you're not reporting.

Remember, the IRS is the arm of the federal government that caught Al Capone, Wesley Snipes, Christina Ricci, and Richard Hatch (from the TV show *Survivor*). The agency has access to substantial internal and external resources about people—especially in today's computer age.

TABLE 13.1 How the IRS Knows More About You Than Your Return Shows

Inside Info: Within IRS Records

W-2s	IRP (Information Returns Program)
1099s	Market Segment Spec Program (MSSP)
Audits of other people's returns	National Research Program (NRP)
Audits of related or pass-through entities	Prior audit(s)
Collections	Prior examiners
Currency and Banking Retrieval System (CBRS)	Tax returns
Casinos	
CTRs (Currency Transaction Reports)	
Customs	
F-Bar (report—foreign bank accounts)	
Form 8300	

Everywhere Else

Agencies	Law enforcement
Bankruptcies	Liens
Better Business Bureau (BBB)	Mortgages
Bureau of Labor Statistics (BLS)	OSHA
Court records (amount/holder)	Permits
Department of Agriculture (DOA)	Probate
Department of Motor Vehicles (DMV)	Property records
Department of Social Services (DSS)	Small Business Administration (SBA)
Department of Transportation (DOT)	Social Media
Divorces	Social Security Administration (SSA)
Fictitious Name Register	US Post Office (USPS)

City and State Information

Employment/unemployment	Permits
Licenses	Sales tax

Other Sources

Banks/S&Ls/credit unions	Informants
City directory	Insurance providers
Corporations (charters, etc.)	Internet searches
Credit applications/reports suppliers	Landlord
Dun & Bradstreet	Legal databases
Employees/contractors	Neighbors
Employer	Newspaper articles
Employer's personnel records	Public utilities
Ex-spouse/children	Third-party contacts—various
Former personal contacts/relationships	Trade associations

How Do You Overcome the IRS's Advantage?

In order to be the most successful in an audit, make sure your representative knows as much about you as the IRS knows. You never want your representative going to an audit only to have him or her learn that the IRS has communications from you that your pro is ignorant of, or that the IRS knows about income or bank accounts that your tax pro doesn't know about.

Be sure to disclose all income sources to your pro. Pull a copy of your own credit report to see what the IRS will find.

If you have unexplained or suspicious transactions that might give rise to IRS criminal scrutiny, you may want to consider hiring an attorney instead of hiring an enrolled agent or certified public accountant.

Keep in mind: your reputation and credibility with the IRS are your best assets if you want to minimize audit damage. If you're caught in a lie, the IRS won't help you reduce the impact of your errors.

If you have inadvertently not reported income, there may be a good reason for your oversight. If the IRS understands it wasn't intentional, the agency may help you avoid fraud and other penalties. Really. I actually had an IRS revenue agent (auditor) help me with a partnership audit. She made me look really good to the partners. (I have lots of stories of getting help from the revenue agents or examiners during audits.)

What Will Happen During the Audit?

First, you should have received a letter telling you what items on your tax return will be examined.

Look carefully at the pages that outline what the IRS wants to see. If you don't understand the letter, you may call the IRS office before you get there and ask for clarification. That ought to shock the office. Few people ever do that besides tax professionals.

During the audit, your examiner will ask a series of questions about you, your past audits, your personal circumstances, and so on. Answer the questions as honestly as you can. Never lie, and don't argue or evade the questions. The examiner is just filling out a form. If you don't know an answer, say so.

Note: When you have a tax professional do this for you, there is one question we generally don't answer. We don't give the IRS your phone number or other contact information. When we have your power of attorney to represent you, we are there to prevent the IRS from bothering you.

Once finished with the general questions, the auditor will focus on the tax return. The first concern is how much income you received. After that number makes sense, then he or she will look at your expenses or the other areas under consideration.

The auditor will have a printout of the 1099s issued to you. Those 1099s show interest-bearing bank accounts and money market accounts, with account numbers. The IRS will already know about your accounts, so bring all the bank statements requested to the audit.

The Most Important Item to Prepare—Proof of Cash

The auditor will look at your income first. To see what the auditor will see, prepare your own proof of cash. When overlooked by taxpayers or tax professionals, this one step can cause more trouble in audits than any other.

When the IRS takes all your bank statements, from all your accounts, and adds up the deposits, what will it find? If you're as casual about what goes into your bank accounts as most people, the IRS will find much more money showing up as deposits than you ever earned.

The total deposits will include loans, gifts, cash advances, inheritances, repayments of loans by family or friends, insurance proceeds. . . . Are you getting the picture? In fact, one of the biggest sources of bank statement inflation is transfers from one account to another. If you leave it up to the auditor, it will look as if you did not report income.

What happens if you leave it up to the IRS? Let me tell you about George.

George owned about 25 low-income residential buildings when he got audited one year. He went to the audit without any real preparation. When the auditor did the proof of cash, she discovered more than half a million dollars of unreported income. The tax, with penalties and interest, was more than $300,000. His tax preparer went back to the IRS and requested an audit reconsideration. While the tax preparer didn't do a great job preparing his second audit, he did get the tax balance due cut by $20,000. That still left $280,000 due. Worse, the state of California would probably add another $100,000 when it was notified about the audit results.

George got lucky. He ran into a sympathetic IRS collections officer—Marta—who had an audit background, too, and listened to George when he insisted that he never had that kind of income. Marta helped us to find the obvious transfers and nonincome items. We found several, including proceeds from mortgages when he refinanced two buildings and pulled cash out. Unfortunately, there was still $300,000 to identify. George was adamant it wasn't income. We found the answer when George remembered that he had borrowed money from the bank using his certificates of deposit as security. We couldn't provide records of the transactions.

He had none. George's bank had burned down in the Rodney King riots in April of 1992.

How did we convince the IRS that the $300,000 wasn't income? We located his old bank manager and had her write a letter saying that she knew he made a regular practice of borrowing against those certificates of deposit. The IRS dropped the rest of the assessment.

In George's case, if he or his tax pro had simply done the proof of cash during the initial audit, they'd have known about the large discrepancy before the audit. They could have rescheduled the audit until he tracked down all the nonincome items. It would have saved him thousands of dollars of professional fees. More important, George would have avoided the stress and fear that comes when the IRS keeps trying to attach your bank accounts, wages, and investment accounts for a year or two.

While this story might seem a bit dated, the concepts are important—and quite current. In fact, trying to reconstruct data is a big part of what tax professionals do when clients are in trouble. This is especially important when dealing with people who have not filed tax returns for many years—often because they were missing information and didn't know how to proceed. If you need more ideas on how to reconstruct missing information, drop by CCH CPELink and take the course I am teaching called "Cohan or Bust: How to Reconstruct Missing Information."

So how do you prepare this nifty proof of cash? It's really easy. See Table 13.2 for step-by-step instructions.

TABLE 13.2 Proof of Cash

Add all the deposits on all the bank statements for all 12 months. Use a spreadsheet like the one in Table 13.3. Make a separate column for each bank account and a "Total" column.

Deduct the following items from the "Total" column:
- ☐ All personal loans
- ☐ Gifts or inheritances deposited to the account (get paperwork to prove it's a gift)
- ☐ Credit card cash advances deposited to the account
- ☐ Bank loans
- ☐ Refinancing proceeds deposited to the account
- ☐ Social Security or disability income
- ☐ Other nontaxable income (IRS tax refunds, certain lawsuit settlements, certain scholarships, etc.)
- ☐ Transfers between accounts
- ☐ Loans repaid to you by family or friends
- ☐ Refunds from stores for personal purchases
- ☐ Reimbursements from employers for your expense reports (be prepared to produce the reports)

Now, take a look at an example in Table 13.3. Prepare it yourself on paper or using spreadsheet software. It makes no difference. Just do it neatly.

TABLE 13.3 Proof of Cash Spreadsheet

Deposits to All Accounts*

	Note	Checking	Savings	Money Market	Total
January		3,345	250	650	4,245
February		3,345	50	650	4,045
March	1	3,815	250	150	4,215
April	2	5,345	250	1,950	7,545
May	3	3,545	250	1,115	4,910
June		3,345	250	1,115	4,710
July	4	45,345	250	41,115	86,710
August		3,345	250	1,115	4,710
September		3,345	250	1,115	4,710
October		3,345	250	1,115	4,710
November		3,345	250	1,115	4,710
December	5	4,345	250	2,115	6,710
Total Deposits		85,810	2,800	53,320	141,930

Less: Deduct All Deposits That Are Not Income

	Note	Checking	Savings	Money Market	
Advances	1	500			From credit card
Transfer	2	2,000			From money market
Advances	3	200			From credit card
Refi (July)	4	42,000			Mortgage loan proceeds
Gift	5	1,000			From family
Transfers			2,800	53,320	From checking
Total nonincome		45,700	2,800	53,320	101,820
Actual income		40,110	0	0	40,110

*Explanation of the cash flow in the table:

All wages are deposited to the checking account.

Transfers are made each month to savings and money market accounts.

The house was refinanced and the credit cards paid off in escrow.

The rest of the money from the refinance was transferred to the money market account.

Looking at the "Total" column, the IRS would have determined that your income was $141,930 based on adding up all the deposits to all the accounts. Look at the actual "income" in the "Total" column. You can see that the net paycheck amounted to $40,110.

Now you understand how the IRS can think you have $100,000 more income than you really do. That's why it's so important to be prepared.

OK. You've established that you didn't deposit more money than you reported on your tax return. What's next during your audit?

Time to Work on Expenses

In ideal situations, when you have a business, you have a profit and loss statement and a balance sheet, along with a detailed general ledger printout. Or you could go in with an accordion file with all the receipts neatly arranged into categories—with each batch of expenses totaled with adding machine tapes attached. You can probably do this when you have receipts that only belong in one expense category. But if the receipt or check needs to be split among several categories, what are you going to do? Think of credit cards. Each statement has auto expenses, office supplies, meals, travel, and entertainment. Unless you can make several photocopies of each statement to attach to each batch, you have a problem.

That's why it's important for you to do your bookkeeping *before* you go to an audit. Do it, even if you never bothered doing it before. (See Chapter 4 for more on record keeping.) Sure, your expenses might come out differently than they appear on the tax return. Don't worry. If your overall expenses are the same, or similar, you'll be fine.

What If, After the Bookkeeping, Your Expenses Are Still Way Off?

You'll need to find ways to come up with additional expenses—legally. Look here:

- **Credit cards.** Did you enter all the business expenses from each statement? From each credit card? Do you have a personal card that you sometimes used for business? Remember to include those business expenses. Did you skip December's bill because it has a January date on it? Grab that bill. If the charges were in December, you may use them.

    Did you have bad credit and have to use someone else's card? Get the other person's statements—and some of the receipts that show you signing for the charges. You may need some proof, but if you show the IRS examiner your really bad credit report, he or she might just smile and understand.

- **Cash.** Did you pay for things using cash in the normal course of the day but there are no receipts? Make reasonable estimates. Look back through your appointment book. If you traveled, make a list of the dates and places. List all the tips you gave out each day. List the cab fares, tolls, public transportation costs, and so on. Did you pay for parking, meters, pay phones? Using a spreadsheet, just list all the different out-of-pocket expenses. Be sure they don't add up to more than the cash you drew from your ATM or bank account.

For expenses where the IRS permits you to use standard amounts (auto, mileage, meals, and travel per diems), compare the actual costs with the standard rates. Often, I have been able to bypass a detailed scrutiny of the expenses via one of these methods. Tables with allowances for several years are available on the Internet. Chapter 6 tells you where to find them.

If you've pulled everything together and you still find discrepancies—call a tax professional. Find a tax pro with experience in audits, bookkeeping, and your industry. A professional may be able to read your mind and help you remember what you were thinking when you originally came up with the numbers on your tax return.

Unless, of course, you either simply made them up—or lied.

Still coming up short? You'll know before you go into the audit what you will lose. It won't be so intimidating when you already know the worst case.

TaxMama's Tips Do Work!

A client of Rita Devlin Zapko recently faced an IRS audit. Rita reports the result: "Thanks in part to your prep, I just had a client dazzle them with organized, reconciled information on his first retail audit. The IRS accepted his past 6 months' records, with zero assessment and agreed not to open 2013–2015."

We get reports like this all the time from graduates of TaxMama's EA Exam Course, and other tax professionals who have attended TaxMama's courses. Neatness counts—and being well-prepared speaks volumes about the taxpayer and the tax pro.

What If You Don't Have Any Receipts?

The Tax Code operates on the "ordinary and necessary" principle. IRC §162 allows the deduction of ordinary and necessary expenses paid or incurred in carrying on a trade or business.[1] If it appears that an activity was entered into for profit, the rules of IRC §162 are applied to each expense.

While the IRS is not always excited about the application of this principle, the courts have ensured that we taxpayers get the benefit of it. There's the old Cohan rule from 1930, when the appeals court decided in favor of entertainer George M. Cohan.[2] Cohan had deducted all his travel, meals, and business expenses without producing receipts. Can't you just see George M. riding around the country on rickety cars, buses, and trains, with his trunks full of vaudeville gear, costumes, props, and all, *and* dragging around another huge trunk just for receipts and accounting records? Well, neither could the court. It determined that if the expenses make sense for your line of work, profession, or trade, you should be entitled to reasonable deductions in line with your industry—even if you don't have receipts.

Beware, though. Current tax law does not allow the use of *Cohan* for certain common business expenses (Section 274 deductions, https://www.law.cornell.edu /uscode/text/26/274), like meals, entertainment, transportation, and travel costs. For those costs, you absolutely must have contemporaneous records.

In addition to the restriction based on IRC 274, and due to abuse of this provision, the courts have ruled that they will not allow the Cohan rule if you have not made every reasonable attempt to re-create your records. If you make no attempt at all, don't count on Cohan to bail you out.

I tested the theory with a client who also happened to be an entertainer. Barry was audited a couple of years ago for his $50,000 worth of business expenses. Well, like good old George M., Barry had nary a receipt for all his travel, meals, and so on. Besides, he had poor credit and paid for everything in cash. So we couldn't reconstruct his expenses using credit card statements. Knowing we needed to provide proof of the travels and costs, I did a lot of work. Using various outside documents, like the *TV Guide* and the postcards he sent me from the road each week, I was able to prove his travels. Using the IRS per diem rates (see Chapter 6), I established reasonable costs. Despite the fact that the records were not contemporaneous, the IRS accepted all the expenses, with no receipts, and better yet, no conflict. It was resolved at the auditor level, right in the office. Of course, it did take a little negotiating. And don't count on today's auditors to be quite this generous, if you don't maintain proper records. As we discussed in Chapter 4, with today's apps, it's really easy to record transactions on the fly.

---

1 IRC §162, available at https://www.law.cornell.edu/uscode/text/26/162

2 *Cohan v. Commissioner*, 39 F.2d 540 (1930)

Negotiating

During an audit, you can negotiate, to some extent, on all levels. You must have a basis for your request. In George's case, discussed earlier, we were able to get the IRS to believe that $300,000 wasn't income because we were able to prove a pattern of behavior. In exchange for a letter from a banker (considered third-party testimony or evidence), I was able to negotiate away $300,000.

Having a basis for your request may involve doing research on similar issues and being able to bring copies of those cases to the auditor. It may involve getting statements from objective third parties. It may involve agreeing to give up one set of expenses so that you can keep others that are more important to you in the future. For instance, I had a client whose tax return included an in-home office, while he was an employee, and $15,000 worth of garments he'd bought as samples. Alex was willing to give up the in-home office for that year, as long as the full amount of the garments was accepted as a deduction. He needed those garments as a deduction to support a Tax Court case. We didn't care about the employee office in home, because the following year he was a full-time independent contractor—and worked from home full-time, in his own business.

The IRS won't do it just because you ask. Not even if you're really cute.

TaxMama's Three Basic Rules of Tax Negotiating (KGB)

When it comes to getting my way, especially with the IRS, or other tax agency, here's my basic strategy. I call it the KGB strategy: Know. Give up. Backup. Here's how it works:

1. **Know.** Before you start negotiating, know exactly what you want to accomplish. (The IRS doesn't need to know that—but it's critical that you have it defined in your own mind.)
2. **Give up.** Have something to give up. (In exchange for giving up some deductions, be so thorough in your audit preparation that you find all expenses the taxpayer overlooked. Look at missed itemized deductions—always a good source of errors in your favor!)
3. **Backup.** Give the auditor or appeals officer something tangible to put into the file to support your position. Providing backup documentation and workpapers saves the auditor or officer time and makes the person look good to his or her superiors on review.

In George's audit, we weren't able to prove that the last $133,000 of deposits were transfers or loans. Since I was able to prove that there was a consistent pattern of behavior, I could negotiate with the IRS about the rest. The IRS would accept the logic and conclude the sum was not income in exchange for my preparing a worksheet with an explanation to provide the auditor for his file. It gave him an excuse to accept my position that the deposits probably were not income.

Office auditors have the discretion to decide what documentation is acceptable. They have to believe the information they see is adequate. Be sure to make an extra set of copies of all the schedules and work papers for the auditor's file. Did I already say this? It provides documentation and makes him or her look better when superiors review the auditor's determination. Besides, the auditor can write notes on it, too.

Audit Reconsiderations, Appeals, and Tax Court: Some Brief Words

An audit reconsideration may be granted when the IRS agrees to reopen an audit that has already been completed and is past all the deadlines for protest on the local level and in Tax Court. It is *not* an appeal. The audit typically goes back to the same level of examination, often the same office that conducted the original audit. The IRS will not give you reconsideration if you have already signed off, agreeing to the original audit. You must have additional information that wasn't presented at the first audit. The IRS will also give you this opportunity if you didn't appear at the original audit. At the time you request the reconsideration, you'd better have at least 80 percent of your material ready. You generally get one shot to present your case. So prepare it well. While the IRS rarely agrees, you *can* get audit reconsiderations. First, you must have the audit report, generally a Form 4549. If you were working with an examiner, ask him or her for help. If you no longer have that contact information, call the IRS's main phone number at (800) 829-1040 (800-TAX 1040) and make the request. If you still have a contact name, ask the auditor's group manager for the reconsideration. If that doesn't work, read this IRS brochure on audit reconsiderations—IRS Publication 3598. It will tell you what steps to follow. Pick up a copy of IRS Form 12661, Disputed Issue Verification. This is where you can outline the parts of your tax return you want the IRS to review—and explain what additional supporting documents you have. The brochure tells you where to submit your request and how to proceed. You will find links to these publications in this chapter's Resources.

Naturally, if you get turned down, you won't be happy. If you're really not in the right, drop it and move on. But if you know that you are justified asking for the reconsideration—move your way through the chain of command:

- Write to the branch chief.
- Have your tax professional contact the Practitioner Priority Service (PPS). (It's a special hotline for the tax professional community.)
- Contact the Taxpayers Advocate at (877) 777-4778.
- Make an appointment at an IRS Problem-Solving Day or Open House if they are still available.
- Contact the Small Business/Self-Employed Operating Division.
- Contact the deputy director, Compliance Field Operations.
- Contact the Commissioner of the IRS.
- Contact your US senator or US representative, or even the President or Vice President of the United States—or all of them. Sometimes, the only thing that will work is political intervention.

Don't ever give up. There's always somewhere to go when you disagree with an audit and you know that you are justified. Sometimes, if it's worth the fight, you will simply have to pay the assessed taxes and file a claim in a federal court to get heard. That's the hard way. Not only do you have to pay the taxes, penalties, and interest first, you will probably also face hefty legal fees.

Decide if the cost to fight your battle is worth what you will win. Sometimes, it's cheaper just to give in to the IRS. But if it's really a matter of principle and all avenues fail, you may want to look for an advocacy group to take on your case. Sometimes what's happening to you is happening to enough other people that it's worth setting up a class action suit or rewriting legislation. You just might end up settling a landmark case—like *Edie Windsor v. Commissioner*, which forced the federal government to recognize same sex marriages for tax purposes.

Should You Use Appeals Only as a Last Resort?

Some tax professionals find the Appeals process is sometimes easier to deal with than the IRS's auditors. While all auditors must have college degrees, the degree does not necessarily have to be in accounting or taxation. Sometimes the auditors are not as well trained as we would like. With the IRS hiring thousands of new employees in this decade, expect to see a lot of people new to auditing.

By the time the IRS agents get promoted to the Appeals level, they have extensive field experience, education, training, and the ability to use and understand tax research and research tools. (Currently, the IRS has started to hire tax professionals from outside the IRS. These are seasoned EAs, CPAs, and attorneys with years of representation experience.) You are dealing with a seasoned professional who has more decision authority than the office auditor and many field auditors.

The goal of the Appeals Office is to settle cases without litigation. The Appeals officers evaluate your case's strengths and weaknesses with an eye to how your case will stand up in court. They will pull the relevant court cases, decisions, and precedents (or at least the items the officers think are relevant). Ask them for their citations when you meet. Most important, have your own research ready. Give them a copy of your cases (not just the citations to cases) with your points highlighted. It will enhance their willingness to cooperate with you. You've done a big part of their job, and they have objective documentation, in your favor, to put into your IRS file.

Remember, an appeal is not about supporting expenses. It is about tax law and precedents. If deductions were not substantiated during audit, expect the appeals officers to kick the audit back to the original auditor to finish. This is now a nationwide policy called Appeals Judicial Approach and Culture (AJAC). If you couldn't resolve it at that level, do you really want to go back to the field office?

Most tax professionals use the Appeals process to their advantage. So can you. When confronted with a particularly troublesome auditor and a group manager who will not intervene, a tax pro would simply call a halt to the whole process. I'd tell the IRS to post its adjustments and walk away.

Before you do that, there is one thing you must take great care to do. As a result of the Appeals current policy, Appeals will no longer accept any new documents about income, expenses, worksheets, bank statements, and so on. If the audit division didn't have those documents in the file, Appeals won't accept them from you. So . . . gather up all the documents and records that you feel you need in order to prove your case and ship them off to the auditor you've been dealing with. Be sure to make two sets of extra copies before sending them. And send them with proof of delivery. One of the extra sets is for you. The other is for Appeals if the field office loses (or claims not to have received) your documents. This way, you won't be bringing Appeals any new documents. And if the original exam group refused to consider your proofs, you can now insist that the Appeals office look over the information.

Why is this step so important? For two reasons. First, Appeals won't look at that mass of data if the examination office has never had a chance to look at it before. Second, by giving the IRS everything it needs to understand your case, and by cooperating with it at every level of the investigation, you have now officially shifted the "burden of proof" to the IRS. Now, if you were to take this case to Tax Court, the IRS will have to defend its position, denying your expenses, or increasing your income. It's the law—IRC §7491.

Then, I'd do one of two things:

1. Request fast-track mediation. This is handled by the Appeals Office. Fast-track mediation is rarely used, even now. The Appeals Office would like to see it used more often. The Appeals officers will work intensely to reach a resolution at that meeting with you and the original examiner (and perhaps the auditor's manager). You can find more information about this program at http://iTaxMama.com/IRS_FastTrack.
2. Wait for the audit determination letter (30-day letter). When it comes, it tells you that you can request an Appeals hearing. If you haven't already done so, get a good tax professional involved. He or she will do a more efficient job at this level.

When writing the letter requesting the Appeals hearing, briefly include specific areas where the auditor is incorrect and outline the documentation you are going to reference for this hearing. *Do not* include a harangue of the auditor's bad qualities or what's wrong with the IRS or the system.

Meanwhile, get all your Appeals documentation and citations together. You already have all the support for the unresolved income-expense issues. Now, you must do in-depth research on the tax law issues involved. This is where all that work you did on your business plan will pay off. If you have losses, the business plan will prove that wasn't your intention. But things do go wrong.

Getting Your Case to Tax Court

If you've missed your opportunity to go to Appeals after the 30-day letter, wait for the 90-day letter (Notice of Deficiency). Owing less than $50,000 means you're eligible to file your petition as a small case. But filing as a small case means you cannot appeal the decision if you lose. So, that may not be your best option. You'll find the most current US Tax Court Petition Kit online at the US Tax Court's website.

You may work with an attorney, a CPA, or an enrolled agent (EA) to represent you. With a CPA or EA, you'll need to sign the petition yourself (in pro per). The CPA and the EA are not admitted to practice directly in the US Tax Court unless they have passed the US Tax Court exam. (Only 122 tax professionals have been admitted since 2000,[3] and they have the letters USTC after their names.) So why do you want the EA or CPA involved, if he or she can't practice in the US Tax Court? Because the case will get kicked back to Appeals before the Court will hear it. That's

---

3 http://taxcourtexam.com/exam-faqs/

when your EA or CPA can step in. He or she will handle the Appeals meetings for you. Tax Court cases usually get resolved at this level. I've resolved all my clients' US Tax Court cases without ever going beyond Appeals. In fact, I have been teaching tax professionals how to handle these cases for over a decade. *However, be warned.* Do not prepare your own US Tax Court petition, or work with an EA, CPA, or attorney who does not have extensive experience with these filings. The most common error when preparing these petitions is that amateurs omit key issues from the petition (like penalties, interest, certain deductions, or credits). If they are not included in the petition in the first place, you cannot add them to the case later.

Reading many Tax Court decisions, it's clear some cases only went to the US Tax Court because the taxpayers were really rude or unpleasant to Appeals—or their representative wanted to make some extra money. There are also those cases that look simple but were pushed up to US Tax Court to establish a precedent.

Strategy: Use as many of the 90 days as you can to get your records and research as ready as possible. Send your petition in at least 10 days before the end of the 90 days. Enclose the $60 filing fee and mail to:

The United States Tax Court
400 Second Street, NW
Washington, DC 20217

Owing Taxes

All right, you've exhausted all logical ways to reduce your audit assessment. Or you filed a tax return and owe money. How do you go about paying it?

Naturally, if you have the money, send the check and get it over with. If you're not liquid right now, the following sections explain some ways to pay.

Credit Cards, Debit Cards, and Digital Wallets

The first three companies that I am about to reference have contracts with the IRS and other government agencies. They have been processing millions of dollars' worth of government credit card payments for about a decade. (The EFTPS program is part of the IRS.) There are two advantages to using credit cards or electronic payments. The first advantage is that you will have immediate proof of payment. The second is the bonus or mileage points you earn for those charges.

- **http://www.OfficialPayments.com.** Pay IRS, state, and local taxes online and pay a "convenience fee."

- **http://www.pay1040.com.** Make federal tax payments online and pay a "convenience fee."
- **http://www.PayUSAtax.com.** Pay federal taxes only, and pay a "convenience fee."
- **https://www.eftps.gov/eftps/.** Pay quarterly estimates, payroll taxes, and business taxes online. Money comes directly from your bank account. There are no fees. But this can take a week or two to set up (see Chapter 1).
- **IRS Direct Pay.** https://www.irs.gov/payments/direct-pay. Pay your federal income taxes, estimated taxes, and a few others directly to the IRS from your bank account without any fees. There is no setup time; just log in and pay on the spot.

When using the first three services, the tax agency doesn't pay the merchant fees—you do. (Merchant fees are the costs the merchants normally pay for accepting your credit card.) The credit card or digital wallet fees will cost about 2.5 to 5 percent of the taxes you pay. (They're called "convenience" fees—that's for the convenience of the tax agency, not you.) Fees for using debit cards are generally a flat fee of $2.00–$3.00.

Suppose you'd like to use your credit cards but don't want to pay online. Here are two other ways to use your credit cards:

- **Alternative 1.** Use your credit card checks (you get all those things in the mail, daily, right?). Read the fine print. See what the company is going to charge you. See if you can get a no-transaction-fee check. Remember to ask for reduced interest or 0 percent interest on the transaction fee. The good news is, with the economy getting better, I have started to see offers with 0 percent fees, and up to 18 months with 0 percent interest. In particular, look for the lower offers at credit unions. You might also get your mileage or rewards points.
- **Alternative 2.** Call your credit card company and request a cash advance to be deposited into your bank account. It will take a week to 10 days, so do it now. If you cajole sweetly, you might get it without transaction fees—otherwise, expect to pay 2 to 3 percent of the amount charged. Look for a card that has a ceiling on the fee (like 3 percent up to $50). Beware. Most don't—so read the fine print carefully. Be sure to request low or 0 percent interest and ask about the mileage or reward points. *Note:* While these 0 percent rates used to be good for up to 18 months, many of them are now only good for 6 to 12 months. In this chapter's Resources, we'll give you a link to the most current 0 percent credit cards.

You Can't Afford to Pay Now, But Will Ultimately

If this is the case, there are three ways to go:

1. **File Form 9465, Installment Agreement Request.** This is the method the IRS suggests. Think twice before requesting an installment agreement (IA). There is a fee for an IA, which you will have to pay again and again if you default on the agreement. The fee ranges between $31 and $225, depending on how you file for the IA, and how you make the payments. The fee is only $32 if payments are deducted directly from your bank account. (You may qualify for a $43 fee if your income is low enough and you file your application on paper.) In addition, you give the IRS your bank account numbers and the right to attach your funds if you're late or miss a payment. In the past, the IRS levied the bank account immediately when you were late. These days, the kinder, friendlier IRS gives you a chance to make good. Or if your financial circumstances have changed, the IRS is willing to revise your IA. If you default, the IRS will levy. Anyone may get an installment agreement, as long as you're not in default on another balance.

2. **Don't file the Installment Agreement Request immediately.** Send the IRS whatever you can afford with the first balance due letter. Save up and send money every time the IRS sends you a balance due notice. If you expect to have enough money to pay the balance off in about six to nine months, this may be cheaper and less invasive than requesting the IA. You'll still be paying interest on the penalties and taxes, but the interest is in the 3 to 4 percent range these days—that's probably less than many credit cards.

3. **Borrow the money from family or friends.** If they love you and trust you—and you're really reliable about paying them back—it's the best option. When you're a few days late, they won't be attaching your bank account. If you're going to flake out on the loan, though, don't borrow the money in the first place. You will destroy valuable relationships and trust. Most important, do not borrow money from family or friends if they have to borrow the money to give to you. After all, if you flake on them, you won't just destroy your relationships, you could damage or destroy their credit. There are still other options.

When the Balance Is Too Large to Pay Off

What happens when the balance is so large that you're just never going to have the money? Perhaps, you're elderly and are living on a fixed income. Or you're insolvent. You can't even afford a bankruptcy attorney. You're not hiding any assets or money. If this is the case, call the IRS and tell the truth. The IRS can put a special collections hold on your balance due for six months or a year and will contact you to review the situation, periodically, for the next 10 years. If, during that time, you can never pay it, you're off the hook.

There is a 10-year limit for the IRS to collect money from you after a tax debt is recorded. Your state may have different limits or no limits at all (meaning they can collect forever). We usually recommend paying off the state. That debt is generally lower, and easier to afford.

Some actions can stop that 10-year clock, but it's best if you get a good tax professional to help you determine where you stand when you're in that situation. I always used to have a tax attorney perform those computations. These days, there's some pretty nifty software available to tax professionals that can help us get definitive information about your deadlines.

Request an Offer in Compromise

Suppose you aren't really insolvent, but the balance is just so unbearable that you feel beaten down by it. Perhaps you have a job or some sort of steady income from your business, but you'll never earn enough to pay all the taxes due.

You do have a way out. The Offer in Compromise (OIC) Program might be able to help you. When you file an offer in compromise, you're asking the IRS to accept a fraction of what you owe on your taxes—and to write off the rest of your debt. But don't get carried away. There is no promise that your tax debt of $50,000 will get cut to $3,000 or $100—despite all those ads you see on television.

The OIC Myth

Washington—The Internal Revenue Service today issued a consumer alert, advising taxpayers to beware of promoters' claims that tax debts can be settled for "pennies on the dollar" through the Offer in Compromise Program. Some promoters are inappropriately advising indebted taxpayers to file an Offer in Compromise (OIC) application with the IRS. This bad advice costs taxpayers money and time. An Offer in Compromise is an agreement between a taxpayer and the IRS that resolves the taxpayer's tax debt. The IRS has the authority to settle, or "compromise," federal tax liabilities by accepting less than full payment under certain circumstances.

As it happens, after the IRS issued that news release in 2004, it shut down several national companies that had been ripping off taxpayers. These days, tax resolution companies are somewhat better regulated. But ever more of them are popping up, as more EAs and CPAs learn how to help you with your hefty tax balances. Please Google the company's name and see if there are records of complaints about them.

Qualifying for an Offer in Compromise

Late-night television, radio, and even some daytime television commercials fill your ears with promises of tax miracles. You're probably getting lots of emails, too. Since the IRS filed a tax lien against you, your mailbox is being filled with solicitations from certain tax firms promising you quick resolution of your problem. Be wary. The truth is most outfits will take far too much of your money—and not help you nearly as much as you'd expect. One promoter even offered a discounted price of $1,500 to give you a do-it-yourself kit, with instructions. That firm was shut down by the IRS, and some members did jail time. Only use firms when you can get a recommendation from someone you know who has used them successfully. Otherwise, go to your own tax professional for help or for a recommendation. If you have no recommendation source, look to smaller, local EAs and CPAs who have experience getting their clients offers in compromise. They won't have massive caseloads and will be able to provide personal service. The two best places to find some reliable help are:

- NAEA (see Chapter 1)—https://taxexperts.naea.org/. Your best bet is someone whose profile shows that he or she is an NTPI Fellow. That means the person has graduated from all three levels of the National Tax Practice Institute.
- ASTPS (American Society of Tax Problem Solvers)—http://www.astps .org/tax-help/. You will find CPAs, EAs, and attorneys with the CTRS (Certified Tax Resolution Specialist, like me) who have graduated from the ASTPS Boot Camps and annual training, or passed their 11-page, in-depth examination.

Fortunately, I have come to know some of the best people in the country because I teach the Tax Practice Series and my EA Exam Courses.

The IRS also offers a do-it-yourself kit. It's free. There's a Form 656 kit (32 pages) that can be downloaded from the IRS's website. This packet generally contains the most updated version of the acceptable forms. The IRS even provides workshops on filling in these forms. Check the IRS website at http://iTaxMama.com/IRS_OIC or call the agency at (800) 829-1040 to see if it is offering a workshop near you. But before you do all that, check to see if you qualify. The IRS has a nifty OIC pre-qualifier tool to help you see if you are a candidate for an OIC.

What if you don't qualify for an OIC? Don't waste your time applying if you don't meet the IRS standards for applying. Here are some general parameters—not the ones the IRS posts—but the reality it uses when considering your offers:

- Are you young, healthy, and able to work?
- Do you have a college education but are choosing not to pursue work in your own field because you'd rather follow your dream?
- Do you have a steady income?
- Do you have equity in your home? Or an IRA or other retirement account?
- Are you expecting a windfall? An inheritance? Or a great job about to start pouring money your way? Don't lie. That's tax fraud. It's one of the few reasons the IRS will send you to jail.

Look at your own earning capability over the next five years. Even though it may be tight, if there's enough left over, by living within your means or restructuring your lifestyle, the IRS will reject your offer. It won't wait while you pursue your dreams and live as a starving artist. It will simply reject your offer in compromise.

Suppose you do qualify and are ready to prepare an OIC. Be thorough. Attach legible copies of all forms, bank statements, and bills requested by the IRS. Enclose three months' worth. Read the information about how it all works on the IRS website. (You'll find a link to at in this chapter's Resources.) If you're not willing to provide the IRS with this much information, don't even start the process. The IRS now requires a fee of $186 that must be sent in with most applications. So you're wasting your money if you don't follow through.

The IRS reports that more than 80 percent of applications for offers in compromise are rejected as incomplete. Another 10 percent are rejected because people don't respond. If you simply attach everything and enclose anything else the IRS wants, you're already in that small minority that might get accepted.

While I warn you away from unscrupulous representatives, I do recommend that you work with a competent tax professional who has a track record of getting OICs for his or her clients. It is a long, complicated process, and having a pro who has gone through it can help. Since you must provide all the documents anyway, you can save yourself dozens of hours of billable time if you gather them all and organize them yourself. I won't go into any more detail here; the application packet is remarkably self-explanatory.

But if you want some in-depth training on how to handle your offer yourself, sign up for one or more of my Tax Practice Series classes. The sessions are taught in plain English, and include tricks and tips for the professionals to use for their clients—best of all, they are available as on-demand video courses. The whole series costs about the value of a one-or-two-hour consultation with a tax professional. You can find the series on my CCH CPELink pages at https://www.cchcpelink.com /teamtaxmama.

The IRS is catching up on to its caseload. The latest news is that offers are being settled in nine months or less. Naturally, the "or less" part is for offers that are presented with complete information. The other good news is, with the Fresh Start Program that the IRS introduced a few years ago, the balances you have to pay to settle the offer are more reasonable than ever. The costs? Even if you hire an ethical tax professional to deal with the IRS on your behalf, expect to pay for at least 10 to 15 hours, if you're organized and cooperative. If you must be chased down and hounded to get documents or if you just dump all your records on the tax pro you hired and expect him or her to do all the work, you're up to 20 to 40 hours.

How About Filing Bankruptcy?

Perhaps you don't want to go through the misery of an OIC. You may not want to subject yourself to remarkable levels of stress and frustration, feeling you're at the mercy of an arbitrary system. You have one last alternative.

Look into bankruptcy. Discharging tax debt isn't easy. When you qualify, it is faster than an OIC, less intrusive—and much cheaper. Attorneys handling this will typically charge about $3,000.

To discharge your taxes in bankruptcy, you must qualify:

- All your returns have been filed.
- If filed, the taxes due were not based on fraud.
- If filed late, the return was filed two years or more before the bankruptcy petition.
- The tax return, with extensions, was due three years or more before filing of the bankruptcy petition.
- Tax liability was assessed more than 240 days before filing of the petition.

All of those requirements must be met in order to qualify.

There are several complications about how the 240 days are counted or what stops the clock. As with all benefits, this one won't come too easily.

The biggest hurdle for many to overcome is the emotional one. There is an intense feeling of failure, of self-denigration when you're reduced to this. But if this is your only—or your best—option, take it. Trust me. I've seen the transformation in people who did. Many people spend years trying to resolve their tax debt through the IRS's channels and simply end up wasting 5 or 10 years feeling worthless, unable to sleep, and unable to maintain their relationships. Yes, taxes do destroy relationships.

Sometimes it's best to just clean the slate and start fresh. But if you do, make sure you don't get into trouble again. Please, don't use tax bankruptcy as part of your regular tax plan.

Summary of IRS Interactions

The information in this one chapter took me more than 20 years to learn—and then another 15+ years of constant research, reading, asking, probing, and pressing IRS managers and executives. Thank goodness, they have been remarkably patient with me. I also have the privilege of consulting some of the top experts in the field. Much of my experience came through sheer stubbornness and the refusal to back down to my fear of the IRS. The rest of the information came through lots of audits and thousands of responses to notices. It helped that in the past few years, we really did get a kinder, gentler IRS. In fact, now, with our new IRS Commissioner, the IRS staff are so much more enthusiastic and optimistic, that they are more helpful than ever.

Using the guidelines provided in this chapter, you'll never have to be afraid of the IRS or mystified by its confusing notices. You have everything you need in order to know how to respond to the usual notices—and audits.

Resources

In this chapter, you saw a variety of resources. Here's a summary of them, so you can find them quickly and easily. The resources are not necessarily in alphabetical order in each category. They are in order of their importance or usefulness, in TaxMama's opinion.

Important Acronyms

- **FYTIN—Form, Year, TIN.** What you write on all checks to government agencies.
- **KGB—Know, Give up, Backup.** An audit negotiating tool.

IRS Resources

- **Main Reference Page to Search for IRS Notices and Explanations.** http://iTaxMama.com/IRS_Notices
- **Internal Revenue Manual, Part 4, Examining Process.** http://iTaxMama.com/IRM_Part4
  - ○ Internal Revenue Manual, Part 4, Chapter 13, Audit Reconsideration instructions. https://www.irs.gov/irm/part4/irm_04-013-001
- **Internal Revenue Service Fast-Track Mediation Process for Audits and Collections Disputes.** http://iTaxMama.com/IRS_FastTrack
- **Internal Revenue Service Offer-In-Compromise Information.** http://iTaxMama.com/IRS_OIC
- **Form 433-A, Collection Information Statement for Wage Earners and Self-Employed Individuals.** https://www.irs.gov/pub/irs-pdf/f433a.pdf
- **Form 433-B, Collection Information Statement for Business.** https://www.irs.gov/pub/irs-pdf/f433b.pdf
- **Form 656, Offer in Compromise Application and Instruction Packet.** https://www.irs.gov/pub/irs-pdf/f656b.pdf
- **Form 2210, Underpayment of Estimated Taxes.** https://www.irs.gov/pub/irs-pdf/f2210.pdf
- **Form 8822, Change of Address.** https://www.irs.gov/pub/irs-pdf/f8822.pdf
- **Form 12661, Disputed Issue Verification.** https://www.irs.gov/pub/irs-pdf/f12661.pdf
- **Publication 3598, What You Should Know About the Audit Reconsideration Process.** https://www.irs.gov/pub/irs-pdf/p3598.pdf
- **IRS Offer in Compromise Pre-Qualifier Tool.** https://irs.treasury.gov/oic_pre_qualifier/
- **IRS Understanding the Offer in Compromise Process.** http://iTaxMama.com/IRS_OIC
- **IRC §7491, Shifting the Burden of Proof to the IRS.** http://iTaxMama.com/Burden_of_Proof
- **IRS Appeals Judicial Approach and Culture (AJAC).** http://iTaxMama.com/AJAC
- **IRS Collections Activities in the Dark Web and Beyond.** http://iTaxMama.com/Child_Porno_Indictment. South Korean National and Hundreds of Others Charged Worldwide in the Takedown of the Largest Darknet Child Pornography Website, Which Was Funded by Bitcoin (October 16, 2019).

- **IRS Statistical Reports—Table 10. Examination Coverage: Recommended and Average Recommended Additional Tax after Examination, by Size and Type of Return, Fiscal 2018.** http://www.irs.gov/pub /irs-soi/18db10ex.xls
- **Table 9b. Examination Coverage: Individual Income Tax Returns Examined, by Size of Adjusted Gross Income, Fiscal Year 2018.** https://www.irs .gov/pub/irs-soi/18db09bex.xls

Online Credit Card Payment Resources

- **IRS Direct Pay.** https://www.irs.gov/payments/direct-pay. Pay your federal income taxes, estimated taxes, and a few others directly to the IRS from your bank account without any fees.
- **Official Payments.** https://www.officialpayments.com/index.jsp. Lets you pay IRS, state, and local taxes online via credit card. There are fees.
- **PAY1040.com.** https://www.pay1040.com/. Make federal tax payments online via credit card. There are fees.
- **PayUSATax.** http://www.PayUSAtax.com. Pay federal taxes only, and pay a "convenience fee."
- **EFTPS (Electronic Federal Tax Payment System).** http://www.eftps.gov. Pay quarterly estimates, payroll taxes, and business taxes online.

General Bankruptcy and Tax Bankruptcy Resources

- **IRS General Bankruptcy Resource.** https://www.irs.gov/businesses /small-businesses-self-employed/declaring-bankruptcy
- **IRS Publication 908. Bankruptcy Tax Guide.** https://www.irs.gov/forms -pubs/about-publication-908. How to discharge tax debt in bankruptcy.
- **Dennis Brager, Tax Attorney.** https://www.bragertaxlaw.com/bankruptcy -the-silver-bullet-of-tax-defense.html. He outlines which taxes qualify for tax bankruptcy.

Credit Resources

- **Best Credit Card Rates.** http://iTaxMama.com/Credit_Cards. Find the most current 0 percent cards.
- **Ilyce Glink—Credit and Finance Books.** http://www.thinkglink.com
- **Liz Weston—Credit Guidance and Resources.** http://asklizweston.com

Tax Information of Interest

- **Kelly Phillips Erb, aka TaxGirl.** http://www.forbes.com/sites/kelly phillipserb. Excellent and interesting tax articles at Forbes.com.
- **Kay Bell's Blog.** http://www.dontmesswithtaxes.com/celebrity/. Love gossip? For more stars in tax trouble,
- **Supreme Court decision in *Edie Windsor v. Commissioner.*** http://www.scotusblog.com/case-files/cases/windsor-v-united-states-2/
- **US Tax Court.** http://www.ustaxcourt.gov/forms/Petition_Kit.pdf. US Tax Court Small Case Petition Kit.
- **IBM on Big Data Analytics.** https://www.ibm.com/analytics/hadoop /big-data-analytics

TaxMama Resources

- **TaxMama's Article on When Filing Bankruptcy May Be Helpful.** http://taxmama.com/tax-bankruptcy/bankruptcy-freedom
- **TaxMama's Courses on Resolving Tax Issues and the Cohan Rule.** https://www.cchcpelink.com/teamtaxmama
- **TaxMama's Course to Become an Enrolled Agent.** http://irsexams.school/
- **TaxMama's Quick Look-Ups.** http://iTaxMama.com/TM_QuickLookUp. You will find all kinds of useful reference materials, webinars you can replay, e-books, and more.
- **Your Business Bible.** http://www.yourbusinessbible.com. Look for worksheets, printable checklists, and other goodies and resources.

EPILOGUE

Some Final Words of Advice— and Resources to Rely On

If a man empties his purse into his head, no man can take it away from him. An investment in knowledge always pays the best interest.

—Benjamin Franklin

All Good Things Must End

You've done a lot of work. Thanks for including me on your journey. I have great confidence in your success. You've done everything right along the way. Your business plan is smashing. You've found some terrific advisors and the right networking groups to join. You worked out some of the kinks in the first few months of operations, so it's been rebalanced. You have learned to be more efficient, so you're earning more money and spending more time living your life. Your tax pro has reviewed your accounting records and budgets, to high praise. Your customers or clients love you.

Most of all, your home and family life has been enriched, through your family's enthusiastic participation in shaping your legacy—and their inheritance.

Let me leave you with this comment from my favorite writer and egotist, Isaac Asimov: "I am at least as intelligent as my tax advisor. So, I should have no trouble understanding the tax laws. But if I were to concentrate my energies towards learning everything I needed to know, the world would be deprived of many of my books."

Follow Asimov's advice. Learn enough about taxes to build a strong foundation. Keep your trusted tax advisor handy, as well as your advisory team. Then concentrate your energies on what you do best—running your business and living your life.

Resources

You've been immersed in tax and business information throughout this book. You've learned so much more than you ever expected. There's so much to learn, to know, about tax law and strategy. This book was designed to be your guide—to lead you to more information. It was designed to open your mind to creative ways of thinking—to bring you perspectives you didn't have before and might not find anywhere else.

You've got power you never had. (Have I said this before? A dozen times perhaps? Oh my goodness, I've become my mother!) But, please, you're in business. Don't prepare your own tax returns. You have an advisory team. Use it. The team and the resources listed throughout the book will help keep you up to date. Most of the resources in these pages are available quickly and freely on the Internet.

Hang on to These Important Phone Numbers

Here are some phone numbers you'll want to have handy:

- **IRS main phone number.** (800) TAX-1040 or (800) 829-1040
- **IRS Forms and Publications Order Line.** (800) TAX-FORM or (800) 829-3676
- **IRS E-Help for Get Transcript.** National toll-free number: 800-908-9946
- **IRS E-Help for EFTPS.** (800) 555-4477
- **Social Security Administration.** (800) 772-1213
- **Taxpayers Advocate Service.** (877) 777-4778

Remember, if you want a little more hand-holding, join me at Wolters Kluwer's CCH CPELink (https://www.cchcpelink.com/teamtaxmama). We are starting a series of classes based on the chapters in this book. You can ask questions about your own business during these classes.

For more resources, please visit the end of each chapter and the wonderful index in this book. Thanks for letting me join you on your new business adventure!

Always leave them laughing when you say goodbye!

—GEORGE M. COHAN OF COHAN RULE FAME

INDEX

ABOUT THE AUTHOR

Taking her first tax class in college, Eva Rosenberg declared she was avoiding this subject—for good. The information changes too much, too often. Who could ever keep up? It's like standing in quicksand—there's nothing solid to hold on to.

Intending to grow up to be Vice President of International Marketing for IBM, Eva took a brief detour spending a couple of years with national CPA firms. Doing taxes temporarily, to earn a living while completing her MBA in international business, Eva kept running into companies and people with tax problems that needed solving. Looking up, more than 20 years later, she finds herself the go-to professional for the tax community. CPAs, attorneys, and enrolled agents call her when their clients get audited—or have tax problems that can't be resolved. Eva finds solutions that surprise even her—or she negotiates a fair resolution. In fact, she recently convinced the IRS to return nearly $100,000 in refunds to a taxpayer who filed far too late to qualify to get her money back. (Now that's a good story!)

Not only does Eva help and advise tax professionals, she trains them. TaxMama's® EA Exam Review Course helps prepare the tax professional community to do more than just pass the tough IRS examinations in order to gain the coveted Enrolled Agent (EA) designation. She actually teaches them fundamental tax laws, tax practice procedures, tax research, and ethics. Never heard of Enrolled Agents or the Special Enrollment Examination (SEE)? Learn more about both at www.IRSExams .school.

Eva has written books, articles, tax columns, and even chapters of tax textbooks. An Internet pioneer and mentor to many, Eva founded the Internet's HelpDesk & WebReview in 1997 to provide a safe place to ask dumb questions about your business website. It lasted for nearly 10 years, and inspired the TaxMama.com® website and persona.

Those years and experiences make Eva a popular resource for journalists. You'll find her quoted in publications as diverse as the *Wall Street Journal, Christian Science Monitor, Chicago Tribune, New York Times, Los Angeles Times, USA Today, Glamour, Woman's Day,* and *National Enquirer.* Her tips appear regularly in banking publications, including those of Wells Fargo, Guaranty Bank, and Bankrate.com. Eva is still awed each time she sees her name in print.

An immigrant to America who has seen life as both a charity recipient and the donor, Eva has the refreshing ability to understand and address the needs of the rich and the poor, as well as the English as a Second Language (ESL) and non-English-speaking community—and to cut through the sob stories to the real issues and problems. She recognizes just how easy it is, in America, to move your address from the backseat of your semi-demolished car to the deck of your 100-foot yacht, with your GPS and satellite-based Internet connection—and to lose it all. Or, to live for free on the kindness of strangers.

Eva's frankness, sense of humor, and casual, stand-up tax delivery make her a popular talk show guest and speaker around the country. Her Dow Jones Market Watch.com tax columns were eagerly anticipated by readers for nearly 15 years, wondering just what IRS button she's going to push next. Eva proudly displays a framed copy of IRS Notice 2004-27 issued as a result of one of her MarketWatch .com articles.

New projects in 2020 include developing and teaching nearly two dozen tax courses at CCH CPELink, and monthly visits with Jim Blasingame, the Small Business Advocate, as part of his Brain Trust and, perhaps, a weekly series of half-hour courses based on her ever-popular TaxQuips.

Known as TaxMama for both her warmth and her nagging, Eva, an enrolled agent, is the publisher of the highly acclaimed TaxMama.com website, author of the Ask TaxMama column, and the voice of the TaxQuips podcast. The TaxMama .com site is a free resource, warmly welcoming questions from all taxpayers and tax professionals. The answers are free—no strings attached. But Eva does ask that you search the site for answers first. Through the site, Eva provides articles, IRS news, links to tax forms for the IRS and all states, and free answers to visitors' tax questions . . . along with her own twist on pending and current legislation. Of course, Eva knows that people really come for the Money Funnies—the jokes pages.

Go to TaxMama.com for your free subscription and access to a continuing stream of tax advice, news, and tips—where taxes are fun.

After all, TaxMama is watching out for you!